This new study of the origins of the English novel argues that the novel emerged from historical writing. Examining historical writers and forms frequently neglected by earlier scholars, Robert Mayer shows that in the seventeenth century historical discourse embraced not only "history" in its modern sense, but also fiction, polemic, gossip, and marvels. Mayer thus explains why Defoe's narratives were initially read as history. It is the acceptance of the claims to historicity, the study argues, that differentiates Defoe's fictions from those of writers like Thomas Deloney and Aphra Behn, important writers who nevertheless have figured less prominently than Defoe in discussions of the novel. Mayer ends by exploring the theoretical implications of the history-fiction connection. His study makes an important contribution to the continuing debate about the emergence of the novel in Britain in the eighteenth century.

CAMBRIDGE STUDIES IN EIGHTEENTH-CENTURY
ENGLISH LITERATURE AND THOUGHT 33

History and the early English novel

CAMBRIDGE STUDIES IN EIGHTEENTH-CENTURY
ENGLISH LITERATURE AND THOUGHT

Some recent titles

Crime and Defoe: A New Kind of Writing
by Lincoln B. Faller

Locke, Literary Criticism, and Philosophy
by William Walker

The English Fable: Aesop and Literary Culture, 1651 – 1750
by Jayne Elizabeth Lewis

Mania and Literary Style
The Rhetoric of Enthusiasm from the Ranters to Christopher Smart
by Clement Hawes

Landscape, Liberty and Authority
Poetry, Criticism and Politics from Thomson to Wordsworth
by Tim Fulford

Philosophical Dialogue in the British Enlightenment
Theology, Aesthetics, and the Novel
by Michael Prince

Defoe and the New Sciences
by Ilse Vickers

A complete list of books in this series is given at the end of the volume

History and the early English novel

Matters of fact from Bacon to Defoe

ROBERT MAYER

Oklahoma State University

CAMBRIDGE
UNIVERSITY PRESS

Published by the Press Syndicate of the University of Cambridge
The Pitt Building, Trumpington Street, Cambridge CB2 1RP
40 West 20th Street, New York, NY 10011-4211, USA
10 Stamford Road, Oakleigh, Melbourne 3166, Australia

First published 1997

Printed in Great Britain at the University Press, Cambridge

A catalogue record for this book is available from the British Library

Library of Congress cataloguing in publication data
Mayer, Robert, 1948–
History and the early English novel: matters of fact from Bacon to Defoe / Robert Mayer.
p.   cm. – (Cambridge studies in eighteenth-century English literature and thought: 33)
Includes bibliographical references and index.
ISBN 0 521 56377 1 (hardback)
1. English fiction – 18th century – History and criticism.
2. Literature and history – Great Britain – History – 18th century.
3. Historical fiction, English – History and criticism.
4. Defoe, Daniel, 1661?–1731 – Knowledge – History.
5. Bacon, Francis, 1561–1626 – Influence.
I. Title.   II. Series.
PR858.H5M39   1997
823′.509358 – dc20   96–9608   CIP

ISBN 0 521 56377 1 hardback

To Elizabeth

"it seemed to them that Fate itself
had meant them for one another"

When I go about a Work in which I must tell a great many Stories, which may in their own nature seem incredible, and in which I must expect a great part of Mankind will question the Sincerity of the Relator; I did not do it without a particular sence upon me of the proper Duty of an Historian

Daniel Defoe, *The Storm* (1704)

It is impossible to imagine what a novelist takes himself to be unless he regard himself as a historian and his narrative as a history. It is only as a historian that he has the smallest *locus standi*.

Henry James, "Anthony Trollope" (1883)

She picks up the notebook that lies on the small table beside his bed. It is the book he brought with him through the fire − a copy of *The Histories* by Herodotus that he has added to, cutting and gluing in pages from other books or writing in his own observations − so they are cradled within the text of Herodotus.

Michael Ondaatje, *The English Patient* (1992)

Contents

Illustrations

Figures 1–3 are reproduced by permission of the Shropshire
Records and Research Centre; Figure 4 by permission of the
History of Science Collections, University of Oklahoma Li-
braries; Figures 5 and 6 and the cover by permission of the
William Andrews Clark Memorial Library, University of Cali-
fornia, Los Angeles; Figure 7 by permission of the Houghton
Library, Harvard University; Figures 8 and 9 with the assistance
of the Audio Visual Center, Oklahoma State University.

Acknowledgments

I wish to thank the following institutions for support and assistance and the following people for comradeship and help. Grants from the William Andrews Clark Memorial Library at UCLA, the Newberry Library, the National Endowment for the Humanities, the Oklahoma Foundation for the Humanities, and the College of Arts and Sciences of Oklahoma State University supported the research and writing of this book. The staffs at the British Library, the Cambridge University Library, the William Andrews Clark Memorial Library, the Newberry Library, the libraries at UCLA and UC-Santa Barbara, the Folger Shakespeare Library, the Library of Congress, and the libraries at Tulsa University, the University of Oklahoma, and Oklahoma State all helped facilitate my research. I am particularly grateful for the many instances of quick work by the Inter-Library Services staff at OSU.

I wish to thank Chris Herbert, Elizabeth Dipple, Martin Mueller, Richard Wendorf, Barbara Foley, and Lawrence Lipking for their help while I was at at Northwestern, and Wendorf, Foley, and especially Lipking for continuing support. The following people kindly responded to requests or inquiries: Terry Belanger, Paula Backscheider, Martine Watson Brownley, Elizabeth Heckendorn Cook, D. F. MacKenzie, Maximillian Novak, and Michael Treadwell. I am particularly grateful to my fellow participants in the 1993 NEH summer seminar at UC-Santa Barbara, directed by Everett Zimmerman, including Alan Chalmers, Lorna Clymer, Peter Cosgrove, Ronald DeAbreu, Charles Embry, Timothy Erwin, Carl Fisher, Jonathan Nielson, John Pier, Treadwell Ruml II, and Cynthia Wall. At OSU, Jeffrey Walker gave me some welcome relief and financial assistance. At Cambridge University Press, Howard Erskine-Hill, John Richetti, and two anonymous readers read and helped improve this book. Earlier versions of chapters 3 and 10 and a portion of chapter 8 appeared in *Studies in Philology*, *ELH*, and *Eighteenth-Century Studies*, respectively; I am grateful to Johns Hopkins University Press (publisher of *ELH* and *Eighteenth-Century Studies*) and to *Studies in Philology* for permission to republish this material. I am also grateful to Alfred A. Knopf, for permission to quote from Michael Ondaatje, *The English Patient* (Knopf, 1993).

Cynthia Wall, Martin Wallen, Elizabeth Williams, Everett Zimmerman, and Linda Zionkowski helped me by reading and criticizing parts or all of the manuscript; they have my profound gratitude and are hereby absolved of responsibility for errors and blindnesses. I want to thank Linda, Martin, and Sam, Lionel and Susan, Marsha and Joe, and especially Bob and Mary Jo for being both serious and comical about the life we all lead. My debt to my family, especially to my mother and father, is great; my mother first taught me the love of books, particularly novels. I can hardly say what I owe to my daughters Eleanor and Susanna for being wonderful companions at home and on the road, tolerating my absences and grumpiness, and teaching me about love. Finally, this book is dedicated to Elizabeth, as a small token of my immeasurable gratitude to her.

Introduction

For a book that is a central text of Western civilization, *Robinson Crusoe* had a strange early history.[1] In the first edition (1719), the title page announced that the work had been written by Crusoe, and the editor's preface asserted that the book was "a just History of Fact" even as it obscurely acknowledged that some or all of the narrative might be fictitious. A number of the early readers of *Crusoe* read the narrative as a factual account; Charles Gildon's famous attack on the book was rooted in his belief that many readers had been deceived by Defoe. Thus, Gildon's "D—l" tells Friday:

> I did not make you speak broken *English*, to represent you as a Blockhead . . . but meerly for the Variety of Stile, to intermix some broken *English* to make my Lie go down the more glibly with the Vulgar Reader.[2]

Having been branded a liar by Gildon, Defoe offered two defenses of his text and his method. The preface to *The Farther Adventures of Robinson Crusoe* (1719) observes that all efforts to "reproach" the earlier work "with being a romance . . . have proved abortive" and further argues that the "just Application" of the work "must legitimate the Part that may be call'd Invention"; the clear implication is that although *some* of the work might be invented, the account is essentially factual, "Contradictions in the Fact" having never been isolated. The preface to the *Serious Reflections of Robinson Crusoe* (1720) also rejects the claims of the "ill-disposed Part of the World . . . That . . . the Story is feign'd" and counters "that the Story, though Allegorical, is also Historical." Thus, the several explications of *Robinson Crusoe* provided by Defoe do not so much shift ground as repeat themselves, and we are left with a paradox: though the work may be regarded as an allegory, it is nonetheless history. So in *Serious Reflections* the editor asserts

---

[1] To cite only two arguments as to its classic status, Samuel Johnson linked it with *Don Quixote* and *Pilgrim's Progress*, and James Joyce called it the "English *Ulysses*." Michael Shinagel, ed., *Robinson Crusoe* (New York: W. W. Norton, 1975), 285, 353.

[2] Paul Dottin, ed., *Robinson Crusoe Examin'd and Criticis'd or A New Edition of Charles Gildon's Famous Pamphlet Now Published with an Introduction and Explanatory Notes* (London and Paris: J. M. Dent, 1923), xvi. On the early reception of *Robinson Crusoe*, also see *The Lives of the Poets* (1753), signed by Theophilus Cibber but now attributed to Robert Shiels, cited in *Defoe: The Critical Heritage*, ed. Pat Rogers (London: Routledge & Kegan Paul, 1972), 49–50.

that "when I mention my Solitudes and Retirements . . . all those Parts of
the Story are real Facts in my History, whatever borrow'd Lights they may
be represented by."[3] Note that Defoe does not simply argue that the work
is "true"; it might well be thought both allegorical and true: Bunyan makes
that claim in his defense of *The Pilgrim's Progress*.[4] Rather, Defoe insists not
only that the text is true but also that it contains "Matter of real History" –
matters of fact – even as he admits that it is a "Fable."

Not only Defoe's repeated, paradoxical defenses of his text but also its
early reception suggest the strangeness of *Crusoe*.[5] Indeed it seems that at
first no one knew what to make of this text – not Defoe, who wrote about it
in such contradictory terms and explicated its generic status again and
again without clarifying the matter; nor Gildon, whose charge that the
book was a lie was wholly lacking in subtlety; nor the early readers who
read the text either as a memoir or as a fable. Subsequent readers
contained the work's strangeness, familiarizing it by classifying the text as a
work of fiction, a "romance" or a "novel," generally without considering
whether such categorizing was justified or whether it resolved formal
questions about the text. The present study, by contrast, begins from the
premise that we can learn a great deal about the nature of *Robinson Crusoe*
as well as Defoe's other narratives and also about the novel in general by
taking Defoe at his word and considering *Robinson Crusoe* as a "just History
of Fact" and then asking how that "History" became part of the canon of
English novels.

In order to take Defoe seriously, however, it is necessary first to
determine what readerly expectations would allow a writer to present such
a text as a history and also allow such a work to be read as a species of
historical discourse. This study, then, is an attempt to delineate a crucial
area of the "horizon of expectations" on which *Robinson Crusoe* appeared in
1719.[6] To describe that horizon one needs to consider both historical and
fictional discourse, since from the seventeenth to the nineteenth centuries,
at least, writers persistently asked readers of fiction to situate their

---

[3] Shinagel, ed., *Robinson Crusoe*, 258–65.
[4] John Bunyan, *The Pilgrim's Progress*, ed. James Blanton Wharey, rev. Roger Sharrock (Oxford:
    Clarendon Press, 1960), 4–5. On the difference between Bunyan and Defoe, see Ian Watt, *The
    Rise of the Novel: Studies in Defoe, Richardson, and Fielding* (Berkeley: University of California Press,
    1956), 80–84; Michael McKeon, *The Origins of the English Novel, 1600–1740* (Baltimore: Johns
    Hopkins University Press, 1987), 121.
[5] On the reception of *Robinson Crusoe* after Gildon, see Rogers, *The Critical Heritage*, 48–51; C. E.
    Burch, "British Criticism of Defoe as a Novelist, 1719–1860," *Englische Studien* 67 (1932), 178–
    98; and chapter 11 below. The concept of the "strangeness" of a literary work is from the
    Russian Formalists; see Viktor Shklovsky, "Art as Technique," in *Russian Formalist Criticism*, ed.
    Lee T. Lemon and Marion J. Reis (Lincoln: University of Nebraska Press, 1965), 3–24.
[6] The term "horizon of expectations" is from Hans Robert Jauss, "Literary History as a
    Challenge to Literary Theory," in *Toward an Aesthetic of Reception*, introd. Paul de Man, trans.
    Timothy Bahti (Minneapolis: University of Minnesota Press, 1982), 22.

imaginative works in relation to the discourse of history, and the history-fiction problematic was, therefore, an ever-present preoccupation of writers and readers of the texts that we now associate with the early English novel.[7] This study arises from the view that Defoe's importance – his centrality – in the early history of the English novel derives from the fact that in the period from the publication of Sidney's *Arcadia* (1590) to the appearance of Scott's *Waverley* (1814), Defoe's narratives constituted the most pointed and significant statement of this history-fiction problematic. Crucial to the definition of the form, Defoe's famous texts laid the basis for a sustained attempt by subsequent novelists and readers to elaborate, comprehend, define, and domesticate the dialogue in the novel between historical and fictional discourse.[8] For this reason, my discussion of

---

[7] Aphra Behn presented *Oroonoko* (1688) as "the history of this royal slave" and asserted that she was herself "an eyewitness to a great part of what you will find here set down"; in *The Secret History of Queen Zarah* (1705) Delarivier Manley distinguished between the popular romances of the day and her own "little histories"; the "editor" of *Moll Flanders* (1722) acknowledged that "the World is so taken up of late with Novels and Romances, that it will be hard for a private History to be taken for Genuine," thereby indicating that Moll's narrative should be read as history; Richardson presented *Clarissa* (1747–48) as "a History," distinguished *Pamela* (1741) from romances, and indicated that he wanted *Clarissa* to be read with a "Historical Faith"; Fielding's narrator in *Tom Jones* (1749) took pains to say "what kind of a history this is"; Sterne likened *Tristram Shandy* (1759–67) to Locke's *Essay*, which Tristram tells us is "a history-book . . . of what passes in a man's own mind," and Tristram addresses "the hypercritick" on the issue of the author's manipulation of time in order to avoid the critic's "rendering my book . . . a profess'd ROMANCE"; Smollett, as I have argued elsewhere, "presses us," in *Humphry Clinker* (1771), "to conceive of the novel as a fictional form that does the work of history"; the preface of Frances Burney's *Evelina or the History of a Young Lady's Entrance into the World* (1778) informs the reader that she or he should not "entertain the gentle expectation of being transported to the fantastic regions of Romance"; Maria Edgeworth presented *Castle Rackrent* (1800) as a narrative "taken from facts" – the kind of history one never finds in historiography; and Scott styled *Waverley* (1814) a "historical romance" and presented it to the reader, in the Magnum edition, with learned introductions and footnotes. See the prefaces or introductions to the works cited, except for *Tristram Shandy*, in which case see vol. II, chapters 2 and 8, and Richardson's comment on *Clarissa*, for which see *Selected Letters of Samuel Richardson*, ed. John Carroll (Oxford: Clarendon Press, 1964), 85. On *Humphry Clinker*, see my "History, *Humphry Clinker* and the Novel," *Eighteenth-Century Fiction* 4 (1991–92), 255.

[8] A fundamental assumption of this study is that fiction and history are qualitatively different forms of discourse. It has not been uncommon for literary theorists to claim that historical discourse is essentially fictive since the historian employs narrative techniques often associated with the fashioning of imaginative stories. See, for example, Roland Barthes, "The Discourse of History," trans. Stephen Bann, in *Comparative Criticism. A Yearbook*, ed. E. S. Shaffer (Cambridge University Press, 1981), 3–20. The work of Hayden White is also apposite; see the discussion of White at p. 90. Recently, however, a number of theoreticians of history and of narrative have insisted upon the essential difference between history and fiction, and all have pointed in different ways to the fact that history-writing is based upon evidence drawn from the historical record while fiction is not. For three such arguments, from very different perspectives, see Arnaldo Momigliano, "The Rhetoric of History and the History of Rhetoric: On Hayden White's Tropes," *Comparative Criticism*, 267–68; Paul Ricoeur, *Time and Narrative*, vol. III, trans. Kathleen Blarney and David Pellauer (University of Chicago Press, 1988), chapter 8; and Dorrit Cohn, "Signposts of Fictionality: A Narratological Perspective," *Poetics Today*, 11 (1990), 775–804. Paul Ricoeur argues that "fiction . . . permits historiography to live up to the task of

"matters of fact" will entail first a fresh look at seventeenth-century historiography and then a reassessment of Defoe's texts – historical and novelistic – in light of a reexamination of both history- and fiction-writing in seventeenth-century England. All this is aimed at illuminating Defoe's crucial role in the creation of the English novel, which derives from his having made the nexus of history and fiction a key element in the theory of the novel elaborated by writers and readers in the eighteenth century. The argument of this study entails, then, a sequence of claims: that the historical discourse of seventeenth- and early eighteenth-century England (what I shall call Baconian historiography) featured a taste for the marvelous, a polemical cast, a utilitarian faith, a dependence upon personal memory and gossip, and a willingness to tolerate dubious material for practical purposes, all of which led to the allowance of fiction as a means of historical representation; that the novel came into being, in important part, because of a "sudden redistribution" within and among discursive fields that occurred in England in the first half of the eighteenth century, and in the process of which the novel hived off from history; that Defoe's most famous narratives – issued as histories, branded as lies, and eventually read as novels – were an important element in that far-reaching discursive realignment; that a key feature of the elaboration of a discourse of the novel was the shift in readerly expectations forced upon readers in the early modern period and after, in important part by Defoe's "novels"; and that the long and complicated history of the reception of Defoe's "novels" signals the fact that the history-fiction problematic in those narratives became a key feature of the emerging discourse of the novel.

I

This study relies heavily on Hans Robert Jauss's perception that literary historians can use the study of reception to describe a form such as the novel as the sum of all questions posed and answers proffered by both the works themselves and the readers of those works. According to Jauss, readers as well as writers theorize forms, and the theory of a form *is* the

memory," and also that "fictional narrative in some way imitates historical narrative," especially insofar as fiction is "internally bound by its obligation to its quasi-past." Ricoeur therefore speaks of an "interweaving of history and fiction," or the

> fundamental structure, ontological as well as epistemological, by virtue of which history and fiction each concretize their respective intentionalities only by borrowing from the intentionality of the other.

Yet even as he argues that these two narrative forms are in important ways inextricably linked, Ricoeur insists on the fundamental difference of the two modes of discourse because "the quasi-past of the narrative voice [in fiction] is . . . entirely different from the past of historical consciousness"; 189, 192, 181.

history of the form "viewed . . . within the horizon of a dialogue between work and audience that forms a continuity." Jauss's call for "an aesthetics of reception" sought to provide a basis for relating historical studies and formalist inquiries: "to bridge the gap between literature and history, between historical and aesthetic approaches." Attention to reception *and* production, he argued, could overcome the limitations of historicist procedures that provided a clear view of the historical context of texts and careers but little means of saying how a work-in-its-historical-context is related to a work-in-its-present-context: "the thread from the past appearance to the present experience of literature, which historicism had cut, is tied back together" by an historical analysis of reception and production.[9] At the same time, attention to reception ensured that formal descriptions would not be severed from historical questions. Jauss's project amounts to the claim that the novel that we study today – the form that we theorize – has embedded within it, for example, Defoe's answers to questions embodied in the works of earlier writers as well as questions propounded within his works and the subsequent answers of Defoe's readers to the questions he posed. Delineating the horizon of expectations of writers and readers of texts associated with the tradition of the novel is a way of describing not only the history but also the theory of the novel.

How does one reconstruct the horizon of expectations against which a work appeared? Jauss has tended to concentrate on individual works as horizonal backgrounds to other works, most recently, for example, on *La Nouvelle Héloïse* and *The Sorrows of Young Werther* as works that responded to the same questions and also as works that were related to each other as question and answer.[10] This method is problematic, however, when one is treating a body of work as initially undifferentiated from a large mass of popular texts as was the work of Defoe. The problem is further accentuated if one is using the equally inchoate set of statements and texts that constituted "history" in early modern England to delineate the horizon against which Defoe's works originally appeared. Faced with this problem of apprehending and describing such a crowded horizon, the discourse analysis of Michel Foucault has at times proved a more productive means

---

[9] Jauss, "Literary History," 19, 18. Writers are readers of earlier works, and thus Defoe's texts are acts of reception in respect to earlier works. As Felix Vodička has argued, the "biography" of a work consists of both its "genesis" and a "greater and more difficult part": the description of "how the work has changed in the minds of those following generations who have dealt with it, who have lived on it, and nourished themselves on it." Thus the views of other readers – critics and common readers – are also valuable evidence for an understanding of the history and theory of the novel; see "The Concretization of the Literary Work: Problems of the Reception of Neruda's Work," in *The Prague School: Selected Writings, 1929–1946*, ed. Peter Steiner, trans. John Burbank, *et al.* (Austin: University of Texas Press, 1982), 105.

[10] Jauss, *Question and Answer: Forms of Dialogic Understanding*, ed. Michael Hays (Minneapolis: University of Minnesota Press, 1989), 148–96.

of seeing Defoe's narratives in relation to historiography. Foucault's work suggests that, rather than focusing on the evolution of a genre from one text to another, the history of the early English novel might better be written as an account of the transformation of an established discursive matrix – history – leading in time to the formation of a new matrix – novel, albeit one with clear links to the older discursive formation.[11] Foucault's concept of discourse shifts the historian away from a history of themes, works, narratological features, authors, and schools of thought toward a "systematic description of the discourse-object" with the aim of describing the statements, actual and possible, that comprise the discourse as well as the "rules of formation" that inhere in those statements: "discourses as practices obeying certain rules."[12] As a history of history, this study does not contain a definitive description of, say, ecclesiastical or natural history; it does not argue for the importance or value of a particular historian or work; it does not seek to praise, damn, or rehabilitate any methodologies, writers, or texts. Rather it examines writers, works, statements, theories, themes, techniques, and types of historiography, as species of historical discourse and as indicators of the rules embedded within and governing that discourse.

Foucault, however, was himself notoriously vague about indicating how a discursive formation could be described; the assertion that a discourse is "a vast field . . . made up of the totality of all effective statements (whether spoken or written), in their dispersion as events" only highlights how difficult the task is, especially since often such a "field" seems to be treated

[11]   Michel Foucault, *The Archaeology of Knowledge*, trans. A. M. Sheridan Smith (New York: Pantheon, 1972), 23–30, 8, 14, 47, 140, 138; for the original French, see *L'archéologie du savoir* (Paris: Gallimard, 1969), 33–43, 16, 24, 64, 183, 182. Foucault argues that a discourse exists if a set of statements refers to the same object, if there is a "system of permanent and coherent concepts involved," if one discovers upon examining a set of statements "the identity and persistence of themes," and if, furthermore, there are "rules of formation" that inhere in the discourse and make possible the objects, types of statements, concepts, and themes that signal its existence. Was "history" a discourse in this sense? One could argue that it was perhaps *the* crucial discourse in the seventeenth and early eighteenth centuries since Bacon's survey of learning identified it as the fundament of all knowledge; on the importance of history to Bacon's "theory of knowledge," see Lisa Jardine, *Francis Bacon: Discovery and the Art of Discourse* (Cambridge University Press, 1974), 123. In addition, since seventeenth-century historiography, after Bacon, was peculiarly aware of itself as a way of knowing and representing the world, one could argue, despite the great diversity of concepts and themes in historical discourse, that it did constitute a discursive formation and that the "object" to which it referred was "matters of fact." Foucault himself seems to have acknowledged the legitimacy of thinking of "history" as a discourse: "If I made a list of all the sciences, knowledges and domains which I should mention and don't, which I border on in one way or another, the list would be practically endless . . . I haven't even attempted an archaeology of history." Foucault, *Power/Knowledge: Selected Interviews and Writings, 1972–1977*, ed. Colin Gordon, trans. Gordon, *et al.* (New York: Pantheon: 1980), 64; for the original French, see *Dits et écrits*, 4 vols. (Paris: Gallimard, 1994), III, 29.

[12]   Foucault, *Archaeology of Knowledge*, 140, 138; *L'archéologie du savoir*, 183, 182.

as if it were roughly unchanging from the beginning to the end of one of Foucault's historical ages or epistemes. Thus, the "totality of all effective statements" potentially includes, for example, all statements made within the discourse of history during a period of approximately 150 to 200 years, if one is considering Foucault's "Classical age." Furthermore, perhaps because Foucault conceived of historical change in terms of discontinuities and ruptures marked by radical transformations of one discursive formation into another, there is little attention paid in his work to the question of how smaller changes within a discursive field inevitably altered that field and affected relations and orientations among the elements within it.[13]

In respect to this problem Jauss can be useful, since he and other like-minded literary historians make us conscious of how every new work alters the horizon against which it appears and thus in its turn creates a new horizon against which other works are viewed. Thus, whereas Foucault provides a spatial frame for plotting the position of Defoe's narratives within the historical discourse of late seventeenth- and early eighteenth-century England, Jauss furnishes a temporal axis along which to chart changes within the discourse of history and between historiography and the emerging discourse of the novel, and this study makes use of both conceptual orientations.[14]

---

[13] Indeed some historians have insisted upon the "utter incompatibility" of Foucault's work and "the practice of history"; see *Foucault and the Writing of History*, ed. Jan Goldstein (Oxford: Blackwell, 1994), 2. Overall, however, this collection of essays argues for the "accessibility" and utility of Foucault for historians; 15.

[14] Foucault seeks not "to rediscover the continuous, insensible transition that relates discourses on a gentle slope to what precedes them, surrounds them, or follows them" but instead simply "to define discourses in their specificity," and yet he acknowledges that he writes "histories of the present." While Jauss focuses our attention upon particular horizons of expectations, he also seeks to link the historical study of reception to the present problem of evaluation and formal definition. Each conceives of the historian's object of study as a verbal field and discusses that field in spatial, even geographical, terms. Each argues that authors, texts, bodies of work, and schools of thought must always be viewed within the matrix of their appearance, operation, or unfolding. One scholar has recently explored affinities between German theory and the thought of Foucault, but he shows that there has been a lack of dialogue between the two; see Robert C. Holub, *Crossing Borders: Reception Theory, Poststructuralism, Deconstruction* (Madison: University of Wisconsin Press, 1992), chapter 4. For some, Jauss is too dialectical a thinker and too focused on authors, genres, and *œuvres* to be compatible with Foucault. I nevertheless use them both in this study because each one's approach seems, for my purposes, incomplete in itself. Foucault seems uninterested in the problem of explaining how shifts take place between discursive formations, and although Jauss focuses on shifting horizons, he does so largely in terms of great authors and major texts and so for all that he is an important theoretician of literary history, his method seems, at least for my purposes, somewhat unhistorical. Foucault's "discursive formation" provides a means of conceptualizing the link among texts, statements, authors, and genres in their "specificity." On the other hand, the present study may seem too traditionally historical – enamored of "matters of fact" – to present itself as written in the spirit of Foucault. Yet Goldstein observes that "a historian need not be . . . a purist who embraces the most radical reading of Foucault . . . in order to find him a . . . stimulating guide to . . . conceptualizing historical phenomena"; *Foucault and the Writing of History*, 15. The present work is, thus, neither a Foucauldian nor a Jaussian study; both models of conceiving of change within

II

"History" was and is a far from simple signifier; in the seventeenth and eighteenth centuries it meant "narrative" as well as "true account," and as "true account" it meant both "essentially or morally true narrative" and "factual account." It also meant both "past events" and an account of such events, what we often call historiography.[15] In the early modern period, as we shall see, "history" often referred to well-made narratives that represented generally accepted versions of events written without reference to any original research, but it also referred to accounts that were rooted in an attempt to establish what was or could be known about a given event or person: "matters of fact." Historical accounts that some early modern readers regarded as masterpieces of historiography were dismissed by other contemporary readers as "romances." Similarly, some historical works that were thought important at the time have been ignored by modern historians of history, while other works that were denounced as "party histories" or propaganda have been celebrated by modern scholars as historiographically innovative. So the "history" that I will argue constituted the matrix of the early English novel is a discourse that is far from easy to describe.

Scholars of early modern English historiography have generally told a familiar story about the history of this discourse: the story of an "historical revolution," effected by antiquarians, in the course of which Elizabethan and Stuart England witnessed a profound and far-reaching transformation of historical practice.[16] The principles and the practice that embodied this great change – a belief that "certitude about what had happened in the past was not unattainable, and, more important, was worth striving for," new attitudes toward evidence and proof, a new devotion to facts rooted in

a literary field are illuminating and useful. Neither is for my purposes an explicit methodology but instead a fruitful theoretical view of the problems associated with writing literary history.

15 *OED*; Raymond Williams, *Keywords: A Vocabulary of Culture and Society*, rev. edn. (Oxford University Press, 1983), 146. I use both "history" and "historiography" to refer to history as account of past events, and also to history as a discursive formation.

16 The principal works are David C. Douglas, *English Scholars, 1660–1730* (1939; repr. Westport, CT: Greenwood Press, 1975); J. G. A. Pocock, *The Ancient Constitution and the Feudal Law: A Study of English Historical Thought in the Seventeenth Century. A Reissue with a Retrospect* (Cambridge University Press, 1987); F. Smith Fussner, *The Historical Revolution: English Historical Writing and Thought, 1580–1640* (New York: Columbia University Press; London: Routledge and Kegan Paul, 1962); Arthur B. Ferguson, *Clio Unbound: Perception of the Social and Cultural Past in Renaissance England* (Durham, NC: Duke University Press, 1979); Joseph Levine, *Humanism and History: Origins of Modern English Historiography* (Ithaca: Cornell University Press, 1987); and Levine, *The Battle of the Books: History and Literature in the Augustan Age* (Ithaca: Cornell University Press, 1991). On antiquarians and antiquarianism, see particularly Fussner, Levine, and Arnaldo Momigliano, *Studies in Historiography* (New York: Harper and Row, 1966), 1–39. For a critique of the historical revolution model, see Joseph Preston, "Was There an Historical Revolution?" *Journal of the History of Ideas* 38 (1977), 362–63.

the conviction that in historical accounts "truth" was equivalent to "fact," and the idea that one of the historian's chief tasks was "the discovery, criticism, and editing of what we would call primary materials" – are all implicit in Barbara Shapiro's assertion that in the seventeenth century "history" was an account of "matters of fact."[17] The story of an historical revolution in early modern England (which in its various tellings extends from the career of John Leland [*c*. 1503–52] to that of Edward Gibbon [1703–92]) undeniably represents an important feature of the history of history in this period, particularly if one focuses on the origins of modern historical practice. In the medieval period, historians were content to present what was generally accepted about the past, but from the sixteenth century certain scholars sought to establish what was known, to criticize that which was believed but seemed improbable, and to uncover new sources of historical evidence. The rejection of conjecture and of invented speeches or scenes, the concentration on secondary (human) rather than primary (providential) explanation, the commitments to impartiality and to a plain style – all these did represent a clear departure from past practice, and many of the best-known historians of the period were in this sense "revolutionaries": Leland, William Camden, Walter Ralegh, John Stow, John Selden, Francis Bacon, Henry Spelman, James Harrington, Robert Brady, William Dugdale, and Thomas Hearne, all have been discussed as "heroes" of the historical revolution by one or more of the students of this transformation.[18] But although there is much truth in the story of the historical revolution, this narrative has been related so often, and so much to the exclusion of other possible narratives, that it is often taken to be the only story that might be told about early modern English historiography, which it decidedly is not.

The history of early modern English historiography is, in short, Whiggish: F. Smith Fussner represents Ralegh as "the heir of a dying medieval tradition"; F. J. Levy discusses "old-fashioned" history as the product of a "cultural lag"; and J. G. A. Pocock treats the failure to arrive at a modern sense of anachronism as a failure to "attain . . . a historical view."[19] To be sure, this Whiggishness is a product of the focus or endpoint chosen by historians of early modern English historiography, most clearly indicated

[17] Barbara Shapiro, *Probability and Certainty in Seventeenth-Century England: A Study of the Relationships Between Natural Science, Religion, History, Law, and Literature* (Princeton University Press, 1983), 120; William Nelson, *Fact or Fiction: The Dilemma of the Renaissance Storyteller* (Cambridge MA: Harvard University Press), 37; J. R. Hale, introd., *The Evolution of British Historiography From Bacon to Namier* (Cleveland: World Publishing Co., 1964), 12; Douglas, *English Scholars*, 16. See also Fussner, *Historical Revolution*, xix. On "matters of fact," see chapter 6 below.
[18] Momigliano, *Studies*, 10–25; Hale, *Evolution*, 9–21; Levine, *Humanism and History*, 73–105; Fussner, *Historical Revolution*; Douglas, *English Scholars*; Pocock, *Ancient Constitution*.
[19] Fussner, *Historical Revolution*, 245; F. J. Levy, *Tudor Historical Thought* (San Marino: The Huntington Library, 1967), 211; Pocock, *Ancient Constitution*, 68, 89.

by Joseph M. Levine who affirms that his subject is "how and why English historiography found its modern method," rather than the product of the scholars' desire to glorify a particular point of view.[20] Still, the "presentist" bias remains.[21] Pocock acknowledges the problem of Whiggishness while also cogently defending his method:

> The history of how these capacities were acquired has to be written somehow, and . . . there is much to be said for starting at a time when they did not yet exist and showing why they did not yet exist and what the changes were which led to their being acquired.

He is right to claim that he avoided the " 'vulgar whiggism' of regarding the time when they [the capacities] did not exist as thereby impoverished," but even Pocock does not suggest that he has avoided privileging modern historiographical practice and thereby at least implicitly depreciating that which seems unmodern. For example, he dismisses the historical work done on English institutions before Spelman's "discovery of feudalism" as something other than "genuinely historical" scholarship.[22] Herein lies the explanation for why important early modern British historians like Thomas Fuller, Edward Hyde, the Earl of Clarendon, and Gilbert Burnet, not to mention popular writers of the late seventeenth and early eighteenth centuries like Sir Richard Baker, Nathaniel Crouch, and John Milton, are consistently ignored by historians of the historical revolution.[23] Fuller's *Church-History of Britain* (1655), Clarendon's *History of the Rebellion* (1702–04), and Burnet's *History of His Own Times* (1724) may have been great works of history, but by the lights of the historians of the historical revolution they are not great *modern* works of history, and they are therefore negligible insofar as the history of history is concerned.

---

20 Levine, *Humanism and History*, 9. See also Douglas, *English Scholars*, 28; Pocock, *Ancient Constitution*, 1; and Fussner, *Historical Revolution*, xxii. Each in his own way has "emphasize[d] certain principles of progress in the past and . . . produce[d] a story which is the ratification if not the glorification of the present"; Herbert Butterfield, *The Whig Interpretation of History* (New York: Charles Scribner's Sons, 1951), v.

21 For this term, see George W. Stocking, Jr. *Race, Culture and Evolution: Essays in the History of Anthropology. With a New Preface* (University of Chicago Press, 1982), 1–12.

22 Pocock, *Ancient Constitution*, 257, 102–03. Pocock's work is, of course, erudite, subtle, and penetrating; his scholarship along with the work of the other historians cited here who treat seventeenth-century historiography justifies Arthur Ferguson's assertion that the history of Tudor and Stuart historiography "has been well and truly written." Arthur Ferguson, *Clio Unbound*, ix. Thus the Whiggishness of the history of seventeenth-century historiography does not derive from inadequate historical imagination but from the inherent limitations of the historical revolution paradigm. As will be apparent, I have learned from and relied upon the scholars whose work I from time to time criticize.

23 Fuller, Clarendon, Burnet, Crouch, and Milton are discussed at some length in chapters 1, 4, 5, 6, and 2 below, respectively; on Baker, see Martine Watson Brownley, "Sir Richard Baker's *Chronicle* and Later Seventeenth-Century Historiography," *Huntington Library Quarterly* 52 (1989), 481–500; on Fuller, see my "The Rhetoric of Historical Truth: Heylyn contra Fuller on *The Church-History of Britain*," forthcoming.

If one is interested in modern historical thought, the use of the historical revolution paradigm is eminently defensible, but if one is interested in the appearance of the English novel, such an approach is likely to be counter-productive: the relevance of historiography to the development of the novel will be understood wholly in light of the historian's devotion to "matters of fact" as that commitment was understood by the small number of historical revolutionaries. The disposition of fiction-writers toward history-writing, in turn, will be seen in terms of the resulting "formal realism" of the early English novel, the implication being that eighteenth-century realism was simply a novelistic displacement of antiquarian practice in a fictional mode.[24] Without a recognition that "history" around 1700 was much more than antiquarian research, any meaningful discussion of the links between historical discourse and the fictional discourse that eventuated in the English novel is almost impossible. Since the aim of this investigation is to stipulate the nature of the link between historical discourse and the novel, my treatment of English historiography in this period differs significantly from that written by the various scholars of the historical revolution. Although the account provided here makes no claim to be definitive, it needs to be related if the history-fiction nexus in the early English novel is to be understood. What I shall demonstrate is that in the historical discourse of the seventeenth and early eighteenth centuries a commitment to the reporting of matters of fact coexisted with a willingness to tolerate or even actively employ fictional elements in history and also with a markedly polemical rhetoric that signaled that history was not a disinterested factual discourse but a means of shaping historical reality.

III

Historians of the English novel – who often begin their consideration of novelistic texts with *Robinson Crusoe* – have generally assumed that Defoe's assertions that his texts were histories have to be read as tropes; they have thus foreclosed the possibility of any genuine inquiry into the nature of the historical claims made by Defoe on behalf of his most famous narrative. As is often the case with the author of *The Rise of the Novel*, Ian Watt actually has more to say about the importance of the history-fiction link in the early history of the English novel than at first appears to be the case. Watt asserts that Defoe and Richardson "were content to be 'mere face-painters and historians'," and in linking historians and Dutch realist painters, he implicitly establishes the figurative nature of any reference to Defoe as a historian. Watt's actual discussion of historical thought and writing is – not

[24] See, for example, Watt, *Rise of the Novel*, 21–24; Barbara Foley, *Telling the Truth: The Theory and Practice of Documentary Fiction* (Ithaca: Cornell University Press, 1986), 109–11; McKeon, *Origins*, 45–63.

surprisingly, given this initial assumption – sketchy; he focuses on changes during the Renaissance in the ways that Europeans conceived of time and argues that the novel reflects these changes. For Watt, the novel is an "historical" form because it discards the "a-historical outlook" of, for example, Shakespeare, or the writers of romance, in favor of narratives that occur "at a particular place and at a particular time." Watt's discussion of the "greater referentiality of language" in the novel as compared with other fictional forms, which he considers one of the principal components of the "formal realism" that constitutes for Watt a virtual definition of the novel, is also tied to the issue of the link between history and the novel. Watt treats the increased referentiality as the result of an appropriation of historiographical practice by the fiction writer: "its [the novel's] formal convention forces it to supply its own footnotes." The "notes," however, illuminate the fictional practice of the novelist; they have only a figurative relationship to historical writing. Thus, even the use of seemingly genuine footnotes by a writer like Scott is to be comprehended under the rubric of "formal realism." So viewed, the claim to historicity can only ever be a figure of speech used by a writer to establish "the novel's air of total authenticity."[25]

By contrast, Lennard Davis has come as close as anyone to a sustained consideration of the history-fiction link in the novel, but his *Factual Fictions* focuses rather narrowly on the link between journalism and the novel. Davis argues that a "news/novel discourse" was the discursive matrix from which the novel emerged. He rightly points out that Defoe's narratives "remain odd to us because they seem not fully novels," in no small part because they "bear the marks of their intimate connection" with the discursive formation to which they were earlier attached. Davis's insightful argument is weakened, however, by his concentration on the "news/novel discourse" – his own construct, of course, the artificiality of which is suggested by its yoking together of "news" and "novel" with a slashmark – rather than "history," the factual discourse with which early modern fiction writers repeatedly linked the new form they were essaying.[26] As Michael McKeon has pointed out, Davis defines the "news/novel discourse" so that "verse ballads play the earliest and most crucial role," but "histories have no importance," and thus Davis brackets the form of discourse most frequently cited as providing a key to the new fiction by the actual writers of "factual fictions."[27]

[25] Watt, *Rise of the Novel*, 17, 21–24, 32. In light of Michael McKeon's work on romance and the novel, some of Watt's assertions seem more problematic than they once did; see McKeon, *Origins*, 3–4.

[26] Lennard J. Davis, *Factual Fictions: The Origins of the English Novel* (New York: Columbia University Press, 1983), 173.

[27] McKeon claims, with some reason, that Davis thereby ignores "his real subject – which might

Despite my differences with Davis, however, this study is akin to his in treating both history and the novel as forms of discourse.[28] Davis conceives of the emergence of the novel not as "a series of genres displacing each other" (romance displaced by novel) but as "a discourse that is forced to subdivide," forcing "news" and "novel" to bifurcate into two distinct discursive formations. Also, Davis describes the discourse from which the novel emerges as one with "a unique and characteristic attitude toward fact and fiction, toward external reality, and the nature of their authenticity."[29] My own view is similar; I see the novel emerging from a historical discourse undergoing change early in the eighteenth century, leading to the emergence of a new, novelistic discourse in which a dialogue between fact and fiction is a key element in the constitution of the form. In discussing the novel, then, I am less interested in traditional generic analysis than in studying the ways in which the new form of fiction emerged from the discursive matrix of history and constituted a new way of knowing, writing about, and acting in the world.

McKeon rejects the idea of a sharp break or rupture between discursive modes such as one finds in most Foucauldian discussions of the novel. His argument in *The Origins of the English Novel*, which posits a challenge to "romance idealism" in the seventeenth century by "naive empiricism" and a subsequent challenge to the empiricist position by an "extreme skepticism" that had much in common with the earlier idealist position, is an argument that the novel was dialectically constituted by a debate between romance and history as well as between competing epistemological and ideological positions.[30] McKeon's construct is rich and compelling but in truth he has taught us a good deal more about the importance of romance to the development of the novel than about the history-fiction link. He discusses "categorial instability" in the early modern period, but too readily identifies historiography with "naive empiricism"; rather like Watt, McKeon accepts the narrative of the historical revolution as an account of the history of history that tells historians and theoreticians of the novel what they need to know in order to account for the development of the English novel. Thus, McKeon's model does not allow one to consider Defoe's historical claim on behalf of fictional texts as the radical, transforming assertion that it was, but instead continues the tradition of familiarizing Defoe's narratives and their editorial assertions.

better be called the 'fact/fiction discourse'"; McKeon, "The Origins of the English Novel," *Modern Philology* 82 (1984), 79.

[28] Others who have used Foucault and the concept of discourse to treat the origins of the novel include Nancy Armstrong, *Desire and Domestic Fiction: A Political History of the Novel* (New York: Oxford University Press, 1987); and John Bender, *Imagining the Penitentiary: Fiction and the Architecture of Mind in Eighteenth-Century England* (University of Chicago Press, 1987).

[29] Davis, *Factual Fictions*, 12.   [30] McKeon, *Origins*, 21.

At least one of the lessons of recent scholarship on the novel is that an event as overdetermined as the appearance of the English novel will never be explained by recourse to any single theoretical approach and that no historical reconstruction of that event can ever hope to be complete. This view is embodied in J. Paul Hunter's cultural (pre)history of the novel, *Before Novels: The Cultural Contexts of Eighteenth-Century Fiction*, where Hunter essentially announces that historians of the novel must begin again: "a mountain of work needs to be done on texts and contexts that the old history (and the new criticism) ignored" in constructing a history of the early English novel.[31] It is the argument of this book that an essential set of these hitherto largely ignored "texts and contexts" is found in the historiography that was actually read and used by novel writers and readers in Defoe's day. To be sure, scholars of the novel have always acknowledged the historical claims of the early novelistic texts, but although there are studies of the novel and epistemology, the novel and life-writing, the novel and travel literature, the novel and guide literature, the novel and the discourse of the prison, the novel and journalism, the novel and conduct books, the novel and the carnivalesque, and the novel and criminal autobiography, there is surprisingly little – no monograph, for example – treating the novel and history.[32] What we lack in particular is a study of the historiography-novel link that moves beyond the assumptions and the findings of the historians of history who have concentrated on the "historical revolution" of seventeenth-century England.

It would be disingenuous of me to suggest, however, that I present this study as simply another examination of "the novel and . . ." Instead, I argue that the present work treats the most important feature on the

---

[31] J. Paul Hunter, *Before Novels: The Cultural Contexts of Eighteenth-Century Fiction* (New York: W. W. Norton, 1990), 3. Admittedly, Hunter is of two minds on the question of the link between history and the novel:

> the writing of history had an impact on the context in which novels began to be written and read, and as an enabling force on the scope of novels it would be hard to overestimate its importance. But it is surprising how little direct influence the writing of history seems to have had on the writing of specific novels.   (341)

Nevertheless, Hunter's observation about the new work to be done on the novel constitutes a virtual call for studies like this one.

[32] In addition to the studies by Armstrong, Bender, Davis, and Watt already cited, see Percy G. Adams, *Travel Literature and the Evolution of the Novel* (Lexington: University Press of Kentucky, 1983); Terry Castle, *Masquerade and Civilization: The Carnivalesque in Eighteenth-Century English Culture and Fiction* (Stanford University Press, 1986); Lincoln B. Faller, *Crime and Defoe: A New Kind of Writing* (Cambridge University Press, 1993); J. Paul Hunter, *The Reluctant Pilgrim: Defoe's Emblematic Method and Quest for Form in Robinson Crusoe* (Baltimore: Johns Hopkins University Press, 1966); Patricia Meyer Spacks *Imagining a Self: Autobiography and Novel in Eighteenth-Century England* (Cambridge MA: Harvard University Press, 1976); and G. A. Starr, *Defoe and Spiritual Autobiography* (Princeton University Press, 1965); for a discussion of the recent, incredibly rich, scholarship on the novel, see Robert Folkenflik, "The Heirs of Watt," *Eighteenth-Century Studies* 25 (1991–92), 203–17.

horizon of expectations against which the novel made its appearance as well as the essential discursive link that led to the rise of the novel. History was the one discourse that virtually all seventeenth- and eighteenth-century fiction writers themselves associated with the novel and identified as the matrix of their fictions. My argument is that the novel is a form that forces the history-fiction problematic on the reader in a way that no other fictional discourse does, and that Defoe was the writer who laid bare the fiction-history link in the novel in a way that no writer did before him or has done since he wrote. Thus the way to the novel lies through the historical study of historiography.

In what follows, I begin, therefore, by reexamining at some length the discourse of history in the century before the appearance of *Robinson Crusoe*. In approaching historical discourse, I have taken the seventeenth century at its word, and have elected to regard for purposes of defining "historical discourse" in this period that which seventeenth-century writers and readers regarded as history. This set of works includes of course the texts that students of the "historical revolution" have taken as their subject, but since those works have already been studied in detail I have tended to examine them principally in relation to the "other history" that is my primary object of study. Some of the authors that I treat are well known while others are almost invisible, even to twentieth-century scholars of early modern England, but I have discussed neither the prominent nor the obscure for their own sake. Instead I have ranged widely – guided mainly by early modern writers, theoreticians, and readers of history, high and low – in order to delineate the borders, rather than to arrive at a definition, of the discourse of history in the years just before the publication of *Robinson Crusoe*. Having thus described historiography, I then look at "histories": fictional texts that asserted their historicity and that have been associated with the tradition of the novel. Works of this type by writers like Thomas Nashe, Thomas Deloney, Aphra Behn, and Delarivier Manley were undeniably important to the history of the novel, but they have not generally been regarded as constitutive events in the emergence of novelistic discourse. I shall argue that this view is accurate, not because Behn or Manley or any other writer wrote "lewd trash" but because the writers of "history" before Defoe, male and female, critiqued the romance tradition without providing any basis for creating a new form of fiction with a new link to historical discourse.[33]

---

[33] The phrase "lewd trash" is a characterization of Behn's fiction from Judith Kegan Gardner, "The First English Novel: Aphra Behn's *Love Letters*, The Canon, and Women's Tastes," *Tulsa Studies in Women's Literature* 8 (1985), 201; for the argument that women's fiction was written out of the canon because, according to subsequent novelists and critics, writers like Behn and Manley "defined 'the novel' as a racy immoral story," see William B. Warner, "The Elevation of the Novel in England: Hegemony and Literary History," *ELH* 59 (1992), 580. While no

I shall then treat in detail the career of Defoe, both as historian and as fiction-writer, demonstrating that the historical claims of Defoe's most famous narratives, when perceived in light of the historiographical practice of the period (and especially in light of Defoe's own version of that practice), appear to be genuine assertions about the set of discursive practices he employed. I shall argue that Defoe's unique position in the history of the novel arises from his having presented richly fictional texts to readers as authentic works of history, works that were only gradually and with great difficulty read into the tradition of the novel. A study of the reception of Defoe's "novels," focusing particularly on *A Journal of the Plague Year*, will then serve to demonstrate that the long and tortuous process by which Defoe's most famous narratives were read into the literary series "novel" unfolded in respect to the question of fact and fiction in his work, and thereby effectively established the nexus of fiction and history as a key feature of the theory of the novel. I shall argue, in short, that Defoe's most famous texts were texts that could plausibly be read as histories when they appeared, but that were subsequently assimilated to the tradition of the novel. Even now there are sound reasons for arguing that one cannot regard some of Defoe's key works as novels, but the process by which they came to be called novels nevertheless illuminates as well as any single development in the history of the form what the word "novel" signifies, at least in respect to the crucial fact-fiction problematic. In closing, I shall theorize the nexus of history and fiction in the novel, arguing that the tradition of the novel is predicated upon at least two related forms of dialogue, one between writers and readers that established the novel as a fictional form that does the work of history and the other between two kinds of discourse – historical and fictional – that by its very enactment in texts like Defoe's created a new discursive formation: novelistic discourse.

Although I aim to illuminate both the history and the theory of the novel, my task in a way is a simple one: first, to suggest how the word "history," when deployed in the preface to *Robinson Crusoe* (and elsewhere in Defoe's works), would have been apprehended by eighteenth-century readers, and second, to see what the practice of the one writer of "novels" whose works were presented to the world as histories and still defy easy classification has to tell us about the dialogue of fact and fiction in the novel form. Jauss argues that through the history of its reception, the

doubt it is true "that women writers in this period were differently situated in relation to epistemological and ethical questions by virtue of their sex," it is nevertheless true that writers like Behn and Manley attempt at least in part to define their fictional forms by linking their fictional discourse with the discourse of history; my view, therefore, is that for both men and women writers the nexus of fiction and history in the novel is a key to understanding the constitution of the novel form. Ros Ballaster, *Seductive Forms: Women's Amatory Fiction from 1684 to 1740* (Oxford: Clarendon Press, 1992), 19.

"revolutionary" work is contained and familiarized and thereby transformed into a "classic," but this description of the process of reception
does not apply to all of Defoe's most famous narratives; *A Journal of the
Plague Year*, for example, has become a classic without ever ceasing to be
"revolutionary," since it persistently raises the fact-fiction question in
respect to the novel in a way that cannot satisfactorily and definitively be
answered.[34] Defoe's works, therefore, more than any texts in the canon of
English novels, force novel readers to come to terms with the link between
the novel and matters of fact that is the focus of the following study.

[34] For Jauss's views on the terms "classic" and "revolutionary," see "Literary History," 25; on the
dual nature of the *Journal*, see chapter 11 below.

1

Baconian historiography: the contours of historical discourse in seventeenth-century England

In 1659 Peter Heylyn, an Anglican divine and well-known historian, launched an attack on Thomas Fuller's *Church-History of Britain* that occupied the better part of two books by Heylyn and elicited a lengthy reply by Fuller in his own defense. This assault was represented by Heylyn as a principled struggle ("Truth is the Mistresse that I serve") to correct Fuller's methodological lapses: his carelessness in regard to the facts, his stylistic idiosyncrasies, and his partiality. In the end, however, Heylyn moved well beyond his particular "animadversions" on Fuller's text, and the attacks on Fuller's *Church-History* served not just a corrective but a delegitimizing function. Heylyn likened Fuller to a "Roman comedian" whose work was interlarded with "*Merry Tales*, and scraps of *Trencher-Jests*," and cited the historian Josephus's observation that "there are some [historians] who do spend themselves on the stile and the dresse, as if their businesse rather were to delight the ear then inform the judgement." Heylyn suggested that Fuller was one such historian and argued that Fuller had failed to ensure that his work was "framed by the Levell and Line of Truth." But despite Heylyn's apparent highmindedness, his aims ultimately were more ideological than methodological. As Heylyn arraigned him, Fuller was not just a writer who was careless with the facts and stylistically flippant; he was also hypocritical and destructive: "[He] hath intermingled his Discourse with some Positions of a dangerous nature, which . . . may not only overthrow the whole power of the Church as it stands constituted and established by the Laws of the Land, but lay a probable foundation for the like disturbances in the *Civil State*."[1]

Heylyn was a Laudian – his biography of the Archbishop treated him as a martyred saint – and he contemptuously rejected Fuller's presentation of himself as a moderate. Despite the fact that Fuller, like Heylyn, had suffered during the interregnum because of his loyalty to the king, Heylyn denounced Fuller's putative evenhandedness as nothing more than a cover for Puritan sympathies, and therefore questioned the reliability of the author of *The Church-History of Britain*. Labelling Fuller a comedian and

---

[1] [Peter Heylyn], *Examen Historicum: Or A Discovery and Examination of the Mistakes, Falsities, and*

arguing that "our Author never meant to frame his History by the line of truth," Heylyn effectively sought to alter the generic status of Fuller's text in the minds of readers, transforming it through a rhetorical barrage from history into fiction.[2] Ann Rigney has argued that historical rhetoric is distinguished by an agonistic element such as one finds in Heylyn's attack on Fuller: "it is through his contradiction of other [putatively] fictional and falsifying versions that the historian accredits himself with the authority to speak for reality."[3] This is the case with Heylyn on Fuller; this particularly contentious – but not, as we shall see, atypical – seventeenth-century historian sought not just to criticize his ideological foe but also to effect a rhetorical transformation of his enemy's historiography into fiction.

The histories of Heylyn and Fuller have essentially been ignored by most historians of seventeenth-century British historiography because their work does not seem to have contributed to the historical revolution, especially as that is identified with the "antiquarian enterprise." As I shall argue in this chapter, however, the dispute of Heylyn and Fuller typifies an important aspect of the historiography of the period. That historiography – which I shall call "Baconian" – is limited neither to the authors and works associated with the historical revolution, nor to those identified by most historians of history with a supposedly moribund historical practice. Rather, Baconian historiography was the discursive meeting ground for all these ways of doing history, a terrain that was also a battleground upon which the right to denominate one's statement or text "history" was the contested prize. One of the aims of this study is to reframe discussions of early modern English historiography in order to focus on this Baconian historiography and thus approach anew the history-fiction question in respect to the early English novel.

This chapter will demonstrate that although there was indeed a great transformation of historical thought and methodology in early modern England, there was also an historical counterrevolution: a concerted assault upon the new history by writers and theoreticians of both history and fiction.[4] For every Camden or Dugdale who employed a new historical method there was a Thomas Nashe or a Winston Churchill who rejected

---

Defects In some Modern Histories (London, 1659), sig. A₄r, A₃r, b₂v–r, A₂v, A₂r, A₃v–A₄r; Heylyn, *Cyprianus Anglicus: or, The History of the Life and Death, of The most Reverend and Renowned Prelate William [Laud]* (London, 1671), sig. A₂v.

2   Heylyn, *Examen*, sig. A₇r.

3   Ann Rigney, *The Rhetoric of Historical Representation: Three Narrative Histories of the French Revolution* (Cambridge University Press, 1990), 48, 61.

4   The idea of such a counterrevolution serves to suggest the limitations of the paradigm of the historical revolution and also to highlight the "otherness" imposed on the historiography treated in this study in accounts where it is dismissed as marginal, vestigial, or moribund. Yet the label also serves to acknowledge that in some cases the texts in question *were* reactionary, often consciously so, in the sense that they were deliberately based on historiographical principles or methodology that had been rejected by the historical revolutionaries.

the new historiographical principles in favor of older historical models and rules. One might classify these various attitudes as reflecting "emergent" or "dominant" or "residual" practices, and thereby contain the strangeness of seventeenth-century historical practice within a satisfying and not inaccurate historical argument, but to do so is to run the risk of valorizing some historians as progressive and prescient while stigmatizing others as reactionary and obtuse.[5] This study seeks to avoid treating the history of history as an unfolding dialectic in the course of which the "emergent" becomes the "dominant" and the "dominant" the "residual," in no small part because in the discursive field that was seventeenth-century historiography, the sense of which historiographical paradigm, at any given moment, was dominant, which residual, which emergent, changes from one text, author, or subspecies of history to another. Neither revolutionary nor "counterrevolutionary" historiography constituted *the* historical discourse of the period; to assert that one or the other did is to claim that writers and readers of history were primarily interested either in developing and promoting a new way of "doing" history or in insisting that the old way of doing history was the only valid way. While some working historians were strongly committed to one or the other of these projects, most producers and consumers of history seem to have been more concerned with what historiography could do in the world at large than with how it should be done. This study examines diverse approaches to the writing of history that, taken together, comprised Baconian historiography.

I

We can begin by stipulating what is meant by the "new history" – the methods, principles, statements, works, and authors that taken together constituted the "historical revolution." This may be economically done by examining the historiographical theory of William Camden, the "greatest practitioner" of the "new history," and comparing his views with those of his contemporaries.[6] In *The History of the Most Renowned and Victorious Princess Elizabeth*, Camden stated his methodological principles in the address of "The Author to the Reader." The historian first discussed the records he "digested" in the course of his work on Elizabeth's reign:

I procured all the Helps I possibly could for writing it: Charters and Grants of King's and great Personages, Letters, Consultations in the Council Chamber, Embassadours Instructions and Epistles, I carefully turned over and over; the Parliamentary Diaries, Acts and Statutes, I thoroughly perused, and read over every Edict and Proclamation.

5   Raymond Williams, *Marxism and Literature* (Oxford University Press, 1977), 121–27.
6   Hale, *Evolution*, 16.

The new historians, above all else, took it upon themselves to find, critically examine, and establish the reliability of documents. Camden asserts that he weighed all potential evidence "in the Balance of mine own Judgment . . . lest I should at any time through a beguiling Credulity incline to that which is False" and also that he had sought to omit from his account "all such things . . . as use to obscure and prejudice the Light of Truth."[7] Insisting that "ignorance," "doubtfull Uncertainty," and "flat Falsity" should be expunged from historical accounts, rejecting "Prejudice" whether arising from fear, greed, or "Affection or Disaffection," and eschewing the use of invented speeches (a regular feature of historiography since antiquity) and "animadverting Observations," Camden declares the historian's task to be the treatment of "Circumstances" so that "not onely the Events of Affairs, but also the Reasons and Causes thereof might be understood."[8] In other words, Camden sought to use matters of fact to establish human, rather than providential, causes of "secular historical problems" and aimed at "writing a history which fulfilled modern rather than medieval norms."[9]

Compare Camden's stated methodology with the views of the writers of chronicles, the dominant historical form in sixteenth-century England. Edward Hall, in his chronicle of the War of the Roses, declared: "I haue compiled and gathered (and not made) out of diuerse writers . . . this simple treatise." For the Tudor chroniclers, histories were narratives constructed from the known "facts," and historians reported what was generally held to be true. From the perspective of many seventeenth-century historians, however, what the Tudor chronicles contained were not facts at all, since "the question 'What is a fact?' . . . one test of the maturity of a period's historiography" never arose for Hall and his fellow chronicle-writers.[10] Historians like Camden, however, made the question "what is a fact?" central to the historiographical enterprise. Thus historians like Degory Wheare canonized Camden's work as the best of the English historiographical tradition because it was "Collected not out of *mere Fictions*

---

[7] William Camden, *The History of the Most Renowned and Victorious Princess Elizabeth Late Queen of England. Selected Chapters*, ed. and introd. Wallace T. MacCaffrey (University of Chicago Press, 1970), 4, 5; on this preface, see Fussner, *Historical Revolution*, 236–38. On the importance of records, see Douglas, *English Scholars*, 16; Fussner, *Historical Revolution*, xix; Levine, *Humanism and History*, 73, 77.

[8] Camden set clear limits, however, to his willingness to speak the unvarnished truth: "Things manifest and evident I have not concealed; Things doubtfull I have interpreted favourably; Things secret and abstruse I have not pried into"; *Princess Elizabeth*, 4–6. This aspect of his practice will be discussed in the next chapter.

[9] Fussner, *Historical Revolution*, 237.

[10] *Hall's Chronicle* (1809; repr. New York: AMS Press, 1965), vii; Hale, *Evolution of British Historiography*, 10. On the chronicle as "an agglomeration of all the known facts," see John Kenyon, *The History Men: The Historical Profession in England since the Renaissance* (University of Pittsburgh Press, 1983), 8; and Brownley, "Sir Richard Baker's *Chronicle*," 484.

and Fables . . . but out of the most sincere and uncorrupted Monuments of Antiquity," and William Dugdale insisted upon "the whole series of publick Records, and . . . multitude of antient and obscure Manuscripts" that he consulted in preparing his seminal *Antiquities of Warwickshire*.[11] Interestingly, the passion for documents and details was also a feature of popular works of history, written by far less "reputable" and "progressive" historians than Camden, Wheare, and Dugdale. In Sir Richard Baker's *Chronicle of the Kings of England* (1643), the most important chronicle of the seventeenth century, for example, the taste for matters of fact in historiography revealed itself in the provision of "picturesque, unusual, and bizarre incidents" and "minor details of character" like a discussion of the page who defended King Canute's daughter, Guinhilda, when she was accused of adultery.[12] Many different kinds of "facts," then, some of which were dubious in respect to both provenance and facticity, were deployed in seventeenth-century English historiography.

What is more, although Camden's *History of Elizabeth* contained a definitive account of the principles of the new history, it was not itself a typical product of the historical revolution, organized as it was annalistically and functioning as it did as a narrative account of a reign. Works that more clearly embodied Camden's principles – Camden's own *Britannia* (1586), John Stow's *Survey of London* (1598), Henry Spelman's *Archaeologus* (1626), Dugdale's *Antiquities of Warwickshire* (1658), Henry Wharton's *Anglia Sacra* (1691), and Richard Bentley's *Dissertation upon the Epistles of Phalaris* (1699) – departed from old models such as annals, chronicles, and the "perfect history" of Renaissance luminaries like Machiavelli or Thomas More, and instead were content to function in important part as collections of data. Stow, for example, undertook the "discovery of London" by reporting what he found in "sundry antiquities" after a thorough "search of records";[13] Spelman set out to account historically for thousands of words crucial to the study of English law;[14] *Anglia Sacra* seemed to a twentieth-century reader "a collection of materials that might subserve a scientific history of the medieval Church in England";[15] and Bentley used his expertise in chronology, epigraphy, numismatics, and philology – all basic tools of the antiquary – to demonstrate that the *Epistles of Phalaris* was a forgery.[16] Thus the "antiquarian enterprise" proceeded by way of

---

[11] Degory Wheare, *The Method and Order of Reading both Civil and Ecclesiastical Histories*, 2nd edn., trans. and enl. Edmund Bohun (London, 1694), 15, 134; William Dugdale, *The Antiquities of Warwickshire* (London, 1661), sig. b3v.

[12] Brownley, "Sir Richard Baker's *Chronicle*," 487–88.

[13] John Stow, *The Survey of London*, ed. H. B. Wheatley, introd. Valerie Pearl (London: Dent, 1987), xxv.

[14] Pocock, *Ancient Constitution*, 94–97.   [15] Douglas, *English Scholars*, 147.

[16] Levine, *The Battle of the Books*, 50–84.

collection, comparison, and criticism, and its essence "lay in the discovery, the criticism, and the editing of materials."[17]

But was this scholarship history? A useful check on the tendency in modern scholarship to regard the "new" history as the "true" history is to recall that even though subsequent readers have declared that such work laid the basis for "genuine" historical study in England, many early modern readers and writers denied that the work of men like Wharton and Bentley constituted even a variety of historiography. Indeed there was a tension between "history" and antiquarian researches from Camden's day down to that of Gibbon.[18] One sees this tension most clearly in the attacks on the new history launched by those whom I call the historical counter-revolutionaries.

Imaginative writers were particularly hard on antiquarian laborers. Sir Philip Sidney depicted the historian as too "loaden with old mouse-eaten records" to be effective teachers of virtue; he ridiculed the historian's "authorising himself (for the most part) upon other histories, whose greatest authorities are built upon the notable foundation of hearsay." Character-istically, Thomas Nashe was even harsher: he called antiquarianism "a musty vocation"; claimed its practitioners "will blow their nose in a box and say it is the spittle that Diogenes spat in one's face"; lambasted "lay chronigraphers, that write of nothing but of Mayors and Sheriffs, and the dear year, and the great frost"; and decried the fact that such writers "cannot sweeten a discourse, or wrest admiration from men reading." Even Milton, in his *History of Britain*, refused to stand "with others computing, or collating years and Chronologies." Antiquaries were a favorite butt of character-writers like John Earle, who declared the antiquary "a man strangely thrifty of Time past . . . whence he fetches out many things when they are now all rotten and stinking." Similarly, Samuel Butler dismissed the type as one who "devours an old Manuscript with greater Relish than Worms and Moths do, and, though there be nothing in it, values it above any Thing printed."[19] As late as the 1740s, furthermore, Fielding attacked "the 'objective' method of factual accumulation used by the antiquarian" and focused "his renovation of reality on private life

[17] Levine, *Humanism and History*, 73; Douglas, *English Scholars*, 16.

[18] Ferguson, *Clio Unbound*, 5; Pocock, *Ancient Constitution*, 102; Shapiro, *Probability and Certainty*, 135. Levine argues that history and antiquities remained more-or-less distinct until Gibbon attempted "nothing less than to put back together what had been torn asunder, to marry literature to erudition, history to antiquities"; *Humanism and History*, 105.

[19] Sir Philip Sidney, *An Apology for Poetry*, ed. Geoffrey Shepherd (London: Nelson, 1965), 105; Thomas Nashe, *The Unfortunate Traveller and Other Works*, ed. J. B. Steane (London: Penguin, 1972), 79, 92; John Milton, *The History of Britain. The Complete Prose Works. Vol. v*, introd. and notes French Fogle (New Haven: Yale University Press, 1971), 37; John Earle, *Micro-cosmographie. English Reprints*, ed. Edward Arber (London: Murray and Sons, 1868), 28; Samuel Butler, *Characters and Passages from Note-Books*, ed. A. R. Waller (Cambridge University Press, 1908), 43.

because he believed that the practice of public history had served primarily to distort people's appreciation of the world and how it works." Thus Fielding's celebrated narrator in *Tom Jones* was presented as a "model historian" who unlike the antiquary understands the proper relationship in historical writing between general truths and particularities.[20]

Historians joined imaginative writers in criticizing the new history. The great Camden himself acknowledged the "musty" character of antiquarian researches in describing his research for the *History of Elizabeth*: "I lighted upon great Piles and Heaps of Papers and Writings of all sorts reasonably well digested in respect of the Times, but in regard of the Variety of the Arguments very much confused. In searching and turning over whereof whilst I labored till I sweat again, covered all over with Dust, to gather fit Matter together."[21] Camden was undoubtedly being ruefully ironic, but his self-deprecating characterization of his own labors did embody the attitudes of both poets and historians who disapproved of the new history. In greater earnest, Winston Churchill, the seventeenth-century politician and historian, argued that some historians were too concerned with their own reputations for accuracy to be of service to their country, and Lawrence Echard, the historian of Rome, derided one historian's "mixing of Critical Learning" with his narrative, which "makes him far less pleasant than he otherwise might be." In addition, Sir William Temple argued that antiquarians had nothing to contribute to the comprehensive history of England that he proposed to compile from the best existing historical works, a project later realized by John Hughes who himself described antiquarian research as "a laborious Plunder of . . . publick Rolls and Records."[22] This same attitude is apparent in Milton's assertions about the kind of history he wrote; the poet asserted that he would avoid "controversies and quotations" that might "delay or interrupt the smooth course of History," implying that the "methods for distinguishing among the materials of history, which were undergoing such radical reconsideration in his own [day] . . . were not among his central concerns" and that instead, he, like the chroniclers, was primarily interested in the rhetorically effective presentation of received historical wisdom. Thus although thoroughly versed in modern as well as ancient historical practice, Milton rejected the new history in favor of a historiography that was mainly indebted to classical models and chiefly concerned with rhetoric.[23] Finally,

---

[20] Leo Braudy, *Narrative Form in Fiction and History: Hume, Fielding and Gibbon* (Princeton University Press, 1970), 121, 179, 180.

[21] Camden, *Princess Elizabeth*, 3.

[22] Winston Churchill, *Divi Britannici: Being a Remark Upon the Lives of all the Kings of this Isle, From the year of the World 2855. Unto the Year of Grace 1660* (London, 1675), 4; Levine, *Humanism and History*, 273–74, n. 39, 166–67, and 170. For a discussion of Churchill, see chapter 2 below.

[23] John Milton, *History of Britain*, 3, xlvii, xlvi, xxiv–xxvii.

Henry St. John, Viscount Bolingbroke dismissed the new historians as "pedants, always incapable, sometimes meddling and presuming."[24]

Joseph Levine treats much of this criticism of the new history as so many salvos launched by proponents of the ancients in the Battle of the Books, and there is much truth in this view. Opponents and critics of the new history like Temple often argued that antiquarian research ("largely pedantry and generally dispensable") was not worthy of being equated with the historical masterpieces of the ancients because classical models of historiography suggested that well-written, rhetorically effective narratives, not citations from "mouse eaten records," constituted creditable historiography. Others, like William Wotton, celebrated antiquarian texts as triumphs of "the magnificent achievement of modern scholarship."[25] Nevertheless, although there are grounds for treating this dispute over the nature of history as a clash between ancients and moderns, this argument tends to obscure the fact that participants on both fronts in that war were advocates of "modern" history and the equally crucial fact that there was more than one "modern" history and more than one "historical revolution" underway during the period under discussion.[26] Often at odds with one another, the different "modern" histories and historiographical upheavals nonetheless were in important respects successive moments in the development of what Joseph Preston calls "Renaissance historiography."[27]

The two types of "modern" history written in the early modern era may be labeled "humanist modern history" and "scientific modern history," although in fact both types were in important respects products of the humanist revival of classical learning.[28] "Scientific modern history" was exemplified by the antiquarian researches of the scholars celebrated by the historians of the historical revolution while "humanist modern history" derived from the efforts of Italian historians like Machiavelli and Guicciardini, who interested themselves in human rather than divine causation and regarded history as a way of writing political philosophy.[29]

---

[24] Henry St. John, first Viscount Bolingbroke, *Historical Writings*, ed. Isaac Kramnick (University of Chicago Press, 1972), 11; for Bolingbroke's views, see Kramnick, "Augustan Politics and English Historiography: The Debate on the English Past, 1730–35," *History and Theory* 6 (1967), 38–40; John F. Tinkler, "Humanist History and the English Novel in the Eighteenth Century," *Studies in Philology* 85 (1988), 514–23.

[25] Levine, *Humanism and History*, 155–77; *Battle of the Books*, especially 7–8 and 42–43.

[26] Tinkler, at 519, cites George M. Logan, "Substance and Form in Renaissance Humanism," *Journal of Medieval and Renaissance Studies* 7 (1977), 13, on this point: "both the rhetorical history and the critical history of the Renaissance are . . . humanist products."

[27] Preston, "Was There an Historical Revolution?," 364.

[28] My argument here owes a good deal to Levine, *Humanism and History*, 123–54, though it differs from his in important respects. See also Momigliano, *Studies in Historiography*, 1–39.

[29] Fussner, *Historical Revolution*, 10–15; Ferguson, *Clio Unbound*, 25–26. On the Italians' view of history, see Peter E. Bondanella, *Machiavelli and the Art of Renaissance History* (Detroit: Wayne

Early practitioners of this type of history in England included Thomas
More and Polydore Vergil; the greatest disciple of the Italian masters in
England was Bacon. "Humanist modern history," with its emphasis on
secondary causation and practical political considerations, represented a
sharp break with the past. Yet, as Stuart Clark observes, historians like
More and Bacon believed that "the task of the true historian, as opposed
to the mere annalist or antiquarian, was the interpretation and explanation of already established facts about the past for the present guidance of
the reader." Practitioners of this type of history did not, therefore,
participate in "the antiquarian enterprise," and if the development of
modern "erudition" is taken as the measure of modernity, More,
Polydore, and even Bacon were not modern historians at all.[30] Indeed in
the *Advancement of Learning*, Bacon distinguished between "Antiquities" and
the kind of history he actually wrote in the *History of the Reign of Henry VII*,
defining the former as "history defaced or some remnants of history
which have casually escaped the shipwreck of time" and the latter as
"just" or "perfect" history.[31]

Bacon's theoretical view of history as opposed to his taxonomy of
historical genres, however, makes it clear why he is seen as a crucial
figure in the making of the historical revolution. In the *Advancement of
Learning* he declared history the basis of all learning because it was the
discourse that did the work of memory and served as the repository of
matters of fact. In the *Great Instauration* he argued for the restoration of
"that commerce between the mind of man and the nature of things,
which is more precious than anything on earth," declaring thereby that
true knowledge was derived from the facts of experience.[32] In his
theoretical works, then, he provided the philosophical rationale for
modern scientific history, but Bacon is nevertheless a problematic figure
in the history of history because although in theory he was a historical
revolutionary, a proponent of modern scientific historiography, in practice
he was a modern historian of the humanist variety. In principle, he
recognized the necessity for research in history but he also thought that
activity "somewhat beneath the dignity of an undertaking like mine." His
Henry VII has been called a masterpiece of historical composition, but it
reveals a carelessness about particulars that is undoubtedly traceable to
the fact that his aims as a historian were primarily political and

State University Press, 1973), 16–25; Pocock, *The Machiavellian Moment: Florentine Political Thought
and the Atlantic Republican Tradition* (Princeton University Press, 1975), 224–25; Shapiro,
Probability and Certainty, 120.

30   Stuart Clark, "Bacon's *Henry VII*: A Case-Study in the Science of Man," *History and Theory* 13
(1974), 99.

31   Francis Bacon, *Selected Writings*, ed. Hugh G. Dick (New York: Random House, 1955), 234–35.
Momigliano shows that the distinction Bacon made is an ancient one; *Studies in Historiography*, 5–7.

32   Bacon, *Selected Writings*, 423; Fussner, *Historical Revolution*, 262–63; Douglas, *English Scholars*, 28.

rhetorical.[33] Levine deftly argues that Bacon was poised at the juncture of two cultures – one humanist, Isocratean-Ciceronian, focused on rhetoric and "practical eloquence," and the other scholastic, Aristotelian, focused on logic and philosophical wisdom – and further that Bacon reconciled these two views in the *Advancement* where he drew upon both the humanist critique of philosophy and the philosophical critique of humanism.[34] In respect to historical thought and writing, we can add a variation on Levine's insight: Bacon was at once a great exponent of "humanist" history and the theoretician who provided the philosophical basis for "scientific" history. Bacon thus had a foot in two historiographical camps, each of which was in its own way "new" and "modern." Moreover, the two groups had much in common, especially a debt to classical models, since the antiquarians had their ancient masters as well.[35]

Nevertheless, humanist historiography was in important ways a counter-revolutionary discourse in respect to the practice of antiquarians like Stow, Camden, Spelman, and Hearne. An historian like Temple, the heir of More and Bacon but determinedly not of Camden and Stow, not only declined to engage in antiquarian research but attacked the antiquarians as fact-grubbers. Throughout the seventeenth century there was tension between these two approaches to history even though both, when seen as part of "Renaissance historiography," were in their own way innovative, and this tension informs the thought of Bacon in a way that makes him particularly instructive for our purposes. Uniting these two different ways of doing history in his own career, Bacon serves as a focal point for apprehending seventeenth-century English historiography as it was actually practiced. At its most characteristic, this was a historiography that partook of both humanist and scientific approaches; it was the product of a dialogue between the historiography now identified with the historical revolution and the sometimes counterrevolutionary historical discourse that has been more or less ignored by twentieth-century scholars. Many crucial historians of this period produced works that embody this dialogue between humanist and scientific approaches. Clarendon, for example, was an historian whose method was rooted in the practice of the ancients and their early modern imitators like Machiavelli and More; he was one of the rhetorically and practically minded modern historians. Indeed most of the historians of the period under discussion sided, whether consciously or not, with the

[33] Fussner, *Historical Revolution*, 258–59, 266–67; the quotation, from Bacon's *Parasceve*, is at Fussner, 259. See also Clark, "Bacon's *Henry VII*," 106; Hale, *Evolution*, 19.

[34] Levine, *Humanism and History*, 147; Tinkler, "Humanist History," 512–14.

[35] Momigliano points out that there was a sharp distinction between "learned research" and "political history" in both the ancient and the early modern period; in that sense the two schools of thought in the seventeenth century were simply drawing on two different aspects of the heritage of antiquity. *Studies in Historiography*, 4.

humanists. Philip Hicks argues that even in the first half of the eighteenth
century "the most pervasive model for historical composition . . . was the
antique one": the account of "great deeds" rendered with sufficient
"rhetorical skills to ensure that the description would be appealing enough
to interest and reach posterity."[36] Yet although Clarendon was in many
ways a historian in this humanist, rhetorical mold, he was also strongly
affected by the historiographical transformations of his time; he was
acutely aware of the views and achievements of scholars like Selden and
Spelman and anxious to do "his best to collect all the written information
necessary for an accurate account of events."[37] Similarly, Bishop Burnet
"had a nineteenth-century reverence for archive or record material," and
Fuller sought "to solve the problem [of bias] by . . . sticking close to his
sources, and engaging in quotation."[38] So seventeenth-century historians
cannot in fact be easily divided into revolutionary and counterrevolutionary camps; those historians who at first glance seem to be humanist
historians in fact owed a good deal to the "antiquarian enterprise"
unfolding around them, and, as we shall see in the next chapter, even the
most celebrated antiquarians were willing for practical purposes to modify
their historiographical principles for reasons of rhetoric or ideology. The
most characteristic historians of this period, then, are neither the "pure"
humanists like Bolingbroke – who was so committed to the idea of history
as a rhetorical performance with a practical end in view that he was willing
to tolerate mendacity in history as long as its use eventuated in the correct
political lesson – nor the "revolutionary" antiquarians theoretically committed to a more severe historical practice, but the historians who drew
upon both of these views of historical practice, the practitioners of
"Baconian historiography."[39]

II

One tends to think of modern humanist historiographers – More, Bacon,
Clarendon – as highly engaged writers who are to be distinguished from
the practitioners of modern scientific history whose antiquarian study was a
more disinterested form of learning. Thus, Stow has been praised for the
"purity of [his] scholarship" and Bentley's *Dissertation* celebrated as a

---

36 Philip Hicks, "Bolingbroke, Clarendon, and the Role of the Classical Historian," *Eighteenth-Century Studies* 20 (1986–87), 446, 447.

37 Shapiro, *Probability and Certainty*, 12, 19, 137, 165; Brownley, "Sir Richard Baker's *Chronicle*," 22. See also Kenyon, *History Men*, 30; Hugh Trevor-Roper, introd., *Selections from Clarendon*, ed. G. Huehns (Oxford University Press, 1978), xi.

38 Kenyon, *History Men*, 36; Joseph Preston, "English Ecclesiastical Historians and the Problem of Bias, 1559–1742," *Journal of the History of Ideas* 32 (1971), 208.

39 D. J. Womersley, "Lord Bolingbroke and Eighteenth-Century Historiography," *The Eighteenth Century: Theory and Interpretation* 28 (1987), 224–26; Tinkler, "Humanist History," 522.

species of "pure scholarship."[40] The antiquarianism of the historical revolutionaries seems to have been designed to ensure that scholars would seek to establish matters of fact and purge their work of bias. This assumption, however, is a fairly dubious one: many counterrevolutionary historians did indeed write with a clear political end in view, but few antiquarian studies from this period were disinterested works of scholarship. Indeed, if the ideal of impartiality is taken as the hallmark of modern method and of participation in the historical revolution, then most historical scholarship from this period was counterrevolutionary since most historians wrote works that were manifestly partial and even openly utilitarian.

For Bacon, historical discourse was, like all learning, not only a way of knowing but also a means of acting in the world. He attacked the "vain" labors of the schoolmen, "laborious webs of learning" that were also "fruitless," and exhorted his readers to "consider what are the true ends of knowledge, and . . . seek it not either for the pleasure of the mind, or for contention, or for superiority to others, or for profit, or fame, or power, or any of these inferior things; but for the benefit and use of life."[41] Since the former Chancellor of England could hardly help but see that working "for the benefit and use of life" generally involved contention and often led to fame and power, he would seem to have meant that men should not use learning for *mere* contention or *mere* power even while clearly indicating that he could not conceive of a form of learning worthy of the name that was not a means to some practical end.

Both before and after the seventeenth century, historiography was regarded as useful, but the idea of utility has had several different senses. Humanist historians argued that history was a storehouse of political and moral lessons, while later the philosophical historians of the eighteenth century came to see history as a means of discerning the principles underlying nature and human nature.[42] In the seventeenth century, however, history was often recommended as an instrument of immediate practical utility. Scholars have pointed out that historical writing was an important weapon for both sides in the English Revolution. Fussner observes for example that Sir Robert Cotton's "influence and patronage . . . helped strike a balance between the study of history as record and the use of history as a weapon," and John Kenyon argues that Clarendon and

---

[40] Fussner, *Historical Revolution*, 220–21; Levine, *Battle of the Books*, 75.

[41] Bacon, *Selected Writings*, 183–84, 193, 437.

[42] Baker, *Race of Time*, 46–52. On philosophical history, see George H. Nadel, "Philosophy of History Before Historicism," *History and Theory* 3 (1963–64), 304–09, 311–14; David Fate Norton, "History and Philosophy in Hume's Thought," in *David Hume: Philosophical Historian*, ed. Norton and Richard H. Popkin (Indianapolis: Bobbs-Merrill, 1965), xxxiii–vi. Nadel shows that history as a way of doing philosophy was a refinement on the view that history was a storehouse of examples.

Burnet wrote their histories to justify the Restoration and the Glorious Revolution, respectively.[43] Less attention has been paid, however, to the fact that the overwhelming majority of seventeenth-century historical works was written with practical ends in view, even those that appear at first glance to be disinterested antiquarian studies. Secret history, virtually by definition, was outlandishly polemical, but even *The Antiquities of Warwickshire*, one of the great local histories of the early modern period, was based on the work of other scholars like Sir Simon Archer, whose work "was motivated by the practical desire to work out his family pedigree and to trace the history of his own estates." Thomas Sprat's *History of the Royal Society*, furthermore, was written as "an Apology" for the new institution.[44] What is more, even theoretical arguments over the nature of history were not infrequently about power. The attack by John Nalson on John Rushworth's *Historical Collections* (1659–92) was a seemingly methodological dispute that was in fact at base ideological. Rushworth presented his *Collections*, a compendium of documents related to important political events in England from 1618 to 1648 tied together by a thin but pointed commentary, as an antidote to "Fancies" and "Contrivances" that fill the "printed Pamphlets in our days." His efforts were criticized by royalist historians, most notably in *Impartial Collection of the Great Affairs of State* (1682–83), where Nalson derided Rushworth's method by proclaiming:

I have not tied my self strictly to the Rules of a Bare Collector, but indulged my self in the Liberty of an Historian, to tie up the loose and scattered Papers with the Circumstances, Causes, and Consequences of them.

On the surface this seems to be a conflict between an historian who espouses a severe antiquarian approach and one who thinks of history primarily as a commentary on the known facts – a dispute, that is, between a modern scientific historian and a modern humanist historian. If one examines the texts that each man produced, however, it is apparent that there is little basis for Nalson's assertion of methodological superiority. Each writer produced a "collection"; in each work the reproduction of documents is at the heart of the author's approach to history. There is more commentary in Nalson's text and many more documents in Rushworth's *Collections*, but qualitatively there is little difference between the two. The title of Nalson's book suggests the real cause of the dispute; declining to fight it out with Rushworth on ideological grounds, Nalson

---

[43] Trevor-Roper, *Selections from Clarendon*, vi; Fussner, *Historical Revolution*, 118; Kenyon, *History Men*, 33.

[44] Stan A. E. Mendyk, *"Speculum Britanniae": Regional Study, Antiquarianism, and Science in Britain to 1700* (University of Toronto Press, 1989), 105; Thomas Sprat, *History of the Royal Society*, ed. Jackson I. Cope and Harold Whitmore Jones (St. Louis: Washington University Studies, 1958), "An Advertisement to the Reader"; Douglas, *English Scholars*, 41. On local history and secret history, see chapters 3 and 5 below; Sprat's *History* is treated in chapter 6 below.

instead maintained that he was primarily concerned with methodological questions, especially his opponent's alleged partiality. But Nalson was no more unbiased than Rushworth had been – he simply took a different view of things.[45] Thus a political dispute was transformed into an argument over whose work deserved to be regarded as genuine history, "history" thereby becoming both a battleground and the prize for the self-proclaimed guardian of legitimate historical practice. Similarly, the clash between Heylyn and Fuller was only partly about method; it was also, and probably primarily, about ecclesiastical politics.

Also, seemingly modern methods could be used by eminent scholars to advance historical views that were little more than mythic tales serving a favored political end. Pocock shows both that Sir Edward Coke's history was "too full of antiquarian learning to be simply a continuation of medieval thought" and also that Coke used his great erudition to advance the myth of the immemorial constitution and of the "confirmations" of the laws of Edward the Confessor by William the Conqueror. The same was true for Spelman, the "discoverer of feudalism" in England, who has been likened by Pocock to Copernicus and Newton for his revolutionary insights. Even though he showed that William I "brought in feudal tenures," Spelman nevertheless argued that the "Conqueror . . . was no conqueror" and that the Norman prince's advent did not fundamentally alter the English constitution.[46] Further complicating the view of seventeenth-century English historiography that emerges from Pocock's great study, Quentin Skinner has argued that the case *for* the historical reality of the Conquest – "a point of view more emancipated than that of Spelman himself" – was made not in the texts of learned antiquaries but in works that formed a "historical tradition" that Skinner himself characterizes as unsophisticated, naive, simple, and old-fashioned: the English chronicle tradition, as represented in the seventeenth century by the works of Baker and William Martyn. Skinner shows that in respect to the Conquest the counterrevolutionary chroniclers were generally correct and the celebrated, revolutionary scholars were willfully wrong.[47]

What is more, Pocock argues that the work of Robert Brady, who was "in the forefront of historical thought of his day" and who showed "that the whole cult of immemorial law was bound up with the fallacy of anachronism," was swept away "when the cause for which they [Brady and

---

[45] John Rushworth, *Historical Collections*, sig. b₁v–b₂r; John Nalson, *Impartial Collections*, ii. Cf. Michael McKeon, *Origins*, 49–50, who is swayed by Nalson's rhetoric into characterizing this dispute as a clash between the "naive empiricism" of Rushworth and the "historical skepticism" of Nalson.

[46] Pocock, *Ancient Constitution*, 51, 103, 105.

[47] Quentin Skinner, "History and Ideology in the English Revolution," *Historical Journal* 8 (1965), 156–60.

others] fought was rejected for ever in 1688 [and] their attitude to history was rejected with it and prevented from exerting its full influence on the course of English thought." For Brady and for his antagonists, in short, historiography was so completely a matter of partisan expediency that political defeat was also historiographical defeat. Thus, advanced historical method could be used in the service of either sound historical scholarship or "bogus" myth, putatively moribund methods led in some cases to superior historical insights, and in either case the historiography that resulted was generally partisan.[48]

Skinner points out that " 'whig' predominance" was so complete that the "conflict of ideas" was not only "suppressed in the politics of the age, but has again been almost completely ignored in works of modern scholarship." In other words, the battle over the "history" of the immemorial constitution led to the triumph of a particular point of view not only in the seventeenth century but also in our own time since the historians who argued that the Conquest had taken place tend to be absent from all accounts of seventeenth-century historiography.[49] In the seventeenth century, then, it was the unreality of the theory of the immemorial constitution that by and large could not be enunciated in historical discourse; in our own time, it is the messy historiographical reality that I have denominated Baconian historiography that has been largely invisible in the scholarship written by historians who undoubtedly see themselves as the heirs of the historical revolution.

Foucault argues that discussions of the nature of "history" and "truth" always entail this kind of triumph and defeat and "truth" always signifies, among other things, the means, the ability, the power of stipulating what can and cannot be enunciated: "Truth is to be understood as a system of ordered procedures for the production, regulation, distribution, circulation and operation of statements." Seventeenth-century English historiography is an extraordinarily clear case in point. Indeed Foucault might have been speaking about early modern English historiography when he observed that

The history which bears and determines us has the form of a war rather than that of a language: relations of power, not relations of meaning. History has no "meaning," though this is not to say that it is absurd or incoherent. On the contrary, it is intelligible and should be susceptible of analysis down to the smallest detail – but this in accordance with the intelligibility of struggles, of strategies and tactics.[50]

[48] Pocock, *Ancient Constitution*, 197, 206, 211; Skinner, "History and Ideology," 160; Pocock, "Robert Brady, 1627–1700. A Cambridge Historian of the Restoration," *Cambridge Historical Journal* 10 (1951), 186.
[49] Skinner, "History and Ideology," 161, 154.
[50] Michel Foucault, "Truth and Power," in *Power/Knowledge*, ed. Colin Gordon, trans. Gordon *et al.* (New York: Pantheon, 1980), 133, 114; *Dits et écrits*, III, 160, 145.

As I have been arguing, seventeenth-century English historians rejected the disinterested stance implicit in the antiquarian ideal even if they embraced the methods of antiquarians; in so doing they implicitly elaborated an engaged and activist version of the Baconian dictum that learning was for "the benefit and use of life." Baconian historiography, therefore, denotes among other things a struggle in which crucial political, cultural, and social issues were at stake and in which, finally, the very word "history" itself as well as other related words like "truth," "fact," "fiction," and "romance" were all contested. To understand early modern English historiography is to understand not only different ways of doing history that sometimes competed with and sometimes complemented each other; it is also to understand the nature and scope of that contest. Heylyn and Fuller, Camden and Clarendon, Spelman and Baker, and many others took part in that struggle; some of its history will be told in the following pages.

2

"Idle Trash" or "Reliques of Somthing True"?: the fate of Brut and Arthur and the power of tradition

In the *History of . . . Princess Elizabeth,* Camden indicated that he thought it improper to invent speeches "of mine own Head." Truth was his "onely Scope and Aim," and truth meant matters of fact: "The bright Lustre of uncorrupt Faithfulness shining forth in . . . Monuments and Records."[1] The historical scholar must not invent, then, but what should the historian do with venerable material that was often dismissed as fabulous but more often included in accounts of the history of England? Such was the "British History," the collections of stories about ancient kings and visits from apostles of Christ, much of which was derived from Geoffrey of Monmouth's *Historia Regum Britanniae* or *History of the Kings of Britain* (c. 1136). Geoffrey's widely read *History* was an important authority on the Trojan Brut and King Arthur for at least four hundred years, but from the first there were skeptics: Geoffrey's contemporary William of Newburgh denounced the former's account as *"Ridicula figmenta."* Yet the Galfridian stories also had credible defenders like Caradoc of Lancarvan, and important historians defended and used Geoffrey's account of British antiquity for centuries.[2] However, the sixteenth century is generally represented as the moment when faith in Geoffrey was undermined, and while it was Polydore Vergil who began the "debunking" of Brut and Arthur, Camden is usually named as the historian who definitively discredited Geoffrey's account.[3]

---

[1] Camden, *Princess Elizabeth,* 6, 4–5.
[2] Geoffrey of Monmouth, *History of the Kings of Britain,* introd. Lucy Allen Paton, trans. Sebastian Evans, rev. Charles W. Dunn (New York: E. P. Dutton, 1958), xx. On Geoffrey, see Thomas Fuller, *The History of the Worthies of England* (London, 1662), 52–53; Caradoc of Lancarvan, *The History of Wales,* augmented and improved, W. Wynne (London, 1697), sig. A5v; T. D. Kendrick, *British Antiquity* (London: Methuen, 1950), 90, 100; Christopher Dean, *Arthur of England: English Attitudes to King Arthur and the Knights of the Round Table in the Middle Ages and the Renaissance* (University of Toronto Press, 1987), 10–11, 15–17.
[3] The word is from Denys Hay, *Annalists and Historians: Western Historiography from the Eighth to the Eighteenth Centuries* (London: Methuen, 1977), 119. See also Levine, *Humanism and History,* 49; Arthur Ferguson, *Clio Unbound,* 111; and Herschel Baker, *The Race of Time. Three Lectures on Renaissance Historiography* (University of Toronto Press, 1967), 93–94. Kendrick acknowledges that Geoffrey had his advocates long after Camden's death, but his discussion of the "eclipse" of the British history focuses on Camden; *British Antiquity,* 108–111. I shall speak throughout

Whoever gets the credit, most historians of English historiography have argued that "reputable" scholars "had decided against Geoffrey" by the beginning of the seventeenth century.[4] Yet, while it is undoubtedly true that by around 1600 the historicity of Brut and Arthur was more problematic than it had previously been, seventeenth- and early eighteenth-century historiography demonstrates that these two putative ancient kings had important champions throughout much of the early modern period. Furthermore, many scholars of the time who acknowledged it to be fabulous were nevertheless willing to tolerate this material in historical texts. In this chapter I will show that the British History endured in a far from moribund state for at least a hundred years after it was supposedly rendered disreputable. If early modern English writers and readers accepted this problematic tradition well into the eighteenth century even in the face of the skepticism of such scholars as Polydore and Camden, that acceptance reveals that the historical discourse of seventeenth- and early eighteenth-century England allowed for the use, or at the very least the tolerance, of admittedly fabulous material in putatively factual accounts. Hence, the fate of the British History illuminates not only the history of history but also the history of the novel and helps us delineate the horizon of expectations of early novel readers.

As I trace changing attitudes toward Brut and Arthur, I will also consider what such a "tradition" entails and what its transmission or endurance signifies, and thereby examine the importance of tradition in early modern English historiography. I will argue that a problematic historiographical tradition like the British History encompasses not only a collection of more or less problematic texts and narratives but also the critique and commentary accruing to those texts over time. I will further argue that the power of tradition led to the use of the British History – skeptically, since the tradition allowed for that – even after the belief that it was largely fabulous became widespread. The discourse of history in the years just before the publication of *Robinson Crusoe*, therefore, admitted fictive material in historical texts when rhetorical or practical considerations argued powerfully for its inclusion. Arthur Ferguson argues that "the controversy over the British History became a classic exercise in the conditioning of modern historical thought."[5] If so, "modern" historical thought is a more perplexing entity than many scholars have acknowledged. English writers and readers accepted the problematic tradition of the British History well into the eighteenth century even in the face of the skepticism of important practitioners of the new history; the fate of Brut and Arthur thus

---

this essay as if belief in Brut implied belief in Arthur and vice versa since "the heritage of Geoffrey was indivisible. If Arthur was to be accepted, so must Brutus and the Trojans"; Ferguson, *Clio Unbound*, 106.

[4] Ferguson, *Clio Unbound*, 107.   [5] *Ibid.*, 105.

demonstrates that the historical discourse of this period did not classify the Galfridian stories as something other than history but, rather, allowed historians to use "pure fable and conjecture" even as they claimed that history should consist solely of matters of fact.[6]

I

Polydore dismissed the story of Brut in his *Anglica Historia* (1534) by pointing out that no writer before Geoffrey made any mention of the Trojan hero. The favorite historian of Henry VII, Polydore treated the question of Arthur mainly by indirection, reproducing William of Newburgh's criticism of Geoffrey and allowing it to speak for itself. Robert Fletcher argues that Polydore's rejection of the British History is to be seen mainly in "his general attitude" toward the material.[7] There is an unmistakable timidity in Polydore's critique, traceable no doubt to the fact that as a foreigner and a papist, he was an easy target for those angered by the new tendency in Henrician historical scholarship to discredit Geoffrey's account. His claims were anticipated by Robert Fabyan and John Rastell in works published in 1516 and 1529, but Polydore is the key figure in the history of the British History because he was the writer most bitterly attacked for criticizing Geoffrey: "The vilification heaped on him for his attack upon the British king went far beyond reasonable scholarly disagreement . . . Vergil was even accused of having burnt priceless sources of English history in order to weigh the evidence in his favour."[8] To be sure, Polydore gave his critics grounds for complaint; although he reproduced much of Geoffrey's material, he did so "with extreme distaste," and called Geoffrey "more a poet than a historian."[9] What is more, scholars have generally judged Polydore's critique effective. Thus, Christopher Dean claims that after Polydore only a small number of historians, blinded by patriotism and a devotion to tradition, were capable of a "head-in-the-sand belief in Arthur" and, further, that "by early in the seventeenth century Arthur was no longer

---

6   The phrase "pure fable and conjecture" is from William Robertson's *History of Scotland* (1759), cited in Hale, *Evolution of British Historiography*, 28; as we shall see, it was not until the era of Hume, Smollett, and Robertson that Geoffrey was finally, simply, and unequivocally put aside by historians.

7   Robert Huntington Fletcher, *The Arthurian Material in the Chronicles Especially Those of Great Britain and France*, 2nd edn., expanded, Roger Sherman Loomis (New York: Burt Franklin, 1966), 259–62.

8   Dean, *Arthur of England*, 20–22. See also Hay, *Annalists and Historians*, 119; Hay, *Polydore Vergil: Renaissance Historian and Man of Letters* (Oxford: Clarendon Press, 1952), 86, 97, 108–10, 113; Ferguson, *Clio Unbound*, 106.

9   Hay, *Polydore Vergil*, 110, 113.

regarded as suitable material for poetry, much less accepted as an authentic historical figure."[10]

Yet in the wake of the attacks on Polydore, many early modern historians were reluctant to reject Geoffrey openly. Although historians of history have seen Camden's comments on Geoffrey of Monmouth as "a watershed" after which one finds only "a few forlorn or angry advocates" for "Geoffrey's fables," Camden's *Britannia* is in truth surprisingly ambivalent on the British History.[11] Although one can argue that Camden demolished Geoffrey's historical authority, there is another side to the story.

First, the demolition. Camden comments on the material from *Historia Regum Britanniae* by saying: "as we cannot choose, but think the fictions of foreigners in this matter extreamly ridiculous, so we must needs own that divers of our own Countreymen give us no very satisfactory account. And indeed, in these and other such like cases, it is much easier to detect a falsity, than a truth." He also asserts that any event as far back as the supposed arrival of Brut in Britain (anything "done before the first Olympiad") is "purely fabulous"; that belief in the very existence of Brut depends on the authority of Hunnibald, "a trifling writer" and the product of "a most barborus and ignorant age"; and that most learned authors say there never was a Brut. Camden is less forthright in dealing with Arthur, but he does express his skepticism more than once. Discussing the antiquities of Winchester, for example, he remarks in respect to "a Round Table which now hangs [in 'an ancient Castle'], and which the common people take for *King Arthur's Table*, I shall observe no more than this, that it plainly appears to be of a much later date."[12] Such statements as these lead Joseph Levine to conclude that "it was William Camden, finally, who set out all the evidence and politely disposed of . . . [the British History] once and for all."[13]

Camden's authority *was* enormous, and echoes of his arguments can be heard throughout the seventeenth century in the assertions of historians who rejected all or part of Geoffrey's account. Peter Heylyn, for example, called his predecessor "Judicious Mr. Camden," and cited him for his own characterization of the story of Brut as "rather a fabulous report, then a well grounded historical truth," and Degory Wheare celebrated *Britannia* as a work collected not out of "*mere Fictions and Fables* . . . but out of the most sincere and uncorrupted Monuments of Antiquity," rejecting Geoffrey "because he seems to write of things that are very obscure and dark

---

[10] Dean, *Arthur of England*, 29–30. [11] H. Baker, *The Race of Time*, 93.
[12] *Camden's Britannia 1695: A Facsimile of the 1695 Edition Published by Edmund Gibson*, introd. Stuart Piggott, bibliog. note Gwyn Walters (New York: Johnson Reprint Corp., 1971), v–vii, 120; see also 205, 921.
[13] Levine, *Humanism and History*, 49.

. . . and are involved with mere fabulous Stories."[14] What is more, the views of others who did not cite Camden also lend credence to the assertion that Camden's treatment of Geoffrey was conclusive. In his popular *Chronicle of the Kings of England*, Sir Richard Baker observed that Geoffrey "makes mention of *Brute*, and of *Merlines* Prophecies, for which he is much taxed by divers Authors of his own time, and after," and Sir William Temple, even though he was openly hostile to antiquarian researches, argued that the story of Brut was "forged at Pleasure" by Monmouth and that much of the Arthurian material was "Idle Trash."[15] Temple's criticism suggests that the tradition of the British History was rejected by a wide range of historians, not just by makers of the historical revolution, and seems to justify the claim that the Galfridian stories were dead after Camden.

But if Camden and other "reputable" scholars of the Tudor and Stuart periods forcibly rejected Geoffrey's account of the British History, many of them did so in such an equivocal fashion as to raise doubts about whether the tradition was, in fact, "disposed of" by the beginning of the seventeenth century. Consider Camden's temporizing, the other side of his treatment of the Galfridian stories. After adducing much evidence for *not* accepting them, Camden declares:

I am so far from labouring to discredit that history, that I assure you, I have often strained my Invention to the uttermost to support it. Absolutely to reject it, would be to make war against time, and to fight against a received opinion . . . I refer the controversie intirely to the whole body of learned Antiquaries; and leaving every man freely to the liberty of his own judgment.[16]

Thus, having laid the basis for rejecting the British History, Camden declines in the end "to make war against time"; his position was one of studied equivocation and in that sense he may indeed have set the standard for discussions of this question in the seventeenth century (albeit in a way most historians of history have not acknowledged) since it is close to impossible to find a historian from this period who rejected the British History outright.[17] Some writers reported the objections to Geoffrey's account but, like Camden, left it to their readers to decide, while others recounted much of the suspect material even though they seemed inclined

---

[14] Heylyn, *Microcosmos. A little Description of the Great World*, 3rd edn. (Oxford, 1627), 25, 455; Degory Wheare, *The Method and Order of Reading both Civil and Ecclesiastical Histories*, trans. and enlarged Edmund Bohun (London, 1694), 134, 139.

[15] Sir Richard Baker, *A Chronicle of the Kings of England, From the Time of the Romans unto the Death of King James the First . . .*, 9th edn. (London, 1696), sig. A₃r; Sir William Temple, *An Introduction to the History of England*, 2nd edn. (London, 1699), 19, 50–53.

[16] Camden, *Britannia*, vi.

[17] There were exceptions, such as Temple and the Scottish historian George Buchanan, discussed below, but by and large the attitude of historians toward the British History was equivocal.

to discredit the *History of the Kings of Britain*. Still others derided the arguments of Polydore, Camden, and the rest, either arguing for the historicity of one or both of the ancient kings or asserting that the existence of those monarchs could not definitely be disproved. And some simply declared a belief in the two kings, arguing for England's right to its own glorious history. In short, the British History endured and even thrived; its proponents were far from being "a few forlorn or angry advocates." Indeed, if one considers all the writers who countenanced use of this material even as they acknowledged it to be fabulous, it can be said that most of the important historians of the seventeenth century were among those historians who have been characterized as outnumbered, obscurantist, and reactionary.

II

The defense of Brut and Arthur against the skeptical arguments of Polydore and others was begun not by chroniclers or annalists (that is, by historical writers employing outmoded forms), but by "the first English antiquary of any consequence," John Leland.[18] In *A Learned and True Assertion of the original, Life, Actes, and death of . . . Prince Arthure, King of Britaine* (1582), Leland acknowledged William of Newburgh's criticism of Geoffrey but cited other sources in support of the *Historia Regum Britanniae* including Nennius (the ninth-century author of *Historia Britonum* and an important source for Geoffrey) and, from Leland's own time, John Stow. Aware of Geoffrey's dubious status as an historical authority, Leland called him "a man not altogether unlearned, what soever otherwise persons ignorant of antiquitie . . . shall say." Declaring that he sought only the truth ("the which one thing, nothing more deare I love"), Leland admitted that fabulous material had attached itself to Arthur's life and reign, and promised "Circumspectly to finde out *Prince Arthure*'s Originall, even from the very egge." Leland then told the story of Igrayne and Uther Pendragon, their adultery facilitated by Merlin's magic, and the birth of Arthur; in retelling this story, Leland cited "the voyce of manie, and also . . . the wrytings of Learned men," Architrenius, Ovid, and Boethius among them. He cited Stow on the time and place of Arthur's coronation and Nennius on the king's twelve epic battles (including the one in which Arthur killed 960 men), asserting that the latter's "wordes although by the negligence of Printers and iniurie of time, they be somewhat displaced, yet not withstandinge because they make much for our present matter, and bring with them a certaine reuerent antiquitie, I will here set them down."

---

[18] Levine, *Humanism and History*, 79. On the obsolescence of the chronicle, see D. R. Woolf, "Genre into Artifact: The Decline of the English Chronicle in the Sixteenth Century," *Sixteenth-Century Journal* 19 (1988), 321–54.

Thus, Leland acknowledged the debatable character of this key source while using it to affirm the historicity of Arthur, and claimed that despite the corruption of Nennius's text over time its very antiquity made it worthy of "reverence." Leland's rationale for this stance is found in his dedicatory epistle, where he argued that Arthur was for the English what Judas Maccabeus was for the Jews, Achilles and Alexander for the Greeks, and Caesar for the Romans:

> Many yeeres surely Arthure hidden lay,
> Of Britons, the Glory, the Light & Honor true:
> Cheerly hath Leland driven darke shadowes away
> And yields the world bright shining Sun to view.[19]

Leland's text was aptly named; it "asserted" the existence of Arthur as well as the value of tradition, without attempting to argue, much less prove, this view.

Leland was not alone; what the *Assertion* aimed to do for Arthur, Richard Harvey's *Philadelphus: or, A Defence of Brutes* (1593) attempted to do for Brut. In the *Defence* Harvey – astrologer, son of a ropemaker, and brother of Gabriel Harvey – attacked historians "who have written more of Brute than behoued them" and thus "behaved unkindly against Brittains, and done less for them than they should." His remarks were aimed particularly at the Scottish historian George Buchanan, whose dismissal of Brut in *Rerum Scoticarum Historia* (1582) made him "as severe a critic as the British History had yet had." Although Harvey claimed to believe that he was "not worthy to be . . . moderator" to such an eminent man as Buchanan, he nevertheless charged that the historian's "invective treatise is in trueth, more factious, then effectuall."[20] Harvey's defense of Brut may seem unnoteworthy since he was so obscure a figure and an astrologer rather than an historian, but in fact such views were widely shared, even among "authentic" scholars like John Stow, who told the story of Brut without qualification in his *Annales of England* (1592) and who also, before relating Arthur's twelve great battles and discussing the importance of the round table, said of Arthur that "there be many fabulous reports, but certaine he was . . . a Prince more worthy to haue aduancement by true histories, then false fables." Stow, of course, was no historiographical quack; Fussner characterizes him as "one of the most accurate and business-like of the English historians of the sixteenth century."[21]

Why would two great antiquaries like Leland and Stow join a writer like

---

[19] John Leyland [Leland], *A Learned and True Assertion of the original, Life, Actes, and death of the most Noble, Valiant, and Renowned Prince Arthure, King of Great Britaine . . .*, trans. Richard Robinson (London, 1582), sig. c₁v, c₂r, c₃r, B₂r.; originally published in Latin in 1544.

[20] *DNB*; R[ichard]. H[arvey], *Philadelphus: or, A Defence of Brutes, and the Brutans History* (London, 1593), sig. A₂r, 1; on Buchanan, see Kendrick, *British Antiquity*, 85.

[21] John Stow, *The Annales of England* (London, 1592), 11, 58, 59; Fussner, *Historical Revolution*, 211.

Harvey in embracing the British History, especially after the attacks on this tradition in both the Henrician and the Elizabethan periods? It has been argued that their views were a product of the Tudors' attempt to present their dynasty as "a return of Arthur's line to the British throne."[22] While this argument may have some validity for the sixteenth century, it certainly cannot explain why there were also, as we shall see, important adherents to the cause of Brut and Arthur throughout the seventeenth century. Fussner argues that many of those who embraced the position of Leland and Harvey shared the antiquaries' instinctive respect for tradition.[23] But what does it mean to say that a scholar respects "tradition"?

In *Keywords* Raymond Williams attributes two conjoined meanings to the word "tradition": on the one hand it refers to "a general process of handing down" and, on the other, it suggests "a very strong and often predominant sense of this [process] entailing respect and duty." Similarly, Edward Shils argues that "there is an inherently normative element in any tradition of belief which is presented for acceptance; it is presented with the intention of producing affirmation and acceptance." According to Williams, the "exhortatory" meaning of "tradition" began to be seen around the beginning of the seventeenth century, roughly the moment when medieval consensus (the Galfridian stories) began to give way in the face of modern critique. The arguments of Leland and Stow indicate that some sixteenth-century historians perceived a clear duty to honor what was handed down to them, even if their antiquarian principles prescribed a skeptical view of traditional material. Respect for tradition, then, could and did entail a willed embrace of the fabulous and a willing suspension of methodological principles. Williams points out that once "the modern" began to be valorized in the nineteenth century, "tradition" and "traditional" were often used pejoratively and "traditionalist" was "almost always dismissive" (as a way of referring, for example, to a slavish respect for the past), but in the seventeenth century a traditionalist was, seemingly, someone who altogether properly defended and even championed the legacy of the past.[24] Indeed, although the careers of Leland, Stow, and Camden are central to any explanation of "how English historiography found its modern method," those historians nonetheless acted in a

---

22 On the "Tudor Cult of the British History," see Kendrick, *British Antiquity*, 34–44; see also Dean, *Arthur of England*, 26.

23 Fussner points out that in the Tudor period "middle-class concern with history was part of a much wider concern with the sanctions of tradition"; 213. Stow asserts, in his *Summarie of Englishe Chronicles* (1570 edition), that those who "scornefully rejected" Geoffrey demonstrated "their greate unthankfulness" to a writer who simply sought to play "only the part of an interpretour"; cited in Fussner at 216.

24 Raymond Williams, *Keywords. A Vocabulary of Culture and Society*, rev. edn. (New York: Oxford University Press, 1983), 319–20; Edward Shils, *Tradition* (University of Chicago Press, 1981), 23, 20.

decidedly unmodern fashion when it suited them to do so. In short they
were true practitioners of what I have labeled Baconian historiography;
their dividedness about a vexed tradition helps to define that ambivalent
historiography.

Camden indicated why he might tolerate fabulous material in historiography in his preface to *Princess Elizabeth* when he distinguished among the
various approaches he took to his material: "Things manifest and evident I
have not concealed; Things doubtful I have interpreted favourably; Things
secret and abstruse I have not pried into." For Camden, practical
exigencies might shape historical practice and the historian might err on
the side of credulity when such considerations suggested the wisdom of
doing so. Camden cited the ancient historian Dionysius of Halicarnassus
who advised historians *not* to " 'pursue . . . the Search' " into " 'the hidden
Meanings of Princes'." Polydore had "pulled the house down on himself,"
and Camden, who if he was the best of the Elizabethan antiquaries was
also "one of the most cautious," presumably regarded the British History
as an occasion when the historian should be mindful of the consequences of
a categorical judgment. The author of *Britannia* expressed his scorn for
"those curious inquisitive people, who will needs seek to know more than
by Law is permitted them," implicitly arguing that a historian could and
should consider what is allowed and what is wanted and approach his
material accordingly.[25]

The view that tradition might be defended and used in a historical text
even when it seemed other than factual is openly advanced in *A Restitution
of Decayed Intelligence in Antiquities concerning the English Nation*, a work by the
antiquary Richard Verstegen first published in 1628, in which the author
discussed the British History in light of questions of honor.[26] Verstegen
gave the kingship of Brut as one of several possible explanations of the fact
that the island was known as Britain and its inhabitants as Britons; he
acknowledged "the doubt many haue conceived of *Brute*, to wit, whether
euer there were such at all," but dismissed such doubts in the name of
tradition:

that there was such a King, and that of him both the countrie and people of our Ile
had heretofore their appellation, it both is and hath beene the common received
opinion: and it is not now rashly to be reiected albeit some things which to some
doe seeme to sound verie fabulously, may haue beene by some few obscure authors
heretofore added vnto his Historie, and so haue made the whole to be doubted.

Verstegen's argument was rooted in his perception of the desire of the

---

[25] Camden, *Princess Elizabeth*, 5–6; Ferguson, *Utter Antiquity: Perceptions of Prehistory in Renaissance England* (Durham NC: Duke University Press, 1993), 89; Ferguson, *Clio Unbound*, 110.

[26] According to the *DNB*, Verstegen's real last name was Rowlands and Verstegen was an "alias"; Anthony à Wood and Thomas Hearne used the alias, as did Ferguson.

English to have a respectable pedigree; he observed, in fact, that this longing was widespread, that the French also traced their ancestry to the Trojans, and that this belief had recently been shown up as "a meere fable and foolerie." He then asked "why this conceit should possesse so many peoples minds" and concluded that both French and British beliefs were rooted in "the lacke of learning in former ages."

Despite his argument on behalf of tradition, Verstegen seemed ready to surrender Brut. Instead, however, he made an unusual and surprising move when he argued that the obstacle to accepting the story of Brut lay not in the assertion that Brut existed and was responsible for the peopling of Britain but in the belief that Brut was a descendant of the Trojan Aeneas. Verstegen argued that "It standeth with farre more likelihood of truth, seeing out of *Gallia* hee came into *Albion*, that we hold him for some Prince of the same countrie and nation." In short, Brut existed and was king of Britain but he was a German, not a Trojan. The *Restitution* thus partook of "the vogue of Germanism [that] had captured the imagination of the English intellectual community" by the beginning of the seventeenth century. Verstegen argued that the assertion that Brut was a German was a "farre more honourable" version of British antiquity than tracing Brut's ancestry back to Troy, but this account of Brut was neither more credible than Geoffrey's nor did it rest on any more evidence. Presumably it was more "honourable" because it transformed Brut into a representative of the people from whom, the Germanists argued, the English received their democratic institutions.[27] In trying to make a historical case for Brut, Verstegen first insisted that tradition should not be lightly discarded and then defended his own views more on the basis of their being "honourable" than on the basis of their being credible. Yet no more than Stow can Verstegen be dismissed as an historical eccentric; Anthony à Wood characterized him as "a great reviver of our English antiquities, and a most admirable critic in the Saxon and Gothic languages." According to Wood, Verstegen's text was "much valued by learned and curious men," and indeed Thomas Hearne, who was just such a man, said of Verstegen in the midst of a discussion of worthy English historians, that the *Restitution* is "proper enough to be read," although he also acknowledged that the author was "guilty of some

---

[27] [Richard Verstegen], *A Restitution of Decayed Intelligence: In antiquities. Concerning the most noble and renowned English Nation* (London, 1628), 89–90, 92, 93, 94. Verstegen's views suggest that we should not be too quick to associate arguments on behalf of the British History with support or flattery of the monarch since interest in Saxon antiquity was rooted first in a desire to defend England's national church and later with the theory of the immemorial constitution. On Germanism, see Ferguson, *Clio Unbound*, 113–16; on the immemorial constitution, see Pocock, *Ancient Constitution*, especially chapter 2.

Faults."[28] In short, an historian could argue for the existence of Brut without being disgraced for taking such a position.

One index of the character of a discourse at a given moment is what kind of statements are permissible within it; at the present time, for example, any discussion of Brut would have to be clearly marked as the treatment of mythic material if it were not automatically to marginalize a text as something other than history.[29] In the seventeenth century, however, despite the fact that historians had argued for a hundred years and more that the Galfridian stories were baseless, an historian could "assert" the existence of Brut and Arthur or at least countenance such assertions in "serious" historiography. Thus we find in the historical discourse of the period a high degree of tolerance for statements that could not be read as unequivocally factual – that could not, that is, entirely escape from the charge of being fabulous; respect for tradition made fiction an "honourable" element in historiography.[30]

Verstegen was far from being alone in asserting such views.[31] Another important advocate of Arthur and Brut was Winston Churchill, the father of the Duke of Marlborough and the author of *Divi Britannici: Being a Remark Upon the Lives of all the Kings of this Isle, From the Year of the World 2855. Unto the Grace of 1660* (1675). Asserting that Churchill's text was accurate and well documented, the *Biographia Britannica* (1747–63) described him as "an eminent Historian" even though it also acknowledged his "Enthusiasm of Loyalty" to the monarchy. The *Biographia* suggested that only its clear bias kept it from being regarded as a "very extraordinary performance."[32] *Divi Britannici* did indeed celebrate monarchy as the system of government that had always held sway in England ("the Government of this Isle was never cloath'd in any other form"), and perhaps for that reason Churchill's text was also the most enthusiastic defense of Geoffrey of Monmouth in the historical literature of the seventeenth century. Churchill opened by comparing British antiquities with the historiography of the ancient world, arguing that the "four great Monarchies of the East . . . need as much the support of Tradition to ascertain their Age, Alterations, and Successions as

---

28 Anthony à Wood, *Athenae Oxonienses. An Exact History of all the Writers and Bishops who have had their Education In The University of Oxford . . .*, 4 vols., ed. Philip Bliss (London, 1813–20), II, 393–94; Thomas Hearne, *Ductor Historicus: Or, A Short System of Universal History, and An Introduction to the Study of it*, 2 vols., 2nd edn. (London, 1705), 198. Printed five times in London between 1605 and 1673, Verstegen's *Restitution* was, according to Kendrick, "a landmark in the history of antiquarian thought"; *British Antiquity*, 119.

29 Foucault, *Archaeology of Knowledge*, 27; *L'archéologie du savoir*, 38.

30 Bacon used "poesy," "Feigned History," and "fable" as more or less synonymous terms for what we would call "fiction"; his seventeenth-century editor referred to Bacon's utopia/imaginary voyage, *New Atlantis*, as a "fable." *Selected Writings*, 243–45, 544.

31 Kendrick, *British Antiquity*, 100–01; he discusses a few defenders of Arthur and Brut from the Elizabethan period down to the Restoration.

32 *Biographia Britannica*, 6 vols. (London, 1747–63), VI, 1330, 1331.

ours." He acknowledged doubts about the historicity of Brut and Arthur, but cited the many historians who treated those stories as true and concluded that "forasmuch as there are some found (and those of Sufficient Credit) that boldly affirm it, and none can make any other conjectural disproof; I conceive Antiquity may reasonably be excus'd, in claiming a Prerogative to uphold, at least for not rejecting so received an Opinion."[33]

Churchill knew his assertion to be controversial and so he adopted a defensive rather than an offensive stance in respect to the British History: the stories of Arthur and Brut, he held, could not be disproved and therefore the tradition should be upheld. But he also had the likes of Leland and Stow on his side, so it is not surprising that Churchill left his defensive posture behind when he turned from historical representations to the historians themselves. Like Verstegen, Churchill attacked English historians who "chose rather to wrong the Age they liv'd in by seeming to detract from the Reverence due to Tradition, then to offer the least violence to their own Credits." Historians, Churchill argued, should be less concerned with their own reputations for veracity or reliability and more careful about honoring received tradition; he cited improbabilities in Herodotus and argued that "even Holy Writ it self, is so hard to digest without a grain of Salt . . . that the quitting of our Reason, is made the merit, as well as the Foundation of our Faith." Naming historians who credited Geoffrey's account of the British History, Churchill argued that many place names (York, Carlisle, Ludlow) lent credibility to arguments in favor of the historicity of other shadowy British kings (Eborac, Caerlile, Lud), and reasoned that Geoffrey was roundly attacked simply because he got his chronology wrong, "which most men make the Touchstone of History, whereas there is nothing more disceptious." With this remark, which echoed Nashe's sneer at "lay Chronigraphers" and Milton's dismissal of historical writers who labored at "computing, or collating years and Chronologies," Churchill dismissed what he characterized as the chief objection to Geoffrey's historiographical method as just so much antiquarian nitpicking. None of these assertions went to the heart of the matter – the lack of evidence or authority for the stories of Brut and Arthur; Churchill's arguments were not so much historiographical as rhetorical and at their core stood the implicit assertion that tradition should be embraced even if that necessitated the "quitting of our Reason." Thus, for both an antiquarian researcher whose work linked him to the parliamentary opposition to the early Stuarts and a politician whose historical text was an apology for the monarchy, the fact that a

[33] Churchill, *Divi Britannici*, 37, 4, 52. A similar argument is made by Robert Sheringham in *De Anglorum Gentis Origine Disceptatio* (1670); see Roberta F. Brinkley, *Arthurian Legend in the Seventeenth Century* (1932; repr. New York: Octagon Books, 1967), 209–10.

narrative was almost certainly fabulous did not bar its inclusion in a historical text.[34]

Further evidence of this aspect of the historical discourse of the period is found in popular texts of the period which demonstrate that in the world of unsophisticated writers and readers the Brut and Arthur stories were produced and received in an untroubled fashion. In William Parsons's *Chronological Tables of Europe*, for example, the account of the British kings begins:

Although we begin ye AEra of our Computation but from ye time of Egbert, & ye Series of ye most Ancient times are very Intricate, & ye Storys somew^t Fabulous, till ye time of Dunwallo: Yet before him occurrs 7 Samotheans, 1 Albionist, and 20 Trojans wch last begin their Dynasty wth Brute, who (an Mundi 2650, before X^t [Christ] 2200) arriv'd in England . . . And (as Tacitus saith) divided ye Island . . . into Great & Little Britain.

Parsons allowed that this material was "somew^t Fabulous," but he also reported and precisely dated Brut's arrival in Britain and gave Tacitus as his source, thereby creating the impression that this information was anything but unreliable. Between 1688 and 1714 there were eight editions of Parsons's handbook, which was itself a reworking of a French text by Guillaume Marcel; the tables were offered to readers as items of "Great use for the Reading of History, and a Ready Help to Discourse," and the *DNB* observes that Parsons's pocket-size text "was regarded in its day as an invaluable vade mecum by the young student."[35] In short, the *Chronological Tables* was a small, presumably cheap, and ostensibly reliable pocket guide to European history – the kind of practically-minded historical text that Louis B. Wright argues had been popular since Elizabethan times.[36] Almanacs were another popular, inexpensive, and utilitarian source of historical information that offered the same view of Arthur and Brut; they contained chronologies of world history that "grafted" British History on to the history of the ancient world, naming "the fall of Troy, Brut's arrival in England (*c.* 1100 BC), and the foundation of London in the same year." Bernard Capp argues that the precisely dated chronologies which constituted the historical component of the almanacs were "linked, however tenuously, to the work of professional historians."[37] Thus,

---

34   Churchill, *Divi Britannici*, 4, 52; on Nashe and Milton, see chapter 1 above.

35   [Guillaume Marcel], *Chronological Tables* . . ., trans. William Parsons (London, 1688), sig. c.1–c.2; Colonel [William] Parsons, *Chronological Tables of Europe*, 6th edn. (London, 1703), title page; *DNB*.

36   Louis B. Wright, *Middle-Class Culture in Elizabethan England* (Ithaca: Cornell University Press; Folger Shakespeare Library, 1935), 100, 297–98.

37   Bernard Capp, *English Almanacs 1500–1800: Astrology and the Popular Press* (Ithaca: Cornell University Press, 1979), 216, 217, 215. Capp asserts that "the great majority of [almanac] buyers were yeomen, husbandmen and artisans"; 60. For a further discussion of popular history, see chapter 8 below.

although the almanacs and Parsons's *Tables* were undoubtedly cheap, popular works, they were presented to readers as genuine sources of historical knowledge. Popular history, then, like the history of high-culture writers such as Leland, Stow, Verstegen, and Churchill, included the stories of Brut and Arthur, so that purchasers of Parsons's *Table* as well as those who acquired Churchill's lavish folio both "bought" the Galfridian stories. In a wide range of texts offered to a heterogenous reading audience, Geoffrey of Monmouth's account of the origins and early history of Britain was given credence. To say that in the seventeenth century only those with their heads in the sand accepted Geoffrey's *History* is to over-simplify a complex historical situation.

Many scholars have pointed out that in the medieval period, historical accounts were not so much summaries of what was known about a given subject as restatements of what was believed by writers and readers; before Leland, Camden, and Verstegen, that is, matters of fact were not the benchmark for judging the historicity of texts that they supposedly became in Churchill's day.[38] Yet the evidence presented here suggests that the putatively medieval habit of reporting general knowledge and belief as "history" endured in the early modern period alongside and often in conjunction with the assertion that truth consisted of matters of fact. Both popularizers and "reputable" historians rejected the standards of the new history – at least when it came to Brut and Arthur – and endorsed what was, in Churchill's words, "approv'd by the Touchstone of universal consent." The invocation of tradition in such matters amounted to an assertion that belief was still an adequate basis for including fabulous material in historical discourse.[39]

III

From Leland to Parsons, then, many historical writers, exalted and humble, argued the case for continued belief in the historicity of Brut and Arthur. There were also others, of course, like Buchanan and Temple, who rejected the British History. But the largest and most important body of historiographers in this period was probably the group that criticized Geoffrey but also temporized, demonstrating a remarkable degree of tolerance for material that many of them clearly believed did not, properly speaking, belong in historical accounts. Such ambivalence goes back, in fact, to Polydore himself since, although he made his skepticism clear, he nevertheless reproduced much of Geoffrey's account "in order not to incur

---

[38] Ruth Morse, "'The Vague Relation': Historical Fiction and Historical Veracity in the Later Middle Ages," *Leeds Studies in English* n.s. 13 (1982), 87–89; Suzanne Fleischman, "On the Representation of History and Fiction in the Middle Ages," *History and Theory* 22 (1983), 305.

[39] Churchill, *Divi Britannici*, 4.

hatred."[40] Camden too sounded much more like Verstegen or Churchill than might be expected from the man who is supposed to have demolished the basis for belief in the British History. The dominant view of the British History into the early eighteenth century, then, was not a skepticism that entailed rejection of this material but a cautious attitude that acknowledged the dubious character of the Galfridian stories while accepting or tolerating all or part of them.

This perspective is clearly embodied in a work that French Fogle calls "the most unified, condensed, and continuous narrative of pre-Conquest England that had yet appeared," John Milton's *History of Britain* (1671). The first book in Milton's *History* consisted largely of material borrowed from Geoffrey's *Historia* even though at the beginning of the second book, when the author turned to events after the descent of Julius Caesar, he informed his readers that they were leaving "a Region of smooth or idle Dreams" and arriving "on the Confines, where day-light and truth meet us with a clear dawn." Despite this dismissal of the stories of Arthur and Brut, Milton recounted them, "in favour of our English Poets, and Rhetoricians, who by their Art will know, how to use them judiciously," and because "seeing that oft-times relations heretofore accounted fabulous have been found to contain in them many footsteps and reliques of somthing true." Fogle suggests that Milton used the British History because it gave him a beginning for his story, something very important to a historian who was preoccupied "with the *manner* of the narrative."[41] The desire for a full account was widespread and helps to explain the use of Milton's account in subsequent histories, even in the eighteenth century, as well as the appropriation of the Galfridian stories by, for example, Stow. Such use of the British History, by Milton and others, resulted from rhetorical concerns that in some cases overruled methodological principles. Thus, rhetoric like politics provided a basis for including fictive material in historical accounts. One might argue that Milton's views on the British History should be discounted since he was so demonstrably a poet even when he wrote the *History of Britain*; after all, he presented the British History for poets and rhetoricians. But Milton was well read in the historiography of his day, and his contemporaries did not view his historical labors so dismissively; Hearne recommended the *History* as a key text for the study of the English past, especially for the period "from the first Tradition beginning to the

---

[40] Hay, *Polydore Vergil*, 110; the phrase, in Latin, is Polydore's.

[41] Milton, *Prose Works*, v, pt. 1:xlvii, 37, 3, xlvi. Nicholas von Maltzahn sees Milton's distancing of himself from Geoffrey as a rejection of that historian; *Milton's History of Britain: Republican Historiography in the English Revolution* (Oxford: Clarendon Press, 1991), 104. I will argue below, however, that Milton's approach to the Galfridian stories is itself very much within the bounds of the tradition.

Norman Conquest," and John Hughes used Milton's *History* for the first section of the *Complete History of England* (1706).[42]

Here again, furthermore, popular works resembled the monuments of elite culture: Milton's view of the British History is also found in a much humbler text, the *Historical Remarques* (1681) of the bookseller and historian Nathaniel Crouch.[43] Crouch cited Roman writers as well as Geoffrey on Brut ("descended from the Demi-God, Aeneas, the son of Venus") before admitting that "Geoffrey's Account has no great Authority." In regard to Arthur, Crouch was both skeptical and credulous; he wrote of the king "of whom so many wonderful Stories are related," and promised an account written "according to true History, passing others over," but then proceeded to relate much if not all (he omitted all mention of Merlin's magic) of the traditional story of Arthur. Although skeptical about some of the details, Crouch related the famous twelve battles. Speaking of one engagement, he observed: "in this Battle, with his Sword called *Callibourn*, some Histories say he slew 800, but this looks something incredible; but certain it is, he returned Victorious from twelve set Battles."[44] As the most successful popular historian of this period, Crouch could be expected to reproduce the British History, but his rendering of these stories is significant because it is so similar to the use of the Galfridian material in the histories of Milton and Camden. The same blend of skepticism and credulity is found in works by the eminent Elizabethan antiquary, the erudite poet and revolutionary Puritan, and the bookseller-historian of the Restoration. That same mix is also found in the work of Thomas Hearne, who derided Crouch while lionizing Camden. Hearne showed considerable tolerance of the Galfridian stories, dismissing Geoffrey with faint criticism:

he affirms, that *Brutus* the Great-grandson of *AEneas*, and from him a Progeny of Sixty Eight Kings Reigned in this Land a Thousand Years before the coming of *Julius Caesar*. He also gives us the story of the *British* Hero King *Arthur*, and the Prophecies of *Merlyn*. But this Author has but slender credit in the World.

This is far from Temple's dismissal of the story of Brut and much of the story of Arthur as "idle Trash," especially since Hearne included an entry

---

[42] On Milton's historical learning, see *Prose Works*, v, pt. 1, xxii–xxix. Hearne also recommended that his readers start with Camden's *Britannia*, and he suggested that they use Samuel Daniel's verse account of the reigns up to Edward III, Bacon on Henry VII, and Camden again on Elizabeth; *Ductor Historicus*, 193. Hughes's *Complete History* was executed according to Temple's plan, as elaborated in the latter's *Introduction to the History of England* at sig. A₃r–v; Levine, *Humanism and History*, 164–71.

[43] On Crouch, see my "Nathaniel Crouch, Bookseller and Historian: Popular Historiography and Cultural Power in Late Seventeenth-Century England," *Eighteenth-Century Studies* 27 (1993–94), 391–419; and chapter 8 below.

[44] Richard Burton [Nathaniel Crouch], *Historical Remarques, and Observations Of the Ancient and Present State of Westminster . . .* (London, 1681), 1–3; on Arthur, see [Crouch], *The Famous and Renowned History of the Nine Worthies of the World* (London, n.d.), sig. C₁v, C₂v.

for Arthur ("King of *Britain*, flourish'd from 516, to 542") in his chronology in the first part of *Ductor Historicus* and also since he reported "the hoary legend of Joseph of Arimathea," another part of the British History, in the same chronology. Hearne gently dismissed Geoffrey but then used him; this man whose work, according to the *DNB*, evidenced his "extraordinary diligence and pains" in antiquarian studies, did not himself unequivocally reject the tradition of the British History.[45]

That not only popular writers but also learned antiquaries continued to embrace or at least to tolerate Geoffrey's stories into the eighteenth century may well be traceable to the very nature of tradition, specifically to the fact that a tradition is far from being invariable but is instead something that changes through accretion and, at least in this case, comes thereby to consist not only of the fundamental elements of the tradition but also of the misgivings, qualifications, and even critiques of those elements that have come to be associated with them. Shils has argued that a tradition "has behind it a process of accumulation of refinements and authoritative arguments" and that a tradition is always "an amalgam of persistent elements, and increments and innovations which have become a part of it." Shils asserts that the blend of original elements and commentary *is* the tradition; in the case of the Galfridian stories, from the very inception of the tradition the "amalgam" consisted of both the stories themselves and of the dubiety with which those stories were sometimes viewed or, more to the point, presented. From the twelfth century on, Geoffrey's stories were regularly reported in the company of the objections made against them by William of Newburgh and others. The British History entailed, accordingly, not just the stories of Brut and Arthur but also the skepticism in respect to those stories; this aspect of the British History was acknowledged by the *Biographia Britannica* when it observed in respect to Arthur that "it is but just, that what is related of him should be told, as also, what is said for and against it."[46] Familiarity with this tradition, then, included an awareness of the fact that the tradition was of uncertain provenance and questionable veracity. Statements about historical "fact" and the qualifying critiques were, taken together, "the given" that constituted the tradition of the British History.[47] So historians who adopted an attitude of skepticism mixed with tolerance (Camden, Hearne), or credulity tinged with caution (Leland, Verstegen), were in fact embracing the tradition of the British history in its complexity. One can speak of an end to the tradition only when one encounters silence in respect to Arthur and Brut, or unequivocal repudiation, and such responses are not regularly encountered until well into the eighteenth century, when Hume

---

[45] Ferguson, *Clio Unbound*, 114. Typically, Hearne observed that Joseph "is said to have preached the Gospel in *Britain*" in 35 A.D; *Ductor Historicus*, 197, 83, 77; *DNB*.

[46] *Biographia Britannica*, I, 197.   [47] Shils, *Tradition*, 44–45.

began his *History of England* with the first Roman invasion of the island and thereby avoided any mention of Brut, briefly treated Arthur as a probable historical figure "whose military achievements have been blended with so many fables as even to give occasion for entertaining a doubt of his real existence," and declared that "the fables which are commonly employed to supply the place of true history ought entirely to be disregarded."[48] Before Hume and other like-minded historians of the later eighteenth century, however, the tradition of the British History endured.

IV

Some historians of the British History have acknowledged that "right to the end of the seventeenth century and beyond, Brut [and Arthur] could still find champions prepared to do battle in this almost hopeless cause."[49] None, however, has focused directly on the peculiar tolerance of fabulous material manifested by so many British historical writers, including members of the pantheon established by scholars of the historical revolution. This tolerance amounted to an assertion that when it was expedient to do so historians could and should make room in their accounts for fiction. Camden acknowledged that "I . . . strained my Invention to the uttermost to support" the British History; Milton used Geoffrey's stories but admitted that they were the stuff of "idle Dreams"; and Crouch labeled the Arthurian material he used as "so many wonderful Stories." All these writers – not just Camden – and many more who championed or tolerated the tradition of the British History, knew of or adhered, if to widely varying degrees, to the principles of the new history, but when it came to Geoffrey of Monmouth's account, they all suspended their embrace of those tenets. They did so for a variety of reasons, the most common of which was probably an inchoate sense that this was what their countrymen wished them to do. Yet this is not a question of well-educated historians pandering to an expanding audience of frequently ill-educated readers. Both Camden's *Britannia* and Churchill's *Divi Britannici* were high culture texts, aimed at wealthy and educated readers. The stories of Arthur and Brut endured not because writers yielded to the credulity of the

---

48 David Hume, *The History of England from the Invasion of Julius Caesar to the Revolution in 1688*, vol. I (New York: Harper and Brothers, 1879), 45, 25–26. One encounters similar views in the work of Robertson (see note 6) and Edward Gibbon, who found the events of Arthur's life less compelling than the tradition of Arthur, beginning with "his romance, transcribed in the Latin of Jeffrey of Monmouth, and afterwards . . . enriched with the various . . . ornaments . . . familiar to the experience, the learning, or the fancy, of the twelfth century." *The History of the Decline and Fall of the Roman Empire*, 3 vols., ed. David Womersley (New York: Penguin, 1994), II, 500. Smollett, like Hume, begins his history with the descent of Julius Caesar.

49 Kendrick, *British Antiquity*, 102. See also Ferguson, *Utter Antiquity*, 90; and Keith Thomas, *Religion and the Decline of Magic* (New York: Charles Scribner's Sons, 1971), 427.

unsophisticated but because both writers and readers were reluctant to sacrifice the British History and settle for mere matters of fact, especially when, in the case of British antiquity, accepting only matters of fact meant, essentially, settling for nothing. The willingness of historians to tolerate this material was also undoubtedly rooted in their sense that these stories had always been used and read skeptically, and could continue to be used in this fashion in respectable historical texts.

Yet the writers' reasons for tolerating the British History are less important than the simple fact of their doing so. In some ways this is an unremarkable aspect of the historical practice of the period; as we shall see, local historians and natural historians also regularly reported fantastic stories in their texts.[50] Still, the fate of Brut and Arthur has generally been pointed to as proof that in this period the medieval tolerance for an undifferentiated blend of fact and fiction became untenable in historical discourse and the medieval historian's embrace of tradition was rendered old-fashioned by the severe methodology of the author of *Britannia* and his successors. But the story is not that simple. Camden did indeed lay the basis for rejecting the British History but then declined to do so himself, and his decision not to repudiate Geoffrey was endorsed throughout the seventeenth century and on into the eighteenth. The British History, then, which has been seen as a test case for demonstrating the emergence of historiographical modernity, reveals instead that although "modern" historians distinguished between fact and fiction and insisted upon reliance on matters of fact in historical writing, they also accepted a modicum of fictional material when practical considerations – questions of honor, the power of tradition – pressed them to do so. In other words, the truth-standard associated with the new history – the commitment to construct historiography on established matters of fact – was subject to revision in the name of tradition, for rhetorical purposes, or because it was the honorable thing to do. Herschel Baker has written of Renaissance histor-ians that "despite their boasted obligation to record the naked truth of things . . . they were at best committed to partial truths, and even the distortions and evasions, of church or state or party."[51] The fate of Brut and Arthur would seem to suggest, however, that historical writers gave their readers not only partial, which is to say biased, versions of events, but also accounts in which fable was blended with fact, and that they continued to do so long after the makers of the historical revolution like Camden had putatively put an end to the practice. Concluding his discussion of the story of Brut, Camden urged: "let antiquity herein be pardoned, if she some-times disguise the truth with the mixture of a fable, and bring in the Gods

---

[50] On local history and natural history, see chapters 3 and 7 below.
[51] Baker, *Race of Time*, 24.

themselves to act a part, when she design'd thereby to render the beginnings, either of a city, or a nation, more noble and majestical."[52] His defense of antiquity might also be extended to his own practice and that of his historiographical successors in England. The new history was very much like the old when it came to Brut and Arthur. The British History prepared readers to approach with a high degree of tolerance apparently historical accounts that nevertheless contained a rich admixture of fiction.

[52] Camden, *Britannia*, ix.

3

The History of Myddle: memory, history, and power

Fiction and fact were, under the proper circumstances, compatible elements in even the most progressive, rigorous forms of historical discourse in the seventeenth and early eighteenth centuries, but history nevertheless was preeminently the form of learning based upon matters of fact. Not all "facts," however, were such as might be obtained from Camden's "Papers and Writings" or "Monuments and Records"; not all of a historian's particulars were the product of erudition and research. Writers of history also depended upon anecdotal information that came to them through their ordinary lived experience; Camden cited his extensive travel throughout England as a major source of material for *Britannia*. Both personal and communal experience and memory were important sources for early modern English writers of history, especially local and natural history. This feature of historical practice meant that there was ample room in the historical discourse of the period for marvelous events and scandalous reports; gossip, hearsay, and rumor were all incorporated in historical texts of the period. But it also meant that history-writing was often an embodiment of power relations and struggles, since, as Patricia Meyer Spacks has argued, gossip and other forms of " 'natural' discourse" are means used by ordinary individuals to affect "the public sphere."[1]

These features of early modern English historiography are vividly revealed in Richard Gough's "Observations concerning the Seates in Myddle and the familyes to which they belong," the second and longest part of a local history about the author's own parish, the Church of St. Peter in Myddle Parish, Shropshire. Written between 1700 and 1709 and left in manuscript when Gough died in 1723, Gough's text first appeared in 1834 under the title *Human Nature displayed in the History of Myddle*, but it is now known simply as *The History of Myddle*.[2] The value of Gough's *History*

---

[1] Patricia Meyer Spacks, *Gossip* (New York: Alfred A. Knopf, 1985), 6–7.

[2] Richard Gough, *The History of Myddle*, ed. David Hey (London: Penguin, 1981), 7, 11–12, 25–26; all citations will be given in the text. The work has seven parts: (1) a description of the parish and many of its principal features and residents (27–75); (2) a discussion of each pew in the parish church and its inhabitants, past and present (76–249); (3) a discussion of eight cases argued on behalf of the parish over the question of poor relief (251–64); (4) a brief discussion of "severall conveniences that beelong to the parish" (265–70); (5) a briefer discussion of

as a source of information about the locale which it treats and rural England generally is suggested by his account of a dispute in 1658 between two parishioners, John Downton and William Formestone, over "the right of kneeling in the sixth peiw on the south side of the north isle." Downton "putt a locke on the pew doore, but William Formestone . . . who claimed a share in that seate, came on the Lord's day following, and giveing the peiw dorre a suddaine plucke, broake off the locke." A meeting was called to settle the matter and also to dispose of a highly-prized pew close to the pulpit, which at the time was wholly given over to the use of young men ("a thing unseemly and undecent that a company of young boyes . . . should sitt . . . above those of the best of the parish"). The meeting of February 7, 1658, attended by the vicar and church wardens and "a considerable part of the parish of Myddle," gave Downton kneelings in two pews, one of them the disputed seat which he had to share with Formeston and two other parishioners. The passage seat, where the "young boyes" had been sitting, was given to two other parishioners, with the proviso that "on sacrament dayes the passage bee allowed to the Communion table" (117–20). This dispute and its seemingly Solomonic resolution (at least two of the orders were abrogated immediately) reveal the centrality of the church in the lives of the residents of the parish, the overwhelming importance of land ownership and tenure, the relentless struggle to achieve or maintain standing in the community, the inescapable link between a stake in the land and standing in the church ("A peiw or seat does not beelong to a person or to land, butt to an house"[77]), and the litigious bent of the parishioners.

Since its initial publication, then, *The History of Myddle* has been a valued source of information about life in early modern England, but it is much more than a source for social historians.[3] This chapter considers *The History of Myddle* first, as a species of local history, a historical form both derided in the early modern period as mere fact-grubbing and also used by many of the greatest historical writers of the time, and, second, as a text that strikingly illustrates early modern English historical practice in general.[4] Gough's brand of local history, concentrating on individuals and families and relying on the author's own and his community's memory, was, to be

"Oswaldstre . . . a Market convenient for the inhabitants of some parts of the Parish" (271–72); (6) an addendum composed in 1706 (275–90); and (7) a glossary (291–306). The first two sections have title pages with monumental ornamentations (discussed below); each has the appearance of an independent text, but the second part is by far the longest section in the *History* and is clearly the heart of the text.

3   David Hey, *An English Rural Community: Myddle under the Tudors and Stuarts* (Leicester University Press, 1974); Roy Porter, *English Society in the Eighteenth Century* (Harmondsworth: Penguin, 1982), 68, 162; Keith Wrightson, *English Society, 1580–1680* (New Brunswick: Rutgers University Press, 1982), 39–41, 82, 100, 102.

4   Fussner, *Historical Revolution*, 211.

sure, highly idiosyncratic, but it was also, in its peculiar way, a highly representative text. Gough's *History* demonstrates that local history was not a disinterested description of land, buildings, and individuals, but an inscription of local power. Saturated by law, Gough's text seems the product of its author's desire to fashion a text that would at least potentially be productive of power; it therefore strikingly illustrates Foucault's assertion that "knowledge functions as a form of power and disseminates the effects of power."[5] The present discussion will show that far from being just an example of local history that is a mine of information about life in early modern England, *The History of Myddle* lays bare essential features of historical practice at the beginning of the eighteenth century.

I

Local history in early modern England had its roots in the labors of Tudor antiquarians: in Leland's *Itinerary* (1530s and 1540s; first published 1710), William Lambarde's *Perambulation of Kent* (1576), Stow's *Survey of London* (1598), and especially Camden's *Britannia* (1586). Gough makes his debt to Camden (particularly to the 1695 edition of *Britannia*) clear, and the *History* also reveals an affinity with such successors to Camden as William Dugdale and White Kennett.[6] Dugdale's *Antiquities of Warwickshire* (1656) is a county history, but it too uses the parochial unit as the fundamental human settlement, and Gough's *History* seems directly imitative of Kennett's *Parochial Antiquities attempted in the History of Ambrosden, Burcester and other adjacent parts* (1695) both in its being a parochial history – Kennett's text was the first local history of this type – and in its ending with a glossary of obscure names and terms (7).[7] The first section of the *History* ("Antiquities and Memoryes of the Parish of Myddle") contains topographical information, details about what is now called infrastructure, and a description of the most important social and political institutions in the parish; thus, the first part of *The History of Myddle* is a reasonably typical local history.[8] The

5   Foucault, *Power/Knowledge*, 69; *Dits et écrits*, III, 33.
6   W. G. Hoskins, *Local History in England*, 2nd edn. (London: Longman, 1972), 17–26; and Hey, *Family History and Local History in England* (London: Longman, 1987), 4–7. On local history, see Fussner, *Historical Revolution*, 211–29; the most comprehensive discussion of "regional history" is Stan A. E. Mendyk, *"Speculum Britanniae": Regional Study, Antiquarianism, and Science in Britain to 1700* (University of Toronto Press, 1989).
7   Hoskins, 24; Dugdale, *Warwickshire*, sig. b₃r.
8   Mendyk identifies "regional study" as practiced by Dugdale, Kennett, and Gough (i.e., those regional historians who did not include natural history) with "chorography," in which, according to a seventeenth-century definition, authors "'describe any particular place . . . delivering all things of note contained therein, as ports, villages, rivers, not omitting the smallest: also to describe the platforme [plan] of houses, building, monuments, or any particular thing: and . . . every particular . . . as being most apt to describe any monument, Tower, or Castle, any Mannour, country, or kingdome'"; *"Speculum Britanniae,"* 21–24. Gough

second part of Gough's *History* is, however, unique, primarily because of two key choices made by Gough in the fashioning of his text. First, there is Gough's inspired decision to structure the manuscript by focusing it on the issue of who sat where in his parish church. The author presents a plan of the church (see figure 1) and writes his history in accordance with that plan (north to south, east to west), explaining who sat in each pew (starting with those pews that were most prized, those closest to the pulpit and the chancel, and then systematically moving away from them), how the seatholders had come to sit there, how long they or their families had held the seats, and how long the seats had pertained to their residences. Gough's second crucial choice – a natural consequence of the first – was to relate the history of his parish primarily in terms of the biographies and family histories of the holders of the seats. He names the various occupants of pews and kneelings and relates important information about their lives: whether and whom they married, how many children they had, on what bases they claimed their seats, how their fortunes fared, and whether they evidenced any notable virtues or vices. Individual lives became family histories and Gough's *History* a form of discourse that might be called historical human topography: "Aubrey's *Brief Lives* on a lower social level, giving us the lives of seventeenth-century men and women who would otherwise be names and dates in a parish register."[9]

The plan suggests that the text functions as both Baconian table and Foucauldian power grid. As a Baconian construct, Gough's plan presents schematically the instances to be used to reveal the "simple nature" of his object of study, in this case "Myddleness."[10] Like a member of the Royal Society, Gough collected and adduced matters of fact in a systematic fashion, working within a broadly Baconian project to provide the reader with empirical data.[11] Gough's scheme also highlights the names of

---

describes the roads, bridges, warrens, "meares and pooles," common land, rectors, parish clerks, and inhabitants of Myddle Castle (29–64).

[9] Hoskins, introd., *Human Nature Displayed in the History of Myddle*, by Richard Gough (Fontwell, Sussex: Centaur Press, 1968), 7. A text that is similar to Gough's in interesting ways is Gilbert White's *Natural History of Selborne*; on White, see *Cultural Landscapes: Gilbert White and The Natural History of Selborne*, with essays by W. B. Carnochan and Elizabeth Heckendorn Cook (Stanford University Libraries, 1989), 3–36. I have also benefitted from Cook's unpublished essay, "Writing the Space of the 'Natural': *The Natural History of Selborne*," which the author has generously shared with me.

[10] Lisa Jardine describes the use of Bacon's tables: "the investigator picks out all occurrences of the simple nature [being investigated] which are particularly informative. He selects instances of the simple nature which are likely to provide useful shortcuts to the discovery of its form . . . These privileged instances are collated and organised so as to provide as clear as possible a picture of the production of the selected simple nature"; *Francis Bacon*, 123. See also Mary Hesse, "Francis Bacon's Philosophy of Science," in *Essential Articles for the Study of Francis Bacon*, ed. Brian Vickers (Hamden: Archon Books, 1968), 120–22.

[11] See Shapiro, *Probability and Certainty*, 19–21, for a discussion of the Baconian project and the centrality of collecting and producing data in the work of the Royal Society.

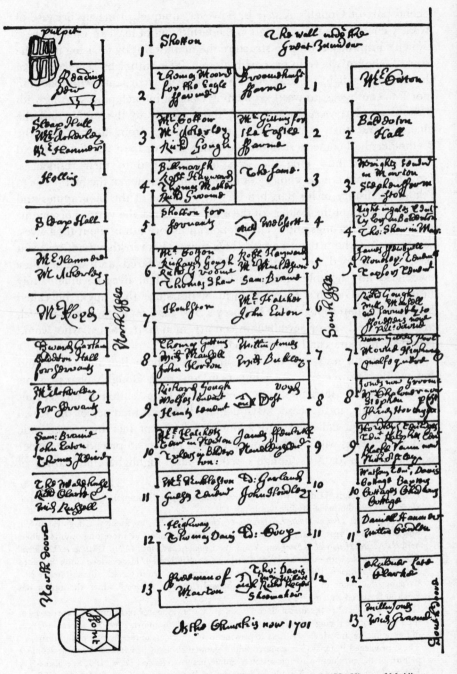

Figure 1 Plan of the parish church in Myddle from Richard Gough, *The History of Myddle*.

individuals and families as well as key socioeconomic units (Balderton Hall, the Castle farm) within the parish, and it also represents power relations among the parishioners ("Mr Acherley for servants," "Wrights tenemt [tenement] in Marton"). The *History*, then, is more than a simple table of data; it is a "technology" of power, encoding "techniques that human beings use to understand themselves" and thereby to "dominate" themselves and others. Revealing the continuity of knowledge and power, it both represents power relations within the parish and turns those relations into discourse; that discourse in turn functions as a means of inscribing and dispersing power.[12]

Since Gough's text is so singular, one might argue that it illuminates only its author's unique practice and does not embody principles and practice governing local history or English historiography in this period. David Hey asserts, however, that the *History* was "like the bulk of local histories . . . [in being] concerned with the manor and its lords, and with the church and its rectors" and was "cast in the same legal mould" as other local histories (8). Thus Gough's history reveals in an unusually clear way the link between questions of truth and questions of power that is implicit in most early modern local histories.[13] There is also another, and more compelling, reason for regarding Gough as an exemplary local historian: unlike Dugdale and Kennett, Gough was not a professional historian (a divine, lawyer, or university scholar) but an amateur who learned Latin, received a modicum of legal training, and knew his Camden (14–16).[14] As a reader of antiquities who briefly became a writer of history, Gough left in his text a clear and unguarded record of an early modern reader's view of historical practice. There are no paeans to objectivity and truth here, no protestations that the *History* is disinterested.[15] Gough's brand of local history is a version of antiquarianism worked out not at the level of the professional writer but at the level of the intelligent consumer of historical and legal studies who decided to make use of his learning and experience to become, for a short span, a historian himself. Gough's text constitutes, therefore, a meeting ground of the professional and the popular in historical practice, and as such it is an invaluable index of the horizon of expectations of history-readers and -writers at the beginning of the eighteenth century.[16]

---

[12] *Technologies of the Self: A Seminar with Michel Foucault*, ed. Luther H. Martin, Huck Gutman, and Patrick H. Hutton (Amherst: University of Massachusetts Press, 1988), 18.

[13] Foucault, *Power/Knowledge*, 132–33; *Dits et écrits*, iii, 159–60.

[14] On professionalism in seventeenth-century antiquarianism and history-writing, see Fussner, *Historical Revolution*, 189–90.

[15] Compare Kennett, who opens his local history with a defense of antiquarian studies and a characterization of the text as "a faithful relation of matters of Fact"; *Parochial Antiquities Attempted in the history of Ambrosden, Burcester and other adjacent parts* (London, 1695), sig. a₂v, a₃r.

[16] For other indicators of popular attitudes toward history in this period, see Mayer, "Nathaniel Crouch, Bookseller and Historian," 391–419; see also chapter 6 below.

II

The History of Myddle is largely a narrative of human affairs; landscape and infrastructure are important only for what they reveal about the lives of women and men. For Gough every pew, every house, every bridge has a history, and the history of those things is the sum total of what human beings have done to or with or in them. Gough, for example, relates that "Chaloner's Cottage, now Highway's . . . was built for a smith's house and shopp on a wast place by the side of Myddle-street" (237). The property was pieced together from parcels of unused land, and an enterprising blacksmith, probably Allen Chaloner, was the first tenant of the cottage and "perhaps" its builder. Once established, a family and a house might become fixtures on the local landscape and then set about acquiring a pew. Chaloner was succeeded as blacksmith by his two sons George and Allen, and the second Allen's daughter married Thomas Highway, who was the tenant of the cottage in 1701. Along the way the Chaloners produced one notably bad offspring, George's first son Richard, who was nearly executed for thievery before being rescued by an uncle, William Tyler, who was himself "a person of the most debauched morals of any that were then in the parish" (124). Still, the family prospered and their success was manifested in the church, where by 1701 they claimed parts of three separate pews on the south wall. For Gough each home in the parish, and the seat attached to it, *is* the lived experience, the successes and failures, of men and women like Chaloner and his descendants.[17]

Gough also represents other physical structures in the parish in terms of human fortune; the bridge over the brook separating Myddle and Baschurch parishes, for example, is treated as the occasion for an argument over who was responsible for repairing the structure (32). The church, of course, as the most important building in the parish, also had a rich history. The building of the pews began with the Reformation, the seats being installed first by the gentry, then by "tenement-farmers," and lastly by cottagers, and the "uniforming" of the seats, mentioned repeatedly by Gough, was a crucial event in the life of the parish.[18] Several seats, including pews assigned to the most important establishments in the community (Broomhurst farm, the Eagle farm) occupied space that was "voyd ground" until "the Church was uniformed with Waine Scott Seates." At that time ("62 yeares past, before this yeare 1701"), a parish meeting authorized the building of two seats in what had been "the Crosse Isle," but the seats were soon after "torne out" by order of another

---

[17] Dugdale focuses on the fortunes of the great men of the parishes; *Warwickshire*, 6–7, 55–56. Similarly, Camden treats only "some of the most ancient and honourable Families; for 'tis impossible to mention them all"; *Camden's Britannia 1695*, sig. d₂v.

[18] Hey, *Myddle under the Tudors*, 219.

meeting, only to be replaced by yet another seat when William Heath, the tenant of Broomhurst farm, obtained an order from "the Court att Litchfield to erect a seate in this vacant place" (185–86, 120). The church was the locus of a constant struggle for priority in the parish; in this case the problem seems to have been that many in the parish wanted this area kept open because it facilitated the celebration of the eucharist, but the space was a desirable one and the better families wanted it for their use.

Yet, despite all the alterations in the church and the parish that Gough details, the author of the *History* conveys little sense of anything fundamental changing over time. Actors changed, power shifted, and new claims of priority came forward, but nothing essential was altered. Neither the rise and fall of individuals and families, nor the catastrophe of civil war, nor the movement of new residents into the community fundamentally changed the parish. Gough accumulates details about human and physical elements in the landscape and for him the parish is the sum total at any given moment of what it has been, but he clearly believes that in essence the parish is always the same. He looks back as far as William the Conqueror, and occasionally even farther, yet never suggests that there was a time when there were not lords and rectors; freeholders, tenants, and squatters; disputes over land or leawans; drunkards, harridans, disappointing children, and hurtful parents. The author of the *History* conveys no conviction that the past was different from the present or that the future would be different from either. Myddle's essential character is apprehended historically by Gough, but what that entails for him is the presentation of matters of fact in an orderly, chronological fashion so as to yield moral or practical lessons for the reader: "Strife brings litigation, harmony fosters love" (141, 321, n. 1). The past thus recorded revealed a great deal about what people were, how they should behave, and what they should avoid, but history did not exhibit a fundamentally different mode of existence or worldview. In certain respects, then, Gough's *History* may seem decidedly premodern. As with the work of other early modern historians, the static view it embodies has sometimes been equated with the lack of a true historical sense. Yet its rich facticity – its commitment to facts as truth – suggests otherwise.[19]

Gough's devotion to facts, however, was of a particular kind; his matters of fact derived mainly from human memory, his own and that of his community (11). Memory is the principal source cited by Gough

---

[19] "English lawyers would never attain to a historical view of their own law by study of its records alone, since these revealed no important changes in the course of their history and nothing interfered with the presumption that the record declared the immemorial custom"; Pocock, *Ancient Constitution*, 68. The view that historiography without a sense of the pastness of the past is not, properly speaking, historical is widespread among twentieth-century scholars of both history and the novel; see, for example, Ferguson, *Clio Unbound*, 423, and, among scholars of the novel, Hunter, *Before Novels*, 340.

throughout the text and thus the basis of his historical authority. To be sure, as one familiar with antiquarian practice, Gough does rely upon documents: parish records, inscriptions, epitaphs, deeds, legal precedents, and warrants (38, 65–67, 188, 78, 261). He is also fond of demonstrating his learning, quoting from the Bible and ancient and modern texts and using his Latin, as well as his familiarity with sound method. Much of his glossary, for example, is taken from Camden's *Remains concerning Britain* (1605), and he also cites Leland, the chroniclers Richard Baker and Robert Fabyan, and the legal scholar John Godolphin (49, 291, 302, 98, 269, 47). Yet despite displays of his intellectual credentials, Gough's most important historical source is personal and communal memory.

The discussion of the clerks of Myddle Parish begins typically with "the first that I remember" (44). The text's temporal span only infrequently extends farther back than the middle of the sixteenth century, when the author's family moved into the parish (12–13). However, Gough possesses not only his own and his family's memories, but also the recollections of his fellow parishioners. He sometimes cites a specific resident of Myddle, such as "Mrs. Aletha Clifford of Lea Hall" who gave him information about a dispute her family had with the rector Ralph Kinaston, or the "soldier dureing the whole expedition" who told him about service in the Protector's army. More often Gough simply asserts "we have a tradition" or "it is thought" (38–40, 104–06, 54, 239). He repeatedly names unspecified "antient persons" of the parish to substantiate his account and more than once acknowledges that he speaks "only from hearsay" (319, 127, 79, 84, 96). He refers to research to justify his implicit claim that he was the master of his community's collective memory, and once even discloses that he has physical possession of the evidence: "These [i.e., the parish] orders were written in the Parish booke of accompts and the leafe was torne out, which leafe I have att last gott the custody of and doe intend to leave it in this booke to be kept in the Parish Chest" (119). The author's ownership of a portion of the historical record indicates the command he brings to his representation of his locality, but it is his personal connection with countless residences, individuals, and pews, finally, that provides the real basis for his historical authority.

One sees this most clearly in Gough's discussion of his own family, which functions as the center of his history of the parish. The principal treatment of the Goughs is in the section on the "Ninth Peiw on the South side of the North Isle," but there is nothing very remarkable about that recitation of marriages, transactions, births, deaths, successes, and failures. The pew in question is close to the center of Gough's church plan, and the treatment of the pew appears almost exactly halfway through his "Observations concerning the Seates in Myddle." The account of Gough's family, furthermore, is the longest such entry in the text and features the only genealogical chart in the *History* (154). But the author and his family are everywhere in the text as they were everywhere in the parish. They are, for example, linked to the first pew treated in the *History*, the one belonging in the author's day to the Hanmer and Acherley farms and to Sleape Hall. Previous residents of Hanmer's farm included the Kinaston family; Thomas Kinaston had a daughter, Jane, who married Robert Corbett. In this discussion of the first pew, Gough introduces and praises another Robert Corbett, even though that Corbett was not a resident of the farm in question but was related to an earlier occupant. The discussion of this individual here makes some sense because Gough often follows family lines until they give out, but the author could just as well introduce Corbett later, when Gough treats himself and his family. Corbett is probably named at this point, however, because Gough was educated by him and "served him as his Clarke," both, that is, because of the author's high regard for his former master and because he wants to introduce himself at this point and demonstrate his connection with powerful residents of the parish.

Similarly, the 1658 Downton-Formeston dispute presumably figured prominently in Gough's mind because his father once sat in the pew at issue, and the author himself therefore claims a title to part of the seat (117, 120). In the discussion of the sixth pew on the north side of the north aisle, the Garlands, who claimed the seat in Gough's day, are given short shrift but the Jukes family is treated at length, presumaby because the Gough family had connections with the Jukeses (96–100). By the time the reader arrives at the discussion of the ninth pew on the south side of the north aisle, the author's lengthy treatment of his family seems wholly justified since through his aunt and uncle, his father, his grandmother, his sister, and his sons, he appears to be linked to everyone in the parish. He has four kneelings scattered throughout the church; only Acherley, who shares a pew with the tenants of Sleape Hall, has as many, and no family has more. Just as Camden claimed to have walked much of Britain, and Dugdale cited the "intricate parts [of Warwickshire] I have walkt in," so Gough establishes his historical authority by demonstrating his personal ties to the places and people he describes.[20]

Since Gough is himself the repository of local memory, it is not surprising that he reports considerable gossip, much of it quite sensational, telling for example "a wounderfull thing" about the Cayhowell farm, which belonged to the in-laws of Gough's sister: "if the chiefe person of the family that inhabits in this farme doe fall sick, if his sicknesse bee to death, there comes a paire of pidgeons to the house about a fortnight or a weeke

---

[20] Camden, *Britannia*, sig. d₂v; Dugdale, *Warwickshire*, sig. b₃v. For both of these historians, however, the documentary record is vastly more important than personal knowledge as a historical source; for Gough the reverse is true.

before the person's death, and then goe away" (87). The instances of this marvel specified by Gough included the death of his brother-in-law, and the negative example of his sister: "Andrew Braddocke died of a sort of rambeling feavourish distemper, which raged in that country, and my sister soone after his decease fell sicke, but she recovered, and dureing her sicknesse, the pidgeons came not" (88). J. Paul Hunter has discussed a "wonders craze" in England at the end of the seventeenth and the beginning of the eighteenth centuries, evident in the outpouring of texts that reported the "strange and surprising"; Hunter argues that this taste for the marvelous was rooted in an "anti-explanatory" impulse, a desire "to find phenomena and events that eluded ready rational explanation" and thereby escaped from a discourse of science "on the way to explaining everything." No doubt this impulse explains certain of the compendia of wonders such as the 1722 purported "advertisement for a carnival magician," cited by Hunter: *The Wonder Of all the Wonders, that ever the World wonder'd at.* But others, like Robert Calef's *More Wonders of the Invisible World* (1700), which contained reports on witches and other diabolical activity in the new world by, among others, Cotton Mather, Puritan divine, historian, and Fellow of the Royal Society, were clearly embedded in historical discourse.[21] Bacon divided natural history into the history of Creatures, Marvels, and Arts, and one finds marvels not only in the works of a writer of "chapbook histories" like Nathaniel Crouch but also in texts by eminent scholars like Robert Plot; in *The History of Myddle* these stories function as matters of fact gleaned from personal or collective memory.[22] But Gough could also be skeptical about this kind of material; he ends the second part of the *History* with a recitation of the signs of an impending disaster but addresses these remarks to "those that are curiouse in Astrologicall speculations" and then adds: "This may cause some that pretend to have a skill in tropomancie [astrology] to say, that the number 8 was criticall to him; butt the numerall letters in his name shew noe such thing" (168, 249). Keith Thomas has argued that by the end of the seventeenth century many historians – rather in the manner of political historians both recounting and questioning the stories of Brut and Arthur – recorded marvels while simultaneously indicating their skepticism in regard to such narratives. Gough's treatment of such curiosities reveals just such a blend of credulity and skepticism.[23]

In addition to recording many wonders, Gough also reports a surprisingly large number of murders; in his treatment of just five pews (the fourth

---

[21] Hunter, *Before Novels*, 215, 209, 216, 385, n. 27.
[22] Bacon, *Selected Writings*, 231; Robert Plot, *The Natural History of Oxfordshire* (Oxford, 1676), 169; Mayer, "Nathaniel Crouch," 405. Crouch and Plot are discussed in chapter 6 below.
[23] Keith Thomas, *Religion and the Decline of Magic* (New York: Charles Scribner's Sons, 1971), 349–52, 452, 643–45.

to the eighth seats on the south side of the north aisle), he discusses four murders, one accusation of murder, and two failed attempts, including a triple murder pact agreed to by "a young wanton widow" and two wives "weary of theire husbands" (148). The most detailed account of a murder is, characteristically, gratuitous. One Richard Eavans, not a resident of the parish, is remembered by Gough simply because he was, for murky reasons ("What passionate words passed I cannot tell, but I have cause to thinke they were such as is too usuall amongst drunken persons") beaten to death "in the lower end of Myddle Towne" by two other drunken outsiders (286–87). Gough acknowledges that several of his accounts of homicide are digressions; in fact, he goes outside the parish for seven of the ten murders he treats (23). After relating one such crime – the murder of a servant girl by Hugh Elks – he tells of "another [that] happened about the same time, by a person of the same name . . . although it was in another Lordship." This second Elks murder must have been irresistible to Gough since the culprit was brought to justice through supernatural intervention, but Gough admits that he includes the story "for the strangenesse of it, though it bee beside the matter" (60).

Gough records no particular sources for these narratives of homicide; one can assume that they were part of the collective memory of the parish and that Gough heard them from his neighbors, that they were, in short, the stuff of gossip. W. G. Hoskins argues that gossip can be serious historical evidence to the local historian, and it certainly was for Gough.[24] If Gough had written for publication, one might argue that stories of murder and the supernatural were included in the *History* to titillate the reader, but there is no sign that Gough wrote to please an audience. Rather, in his principal defense of his text, Gough argues that everything in the book is at least potentially useful (78). His inclusion of such material was, thus, a kind of popular antiquarianism since in reporting gossip and hearsay, Gough turns the popular memory into matters of fact recorded and presented by the historian.[25] David Carr, taking issue with Hayden White's argument that the writing of history involves the imposition of narrative upon inchoate material drawn from the historical record, argues that narratives are as much a part of the historical record as documents, dates, names, and events:

Storytelling is pervasive . . . and it is practical before it is ever poetic. To address the world of practical action with a view to telling a story about it, in the literary sense, is not to encounter a world of disjointed actions, of confusion and

[24] Hoskins, *English Local History: The Past and the Future. An Inaugural Lecture Delivered in the University of Leicester, 3 March 1966* (Leicester University Press, 1966), 8.

[25] On the popularization of natural history, see J. Paul Hunter, "Boyle and the Epistemology of the Novel," *Eighteenth-Century Fiction*, 2 (1990), 278–79; and *Before Novels*, 197; see also Michael Hunter, *Science and Society in Restoration England* (Cambridge University Press, 1981), 85.

discordance, a mass of elements to which one brings the clarity and organization of a narrative account. It is to encounter a world already narrativized, singly and collectively, by the persons involved.[26]

This "narrativized" world is the basis of Gough's *History*; in his text "history" as it existed in the popular mind meets and blends with the "history" uncovered and reported by the antiquarian.

Spacks argues that gossip "inculcates the same knowledge" that is conveyed by novels, a knowledge that derives from "attentiveness to human . . . detail."[27] This suggestion that gossip is a form of discourse akin to novelistic discourse needs to be coupled with the qualification that especially in Gough's day such material could be the stuff of history. For Gough, wonders and murders, like everything he reports, are legitimate material for the historian. He recognizes that "some persons will thinke that many things I have written are alltogaether uselesse," but he argues: "I doe believe that there is nothing herein mentioned which may not by chance att one time or other happen to bee needfull to some person or other" (78). Given this belief, all matters of fact repeated by one's neighbors were inescapably part of historical discourse.

III

The reasons for this belief in the utility of such information is apparent when one attends not only to the popular narratives but also to the communal judgments that are inscribed in Gough's text. Spacks observes that "gossip consolidates and uses social power to affect status and opinion in a community," and Gough, in recording his parish's views on individuals, families, and situations, represents unfolding power relations within the community.[28] Ralph Kinaston, one of the rectors of Myddle parish, is depicted as "bold and undaunted," and celebrated for his charity, because he sued a great man on behalf of the parish. Gough's praise of the rector echoes the community's judgment, registered on the clergyman's gravestone in the chancel of the church (38, 41). The community also speaks on the question of disinheritance; Thomas Acherley had three sons, and "gave all his lands" to his third son, Richard, but this action was disapproved of "by many persons, who said, that this was a disinheriting of the elder son, and that such things doe seldom prosper." As if to prove the wisdom of this judgment, Gough relates that Richard died "without ishue male" and "the antient inheritance" of his family reverted to a collateral line (90).

Nevertheless, although throughout the text Gough speaks for and judges

[26] David Carr, "Review Essay, *Temps et Récit. Tome 1.* By Paul Ricoeur," *History and Theory* 23 (1984), 368–69; for an extended discussion of this issue, see Carr, *Time, Narrative, and History* (Bloomington: Indiana University Press, 1986), chapter 6.

[27] Spacks, *Gossip*, 20.   [28] *Ibid.*, 22.

in the name of his parish, *The History of Myddle* is clearly Gough's and not the parish's work; the text is indisputably "Goughean" in character, embodying as it does the point of view of Gough and other similarly minded members of the parish, especially Gough's view of existing relations of power within the parish. His treatment is different from the representation of the parish that might have been fashioned by one of the notorious Tylers and probably also from the kind of history that would have been written by the scholarly Gittinses (187–90). Gough is aware that he might be criticized for giving an incomplete or biased view of the life of his parish: "I hope noe man will blame mee," he wrote, "for not nameing every person according to that which hee conceives is his right and superiority in the seat in Church." He defends himself by suggesting that a careful reader would "first take notice of every man's church *leawan*, and then look over what I have written concerning the descent and pedigree of all," but his defense reveals that for him the importance of individual parishioners depends on the church rates they paid and and on their "pedigrees" (78). In short, Gough is completely wedded to the hierarchies in place on the land and in the church. He often rails against the poor who, as he sees it, have too many children and burden the public with their care; such were Thomas Davies and his wife from whom "hath proceeded such a numerouse offspring in this parish, that I have heard some reckon up . . . noe less than sixty of them and the greater part of them have been chargeable to the parish. Many great familyes in this parish have been extinct, but this has gott soe many branches that it is more likely to overspread it" (243).

This is more than mere bias on the part of the historian. The concept of bias generally assumes a typology of particular perspectives found in accounts of frequently represented events from particular perspectives, such as royalist, parliamentary, and Whig histories of the English civil war.[29] But Gough's *History* is not in any meaningful sense an interpretation of the history of his parish even though, as the work of a well-to-do landholder who was not a member of the gentry, the text embodies a specifiable ideological position. The *History* is more than an interpretation; the author is doing more than simply recording information and casting it in a certain light. He is inscribing his community, turning one form of discourse (gossip) into another (history) and in the process embodying not only "relations of meaning," as Foucault calls them, but also "relations of power."[30]

In Gough's text the church is the site of an endless struggle for priority;

29 Royce McGillivray, *Restoration Historians and the English Civil War* (The Hague: Martinus Nijhoff, 1974), 1–3; Joseph H. Preston, "English Ecclesiastical Historians and the Problem of Bias, 1559–1742," *Journal of the History of Ideas* 32 (1971), 203–20.
30 Foucault, *Power/Knowledge*, 114; *Dits et écrits*, iii, 145.

parish meetings, physical conflict, and litigation were all elements of the struggle, and not just the rich and powerful were involved. Two members of a squatters' colony that expanded slowly from 1581 to 1701 claimed

an old Pew which was not broaken att the uniforming of the seates . . . Eavan Jones, and Francis Davis who had built new houses upon lands taken out of Myddle Wood, did sitt in this Pew, beecause they had no seates in Church; and now Richard Rogers who has Eavan Jones' house, and Thomas Davis, who has Francis Davis' house, doe claime a right in it by long usage.   (22, 211)

Like Chaloner, these two gained a toehold in the community by appropriating common land, and in the church they claimed a pew, an old one that was not "uniformed" with the others; the heirs of Jones and Davis eventually claimed the seat "by long usage." Squatters in both the wood and the church, men like Harris and Rogers were set apart, but even so they eventually achieved a modicum of legitimacy. Since the seating scheme in Myddle church, which before Gough's time existed in the church itself and in inchoate form in the minds of the parishioners, always represented from moment to moment the ongoing struggles in the parish as well as the winners and losers of earlier fights, Gough inscribed power relations that the parishioners never lost sight of. Hey has examined the issues of power and authority in Gough's text but mainly in terms of how the *History* registered "social gradations within the community"; indeed, he argues that the church was the only institution in Myddle where such gradations could be expressed.[31] Parochial hierarchies are indeed apparent: the orders issued after the Downton-Formeston dispute demonstrate, for example, the widely held view that "the best of the parish" should be "above" their social inferiors (20, 117). Yet much more than hierarchy is inscribed in Gough's text. The means of asserting one's very existence in the parish; the seizing of a portion of local power; the expansion from one holding to many, outside and inside the church; the loss of property and priority; and the constant representation of power relations on the land and in the church are all written in Gough's history. The text, in short, is a complex grid of multivalent power relations.

What makes the *History* remarkable in respect to the issue of historical discourse and power is not that Gough inscribed local power relations in his book, but that the author himself was apparently so lucid about the functioning of his text as an embodiment of power relations within his community. Despite the fact that the text is premised upon a fundamentally static view of history, it represents a world of constant strife and flux in which power and priority are constantly at stake, and Gough clearly believed that his *History* was germane to that struggle. The text, in short,

---

[31] Hey, *Myddle under the Tudors*, 230.

was produced "in accordance with the intelligibility of struggles, of strategies and tactics."[32] One sees this most clearly in the author's attention to questions of law.

A contested claim to a piece of property or a seat in the church was often a cause for legal action, and the *History* represents one such legal battle after another (68, 184–85). It is as a text saturated with law that this local history most clearly and self-consciously reveals its inscription of local power. The author cites case law in specifying who had the right to dispose of certain seats. He invokes the authority of Godolphin (author of *An Abridgement of the Ecclesiasticall Laws of this Realm* [1678]), of Sir Edward Coke, and of Sir John Doddridge (author of *The English Lawyer* [1631]). Deeds are reproduced, parish orders transcribed. An entire section of the *History* is devoted to "Certaine Cases and Controversies Which Have Happened Betweene This Parish and Other Parishes," mainly concerning the question of responsibility for paupers. Most tellingly, at the end of the first section of the text, Gough treats "Customes in this Lordship of Myddle" and defines a custom as "a law or right, not written, which being established by long use and the consent of our ancestors hath been and is dayly practised" (64). In other words, custom was unwritten law encoded in memory.[33] Since Gough records the memory of his community, much of it focused on land ownership or claims on pews, the entire text is potentially a legal document, and thus his belief "that there is nothing herein mentioned which may not . . . happen to bee needful." Gough presents the *History* as a work that can be read and used by his litigious neighbors in a very practical sense.[34] He conceives of his text as a legal tool, one might aptly say a weapon, available to the residents of Myddle – a record and therefore evidence of what has passed and what has been believed in the parish, and, therefore, the basis for the settlement of future disputes. All memories were potentially useful; if memory was ultimately law, no memory could be regarded as negligible.

Thus, Gough indicates that his text not only records power relations but, potentially at least, also produces power. Local historians, by focusing on property rights, putatively beneficent hierarchies, and struggles for power and priority, valorized existing power relations and disempowered all persons and social forces they did not treat. Thus, Gough's text ensured that both poverty and nonconformity rendered a resident of Myddle history-less. Gough clearly believed that much could not or ought not to be

---

[32] Foucault, *Power/Knowledge*, 114; *Dits et écrits*, III, 145.

[33] On the "customary" nature of English law generally, especially as revealed in the debates over the nature of the English constitution, see Pocock, *Ancient Constitution*, especially 15, 30–31.

[34] Gough's discussion of the parish's disputes over poor relief establishes his own legal credentials; the eight cases he treats are ones that he helped to argue, and he proudly informs the reader that although the first was lost, "thanks be to God wee never lost any afterwards" (252).

known about his community; what needed to be known was whatever made possible the distribution of the seats in the parish's central institution in a fashion that was "seemly" and "decent."

The "frontispieces" for three different sections of Gough's book participate forcefully in the text's representation and production of power. Each of the three has a monumental quality, with columns, arches, decorative features, and a generally architectural appearance (see figures 2 and 3). The first two, appearing at the beginning of the first and second sections of the text respectively and featuring the titles of the sections, the name of the author, and the year in which each section was written, have the appearance of headstones. Hoskins points out that although "no monument commemorates Richard Gough in the [Myddle] parish church," his book is his "true memorial," and Gough's frontispieces suggest that the author himself might also have considered the text in that light.[35] This seems especially apparent in the third such decoration, which has the same monumental quality as the first two and also contains what we can assume is a self-portrait of the author. This third drawing looks like a design for a Richard Gough memorial that was never built. But there is more to these illustrations than mere narcissism; their monumental quality is consonant with the instrumental function the author seems to have envisioned for his text. Antiquarians treated headstones as an important part of the historical record, and as a reader of antiquities Gough could hardly have been unaware of the evidentiary value of such monuments.[36] The frontispieces thus invite us to read the *History* not just as a piece of historical writing but as the historical record itself.[37] As such, the text could function as a focal point (perhaps Gough believed it would be *the* focal point) within "a productive network [of power] which runs through the whole social body"; the *History* presents itself, in short, as the center of the nexus of power within the community it represents.[38] As a text that turns memory and gossip into history and law, the *History of Myddle* might well have been considered the discursive center of the parish by its author just as Myddle Church provided a physical basis for community.

Gough's is not the only text from this period that reveals the ways in which seventeenth-century historical discourse functioned not only as a

---

[35] Hoskins, *Human Nature Displayed*, 7.   [36] Momigliano, *Studies in Historiography*, 11–13.

[37] The text would have been particularly useful to Gough's family, since their holdings were described in great detail, and the monumental quality of the *History* would also have had the effect of memorializing – fixing in the local memory, protecting with customary law – the history and standing of the author's family. Perhaps Gough's family so viewed his efforts, since almost two centuries later two of his descendants used the *History* as the starting point for a history of the family; see F. H. and A. V. Gough, "The Goughs of Myddle and Their Descendants," *Transactions of the Shropshire Archaeological and Natural History Society*, 2nd ser., 5 (1893), 261–92.

[38] Foucault, *Power/Knowledge*, 119; *Dits et écrits*, iii, 149.

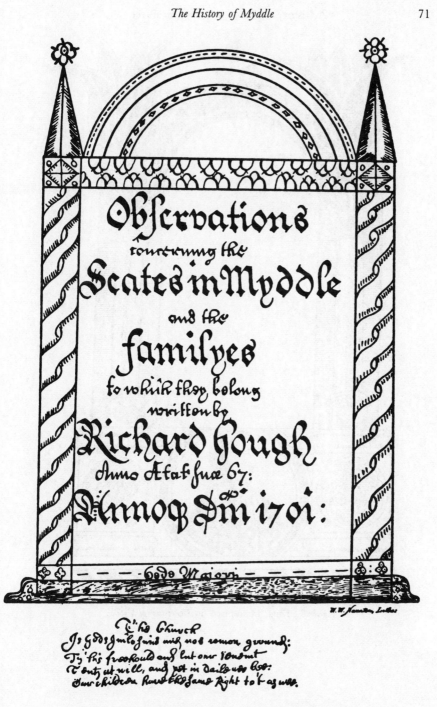

Figure 2 "Frontispiece" to the second section of *The History of Myddle*.

Figure 3   Final "frontispiece" in *The History of Myddle*.

record of the past but also as an embodiment of "relations of power." David C. Douglas argues that "like his predecessors," Dugdale "approached his subject in the interests of his class," and the *Antiquities of Warwickshire* was dedicated to the gentry of the county. Dugdale's *Monasticon*, furthermore, was not only " 'productive of many lawsuits' " but also "had been admitted in the courts of Westminster as 'good circumstantial evidence'." Hey points out that antiquarian researches were sponsored not just out of pride but "to protect descendants from legal claims on property," and in fact local history was often written by lawyers or scholars with legal training (Dugdale's father was a lawyer and had his son read law).[39] Sir Henry Chauncy, author of *The Historical Antiquities of Hertfordshire*, was also a lawyer, and he established a close affinity between the law and local history when he argued that those gentlemen who failed to cooperate with him might regret having done so because they "deny'd me the opportunity of Asserting their Rights." Similarly, Kennett claimed that his *Parochial Antiquities* constituted the greatest service he could perform for his parish (except for "the immediate discharge of my Holy Office") and informed his readers that his antiquarian labors began in an attempt to defend the parish's right to revenues from certain lands.[40]

Local historians were not alone in conceiving of historical discourse as productive of power. Fussner calls Sir Robert Cotton's library "the arsenal of the Parliamentary opposition," and it has frequently been argued that Clarendon's *History of the Rebellion* was written as an extension of Clarendon's service to the king.[41] In addition, the putatively methodological dispute between Thomas Fuller and Peter Heylyn over the former's *Church-History of Britain*, as we have seen, was really a struggle between representatives of two factions within the English church over, among other things, the meaning of the Civil War. Indeed, to an unusual degree, seventeenth-century historiography was predicated on the belief, conditioned both by the various crises of the century and by the Baconian faith that learning must be for "the benefit and use of life," that history was inevitably a tool or a weapon in the hands of those who wrote it and those who read it.[42]

Gough's *History* is important because it lays bare this tendency; his text "defamiliarizes" both local history and seventeenth-century historiography in general. Shklovsky, in discussing the defamiliarizing function of poetry, has argued that it is a poet's innovative "technique" that renders that

---

[39] Douglas, *English Scholars*, 41; Dugdale, *Warwickshire*, sig. a₃r; Hey, *Family History*, 4, 5; *DNB*.

[40] Henry Chauncy, *The Historical Antiquities of Hertfordshire* (London, 1700), sig. B₁r; Kennett, *Parochial Antiquities*, sig. a₂v, b₁r–b₂v.

[41] Fussner, *Historical Revolution*, 118; George Watson, "The Reader in Clarendon's *History of the Rebellion*," *Review of English Studies* ns 25 (1974), 396–99.

[42] Bacon, *Selected Writings*, 437.

poet's discourse capable of "making objects 'unfamiliar'."[43] Gough's text
indicates how new techniques in other forms of discourse can also have a
defamiliarizing effect. *The History of Myddle* was in some ways the work of a
naif, a reader of antiquities and law who became a one-time writer of local
history, but because it was so cleverly and peculiarly conceived, the *History
of Myddle* reveals with unusual clarity the nature of early modern historical
discourse in England. Dugdale worked on behalf of the gentry of Warwickshire, yet his rigorous adherence to the canons of antiquarian scholarship –
which is to say, his technique – led to his being canonized as a grave,
severe, scrupulous, methodical, and accurate historian.[44] Gough, with his
odd map of his parish church, his gossip, his family histories, and his
fascination with the settlement of apparently petty disputes, may seem far
removed from the great "antiquarian enterprise," but his technique – to
draw upon Shklovsky again – succeeds in making early modern historical
discourse "difficult" in a way that Dugdale's weighty tomes never have.[45]
It is Gough, in short, who forces us to see that seventeenth-century
historiography is a discourse notable less for its "purity of scholarship" or
its "astonishing variety of historical materials" than for the unabashed way
in which it asserts that historical writing is and ought to be an essay in
power.[46]

Baconian historiography – of which Gough's history was a part – was a
way of acting in the world. The novel shared this feature of historical
discourse; Hunter suggests that "the new fiction" tends to partake of
history's "tendency to organize narrative along . . . ideological lines."[47]
Local history, like other types of history examined below, suggests that
historical discourse constantly abetted early modern readers – especially
the new readers who became novel readers – in their view that reading was
and should be a highly utilitarian affair.[48] Thus, once again, history can be
seen as creating the readerly expectations of Defoe's audience.

---

[43] Shklovsky, "Art as Technique," 12.   [44] Douglas, *English Scholars*, 41–43.
[45] Shklovsky, "Art as Technique," 12.   [46] Fussner, *Historical Revolution*, 220–21.
[47] Hunter, *Before Novels*, 344; it should be said that Hunter also argues that "this tendency . . .
probably is not imitated from histories."
[48] On the utilitarian cast of mind of the new readers of the late seventeenth and early eighteenth
centuries, see Hunter, *Before Novels*, 84; Mayer, "Nathaniel Crouch," 410–12; and chapter 6
below.

4

Lifewriting and historiography, fiction and fact: Baxter, Clarendon, and Hutchinson on the English Civil War

The editors of the *Norton Anthology of English Literature* assert that Clarendon's *History of the Rebellion*

was remarkable not only for the largeness of its canvas but for the force and coherence of the social philosophy informing it – which, under the name of Toryism, retains an influence even to the present day. As an historical rhetorician and portrait painter, Clarendon ranks with . . . Thucydides and Tacitus.[1]

High praise indeed, but also equivocal praise. Clarendon, it seems, like Shakespeare in Johnson's famous "Preface," deserves to be classed with the ancients, but he merits this honor because of the breadth of his vision, his rhetorical skills, and his character studies; he is praised more for his rhetoric than for his contribution to the historical literature on the Civil War. This ambiguous praise is wholly in keeping with the treatment of Clarendon in twentieth-century scholarship on historiography, since aside from rather formulaic praise for his character sketches, he is largely ignored in the history of history.[2]

The eighteenth century, of course, did not ignore Clarendon; the *History of the Rebellion* was an immediate "bestseller," and although some condemned it as fatally flawed by partiality, "it was widely recognized as a masterpiece."[3] The twentieth century, however, has been more dubious. John Kenyon declines even to regard Clarendon's *History* as "the real thing": declines, that is, to consider the best-known historical work published in England in the century before the appearance of *Robinson Crusoe* as a genuine work of history.[4] And if Clarendon is slighted, Richard

---

[1] *The Norton Anthology of English Literature*, 6th edn., 2 vols., ed. M. H. Abrams, *et al.* (New York: W. W. Norton, 1993), I, 1752.

[2] "Over the centuries the substantial literary merit of Clarendon's *History* has become a critical . . . commonplace," but the twentieth century has done little more than pay "lip service" to Clarendon; Martine Watson Brownley, *Clarendon and the Rhetoric of Historical Form* (Philadelphia: University of Pennsylvania Press, 1985), xiii.

[3] On the *History* as a bestseller, see Hugh Trevor-Roper, introd., *Selections from The History of the Rebellion and The Life by Himself* by Clarendon, ed. G. Huehns (Oxford University Press, 1978), x; Brownley, *Clarendon*, 27.

[4] Kenyon, *History Men*, 29; Kenyon is quoting and disagreeing with Trevor-Roper's assertion that Clarendon effects the transition from "quasi-history" to "the real thing."

Baxter, author of *Reliquiae Baxterianae*, with its "dissection of the Civil War parties [upon which] an almost religious reliance has been placed," and Lucy Hutchinson, author of *Memoirs of the Life of Colonel Hutchinson*, which, according to the *DNB*, "possesses a peculiar value among seventeenth-century memoirs," are both consigned to oblivion. There is but one reference to either writer in the five best-known studies of seventeenth- and early eighteenth-century English historiography.[5]

The reasons for the neglect of these texts by historians of history are several, including the dominance of the historical revolution paradigm in the scholarly literature on the historiography of the period, a difference in early modern and twentieth-century views of the relationship between lifewriting and history-writing, and a modern consensus, at least among literary scholars and critical theorists, that autobiographical writing is by definition fictive. Moreover, the eclectic nature of these works – part autobiography and part historiography, indebted both to classical models and to the new history, and blending records of matters of fact with personal reminiscence – makes them texts that scholars of historiography have trouble classifying and that they therefore mostly ignore. In the last chapter we considered a work that is remarkable for its tendency to turn personal and communal memory into historical discourse that aspired to the status of law. The works to be discussed in this chapter were also rooted in memory, to such a degree that they all occupy a borderline position between lifewriting and historiography. As a result, the qualities that make the "Lives" of Baxter, Clarendon, and Hutchinson representative of seventeenth-century historical discourse – the rootedness in personal experience, the eliding of formal barriers, the utilitarian cast, the polemical stance – are exactly the qualities that make them suspect as history to twentieth-century scholars investigating the origins of modern historical practice.[6]

---

[5] Joyce L. Malcolm, "A King in Search of Soldiers: Charles I in 1642," *Historical Journal*, 21 (1978), 252–53; *DNB*. The studies to which I refer are Douglas, *English Scholars*; Ferguson, *Clio Unbound*; Fussner, *Historical Revolution*; Levine, *Humanism and History*; and Pocock, *Ancient Constitution*. Studies of Baxter and Hutchinson include N. H Keeble, *Richard Baxter: Puritan Man of Letters* (Oxford: Clarendon Press, 1982); Keeble, "The Autobiographer as Apologist: *Reliquiae Baxterianae*," *Prose Studies* 9 (1986), 105–19; Sandra Findley and Elaine Hobby, "Seventeenth-Century Women's Autobiography," in *1642: Literature and Power in the Seventeenth Century. Proceedings of the Essex Conference on the Sociology of Literature. July 1980*, ed. Francis Barker, *et al.* (Colchester: University of Essex Press, 1981), 11–36; and N.H. Keeble, "'The Colonel's Shadow': Lucy Hutchinson, Women's Writing and the Civil War," in *Literature and the English Civil War*, ed. Thomas Healy and Jonathan Sawday (Cambridge University Press, 1990), 227–47.

[6] When I use the term "Life" in this chapter and hereafter, I am referring to a written account of the life of an individual, either of the author or of some individual other than the author. By "lifewriting" I mean texts that tell the life-stories of historical individuals, generally biographies, autobiographies, memoirs, and so forth, but, as this chapter argues, history can also be a species of lifewriting, as can texts like Delarivier Manley's *Memoirs of Rivella* (1714), which

In this chapter, the relationship between lifewriting and historiography will be explored, along with the presuppositions governing the reception of historical and biographical texts by early modern and by twentieth-century readers. The works of Baxter, Clarendon, and Hutchinson will demonstrate that around 1700 historical discourse included highly personal life-histories primarily focused on public matters. This study will also show that many seventeenth-century works of history partook of the personal and the polemical to such a degree as to suggest to later readers that they ought not to be read as species of historical discourse, even though that does not seem to have been the perception of most early modern readers. Histories rooted in life-stories, although sometimes challenged by critics as unreliable or even fictional, were generally acepted as part of historical discourse; thus readers were habituated to accepting highly personal, even clearly biased, accounts as works of history.

I

Baxter, Clarendon, and Hutchinson claim our attention as historians of the Civil War because they write about events they witnessed and in which they participated. Each of them approaches the representation of historical events by way of lifewriting, specifically autobiography. Having been exiled twice, Clarendon had to rely mainly on his own memory of events for his account of the Civil War in *History of the Rebellion*; what is more, the published version of the *History* consisted in important part of material that Clarendon first wrote for use in his *Life . . . By Himself*. Not surprisingly, therefore, Clarendon's account of the rebellion is highly personal: 75 percent of the text focuses on only nine of the twenty years that he ostensibly covers, the years when he was most active.[7] Clarendon bases his authority as an historian on his own involvement in the Civil War, declaring: "I may not be thought altogether an incompetent person for this communication, having been present as a member of parliament . . . before and till the breaking out of the rebellion, and having since had the honour to be near two great kings in some trust."[8] Thus, "the validity of . . . [Clarendon's] personal vision of events" is one of the central thematics

---

species of lifewriting, as can texts like Delarivier Manley's *Memoirs of Rivella* (1714), which presents itself as a work of fiction.

[7] Begun in the 1640s but written mainly in the 1660s, the *History* was composed not while Clarendon was active in English politics and government but while he was in exile. Having finished the *Life* by 1670, Clarendon decided to combine it with an account of events up to 1648 that he had drafted twenty years earlier, and the result was the *History*. See C. H. Firth, "Clarendon's *History of the Rebellion*," *English Historical Review* 19 (1904), 26–54, 246–62, 464–83; Brownley, *Clarendon*, 22–27.

[8] Edward, Earl of Clarendon, *The History of the Rebellion and Civil Wars in England Begun in the Year 1641*, 6 vols. (Oxford: Clarendon Press, 1888), I, 3; hereafter citations will be given in the text.

of the *History*, and for the former chancellor "the true history of the civil wars was . . . a history of himself."[9]

Baxter's text, too, is decidedly autobiographical; it opens with a discussion of the author's youth, including a famous "account of heart-occurrences, and God's operations on me."[10] The text functions both as a spiritual autobiography, tracking the author's "development as a Christian soul," and as a history, specifically an ecclesiastical history, of England during and after the Civil War.[11] One is highly personal, the other treats public events, but the two are, in Baxter's view, inseparable. In the midst of the discussion of his early years of ministry in Kidderminster, Worcestershire, when Baxter is supposed to have accomplished a legendary moral transformation of that community in 1641–42, the author of the *Reliquiae Baxterianae* suddenly turns to political events, remarking "I must return to the proceedings of the parliament, because the rest will not be well understood without connoting the occasions of them which were administered" (28–29). Driven from his living for suspected nonconformity, later a chaplain to Charles II, and finally a key figure at the conference called by the King in 1661 to find common ground between the Anglicans and the Presbyterians, Baxter writes as one whose private, spiritual life is inextricably bound up with the great events he represents.[12]

Hutchinson is ostensibly writing a life of her husband rather than an autobiography, but scholars have treated her text as a species of autobiography because in the seventeenth century the biography of one's deceased husband was a "seemly" vehicle for a woman's autobiography and because she herself figures so prominently in the work: "She, not he, animates a text devoted to him."[13] The seventeenth century recognized no clear generic or formal distinction between the writing of a life and the writing of one's own life; Bacon discussed only "Lives," and autobiography, strictly speaking, did not exist at the time, although it was coming into being.[14] In

[9] Braudy, *Narrative Form*, 15, 14.
[10] *The Autobiography of Richard Baxter*, abr. J. M. Lloyd Thomas, ed. and introd. N. H. Keeble (London: Dent, 1985), 103; hereafter citations will be given in the text. I will generally refer to this text as the *Reliquiae Baxterianae* even though I will be citing the readily-available modern abridgment because the modern version follows the 1696 version of Baxter's text quite closely. All of the published versions of the *Reliquiae* are editors' reconstructions of Baxter's text (v–vi).
[11] Margaret Bottrall, *Every Man a Phoenix: Studies in Seventeenth-Century Autobiography* (London: John Murray, 1958), 112.
[12] Baxter represented "the Presbyterian case" at the conference, although not very effectively ("inexpert negotiating skills seem to have helped to close the episcopal ears"); Keeble, *The Literary Culture of Nonconformity in Later Seventeenth-Century England* (Athens GA: University of Georgia Press, 1987), 30.
[13] James R. Sutherland, *English Literature of the Late Seventeenth Century*, vol. VI, *The Oxford History of English Literature* (Oxford University Press, 1969), 260–61; Donald A. Stauffer, *English Biography before 1700* (Cambridge MA: Harvard University Press, 1930), 154. The quote is from Keeble, "Lucy Hutchinson," 244.
[14] On the near-identity of biography and autobiography before 1700, see Wayne Shumaker,

any case, although Hutchinson informs her readers that she examines "the state of the kingdome" in 1641 merely to make comprehensible her and her husband's "part in this greate Trageddy," thereby suggesting that her concerns are primarily personal, she in fact focuses to an overwhelming degree on public events.[15] After a playful account of Hutchinson's courtship of her, the author of the *Memoirs* treats not the private lives of husband and wife (omitting, for example, any substantial discussion of the lives of their many children) but the role that they played in the Civil War.[16] Great upheavals of seventeenth-century English history were represented in terms of the life of Hutchinson and his wife; thus, the degree to which "all the Parliament Garrisons were infested and disturb'd with like factious little people" was suggested by the long-running dispute between John Hutchinson as Governor of Nottingham Castle and the committee "elected to act with him when he became Governor" (158). In a text that numbers 277 pages in its most recent edition, Hutchinson devotes only 37 to the history of the Hutchinson family before the beginning of the Civil War, and half of the *Memoirs* focus on the years 1642 to 1648 even though the author's husband lived from 1615 to 1664 (xii). Thus, Hutchinson, like Clarendon and Baxter, uses lifewriting as a means of writing the history of her time; all three authors explicitly or implicitly establish their authority as historians by relying heavily upon their own experience of events represented in the texts.

Baxter in particular is at pains to justify lifewriting as a legitimate historical form. To ensure that he will be read as a truthful historian, he asserts:

I have purposely omitted almost all the descriptions of any persons that ever opposed me, or that I ever or my brethren suffered by, because I know that the appearance of interest and partiality might give a fair excuse to the reader's incredulity.   (128)

Baxter's primary concern here, of course, is to convince his readers that he is a credible historian, but a subtext is his assertion that his life-story can and should be read as a history of his age. He denies himself what he sees as one of the most important historical tools ("the true description of persons is much of the very life of history"), and he does so to demonstrate

English Autobiography: Its Emergence, Materials, and Form (Berkeley: University of California Press, 1954), 5; Shumaker argues that autobiography did not exist in England before 1600 and that it was not until around 1800 that "authors seem to be writing in a tradition instead of feeling their way into a new literary genre." See also Stauffer, *English Biography*, 175.

[15] Lucy Hutchinson, *Memoirs of the Life of Colonel Hutchinson with the Fragment of an Autobiography of Mrs. Hutchinson*, ed. James Sutherland (London: Oxford University Press, 1973), 37, 53; hereafter citations will be given in the text.

[16] The children are the recipients, not the subject, of the *Life*; Hutchinson begins with a prefatory address "To My Children" and seeks "to commemorate" her husband to them (2).

that his aim is to function as an even-handed historian. So "though the form is autobiographical, the theme is not," as N. H. Keeble observes, "for throughout [the *Reliquiae*] Baxter's own personal experience serves to particularize and typify that of the Puritans at large" (xxvii, xxvii).

From a seventeenth-century perspective, the assertion that lifewriting is a historical form was entirely unremarkable. In the early modern period the two forms of writing were regarded not just as compatible but as essentially identical. In Bacon's taxonomy of the forms of learning, "Lives" is one of the three principal subdivisions of "Perfect History."[17] Arnaldo Momigliano does argue that lifewriting and history-writing were distinct in antiquity because "the borderline" between fact and fiction was thought by the Greeks to be "thinner in biography than in ordinary historiography," but in the early modern period an account of an individual life was regarded as a legitimate form of history-writing.[18] In fact, before 1660 a writer of a "Life" was denominated not a biographer but a historiographer.[19] There were, of course, well-known classical precedents for writing history from the perspective of a single individual; Thucydides informed readers "either I was present myself at the events which I have described or else I heard of them from eye-witnesses," thereby establishing a tradition that history was best if written by those who had participated in the events described.[20] Indeed Philip Hicks argues that well into the eighteenth century the most common model for a historical writer was the classical historian, typically understood to be "a man of action now retired, who wrote a truthful account of contemporary politics and war for men of similar station."[21] Thus, although the Greeks may have regarded biography as a form tending more toward fiction than history, they also understood that the historian often wrote from what we would consider an autobiographical perspective, and profitably so; in the early modern period this aspect of ancient thinking about the link between lifewriting and history-writing had become an article of faith. In the seventeenth century a Life was a work of history, not a form of fiction, and, indeed, as Bacon saw it, Lives might well be regarded as the most important historical form:

[17] For Bacon history was of four types (natural, civil, ecclesiastical, and literary), civil history was divided into three classes ("Memorials, Perfect Histories, and Antiquities") and perfect history consisted of "Chronicles," "Relations," and "Lives"; *Selected Writings*, 230–35. On the conventional cast of Bacon's classification, see Arnaldo Momigliano, *The Development of Greek Biography. Four Lectures* (Cambridge MA: Harvard University Press, 1971), 2.

[18] Momigliano, *Greek Biography*, 57, 102; he discusses both the story of one's own life and the story of another's life as essentially equivalent within the ancient Greek context.

[19] Stauffer, *English Biography*, 220.

[20] Thucydides, *History of the Peloponnesian War*, trans. Rex Warner, introd. and notes M. I. Finley (London: Penguin, 1972), 48.

[21] Hicks, "Bolingbroke, Clarendon, and the Role of the Classical Historian," 447–48; see also, Braudy, *Narrative Form*, 10–11.

For the History of Times representeth the magnitude of actions and the public faces and deportments of persons, and passeth over in silence the smaller passages and motions of men and matters. But such being the workmanship of God as he doth hang the greatest weight upon the smallest wires . . . it comes therefore that such histories do rather set forth the pomp of business than the true and inward resorts thereof. But Lives . . . propounding to themselves a person to represent in whom actions both greater and smaller, public and private, have a commixture, must of necessity contain a more true, native, and lively representation.[22]

Given his belief that the value of the lifestory as an historical representation derives from the blend of "greater and smaller, public and private," it would seem that Bacon recognized that such accounts would be highly subjective representations of historical events and accepted that aspect of Lives as the inevitable effect of a powerful individual writing history in the form of his or her Life. Certainly, each of the texts under discussion here embodies a far from disinterested view of the events represented. Hutchinson's perspective is singular in a number of ways. Her account is the most important memoir of the Civil War written by a woman. She is assertively a Puritan; her husband, she tells us, "was a man of a most moderate and wise spiritt, but still so enclin'd to favour the oppressed saints and honest people of those times that, though he conform'd to their governments, the licentious and profane encroachers upon common native rights branded him the reproach of the world, though the glory of good men, Puritanisme" (17). Writing in defense of her husband, she incorporates in her Life a sympathetic portrait of a stiffnecked Puritan, whom Sutherland characterizes as "at once intellectually attractive and socially repellent" but whom the author not surprisingly represents as being of "noble spiritt," "native majesty," and "sweete greatnesse" (xii, 8). Hutchinson's point of view is even sharply defined in geographical terms. Her husband was largely responsible for holding Nottingham for the parliamentary side when most of the rest of the shire sided with the king, and although her account of events outside of Nottingham is "of little value," the treatment of the civil war in Nottingham is "full and accurate" and "as a picture of the life of a puritan family . . . it is unique."[23] Hutchinson, then, gives us a view of "English democracy in action," representing the experience of "the common man" far from the center of things (xii, xiv).

Baxter, for his part, writes as a churchman with a clear sense of the proper course, past and present, for the various English ecclesiastical factions, and yet his view was so singular that more than one observer simply labelled it "Baxterian" (xx, xxiv). He praises Presbyterians and Independents, calls Quakers and Anabaptists "proper fanatics," and

---

[22] Bacon, *Selected Writings*, 235.   [23] *DNB*.

reviles Papists; nevertheless, his proposal for church government calls for
a "primitive Episcopacy" (a "moderate episcopacy" that was also to be
"a Presbytery"), and he is capable of commending the Quakers because
they "did greatly relieve the sober people" persecuted after the Restoration. Baxter even acknowledges that "God hath many sanctified ones"
among the Papists, people "who have received the true doctrine of
Christianity" (179, 189, 171).[24] Of course, Clarendon was "the greatest
English statesman on the royalist side in the period of the English . . .
Revolution," and his account begins with the assertion that "a general
combination, and universal apostasy in the whole nation from their
religion and allegiance" led inevitably to "a total and prodigious altera-
tion and confusion over the whole kingdom" (I, 1).[25] Although Clarendon
is at times remarkably candid about the faults of the king and his
ministers and about the strengths of such men as Hampden or Cromwell,
he never ceases in the text to be the loyal subject and servant of his king.
Thus, each of the authors writes from a clear and distinct position, both
biographical and ideological; one is a statesman, one a churchman, one a
wife; two were dissenters while one was an Anglican; two were revolutionaries, one was a royalist; one of the revolutionaries nearly saw her
husband executed as a regicide after the Restoration, the other was a
major conciliator.

The value of these works derives largely from the representation of the
very particular lived experience of each author and thus of a particular
point of view embodied in the text. This is evident when one compares the
different treatments of the same issues in the three texts. Consider, for
example, Baxter, Clarendon, and Hutchinson on the Presbyterian-Independent split within the parliamentary camp. Clarendon views this split
from the point of the view of the king, seeing the Presbyterian-Independent
split as a corollary of the division between the army and the parliament; he
points out that "the parliament . . . prosecuted a presbyterian settlement
as earnestly as they could" and "punished . . . and discountenanced" the
Independents, "which the army liked not as a violation of the liberty of
tender consciences." He also represents monarch and legislature as joint
victims of the army; the leaders of the army appear as "more brisk and
contumacious" with the parliament, once the king was in their hands, than
they had ever been before. Furthermore, once "the army had . . . subdued

---

[24] William M. Lamont claims that a key feature of Baxter's representation of the Civil War is his
"magnanimity"; *Richard Baxter and the Millenium: Protestant Imperialism and the English Revolution*
(London: Croom Helm, 1979), 78.

[25] Trevor-Roper, *Selections from Clarendon*, v. Braudy argues that in the *History* "the problem of
ruptured continuities" is solved by "Clarendon's own perspective": "He is there, the King is
there, and . . . history is there too. The Commonwealth government is an aberration. Here is
the true continuity" (18–19).

all opposition, and the parliament and they seemed all of a piece . . . the army seemed less regardful of the king than they had been" (IV, 257, 228, 256). Clarendon analyzes the relative political effectiveness of the Prebyterians and Independents, and although he accused both of "dissimulation," "malice," and "wickedness," it is the former that he finds wanting in practical terms. He notes "a wonderful difference" between the two groups:

the independents [were] always doing that, which . . . contributed . . . to the end they aimed at, and to the conclusion they meant to bring to pass; whereas the presbyterians, for the most part, did always somewhat that reasonably must destroy their own end.   (IV, 303)

Citing Machiavelli, Clarendon treats this contrast in some detail, attributing it to the fact that the Presbyterians were "distracted and divided" among themselves and "formed their counsels by . . . the affections of the people," whereas Cromwell and a few others made policy for the Independents: "the one resolved, only to do what . . . the people would like and approve; and the other, that the people should like and approve what they had resolved" (IV, 303, 304). In short, the author of the *History of the Rebellion* disapproves of Cromwell and his adherents but recognizes political effectiveness when he sees it. Ever the politician, Clarendon's knowing assessment of the motives and skill of the various political actors enriches his account of the Civil War, even though his analysis is never wholly separable from his royalist stance.

Not surprisingly, Baxter's approach is different. At the beginning of the second part of *Reliquiae*, he lists "the truth or good" in which each of the "contending parties" was "more eminent than the rest" and discusses his efforts at creating "concord and pacification" (135). In his "Self-Analysis," furthermore, he makes much of the fact that he was less of a controversialist in the 1660s than he had been in the 1630s and 1640s; he argues that one of his strengths was to work at "narrowing controversies by explication, and separating the real from the verbal, and proving to many contenders that they differ less than they think they do" (107, 125). This assessment indicates why Baxter focuses as he does on his own and others' attempts to arrive at a religious settlement; he sees most religious antagonists, including the Presbyterians and the Independents, as Christians who, from a want of clarity, focus on differences that need not divide them. The author of the *Reliquiae* contrasts his own desire to reconcile the contending religious parties ("we made our Terms large enough for all, Episcopal, Presbyterians and Independants") with what he sees as Cromwell's cynical use of confessional divisions to serve his own political ends. Thus Baxter argues that Cromwell treated the Vanists, Independents, and others left in the parliament after Pride's Purge just as he had earlier treated the Presbyterians: "mak[ing] them odious by hard speeches of them throughout his army" (84, 63, 68, 153, 211).[26]

Hutchinson is no peacemaker; she sides unabashedly with the Independents, observing that when her husband went up to London in 1644 to take his seat in Parliament, "he found a very bitter spiritt of discord and envie raging . . . and the Presbiterian faction . . . endeavouring a bitter persecution . . . against those who had in so short a time accomplisht by God's blessing that victory which he was pleas'd to bestow on them" (166). What is more, Hutchinson treats the Presbyterian-Independent split by focusing more than once on how that division was registered in the married life of Sir Thomas Fairfax. During the time that Fairfax convalesced at Nottingham Castle, we are told:

The Generall's Lady was come allong with him, who had follow'd his camp to the siege of Oxford, and layne at his Quarters there all the while he abode there, and was exceeding kind to her husband's Chaplaines, Independent Ministers, till the Armie return'd to lie neerer London; and then the Presbiterian Ministers quite chang'd the lady into such a bitter aversion against them [i.e., the Independents] that they could not endure to come into the Generall's presence while she was there, and the Generall had an unquiett, unpleasant life with her, who drove from him many of those friends in whose conversation he had found much sweetenesse. (168)

Hutchinson later attributes Fairfax's decision not to lead his army against the Scots to the unfortunate influence of his wife and "her Presbiterian Chaplains" (195).[27] Writing as a woman and as a wife, Hutchinson is free to treat the personal ramifications of political and religious questions.

Each of these works, then, substantiates Bacon's assertion that Lives contain the "true and inward resorts" of events; each, that is, contains a unique representation of the Civil War inextricably tied to the lived experience of the writer. From an early modern perspective, these Lives from the Civil War were exemplary species of historical discourse. Such texts helped to create certain important expectations in the reader; what J. Paul Hunter says about works by Burnet and John Oldmixon applies equally well to these Lives: "they legitimized the subjective structuring of history as a way of seeing a certain historically definable culture."[28]

II

The twentieth century's view of the relationship between lifewriting, especially autobiography, and history-writing, however, is radically dif-

---

[26] Clarendon, by contrast, does not discuss Pride's Purge in terms of religious factions; see IV, 465–66.

[27] Cf. Clarendon, *ibid.*, 356–58; on this aspect of Hutchinson's account, see Keeble, "Lucy Hutchinson," 233–35.

[28] Hunter, *Before Novels*, 342.

ferent from the one that prevailed in the early modern period, and this striking difference helps to explain why these important seventeenth-century texts have been ignored by students of early modern English historiography. According to twentieth-century theorists, individuals who undertake to write their own lives are engaged in a literary activity wholly distinct from the writing of history. In a typical work, Roy Pascal discusses autobiography as "a search for one's inner standing," arguing that the form "often acquires the meaning of a theodicy"; ultimately Pascal defines the writing of one's own life as a work of art, not a type of historiography.[29] Similarly, although the historian Georges Gusdorf distinguishes between autobiographies that focus on public events and those that treat mainly private affairs, the distinction gets lost when he defines autobiography as "a kind of apologetics or theodicy of the individual being" and asserts that "the significance of autobiography should . . . be sought beyond truth and falsity . . . [since although] it is unquestionably a document about life . . . it is also a work of art."[30] The argument of both of these theoreticians of autobiography is that in this species of lifewriting the narrator-subject creates not only a narrative but also a vision of the self, and that this aspect of autobiography transforms what might otherwise be regarded as a factual relation into what Gusdorf finally describes as a "mythic tale."[31]

In a way, then, twentieth-century theorists have returned to the view of the Greeks, at least in respect to autobiography, and as a result contemporary scholarship has been disinclined to classify autobiographical texts as works of history. If autobiography is an essentially imaginative form, historiography written from an autobiographical perspective is suspect and therefore unlikely to play an important role in any history of history focusing on the development of modern historical practice with its rules of evidence, encomia to objectivity, and devotion to fact. Lifewriting is closer to fiction than to historiography.[32] Yet although this line of argument may problematize the status of autobiography for the twentieth-century reader, it should not prevent our considering such works as species of historical discourse within an early modern context, especially if our interest in them arises from the desire to stipulate the horizon of expectations of readers of history around 1719. For the seventeenth-century reader, biography and

---

[29] Roy Pascal, *Design and Truth in Autobiography* (Cambridge MA: Harvard University Press, 1960), 182, 183, 186.

[30] Georges Gusdorf, "Conditions and Limits of Autobiography," trans. James Olney, in *Studies in Autobiography*, ed. Olney (New York: Oxford University Press, 1988), 36, 39, 43.

[31] Gusdorf, "Conditions and Limits," 48. See also Olney, *Metaphors of Self: The Meaning of Autobiography* (Princeton University Press, 1972), 35; Paul de Man, "Autobiography as De-facement," *MLN*, 94 (1979), 921–22; and Paul John Eakin, "Narrative and Chronology as Structures of Reference and the New Model Autobiography," in Olney, ed., *Studies*, 38.

[32] Bottrall argues that truth in autobiography is not equivalent to truth in historiography, but possesses, rather, "the same kind of truthfulness as poetry possesses"; *Every Man a Phoenix*, 9.

autobiography were essentially one, and both were assimilable to historiography. Nevertheless, it seems clear that the problematic character of autobiographical writing in the twentieth century is partly responsible for the treatment of texts such as those by Baxter, Clarendon, and Hutchinson as works of marginal importance in the history of history.

Admittedly, such works were sometimes dismissed as essentially fictive texts even by early modern readers. This was so, however, not because the texts created versions of the writers' selves but because they were perceived as partial. In the 1720s, for example, John Oldmixon argued that the *History of the Rebellion* was "the least Historical of any that ever deserv'd the Name of History" because it was filled with stylistic "Flourishes" and "Tricks" designed to conceal from the reader "the Rottenness," that is, the bias, at the heart of the text. Oldmixon compared Clarendon to "those Painters who can perform well when they paint after Fancy, but never succeed when they are to follow Likeness."[33] As in the case of the attack upon Thomas Fuller by Peter Heylyn, the charge of bias is combined with the dismissal of a text as fictive, but generally only when a critic of a particular historian took a different view of events. Thus, Oldmixon's attacks on Clarendon have been explained as one of his "splenetic outbursts against . . . anyone . . . who did not read history, especially recent history, through the most strongly Whig-tinted spectacles."[34]

The histories of Clarendon, Baxter, and Hutchinson, however, demonstrate that at least for the seventeenth-century reader, such charges of partiality did not necessarily preclude a work's being read as history. These writers openly displayed their biases and their practical goals and yet defended their works as matters of fact. Hutchinson wrote for her children, that they might know their father, but also "to discover the deformities of this wicked age, and to instruct the erring children of this generation" (1). To that end, she depicted her husband heroically against a corrupt background in order to vindicate him and his cause; he was represented as a deliverer of his people and likened (because of his years of retirement in the country before the Civil War began) to Moses in the wilderness: "Mr. Hutchinson . . . was sequester'd from a wicked court and . . . exercis'd himselfe in contemplation of the first workes and discoveries of God. Here he . . . had a call to goe back to deliver his country, groaning under spirituall and civill bondage" (35–36). Hutchinson made no attempt to disguise her championing of the cause of her husband and his faction. Clarendon, too, announced to his readers that he became an historian so

[33] [John Oldmixon], *Clarendon and Whitlock Compar'd* . . . (London, 1727), x–xi; [Oldmixon], *The Critical History of England Ecclesiastical and Civil* . . . (London, 1724), 165.

[34] Bonamy Dobrée, *English Literature in the Early Eighteenth Century 1700–1740*, vol. VII, *Oxford History of English Literature* (Oxford: Clarendon Press, 1959), 386; on Fuller and Heylyn, see chapter 1 above.

that "posterity may not be deceived" as to the "wickedness of these times";
indeed, Clarendon began the history "as a state paper for the eyes of the
King."[35]

The comments of twentieth-century students of historiography suggest
that the blatant prejudices acknowledged by these authors have served to
eliminate their works from consideration as "serious" works of history.
Fussner, for example, argues in one of his few comments on Clarendon
that the *History of the Rebellion* has been "often criticized for its partiality,"
and Keeble acknowledges, despite his claims about Baxter's attempt to
write a well-documented "chronicle," that the author of the *Reliquiae*
actually wrote a work of apologetics: "the moderate persona, the general-
ising of personal experience, the marshalling of evidence, all are deployed
in the service of an interpretation of events."[36] Yet the admissions of these
writers that their accounts were not disinterested coexisted in their texts
with claims that they relied primarily upon "particulars," as Clarendon
expressed it, "exposed to the naked view." The author of the *History of the
Rebellion* identified his history as a "relation of matter of fact" and
promised: "I shall . . . preserve myself from the least sharpness that may
proceed from private provocation or a public indignation" (IV, 3, 2, 4;
I, 3). Baxter decried "the prodigious lies which have been published in this
age in matters of fact," implying that he aimed to publish the simple truth
(126). Both historians were indebted in important ways to contemporary
antiquarians. Baxter's consciousness of the need to substantiate his claims
with credible evidence, for example, is revealed by his interlarding of his
text with many documents. This feature of the *Reliquiae* is almost totally
obscured in the most recently available Everyman edition of Baxter's
history, which omits his documentation, but Joan Webber argues that for
Baxter such documents were "the simplest way of assuring oneself and
one's readers that the literal truth has been recorded." Similarly, Clarendon was influenced by the antiquarians Spelman and Selden and "did
his best to collect all the written information necessary for an accurate
account of events." Martine Brownley argues in fact that at times
Clarendon's "antiquarian desire to assemble factual information over-
whelmed his literary control."[37] To be sure, these writers relied heavily
upon their own memory of events, but Bacon did not distinguish between

---

[35] Trevor-Roper, *Selections from Clarendon*, vi; Kenyon, *History Men*, 3. See also Sir Charles Firth,
"Edward Hyde, Earl of Clarendon, as Statesman, Historian, and Chancellor of the University," in *Essays Historical and Literary* (Oxford: Clarendon Press, 1938), 115; Firth argues that
Clarendon wrote "with a definite practical purpose . . . to point out the errors of policy
committed on the King's side."

[36] Fussner, *Historical Revolution*, 160; Keeble, "Autobiographer as Apologist," 114.

[37] Joan Webber, *The Eloquent 'I': Style and Self in Seventeenth-Century Prose* (Madison: University of
Wisconsin Press, 1968), 120–21; Brownley, *Clarendon*, 22. See also Trevor-Roper, *Selections from
Clarendon*, x–xi.

"the facts of experience and historical facts" and "took seriously the
ancient identification of history and memory," and, as we saw in the
previous chapter, a reliance upon personal and communal memory was
not inconsistent with the principles governing "scientific" history around
1700.[38]

Although Hutchinson makes almost no theoretical observations, apart
from a promise to use "a naked undrest narrative, speaking the simple
truth" to reveal her husband's character, she relies heavily on a simple,
detailed narration of events as they transpired in and around Nottingham
Castle. She also explicitly distinguishes her practice from romance-writing.
Trying to explain the "strange ebbe and flow of courage and cowardize
there was in both parties" in the battle for Nottingham, she comments "if
it [her memoir] were a Romance, wee should say . . . that the Heroes . . .
[acted] out of excesse of gallantry," but she insists instead on naming what
she regards as the real cause. That this cause was, as Hutchinson saw it, the
"wonders of Providence . . . the beames of the Almighty" – another
element of early modern historiography associated with a "dying tradition"
by the historians of the historical revolution – does not alter the fact that
Hutchinson rejects romance as her model in favor of "true history" (1,
114–15, 32).[39]

How can one square the blatant partiality of these writers with their
commitment to matters of fact? The apparent contradiction can be
explained by pointing to the belief, sometimes explicitly asserted and
sometimes only implicitly acknowledged by virtually all historians of the
period, that one always, necessarily, wrote history with an end in view. For
Bacon learning was "not an opinion to be held but a work to be done,"
and works written, again in Bacon's words, "for the benefit and use of life"
were not likely to be disinterested, especially if they treated recent
controversial events.[40] History and polemic, then, were not mutually
exclusive. Baxter, more concerned than the other two writers discussed
here with the issue of belief in historiography, examines the question of the
engaged historian in a fascinating discussion of "what History is Credible,
and what not" at the beginning of his *Church-History of the Government of
Bishops*.[41] Focusing on the character of the historian, first by discussing the
nine points that he believes establish "the Veracity or credible fitness of the
Reporter" and then by indicating fourteen ways to recognize the historian

---

38　Fussner, *Historical Revolution*, 260.

39　*Ibid.*, 193–94; he treats Ralegh as one of the makers of the historical revolution *in spite of* his
　　being wedded to the delineation of primary or providential, rather than secondary or human,
　　causes.

40　Bacon, *Selected Writings*, 437.

41　Baxter, *Church-History of the Government of Bishops and Their Councils Abbreviated* (London, 1681), sig.
　　a₄v; the title page informs the reader that the text was written by "Richard Baxter, a Hater of
　　False History." See also a similar comment in the *Reliquiae* at 126–28.

"who is not worthy of belief," Baxter suggests that the embrace of a particular point of view or a clear goal is not incompatible with the responsibility of the historian to tell the truth. He asserts that the believable historian must be "impartial, a lover of peace, and not ingaged by faction," but his subsequent comments on the "lying Historian" reveal that, as he sees the matter, impartiality and freedom from faction are at best achieved incompletely and with difficulty. Baxter warns his readers not to believe a historian who is "*deeply* ingaged in a Party [emphasis added]," suggesting thereby that attachment to some party is inevitable but that nevertheless the historian must be free from excessive devotion to the interests of his or her group.

An admission that every historian belongs to some faction is also implicit in Baxter's assertion that a historian cannot be trusted if "sober moderate men of his own party contradict him." Baxter cautions against an historian with "a malignant spirit"; readers, therefore, have a right to expect historians to be moderate ("sober, calm, considerate"), relatively benign, reasonably impartial, and not too deeply attached to a particular point of view. Yet the author of the *Reliquiae* also implies that no one can expect any historian to be entirely free from bias. He treats the problem of credibility in personal terms, arguing that a judgment about the veracity of a work of history is equivalent to a judgment about the integrity of the author, thus making all historiography inescapably personal.[42] Clarendon, too, tells his readers, "I shall . . . preserve myself from the least sharpness, that may proceed from private provocation, or a more public indignation, in the whole observing the rules that a man should who wishes to be believed" (3). For both writers, the reader's decision whether or not to believe a historical narrative is equivalent to an assessment of "the man" or "the woman" who has written the history – his or her tone and demeanor – and not a simple evaluation of the text with its evidence or lack thereof. One judges the text by judging the person revealed in the text. Thus for early modern historians and their readers, the best history was written by participants in the events described, and the best measure of an historical account was the integrity of the individual whose experience and (admittedly partial) views were embodied in the text.

III

Baxter's argument is surprisingly akin to the views of a twentieth-century "metahistorian" like Hayden White, even though White does not explicitly

---

[42] *Ibid.*, sig. a₁v–a₂v. For a related argument, see Steven Shapin, *The Social History of Truth: Civility and Science in Seventeenth-Century England* (University of Chicago Press, 1994), xxvii; Shapin argues that in early modern England "the gentleman was recognized as, and enjoined to be, a truth-teller."

focus on the issue of belief on the part of the reader of history. White argues, at the end of *Metahistory*, that the "explanatory strategies" in any historical narrative are shaped by "the imperatives of the trope which . . . [the historian] has used to prefigure the field of historical occurrence singled out by him for investigation"; White argues, furthermore, that the decision to employ one trope or another is entirely the writer's choice. White suggests that recognizing this aspect of history-writing can potentially have a liberating effect on students of history: "Historians and philosophers of history will then be freed to conceptualize history, to perceive its contents, and to construct narrative accounts of its processes in whatever modality of consciousness is most consistent with their own moral and aesthetic aspirations."[43] Both Baxter in the seventeenth century and White in the twentieth grant that a historian can never achieve objectivity; the principal difference between the two is that Baxter apparently believed an historical account could be truthful and indeed factual, even though the text reveals the author's allegiance to a particular perspective or party, whereas White seems to suggest that once historians admit what it is they are really doing they are then free to imagine history ("perceive its contents") as they so desire.

White's metahistorical criticism leads him in the end to argue that even the historian's use of facts has to be seen as a process shaped by an ideologically and tropologically determined "prefiguring" of the narrative in the initial response to the historical record. Baxter, by contrast, suggests that although the historian does indeed select "facts" and fashion "conceptualizations," these elements can still combine in a narrative that can be read as factually true. Thus despite the acknowledged impossibility of being anything more than free of excessive attachment to a faction, Baxter argues that the facts of some historians are credible:

When History delivereth a matter of fact and sense, by the common Consent of all men that knew it, though of contrary minds, dispositions, and interests, it giveth us a certainty which may be called Natural.[44]

For Baxter, then, belief in history as matters of fact is possible and the measure of whether a work of history is credible is always the character of the person who wrote it.

Baxter's position in respect to the issue of partiality in history is not, however, exclusively a view of the seventeenth century. The most sustained philosophical examination of the complex relationship between history and fiction in our time – Paul Ricoeur's *Time and Narrative* – acknowledges the value of White's work but also objects that "White's recourse to tropology

43 Hayden White, *Metahistory: The Historical Imagination in Nineteenth-Century Europe* (Baltimore: Johns Hopkins University Press, 1973), 427, 434.

44 Baxter, *Church-History*, sig. a₁r.

runs the risk of wiping out the boundary between fiction and history."
Ricoeur's view is that although one must acknowledge the inescapably
rhetorical – ideological, tropological – nature of all historical narrative,
one must also acknowledge that the historian begins from and has a
profound responsibility to the "marks" or "traces" of the past that
constitute the inescapable basis for any historiographical narrative:

the concern for "returning history to its origins in the literary imagination" must
not lead to giving more weight to the verbal force invested in our redescriptions
than to the incitations to redescription that arise from the past itself. In other
words, a sort of tropological arbitrariness must not make us forget the kind of
constraint that the past event exercises on historical discourse by way of the known
documents.

Ricoeur acknowledges "the interweaving of fiction and history" in both
fictional and historical narratives, *and*, at the same time, asserts the reality
of the boundary between the two.[45] Although it is indeed fashioned
according to the lights of the shaping individual who is the historian,
history does not cease to be history; historiography, while never completely
separable from rhetoric or fiction, is nevertheless not reducible to either or
to both.

Something like Ricoeur's view, I would argue, is implicit in Baxter's
apparently contradictory assertions that a credible historian must, on the
one hand, be impartial and, on the other, not be *too* partial. Early modern
English historians, working during or after the Civil War and as a result
imbued with the principle that historiography was both a way of knowing
and a means of acting, believed that historiography could be, perhaps had
to be, both partial *and* true. Works of history that owed much to lifewriting
embodied this doubleness of early modern historiography particularly
clearly; the works of Baxter, Clarendon, and Hutchinson were of unique
value as accounts of the Civil War because of the lived experience of their
authors, and such works could never be separated from those lives or from
the views that they had engendered.

Such works might inevitably partake of the fictive as well as of the
programmatic; there are grounds for making this claim in respect to the
works of Baxter, Clarendon, and Hutchinson if for no other reason than
because the texts were so much indebted to antique models. Thus
important elements of Clarendon's *History* – its point of view, its style, and
its conception of historiography as a grand rhetorical performance – have
been attributed to the influence of Clarendon's classical model, Thucydides.[46] Even Baxter, who seemingly owed little to the ancients, also
apparently had a model from late antiquity for his text, one that he was

45 Ricoeur, *Time and Narrative*, 3:154–55 and chapter 8.
46 Braudy, *Narrative Form*, 11, 15, 17; Levine, *Humanism and History*, 161–62.

willing openly to imitate: Augustine's *Confessions*. Baxter's account of his spiritual progress included among the sins of his youth the following:

2. I was much addicted to the excessive gluttonous eating of apples and pears; which I think laid the foundation of that imbecility and flatulency of my stomach which caused the bodily calamities of my life.
3. To this end, and to concur with naughty boys that gloried in evil, I have oft gone into other men's orchards and stolen their fruit, when I had enough at home. (5)

The kinship between this passage and a similar one in the *Confessions* is manifest:

I lusted to thieve, and did it, compelled by no hunger, nor poverty, but through a cloyedness of welldoing, and a pamperedness of iniquity. For I stole that, of which I had enough, and much better . . . A pear tree there was near our vineyard, laden with fruit, tempting neither for colour nor taste. To shake and rob this, some lewd young fellows of us went, late one night . . . and took huge loads, not for our eating, but to fling to the very hogs.[47]

Here we see Baxter appropriating both "facts" and "explanatory strategies" – stolen fruit, spiritual progress – from his ancient source, just as Hutchinson, thinking typologically, finds elements of the story of Moses in the life of her husband. This debt to an ancient text – this sin reported by Baxter, echoing Augustine's own sin – might be used to argue that the *Reliquiae* cannot possibly be read as history, especially if one argues as White does that the importation of elements of other stories into historical representation "arises out of a desire to have real events display the coherence, integrity, fullness, and closure of an image of life that is and can only be imaginary."[48]

Much the same point can be made by looking at the utilitarian quality of these texts. Pocock judges Bolingbroke harshly because, as he sees it, Bolingbroke, for whom "the function of historical study is not to discover how men have lived . . . but to inculcate the moral and practical lessons of statecraft," had no interest in the history of remote times. This "theme [of] history as a school of politics" was of course widespread in Renaissance Europe, yet Pocock describes Bolingbroke's version of it as "a deplorable attitude," since the "man of affairs need concern himself only with those periods likely to contain examples relevant to his own situation" and therefore "ends by ruling out the greater part of recorded history" as fit matter for the historian. What is missing from Bolingbroke's sense of history, according to Pocock, is the capacity "to see the present state of mankind as emerging from the

---

47 St. Augustine, *Confessions*, trans. and introd. R. S. Pine-Coffin (Harmondsworth: Penguin, 1961), 25–26.
48 White, "Value of Narrativity," 27.

whole of its past experience."[49] Yet the fact is, as Charles Webster has stated the matter, that "science [in the seventeenth century] was pursued not as an end in itself, but for its value in confirming the power of providence and for its applicability to social amelioration."[50] For an early modern historian, then, "the function of historical study" was naturally and properly utilitarian.

Historians like Baxter, Clarendon, and Hutchinson, therefore, wrote history that was strikingly partial in an untroubled fashion. Baxter might well have argued that a historical writer could import details and devices from other texts and authors and still be believed by the reader if the reader made the judgment that "the credible fitness of the Reporter" ought to be accepted. The histories of Hutchinson, Baxter, and Clarendon – with their formal and stylistic similarities to ancient texts, their blatantly polemical aspects, their highly individualized points of view, and their utilitarian features – may easily be dismissed as unmodern and unscientific works of historiography, particularly if one argues on behalf of a modern historical method that has managed to escape from the utilitarian cast of mind of earlier historians. Nevertheless, these are eminently representative examples of Baconian historiography, examples which demonstrate that in the century before *Robinson Crusoe* the rules of historical discourse allowed writers who were unabashedly partial and who shaped their texts accordingly to represent their narratives as matters of fact. Yet how were such texts apprehended by readers? We shall have more to say about this below, but for the moment we can observe that Patricia Meyer Spacks argues that the writer of his or her own Life "assumes, and assumes that the reader will assume, that a person can be known through his story." She argues further that the "role of the writer" also reveals that "the historian like the fictionist forms his record to reveal the meaning he wishes to impart." Yet Spacks acknowledges that "the rhetoric of eighteenth-century autobiographies . . . refers to history rather than story."[51] Thus Lives in which the writer can be seen as acting like a polemicist or a fictionist were, for the early modern reader, situated within historical discourse. Such works forcibly suggested to those readers that history could and did come in the shape of a Life and that the far from disinterested life story – rich in matters of fact, partaking perhaps of the fictive and certainly of the polemical – was nevertheless recognizably historical.

[49] Pocock, *The Ancient Constitution*, 246–50. Pocock does admit that Bolingbroke's detachment from the past, in its own way, contributed to the development of modern historicism because it "gave him the power to reflect on the historical process . . . which was beyond better scholars."

[50] Charles Webster, *The Great Instauration: Science, Medicine and Reform, 1626–1660* (New York: Holmes and Meier, 1975), 30.

[51] Spacks, *Imagining a Self*, 301.

5

The secret history of the last Stuart kings

Up to this point in the examination of seventeenth-century historiography, the argument has focused on the debate over the British History, which revealed a surprisingly high tolerance for elements of fiction in historical discourse; on local history, which drew upon gossip and hearsay and functioned as an essay in power; and on histories of the Civil War, which indicated a strong bias in favor of narratives written from the point of view of an engaged individual, so much so that these works have not infrequently been read as works too partial to be regarded as genuine history. In this chapter the focus will be on secret history, where the various features of early modern historiography so far singled out come together. An examination of secret history is crucial to the attempt made in this study to stipulate how late seventeenth- and early eighteenth-century historical discourse functioned as the matrix for the development of the early English novel; the form occupies a position in the discursive terrain where historical and fictional discourse can be viewed in closest conjunction. There were at least three different types of secret history, one that was distinctly historical in character, one that constituted essentially a sustained rhetorical blast, and one that was a fictive form often associated, then and now, with the popular French form, the *chronique scandaleuse*. Readers were quite capable of sorting out the three different types. The closeness of historical and novelistic discourse at the beginning of the eighteenth century in England should not be taken to indicate that readers were confused about the difference between the two. Early modern writers and readers, as Barbara Foley has observed, did not live "in some sort of epistemological haze."[1] The essential feature of historiography in this period was not confusion; the novel was not based upon a muddle. The reception of certain key secret histories reveals that readers could and did make fine distinctions among different texts that bore the same label.

The present chapter centers on the type of secret history that belonged to historical discourse, first defining the historiographical form and then indicating why Bishop Burnet's *History of His Own Times* and Anthony

---

[1]   Foley, *Telling the Truth*, 110.

Hamilton's *Memoirs of Count Grammont* are telling examples of the form. The discussion then turns to the ways in which these texts invited readers to concretize them both as works of fiction and as works of history. Finally, it considers how readers in fact made the distinctions that these texts forced upon them.[2] It is by studying such moments in the history of reading that one can stipulate the horizon of expectations of early modern readers who would soon find it necessary to make sense of Defoe's narratives and who, along with later writers, would use these and similar reading experiences to begin to theorize the "new species of writing" that emerged in the middle of the eighteenth century.

I

Secret history is an historiographical form with a long but shadowy formal history. At least one secret history was written in antiquity and some have appeared in the modern period, but the end of the seventeenth and the beginning of the eighteenth centuries was undoubtedly the "golden age" of secret history in English letters. Secret histories were produced by now mostly forgotten writers like Nathaniel Crouch, Ned Ward, and John Oldmixon as well as by such better-remembered denizens of Grub Street as Defoe, Eliza Haywood, and Delarivier Manley.[3] Procopius's *Anecdota* or *Unpublished Notes*, first published in translation in England in 1624 and since then known as the *Arcana Historia* or *Secret History*, was the most important ancient example of the form,

2   On the concept of the "concretization" of a literary work, see Vodička, "The Concretization of the Literary Work," 110–12. For Vodička, concretization is "the reflection of a work in the consciousness of those for whom it is an esthetic object." He thinks of such reflections (of which there can be many, although the nature of any concretization is controlled by both "the properties of the work" and "the period's literary requirements") largely in terms of the application of prevailing "literary values." As is true for Jauss, the work of the Russian Formalists is crucial for Vodička, who argues "that after a certain hesitation caused by the novelty of the work, it is accepted into literature in a certain concretized appearance" that endures until "a new concretization is recorded and publicized." It might be argued that Vodička's formulations are not suited to the discussion of works like the secret histories considered here, since their status as "esthetic objects" is at issue. But surely an initial, although generally unstated, step in the process of concretization is perceiving a work in terms of one of the "totalizing frames" – fact or fiction – that Foley argues must be employed by readers if they are successfully to apprehend texts; *Telling the Truth*, 40. The question of whether a work is fact or fiction may rarely be at issue, but when it is, we can expect it to be the crucial question in the minds of readers. This is the case, for example, with several of Defoe's narratives, as we shall see in chapter 10. Neither Vodička nor Jauss considers the possibility that his method can be used to investigate the boundaries between forms of discourse, but secret histories and Defoe's narratives seem to demand that we do so as we study how readers have read these texts.

3   In addition to authors and works discussed here, see, for example, [Ned Ward], *The Secret History of Clubs* (London, 1709); [John Oldmixon], *Arcana Gallica: Or, The Secret History of France, For the Last Century* (London, 1714); [Eliza Haywood], *The Secret History of the Present Intrigues of the Court of Caramania* (London, 1727).

although early modern writers sometimes cited Suetonius's *The Twelve Caesars* as another forebear. The form, furthermore, has never really gone out of use; in the nineteenth and twentieth centuries, there have been a few notable secret histories, including Karl Marx's *Secret Diplomatic History of the Eighteenth Century*.[4] The fact that there have been many secret histories in the English tradition and that the form has roots in antiquity has not meant, however, that scholars and critics have known what to make of them. Quite the contrary; secret history is rarely discussed and almost never defined. Historians of history ignore it altogether while students of the novel refer to it in passing as a fictive form, identifying it with the scandal chronicle, and thereby begging all questions as to its categorial status.[5] It is necessary to begin, therefore, with a definition of the form, using works by Procopius and Marx as well as a number of early modern secret histories as exemplars.

Secret history typically has been offered to readers as a species of history-writing that contains material not obtainable in other historical works. Procopius presented *Anecdota* as a supplement to his more traditional *History in Eight Books*, containing "those things which have hitherto remained undivulged," and Marx began his text by reproducing four secret, eighteenth-century dispatches that demonstrated, as Marx saw it, that the British government was a "tool and accomplice" of Tsarist imperialism, hardly a standard view in the historiography of Marx's day.[6] What was revealed by the writers of secret history was of a scandalous nature, formerly hidden because its revelation would have disgraced important individuals or institutions or endangered the writers themselves. Thus Marx argues that his revelations nailed the British government "for ever to the pillory of history," and Procopius brought to light the "base deeds" of the Emperor Justinian, his wife the Empress Theodora, and their greatest general (and Procopius's patron) Belisarius, suggesting the literally unspeakable nature of his material when he asserted that revealing them

---

4 Other modern examples include Walter Walsh, *The Secret History of the Oxford Movement*, 4th edn. (London: Swan Sonnenschein, 1898), a Protestant attack upon Newman and his followers; and Peter Bushell, *London's Secret History* (London: Constable, 1983), an "anecdotal" treatment of the "sometimes bizarre and often amusing aspects of the metropolis" (1).

5 All three forms of secret history figure in this study, and each will be examined in its turn, the second type (briefly) in the course of the discussion of Defoe and the third type in the discussion in chapter 8 of "history"-writers before Defoe. The best discussion of secret history is in John Richetti, *Popular Fiction Before Richardson: Narrative Patterns, 1700–1739* (Oxford: Clarendon Press, 1969), chapter 4; Richetti, however, treats only the manifestly fictional narratives of writers like Manley and Haywood. For scholars of the novel who automatically classify secret history as a scandal chronicle, see McKeon, *Origins*, 54–55; Jerry C. Beasley, *Novels of the 1740s* (Athens GA: University of Georgia Press, 1982), 53–54.

6 *The Anecdota or Secret History*, vol. VI of *Procopius*, 7 vols., trans. H. B. Dewing (Cambridge MA: Harvard University Press, 1935), 3; Karl Marx, *Secret Diplomatic History of the Eighteenth Century and the Story of the Life of Lord Palmerston*, introd. and notes Lester Hutchinson (New York: International Publishers, 1969), 48–61, 14–15.

earlier would have led to his "most cruel death."[7] The secret histories of the late seventeenth century focused mainly on the reigns of Charles II and James II, representing the last Stuart kings as tools of Louis XIV, exposing them as secret adherents to the Church of Rome, and revealing the corrupt nature of their private lives. David Jones's secret histories, for example, presented "an Exact Account of the *Private League* between King *Charles* the Second and the French King," while Crouch, like Procopius, concentrated on the private sins of the monarchs.[8] Crouch depicted Charles as a liar, a fornicator, an adulterer, and a tyrant, a man who mouthed "pious Ejaculations," but "on the very first Night that his Sacred Majesty was to lie at *White-hall*," arranged "to have the Lady *Castlemain* seduc'd from her Loyalty to her Husband."[9]

The sensational nature of these works often threatened to undermine the historical claims of their authors; the scandalous material presented in the secret histories tended to attach itself to the text and to the writer, raising the possibility that what was revealed "will seem neither credible nor probable to a later generation." Thus, Procopius feared he would be read not as a historian but as "a narrator of myths." The fact that secret history was supplemental – intended to correct a mistaken view or to complete an unsatisfactorily partial picture – and therefore generally anecdotal, impressionistic, and suggestive rather than systematic increased the likelihood that the text might be read as a work of fiction.[10] The secret historian's penchant for the telling of curious or shocking anecdotes, furthermore, frequently led him on to dubious historiographical ground; Procopius's twentieth-century editor argued that outlandish stories about Theodora had the effect of "discrediting his [Procopius's] own testimony . . . which falls to the ground through the weight of its own extravagance."[11]

Another reason why the reader might doubt whether the secret historian actually wrote history was that the author of these works was always a highly engaged writer whose main goal was to discredit his historical subject in the furtherance of a political agenda. Procopius hoped his stories would restrain future rulers, and Marx sought to demonstrate that the

---

[7] Marx, *Secret Diplomatic History*, 14–15, 63; Procopius, *Anecdota*, 3, vii. The *Anecdota* begins with the story of the love of Antonina, Belisarius's wife, for her adopted son, Theodosius, at first the "natural" love of a mother for a son, but later an uncontrollable erotic passion; subsequently, the misogynistic Procopius identified Theodora as the source of corruption in the royal family, coming as she did from a family of whores (11, 105).

[8] David Jones, *The Secret History of White-hall, From the Restoration of Charles II, Down to the Abdication of the late K. James* (London, 1697), sig. A₄v–A₅r; [Nathaniel Crouch], *The Secret History of K. James I. and K. Charles I. Compleating the Reigns of the Four last Monarchs* (n.p., 1690), sig. A₂r.

[9] [Nathaniel Crouch], *The Secret History of the Reigns of K. Charles II. and K. James II* (n.p., 1690), 21, 22.

[10] Dewing argues that the anecdotal character of Procopius's secret history has caused it to be read as a scandal chronicle; Procopius, *Anecdota*, ix.

[11] *Ibid.*, ix.

British government was still in his own day a pillar of reaction.[12] The secret histories by Crouch and Jones and their contemporaries were generally written to defend the Revolution of 1688, primarily by discrediting the monarchs who immediately preceded William and Mary on the throne. Crouch's texts contrasted "the unparalleled Vertues, that are so Resplendent in our Gracious Soveraigns, in opposition to those Ignominious Vices that reigned in the Other."[13] Jones concentrated on the destructive ties between the Stuarts and the French court, arguing that the French ministers opposed Charles II's return to England "to keep us Embroiled at Home"; that the French paid "those Incendiaries" who were responsible for the great fire of London; and that at the time of James II's abdication the French again attempted "to embroil the Nation," principally by encouraging the "Republican Party."[14] The clear political goals of the secret historians inspired the use of a harsh, condemnatory rhetoric; Marx's characterization of the communications of the British diplomats is typical:

The secret despatches of Russian diplomatists are fumigated with some equivocal perfume. It is one part the *fumée de fausseté*, as the Duke of St. Simon has it, and the other part that coquettish display of one's own superiority and cunning which stamps upon the reports of the French Secret Police their indelible character . . . In this point the English secret despatches prove much superior. They do not affect superiority but silliness. For instance, can there be anything more silly than Mr. Rondeau informing Horace Walpole that he has betrayed to the Russian Minister the letters addressed by the Turkish Grand Vizier to the King of England, but that he had told . . . their excellencies not to tell the Porte that they had seen them (those letters)! At first view the infamy of the act is drowned in the silliness of the man.[15]

Histories couched in this kind of rhetoric were bound to be dismissed as fiction by readers who did not share the writer's politics, and while the early modern reader was accustomed to reading polemical history, there were students of historiography, such as Camden, who argued that unabashed bias disqualified a text from being read as history.

There were, then, a number of reasons why secret histories were likely to be read as fictional discourse: scandalous material, anecdotal method, and unmistakable bias. Yet the posture of these writers was that of a historian, and secret historians often went to some lengths to defend their practice as being legitimately historical. Marx reproduced and commented upon contemporary sources, observing "at the head of the historical evidence we

---

[12] *Ibid.*, 7; Marx, *Secret Diplomatic History*, 14–15.
[13] Jones, *White-hall*, sig. A4v–A5r; Crouch, *James I*, sig. A2v–A3r
[14] Jones, *White-hall*, Letters II, VI, VII, and LXV.
[15] Marx, *Secret Diplomatic History*, 61–62. According to Dewing, Procopius also wrote out of disgust and bitterness; *Anecdota*, vii.

have to sift, we place . . . long-forgotten English pamphlets printed at the very time of Peter I," and while Procopius offered no documentation, his fear that he would be read as a fiction-writer amounted to an implicit claim that the author of *Anecdota* should be understood as the same writer who wrote the *History*, an adviser to Belisarius who was also "the most notable Greek historian of the Later Roman Empire," one who wrote "with great attention to accuracy and with a high degree of objectivity."[16]

Similarly, Crouch and Jones acknowledged that their historical practice was highly suspect, and sought to defend themselves and their form. Generally, Crouch commented very sparingly on such questions in his cheap, popular histories, but the secret histories featured what were for him extended theoretical remarks.[17] Crouch cited the classical precedent for his labors, describing Suetonius as one who also "made Publick to the World the Vices and Miscarriages" of corrupt monarchs "with the same freedom with which they were by them Committed."[18] The bookseller-historian acknowledged the indecorousness of what he was doing ("we ought not to rake into the Ashes of Princes, and expose either their Personal Miscarriages, or their Failures in Management of Government") but argued that "the making them Publick may sometimes contribute . . . to the General Good," citing the need to refute "the French King's most Scandalous Libels" against William.[19] Jones's defense of his secret histories centered on the fact that they were written in the form of letters; he asserted that the texts were originally executed as a series of letter-reports of "Intelligence" to an unnamed English lord and argued that the epistolary method was both useful and natural:

there is a very engaging part naturally couched under such a method of bringing *State-Arcana's* to light by way of Letters, which, in the very Notion of them carry something of secrecy.[20]

The use of letters, then, made the text more "engaging" and at the same time nicely conveyed the secret nature of the text. Jones asserted that "the Reader cannot but observe an Air of History to run . . . through the whole composition."[21] Each author, furthermore, defended the historical claims of his texts by citing his sources; like Procopius, Jones pointed to his familiarity with powerful individuals as well as his resulting access to a store of documents relating to French-English affairs.[22] Crouch had no powerful

---

[16] Arthur E. R. Boak, ed., Procopius, *The Secret History* (Ann Arbor: University of Michigan Press, 1961), vi–vii.

[17] Mayer, "Nathaniel Crouch, Bookseller and Historian," 397, 405–06.

[18] Crouch, *Charles II and James II*, sig. A₂r.   [19] Crouch, *Last Four Monarchs*, sig. A₂v.

[20] Jones, *White-hall*, sig. A₆r.   [21] *Ibid.*

[22] In Jones's case his special knowledge resulted from his employment by the Marquis de Louvois as an interpreter. Jones also claimed that "the reader will be . . . perswaded of the verity of the Facts . . . by the perusal of the work" itself, especially since Jones's own text accorded with

friends or insider information, so instead of citing a privileged position, he
referred his readers to general knowledge ("the loud and General Com-
plaints of the Kingdom") and argued that subsequent events bore out his
representation of the reigns of the Stuart kings ("as to the more secret
Transactions; the Consequences and Events are my Testimonies").[23]

Although Crouch cites common knowledge, secret historians generally
write from the perspective of an insider, not as one who has participated in
the events but as one who has heard what happened from well-placed
informants. If the secret historian was not privy to the facts, he had close
ties to others who were; he wrote, as John Robert Moore once observed of
Defoe, from "within-doors."[24] Procopius lived close to the center of power
during the reign of Justinian, and even Marx, after a fashion, wrote from
the perspective of an insider since he reproduced the private communications of British diplomats and allowed these and other documents to
"speak" for themselves in the text. This aspect of the secret historian's
practice can lead to these texts being dismissed as mere scandalmongering,
and yet, although Procopius's modern editor acknowledges that "the book
is often characterized by malicious exaggeration," he also observes that
scholars have shown "that Procopius often has the support of the testimony
of other writers of his time."[25] Gibbon made a similar point in respect to
Procopius; commenting on the scandalous discussion in *Anecdota* of Antonina, the wife of Belisarius, Gibbon observed that

> the generous reader may cast away the libel, but the evidence of the facts will
> adhere to his memory; and he will reluctantly confess that the fame, even the virtue
> of Belisarius were polluted by the lust and cruelty of his wife; and that the hero
> deserved an appellation which may not drop from the pen of the decent
> historian.[26]

Whether the Procopius of the *Secret History* seems entirely "decent" or not,
Gibbon treated him as a fellow historian, not as a writer of fiction. Indeed
the author of the *Decline and Fall* inadvertently suggests that the tendency to
regard secret histories as fictional works arises from the secret historian's
willingness to present material that more decorous historians avoid. Nevertheless, making it clear that Procopius was the chief source for his
treatment of the reign of Justinian, Gibbon declares that Procopius was
reliable as long as the ancient historian's prejudices were recognized:
"after the venom of his malignity has been suffered to exhale . . . the
anecdotes . . . are established by their internal evidence, or the authentic

---

    other, better known works, such as "Sir *William Temple*'s *Memoirs*, Mr. *Coke*'s *Detection of the Court
    and State of England during the Four Last reigns*, &c."; *ibid.*, 2, sig. A₅v.
[23] Crouch, *Charles II. and James II*, sig. A₂v.
[24] J. R. Moore, introd., *A Brief History of the Poor Palatine Refugees (1709)*, attrib. to Defoe (Los
    Angeles: William Andrews Clark Memorial Library; University of California Press, 1964), vi.
[25] Procopius, *Anecdota*, xiii.   [26] Gibbon, *Decline and Fall*, II, 680.

monuments of the times."[27] This comment by an historian who was notoriously scrupulous about his sources demonstrates that although early modern readers of secret history recognized that this historical form always featured a heavy admixture of dubious material and was highly polemical, they nonetheless judged that some secret histories deserved to be read as matters of fact.

II

Two eighteenth-century works that are not often thought of as secret histories but that correspond to the definition delineated in this chapter – Gilbert Burnet's *History of His Own Times* and Anthony Hamilton's *Memoirs of Count Grammont* – demonstrate why readers might be tempted to read secret histories as works of fiction and at the same time show that readers in fact read them as species of historical discourse when they regarded them as being constructed of matters of fact. Burnet first conceived of the *History of His Own Times* as a secret history or memoir but apparently decided to recast the work after reading the first volume of Clarendon's *History of the Rebellion* in 1702; he then took Jacques-Auguste de Thou's *Historiarum sui Temporis* as the model for the newly conceived work. H. C. Foxcroft argues that Burnet abandoned the idea of writing secret history so as to seem less of a controversialist, and further argues that "his change of plan probably enhanced the vogue and influence of his narrative. A work under the graver style of *History* imposes more than very artless memoirs."[28] Yet the irony is that Burnet is now best remembered for the *History of His Own Times* rather than for "graver" histories like the *History of the Reformation*, and, further, that however Burnet may have changed his mind in respect to this text, the *History* remained in important ways exactly what it started out being – a secret history.

In the preface Burnet asserts that he had set out "to look into the secret conduct of affairs amongst us," and like a true secret historian, he leaves "public transactions to gazettes and the public historians of the times."[29] Also, Burnet was clearly partial; Swift attacked him as "the most partial of

---

[27] *Ibid.*, II, 563.

[28] T. E. S. Clarke and H. C. Foxcroft, *A Life of Gilbert Burnet, Bishop of Salisbury*, introd. C. H. Firth (Cambridge University Press, 1907), 187, 403–04. According to *The Oxford Companion to French Literature*, comp. and ed. Paul Harvey and J. E. Heseltine (Oxford: Clarendon Press, 1954), 709, de Thou's work is notable for "a scrupulous justice and tolerance" in regard to the Reformation and the wars of religion before in France, showing an impartiality which "brought him into disfavor with Rome." As we shall see, no one ever argued that Burnet's work was unbiased.

[29] The principal edition of Burnet's *History* used here is *History of His Own Time* (London: William S. Orr, 1850), hereafter cited in text. For the preface, however, which is not in the above text, references are to Burnet, *History of His Own Time With the Suppressed Passages of the First Volume*, 2 vols. (Oxford: Clarendon Press, 1873), I, 4; hereafter cited, in notes, as "Preface."

all writers that ever pretended so much to impartiality," and from the
eighteenth century onward it was acknowledged that he wrote to justify the
Glorious Revolution.[30] Burnet was also a typical secret historian in that he
wrote as an insider, pointing to his "intimacy" for more than thirty years
"with all who have had the chief conduct of affairs." These connections
allowed him "to penetrate far into the true secrets of counsels and
designs."[31] Burnet's treatment of the end of James II's reign, for example,
derives from his acquaintance with that king as well as with William and
Mary. He met the latter monarchs, he informs us, when he was summoned
to The Hague by them, and found that "they had received such characters
of me from England . . . [that] they resolved to treat me with great
confidence." Burnet observes, "I found the prince was resolved to make
use of me," but he himself first "had a mind to see a little into the prince's
notions before I should engage myself deeper into his service" (439).

Burnet and the king discuss theological questions, and William assures
the clergyman of his desire for tolerance in religious matters and also of his
intention that "he should never be prevailed with to set up the Calvinistical
notions of the decrees of God." Burnet becomes particularly intimate with
Princess Mary and even manages to settle in advance and with absolutely
no fuss the question of William's role if he and Mary should ever be invited
to reign in England. The prince is impressed, the author of the *History*
continues, and although he says nothing to Burnet directly ("such was the
prince's cold way"), he tells associates that "he had been nine years
married, and had never the confidence to press this matter on the queen,
which I [Burnet] had now brought about easily in a day" (440–41). Later,
Mary and her father exchange letters about "the grounds upon which the
king himself had changed his religion" and the prince sends Burnet the
letters, the substance of which Burnet reports in the *History*, offering
evidence of his accuracy that is both unverifiable and somewhat suspect:

The prince sent it [the king's letter] to me together with the princess's answer, but
with a charge not to take a copy of either, but to read them over as often as I
pleased; which I did till I had fixed both pretty well in my memory. And, as soon as
I had sent them back, I sat down immediately to write out all that I remembered,
which the princess owned to me afterwards, when she read the abstracts I made,
were punctual almost to a tittle.   (458)

Why would the prince forbid Burnet to make copies of the letters but then
tell him that he could read them as many times as he wanted, thereby

---

[30] "Editor's Note," Thomas Stackhouse, abr. *Bishop Burnet's History of His Own Times* (London:
J. M. Dent, 1906), vii; Kenyon, *The History Men*, 33.

[31] Like Jones, Burnet also cited his familiarity with an important set of documents, in this case the
papers of the dukes of Hamilton, whose biographer Burnet was, but in the preface Burnet
makes it clear that the ultimate basis for the *History of His Own Times* was his personal knowledge
of men and events; "Preface," 4.

inviting him to memorize them? Why would Burnet not simply write accurate summaries of the letters while they were in his possession, since this was not forbidden? Why would Burnet show Mary his abstracts, since summaries that were accurate "to a tittle" violated at least the spirit of the prince's injunction against copying the letters? Why would Mary read and approve them?

If one encountered this recital of how such crucial documents came into the hands of a writer in an eighteenth-century novel, one might well read these curious assertions as figurative elements of the text that comment upon the author's fictional project.[32] Burnet's text is, however, unequi-vocally presented to readers as historical discourse. This account of Burnet's use of the princess's correspondence suggests why Burnet's text has troubled readers ever since its publication: not only because it is a highly biased account but also because at times it seems methodologically unsound. Thus even those who admired Burnet and his book tended to celebrate the *History* as a delightful work rather than as a reliable account of matters of fact. According to Boswell, Dr. Johnson thought it "one of the most entertaining books in the English language" and "quite dramatic," but he also observed that Burnet "was so much prejudiced, that he took no pains to find out the truth" and declared that the text was "mere chit-chat." Macaulay also thought Burnet "a most entertaining writer – far superior to Clarendon in the art of amusing – though of course far Clarendon's inferior in discernment, dignity, and correctness of style." Similarly, Horace Walpole's comment on the *History* indicates both why it has become Burnet's most celebrated text and why it might be regarded as a fictionalized political history: "it seems as if he [Burnet] had just come from the King's closet or from the appartments of the men whom he describes, and was telling his readers, in plain honest terms, what he had seen and heard."[33] Burnet might be credited with "writing to the moment" decades before *Pamela*. Frederick Jackson has acknowledged that Burnet "gives not only a self-revelation of the author, but also brings the reader into close connection with [momentous] times," and Jackson further observes that one "needs some boldness to recommend it" as history because "its statements and accuracy have long been the subject of severe criticism."[34]

The representation in the *History* of Burnet's arrival on the London

---

[32] The many tasks that Clarissa performs in respect to her letters make "the production of writing . . . a central topic" of that novel; Everett Zimmerman, "*A Tale of a Tub* and *Clarissa*: A Battling of Books," in *Critical Essays on Jonathan Swift*, ed. Frank Palmeri (New York: G. K. Hall, 1993), 154.

[33] David Allen, introd., *History of His Own Times* by Burnet (London: Dent, 1979), i, vi, xi–xii.

[34] Frederick John Foakes Jackson, *A History of Church History: Studies of Some Historians of the Christian Church* (Cambridge: W. Heffer and Sons, 1939), 158.

scene in 1673 illustrates the ways in which this text invites us to read it as a work of fiction. Burnet first relates that he came to London to attend to the publishing of his *Memoirs of the Dukes of Hamilton*, and then describes an interview between himself and the duke of Lauderdale during which the latter "took me into his closet, and asked me the state of Scotland" and Burnet "gave him a very punctual and true account of it." Then the duke

carried me to the king, and proposed the licensing my "Memoirs" to him. The king bid me bring them to him, and said he would read them himself. He did read parts of them, particularly the account I gave of the ill-conduct of the bishops, that occasioned the beginning of the wars; and told me he was well pleased with it . . . Sir Ellis Leighton carried me to the duke of Buckingham, with whom I passed almost a whole night, and happened so far to please him that he, who was apt to be fired with a new acquaintance, gave such a character of me to the king, that ever after that he took much notice of me, and said he would hear me preach. He seemed well pleased with my sermon; and . . . ordered me to be sworn a chaplain, and admitted me to a long private audience, that lasted above an hour, in which I took all the freedom with him, that I thought became my profession. He run me into a long discourse about the authority of the church . . . [and] I went through some other things with relation to the course of his life, and entered into many particulars with much freedom. He bore it all very well, and thanked me for it . . . He seemed to take all I had said very kindly; and during my stay at court he used me in so particular a manner, that I was considered as a man growing into a high degree of favour.   (236)

Everyone at court, it would seem, was pleased with the Scottish cleric; everyone sought him out; and he was able to speak frankly with all of them, even his sovereign, who in fact thanked Burnet for lecturing him about his personal life. Like Boswell in the next century, Burnet reveled in the company of the great, and took pride in pleasing them; the author of the *History* presents himself as the confidant of kings, and it all sounds a little too good to be true.[35] One of Burnet's earliest critics questioned Burnet's veracity because of such scenes:

I cannot work myself up to a Belief, that he ever reproved his Majesty . . . in the manner he relates: He might indeed dream or meditate of such an Undertaking, and imagine he should acquire everlasting Fame among the Godly, if he could procure the Reputation of having performed so heroical an Undertaking. But impartial People will be apt to conclude, that he really mistook his Dreams, or waking Whimsies for real Facts, and had related them so often, that he came at length to believe them true himself.[36]

[35] This moment in the narrative is reminiscent of Boswell's account in the *London Journal* of his own early career in London, and especially his entry into the life of the man whose biography he would later write.

[36] Thomas Salmon, *An Impartial examination of Bishop Burnet's History of His Own Times*, 2 vols. (London, 1724), II, 709; see also a similar assertion at II, 711.

This critic anticipated Johnson, who averred that Burnet believed the false statements he made, as well as Charles Lamb, who likened the bishop to a garrulous old man endlessly repeating fanciful stories to his sons.[37] Others attacked the author of the *History of His Own Times* as a romancer because of the bias in his text, just as Heylyn had argued that Fuller did not fulfill the true duty of an historian.[38]

The best index of how suspiciously Burnet has been regarded by many readers is the abridgment of the work by Thomas Stackhouse, which was undertaken almost immediately after the work's publication and which has endured down to the present day, despite the fact that it is a very dubious piece of work. Stackhouse altered the text in such a way as to rob it of its "secret" aspect and transform it into little more than a bland recitation of historical events; he believed that Burnet's "Deviations into his own Life and family savour of Vanity" and systematically eliminated them. Indeed Stackhouse cut Burnet out of his own text. The abridger removed, for example, Burnet's account of his triumphal arrival in London as well as many other such scenes.[39] Cutting the material that made Walpole feel as if the narrator of the *History* had written a breathless account of events that had just transpired, and at the same time eliminating portions of the text that made readers judge the text to be fictional, Stackhouse argued that the *History* was lacking in "its form and composition," not in its "truth and solidity."[40] This observation suggests that insofar as Burnet's text remained a secret history, Stackhouse objected to it and sought to eliminate that element in the text in order to highlight what Stackhouse apparently regarded as its real claim to historicity – its simple narrative of events.

Yet in altering the text as he did, Stackhouse also stripped it of its raison d'être by systematically deleting those parts of the narrative that justified Burnet's claim that he presented "the secret of affairs." If at times Burnet puts us in mind of eighteenth-century fiction writers or such writers of "fact" as Boswell – stretching credulity and apparently shaping events so as to cast himself in a favorable light – that is one reason why this history merits the attributive "secret." Often based upon the personal knowledge of the narrator, often scandalous, sensational, and polemical, secret histories seem almost to defy readers to construe them as works of fiction. Yet readers generally judged Burnet's *History of His Own Times* to be genuinely historical. Hume used the work extensively for the *History of*

---

[37] Both observations are reported in Allen, introd., *History of His Own Times*, v, vi.

[38] See, for example, B. Higgins, *Historical and Critical Remarks on Bp. Burnet's History of His own Time* (London, 1725), sig. A$_2$r, A$_3$r.

[39] Such as, for example, Burnet's conversations with the duke of York concerning religious questions (237–38).

[40] Thomas Stackhouse, *An Abridgement of Bishop Burnet's History of His Own Times* (London, 1724), x.

England; the *General Biographical Dictionary* observed that as "the strong party zeal . . . of the last century becomes . . . less . . . bishop Burnet's works seem to rise in public estimation," and Charles Firth argued that Burnet was superior to Clarendon in terms of his grasp of the problem of causation and his ability to clarify the nature of complicated political events. Similarly, Harry Elmer Barnes credited Burnet, as well as Clarendon, with contributing to the rise of "modern political and party history." Even Francis Atterbury, Burnet's contemporary and political foe, exclaimed, "Damn him, he has told a great good deal of truth."[41]

One recognizes the potential for reading early modern secret history as fiction even more clearly in Anthony Hamilton's *Memoirs of Count Grammont*, a text sometimes classified as a work of fiction but one that satisfies our working definition of secret history and that has generally been read, at least by English readers, as authentically historical. Although the *Memoirs* contain some account of Gramont's life before his sojourn at the court of Charles II, the bulk of the text focuses on his visit to England during the years 1662–64. Like other secret histories, Hamilton's text contains material not to be found in other histories; seemingly, the author resolutely ignores any and all serious political issues in favor of "trifling incidents," and when he introduces great men into his narrative, he writes almost exclusively of the figure they cut at court, especially in comparison with the "indefinable brillancy" of the count. Thus, Hamilton reports that the duke of Buckingham and the earl of St. Albans "were the same in England as they appeared in France: the one, full of wit and vivacity, dissipated, without splendour . . . the other, a man of no great genius, [who] had raised himself a considerable fortune from nothing, and by losing at play, and keeping a great table, made it appear greater than it was." Hamilton's attitude toward such men and their love affairs, contests of honor, and feats at the gaming table is somewhat difficult to discern. Many English readers have found a "disgusting picture of depraved manners" in the text, but "no condemnation of the prevalent code of morals," and yet Hamilton's treatment of his material is almost invariably described as brilliant, vivacious, witty, and entertaining. Still, the publishers of Bohn's Standard Library (which featured works by Bacon, Lucy Hutchinson, and Adam Smith, editions of the works of Milton, Sheridan, and Cowper, and "others of the same sterling character") decided not to include Hamilton's *Memoirs* in that series because they feared that to do so would offend readers by seeming to endorse a work "which may not unhesitatingly be put into the hands of the most

41 Hume, *History of England*, VI, chapters 70 and 71; *General Biographical Dictionary*, VII, 379; Firth, "Burnet as Historian," in *Essays Historical and Literary*, 208 (Atterbury cited at 198); Harry Elmer Barnes, *A History of Historical Writing*, 2nd edn. (New York: Dover, 1963), 116.

fastidious."[42] So, as in other secret histories, the scandalous nature of the material was seen as contaminating the text itself.

One cannot argue that Hamilton, like the other historians treated in this chapter, couched his text in a harsh rhetoric or heaped contempt on the historical subjects he treated in the secret history. Apparently, Hamilton genuinely admired Gramont and thought him one of the most brilliant men of his age. Of the late seventeenth- and early eighteenth-century secret histories that have been examined in this chapter, only Hamilton's took a benign view of Charles II, and indeed Hamilton's perspective was that of not only a Tory but a Jacobite since he and his family went into exile with James II and the author of the *Memoirs* spent the rest of his life in France. Nevertheless, there *was* scorn and even a clear political bias in this text, although it was either expressed negatively or remained unspoken. One glimpses it in Hamilton's brief discussion of Count Gramont's previous visit to England, during the interregnum:

Curiosity to see a man equally famous for his crimes and his elevation, had once before induced the Chevalier de Grammont to visit England . . . and Cromwell . . . was at his highest pitch of glory when he was seen by the Chevalier de Grammont; but the Chevalier did not see any appearance of a court. One part of the nobility proscribed, the other removed from employments; an affectation of purity of manners, instead of the luxury which the pomp of courts displays, all taken together, presented nothing but sad and serious objects in the finest city in the world; and therefore the Chevalier acquired nothing by this voyage.   (103)

Hamilton's representation of the gallantry and devotion to pleasure, the delicate manners and endless play, at the court of Charles II is here implicitly set against the dour, dull, and sanctimonious non-court of Cromwell. His text, then, is a secret history written against all the other secret histories that condemned Charles II and his brother. Talleyrand is reported to have said that anyone who did not live before the French Revolution could not know the sweetness of life; Hamilton seems to argue in this text that anyone who did not live before the Restoration could not know how profoundly unpleasant life could be. Thus, Hamilton's great subject in the *Memoirs* – the gaiety and delicacy of Charles's court, where "the nation . . . tasted the pleasure of a natural government, and seemed to breathe again after a long oppression" – is a constant implicit reproach to the Puritans who provided such a poor setting for the count when he first visited England (104). The scorn one expects to find in a secret history

---

[42] *Encyclopedia Britannica*, 11th edn. (New York: Encyclopedia Britannica Co., 1910), XII, 333; [Anthony Hamilton], Memoirs of the Court of Charles the Second, ed. Sir Walter Scott (London: Henry G. Bohn, 1853), 34, 106; hereafter cited in the text. *DNB* entry on Hamilton; Cyril Hughes Hartmann, ed., *Memoirs of the Comte de Gramont*, trans. Peter Quennell (New York: Dutton, 1930), 1–2. See the note, "Bohn's Extra Volume," at the front of the 1853 edition of the *Memoirs*.

is, therefore, present in Hamilton's text, but it is aimed not at those who surrendered themselves to luxury and play but at the enemies of pleasure and indulgence.[43] Hamilton's *Memoirs* were more typical of secret history in being based upon the testimony of a person with intimate knowledge of private affairs at the court of Charles II, in this case Count Gramont himself, but several readers of the *Memoirs* have pointed out that Hamilton himself knew the court better than Gramont did.

Yet in asserting that the only sort of reader who interests him is one who reads for amusement, Hamilton almost willfully undermines the historical status of the text. At one point Hamilton describes the preparations for a masquerade given by the queen that became an occasion for one of the "little tricks . . . for turning into ridicule the vain fools of the court," for which "Miss Hamilton," the sister of the author and the future wife of Count Gramont, was well known (125). On the evening of the ball, the count arrives late and "everybody was astonished that he should be one of the last at such a time, as his readiness was so remarkable on every occasion." All were again surprised when the count appeared in "ordinary court-dress"; the king himself intervenes:

The king immediately took notice of it: "Chevalier," said he, "Termes [Gramont's valet] is not arrived [from France] then?" "Pardon me, Sire," said he, "God be thanked!" "Why God be thanked?" said the king; "has anything happened to him on the road?" "Sire," said the Chevalier de Grammont, "this is the history of my dress, and of Termes, my messenger." At these words the ball, ready to begin, was suspended: the dancers making a circle around the Chevalier . . . [who] continued his story.   (133)

And the count tells a tale in which Termes (labeled "Mr. Scoundrel") describes his efforts at obtaining for the count " 'the finest suit in the world . . . which the Duke of Guise himself was at the trouble of ordering' "; the suit is lost, however, when Termes sinks into quicksand (134). James Sutherland observes that "such situations are . . . the raw material of Restoration comedy," thereby suggesting how like a comedy of manners Hamilton's work sometimes seems.[44]

The problem of stipulating the generic status of Hamilton's *Memoirs*, however, is a complicated one, and, intriguingly, the solution has been different in different national settings. Hamilton's work has its roots in French rather than in English literature; the model that Hamilton probably had in mind was Bussy-Rabutin's *Histoire Amoureuse des Gaules*, a " '*roman satirique*' " that reports the scandalous exploits at the court of Louis XIV

[43] *Memoirs of the Court of Charles II by Count de Gramont*, anon. ed. (New York: Collier and Sons, 1910), 6.
[44] James Sutherland, *English Literature of the Late Seventeenth Century*, vol.vi, *The Oxford History of English Literature* (Oxford University Press, 1969), 266.

(including those of Gramont) in such rich detail and with such accuracy that it led to the author's exile from court.[45] Despite the fact that Bussy-Rabutin's text was thus implicitly held to be referential (by the king and his agents), Hamilton's text has generally been described, by French readers at least, as an example of the French "romans prétendus historiques" or scandal chronicle, known to the English as secret history. It was first published in France as the *Histoire Amoureuse de la Cour d'Angleterre*, and a nineteenth-century French editor referred to the text as "ce chef-d'œuvre de notre littérature" and asserted that it had been written in imitation of *A Thousand and One Nights*. A later French editor argued that Hamilton wrote the *Memoirs* "usant de son droit de romancier."[46]

But while the French by and large have read the *Memoirs* as fiction, the English have read the work as history, and Hamilton clearly provides a basis for doing so in his preface where he claims that the text was entirely derived from Gramont's testimony: "It is . . . to the Count that we must listen . . . and it is on him that we must rely for the truth of . . . these memoirs, since I only hold the pen, while he directs it to the most remarkable and secret passages of his life" (35). Hamilton represents himself as a mere amanuensis, Gramont as the true author of the work, and the *Memoirs* as authentic, and many English readers have accepted these assertions. The *General Biographical Dictionary* declared that Hamilton's text contained "a striking and too faithful detail" of Charles II's court, and an unnamed editor at the beginning of the twentieth century judged that "the essential value of this *chronique scandaleuse* is that it is true, and presents a genuine depiction of a phase of English Court life." What is more, Sutherland makes essentially the same point about Hamilton's *Memoirs* that Gibbon made about Procopius's secret history: "much of what we are told can be corroborated." Thus Hamilton's text has been concretized in radically different ways in two different literary traditions: "the French . . . class the book as a novel" whereas "in England the historical importance of the book has always been insisted upon."[47]

Both Burnet's and Hamilton's texts, therefore, have been read in peculiarly complicated ways. The Stackhouse abridgment, which has been the most widely available version of the *History of His Own Times* almost from the moment it was published, attempted to salvage the "history" in Burnet's text by sacrificing its "secret" aspect, and Hamilton has been read

---

45   On Bussy-Rabutin, see Elizabeth C. Goldsmith, *Exclusive Conversations: The Art of Interaction in Seventeenth-Century France* (Philadelphia: University of Pennsylvania Press, 1988), chapter 3.

46   Benjamin Pifteau, *Mémoires du Comte de Grammont* (Paris: Jules Bonnassies, 1876), xi, xvii; Claire-Eliane Engel, ed., *Mémoires du Chevalier de Grammont* (Monaco: Editions du Rocher, 1958), 41. See also Antoine Adam, *Histoire de la littérature française au XVIIe siècle*, 5 vols. (Paris: Editions Domat, 1948–1951), v, 308–09.

47   *General Biographical Dictionary*, XVII, 89; anon., ed., *Memoirs*, 6; Sutherland, *English Literature*, 265; Hartmann, ed., *Memoirs*, 2–3.

by some as a fictionist and by others as a historian. These reading histories demonstrate how problematic secret history is as historiography, and yet they also demonstrate that in each case a decision was made by readers that led to the repeated concretization of these texts as either fiction or history. A closer look at how and why readers made these decisions will illuminate both the boundary between fiction and history around the time that Defoe published *Robinson Crusoe* and the horizon of expectations of early modern readers who had to concretize both the secret histories of Burnet and Hamilton and the "histories" of Defoe that are often regarded as the first English novels.

III

The remarkable difference between the way that French and English readers have concretized the *Memoirs of Count Grammont* seems traceable to the fact that in France the work has been seen as a triumph of style ("Quel badinage fin et léger! quel mélange de grâce et de malice!") whereas in England the *Memoirs* have been assimilated to a number of similar works that tell the nasty story of "the licentious court of Charles II."[48] It would seem the French reader has regarded Hamilton's treatment of his material – his use of dialogue and scene and the text's seeming to be "characteristically and exquisitely French" – as determinative, while the English reader has instead focused upon Hamilton's assurance that he merely reports the count's (and, it is understood, his own) experience. Yet, as we have seen, there are moments in Hamilton's text that encourage readers to apprehend the work as fictional discourse. Why then read him as a historian? One can begin to say why if one compares Hamilton with Burnet and also with Manley, whose *New Atalantis* has generally been compared with the scandal chronicle or secret history of Bussy-Rabutin.[49]

Like Burnet, Hamilton asserts the veracity of his account. Like Burnet, Hamilton limits his relation to known habitués of the court. Like Burnet, Hamilton reports dialogue between the king and Gramont that the author asserts was actually spoken. Unlike Manley, Hamilton does not adopt the conventions of the *roman à clef*. Unlike Manley, he does not use the language and character names of myths and romances, choosing, rather, to give historical actors their real names. Manley begins her "adventures" by recounting an earthly visitation of the goddess Astrea who engages in a dialogue with Virtue. Hamilton, by contrast, opens his "register" of "the remarkable particulars" of Gramont's life with a discussion of how "affairs

48 Pifteau, ed., *Mémoires*, xii; *Encyclopedia Britannica*, 11th edn., XII, 333. The author of the *Britannica* article observes: "The book is the most entertaining of contemporary memoirs, and in no other book is there a description [of Charles's court] so vivid, truthful, and graceful."
49 Richetti, *Popular Fiction before Richardson*, 119–20.

were . . . managed" when Louis XIII was king of France "but the Cardinal de Richlieu governed the kingdom" (20, 36).[50] Hamilton's practice, therefore, set his work apart from *New Atalantis* and other secret histories that flaunted their fictionality as well as their polemical function. Thus, whether consciously or no, Hamilton provides a basis for accepting the claim of the author of the *Memoirs* that the text consists of matters of fact. An understanding, it would seem, was forged between readers and writers like Hamilton, Jones, Crouch, and Burnet that was different from the understanding that existed between Manley and her readers: works by the first set of writers were to be read as history while works of the second were to be read as fiction.

The status of this understanding needs to be explored. How could French and English readers read this same text as fiction and history respectively? The most recent discussions of the relationship between these two modes of discourse suggest that readers in fact concretize works as *either* fiction *or* history with a clear sense of the difference but also of the closeness of the two forms. Indeed, as we have seen, Paul Ricoeur argues that "fiction . . . permits historiography to live up to the task of memory," and also that "fictional narrative in some way imitates historical narrative," especially insofar as fiction is "internally bound by its obligation to its quasi-past." Ricoeur therefore speaks of an "interweaving of history and fiction," or "the fundamental structure, ontological as well as epistemological, by virtue of which history and fiction each concretize their respective intentionalities only by borrowing from the intentionality of the other." Yet even as he argues that these two narrative forms are inextricably linked in respect to their separate "intentionalities," Ricoeur insists on the absolute difference of the two modes of discourse because "the quasi-past of the narrative voice [in fiction] is . . . entirely different from the past of historical consciousness."[51]

If there has been a difference between the ways that English and French readers have concretized Hamilton's text, the difference is obviously not a result of one nation of readers being right and the other wrong. It is the result, rather, of the ways in which different sets of readers weighed the historical claims and the literariness of the *Memoirs*, with the French apparently deciding that the celebrated literary virtues of the text ("the truest specimen of perfect French gaiety") as well as the kinship between Hamilton's text and similar works like those by Bussy-Rabutin and Mme. D'Aulnoy indicated that Hamilton was acting as a writer of fiction, and the English deciding that the apparent accuracy of the text ("its striking and too faithful detail"), its constant reference to historical figures, and its lack

[50] Delarivier Manley, *The New Atalantis*, ed. Ros Ballaster (London: Penguin, 1991), 3, 4, 6–9.
[51] Ricoeur, *Time and Narrative*, III, 189, 190, 181, 191.

of overt fictional devices, authorized the reader to accept the author's claim that he was telling the truth despite the artful dialogue and playful scenes. The early modern reader, then, was used to close calls, and made them all the time. Readers judged the difference between types of secret history, apprehending some as fiction and others as history. But whatever the judgments, the reception of texts was, as this study demonstrates, contingent upon the historical particularities and peculiarities of a given discursive context; different decisions could be made about the same text and could endure in different settings.

In any case, it seems certain that ascertaining and indeed stipulating the rules governing the reception of secret history rendered these readers better equipped (if not fully prepared) to recognize a novel when that form of discourse began to be differentiated from the larger discourse of history. The years just before the appearance of *Robinson Crusoe* were undoubtedly demanding for readers, as the reception of the *Memoirs of Count Grammont* suggests. Some readers concretized the *Memoirs* as history at least in part because the nature of the discourse of history allowed a form like secret history to exist for a time. The fact that secret history flourished in this period and the additional fact that readers clearly recognized certain varieties of it as works that could plausibly be read as history helps us to understand why readers hesitated when confronted with *Robinson Crusoe*: they were used to narratives that claimed to be historical and to be based on personal knowledge but that felt like fictional texts. Readers needed to weigh the evidence and make a choice, and thereby participated in the definition of a form. That hesitation, I shall argue, can be seen as the moment of the novel's constitution.

6

"Knowing strange things": historical discourse in the century before *Robinson Crusoe*

In the Folger Shakespeare Library in Washington, D.C., one can read a fascinating register of the intellectual interests of an anonymous writer of the first three decades of the eighteenth century who recorded his or her reading and thoughts in 296 hand-numbered pages entitled *The Second book of history. 1701–1722*. The writer discusses British historians from Geoffrey of Monmouth to Bishop Burnet, declaring Milton a good historian, Cotton a "famous Antiquary" with "a noble library," and Rushworth a historical writer whose "falshoods" necessitated the "impartial collections" of Nalson. The author of the *Second book* records information from historians and antiquaries like Clarendon (on "the vile artifices of the Scots Comissioners" who turned Charles I over to his enemies) and Anthony à Wood (on the "ill end" of Samuel Butler), and once even discusses history in theoretical terms, citing Paolo Sarpi in support of the view that "A good historian should not only relate the events of things, but also the causes & motives wch produced them." If this were all that one found in the *Second book*, it would seem like little more than a private and personal version of the historiographical criticism in the various *Historical Libraries* (1696–1724) of William Nicolson or Thomas Hearne's *Ductor Historicus* (1705). But there is more. Alongside the comments on historians, one also finds accounts of wonders or marvels that are in their own way just as representative of the discourse of history in this period as the discussions of Geoffrey, Buchanan, Bacon, and Selden. The marvels reported included a woman forced to mate with a bear who produced a son who himself later married and had children of his own, gnats that could kill a lion, a woman in her sixties who gave birth to a child, the skeleton of a giant found in Northumberland, and "myriads of animals that swime in those little seas of Juices, that are contained in the several vessels of an human body." Sources for these reports included Saxo Grammaticus, the *History of the Works of the Learned*, the *Turkish Spy*, Locke's *On Education*, the *Athenian Oracle*, and *The Tatler*.[1]

This taste for the arcane, the marvelous, the incredible, and the curious,

---

[1]   *The Second book of history. 1701–1722*, Folger MS. M.b.7, fos. 17, 102, 98, 167, 105, 110, 73–85, 121, 212.

an important feature of the historical discourse of this period not yet treated here in any detail, is all but completely ignored in the history of history, undoubtedly set aside as a vestige of a credulity more or less eliminated from "serious" historical writing by the beginning of the eighteenth century.[2] Even Foucault, who is often at odds with other historians of thought and culture, argues in *The Order of Things* that "the Classical age" – roughly the seventeenth and eighteenth centuries – was sharply distinct from the Renaissance because in the latter period historians of nature sloughed off the habit of "reading" nature in terms of "the resemblances that could be found in it, the virtues that it was thought to possess, the legends and stories with which it had been involved, its place in heraldry . . . what the ancients recorded of it, and what travellers might have said of it." Foucault argues that until the mid-seventeenth century historians sought "to establish the great compilation of documents and signs . . . that might form a mark," but that afterwards they undertook the "meticulous examination of things themselves" and the transcription of what was "gathered in smooth, neutralized, and faithful words" and that in the latter age "observation . . . is a perceptible knowledge" from which hearsay and much else was excluded. Using even Foucault's construct, then, it is possible to argue that Robert Plot's fondness for dubious material identifies him as too much under the sway of "the theory of the mark" to be regarded as a "serious" natural historian, a true creature of the Classical age. Yet, as we have seen throughout this study, the commitment to collecting and ordering facts coexisted in this period with a conviction that such material as hearsay and fabulous narratives ought to be accepted as matters of fact. Furthermore, principles governing historiography were subject to qualification or revision in light of the instrumental ends of a given historical text. Thus although the transformation that Foucault describes undoubtedly took place, it does not seem to have been the sharp "discontinuity" that he imagined since, as late as the end of the seventeenth and the beginning of the eighteenth centuries, the reading of "marks" in natural history coexisted in historical discourse with the "mathesis" and "taxinomia" that, for Foucault, characterized the Classical age.[3] The taste for the marvelous cannot, therefore, simply be dismissed as the preoccupation of hopelessly naive or reactionary historical writers. Rather, in the

---

[2] On the taste for the marvelous, see Hunter, *Before Novels*, chapter 8.

[3] Michel Foucault, *The Order of Things: An Archaeology of the Human Sciences* (London: Tavistock/ Routledge, 1970), 129–132, xxii, 71; for the original French, see *Les mots et les choses: une archéologie des sciences humaines* (Paris: Gallimard, 1966), 140–44, 13, 86. In the *Archaeology of Knowledge*, 169 (*L'archéologie du savoir*, 221), Foucault uses the phrase "sudden redistribution" in such a way as to suggest that it is roughly analogous to "discontinuity," "rupture," or "gap." The idea of a redistribution within and among discursive formations seems to allow for abrupt change *and* evident continuity and in that sense seems more satisfactory for the present purposes than the other terms listed above.

historical discourse of late seventeenth-century England many "facts" that even then seemed dubious were treated as the legitimate stuff of history, and the fictive at times functioned as a subspecies of the factual.

In bringing this examination of the history of English historiography to a close, then, it is necessary to insist upon the strangeness of historical discourse in the decades before Defoe wrote such "histories" as *Crusoe, Moll Flanders*, and *A Journal of the Plague Year*. To that end, I range somewhat more widely in the discourse of history than I have done to this point, looking at popular historiography, at natural history, and at a wide variety of isolated statements drawn from both treatises on history and discussions of history in commonplace books and diaries. In the course of this examination, I shall reprise such issues as the belief in the utility of history, the tolerance of the fictive, and the devotion to the factual that were prominent features of historical practice in Defoe's day. I shall also treat the issue of how Baconian historiography was presented to the readers to whom Defoe addressed himself in his most famous narratives. Insisting on the strangeness of the historical discourse of this period may seem odd since throughout this study I have criticized the tendency to stigmatize Baconian historiography as the historiographical "other." Yet only by insisting on the difference of Baconian historiography from modern historical thought and writing can one actually glimpse early modern English historical discourse in its historical specificity, and only by insisting that the historiography of the first decades of the eighteenth century was decidedly *not* modern can one apprehend how Defoe could have deployed the word "history" in defining and defending the narratives that have become so crucial a part of the tradition of the English novel. By making history strange, in short, we can see the novel anew.

I

The intense and almost universal interest in history at the end of the seventeenth and the beginning of the eighteenth centuries, traceable in important part to Bacon's having made it the foundation of all learning, can be discerned in the diary of Samuel Pepys. In the diary, Pepys displayed a voracious curiosity and love of facts combined with the practical, technical interests of a man who was both secretary to the admiralty and president of the Royal Society. Pepys read Camden, Cotton, Heylyn, and Hooke; Fuller was his favorite writer. His love for matters of fact led him to praise Dugdale's *Origines Juridiciales*, to exclaim that *Micrographia* was "the most ingenious book that ever I read in my life," and to declare that John Graunt's book on the bills of mortality ("one of the earliest English treatises on vital statistics") was "very pretty." For Pepys such texts were both entertaining and serviceable: Coke on treason in the

Institutes was "well worth reading" because "it is useful now to know what these crimes are" and Rushworth's *Historical Collections* was "the best worth reading for any man of my condition, or any man that hopes to come to any public condition in the world."[4] Pepys embraced the principal canons governing the activity of the Royal Society and embodied in the historical discourse of the period: matters of fact were by definition worthwhile but always because they had the potential of providing men and women with a basis for acting efficaciously in the world.

These views are echoed again and again in the diaries and commonplace books of the period.[5] Even more than his friend Pepys, John Evelyn, another member of the Royal Society, evinced a belief in the "almost mystic vitality of facts," recording endless information in his diary about such topics as food, flowers, architecture, horses, furniture, diseases, cures, trees, and weather. Evelyn reported his inspection of collections of curiosities, including the one belonging to Elias Ashmole, and regretted that Robert Plot's labors had not eventuated in a natural history of the whole of England, "since [if it had] it would be one of the most useful and illustrious workes that was ever produc'd in any age or nation."[6] The age, then, delighted in collecting and reporting matters of fact and was convinced that facts were always at least potentially useful. Thus when the *General Biographical Dictionary* (1812–17) observed in respect to Thomas Hearne's antiquarian efforts that "he would have been more generally useful had he now and then questioned the importance of what he was about to publish," its criticism of Hearne, while reflecting the widespread view that antiquarian texts were little more than "laborious Plunder . . . of Rolls and Records," failed to acknowledge that in the century after Bacon the collection of matters of fact seemed a duty of the highest intellectual and even religious significance.[7]

---

4   *The Diary of Samuel Pepys*, 11 vols., transcription ed. Robert Latham and William Matthews (London: G. Bell and Sons; Bell and Hyman), vi, 2, 17, 18; viii, 547; ix, 291; viii, 170; iii, 53; vi, 18; viii, 284; iv, 395. Richard Ollard, *Pepys: A Biography* (New York: Holt, Rinehart and Winston, 1974), 107–09.

5   See, for example, *The Diary of Ralph Josselin 1616–1683*, ed. Alan Macfarlane, (London: British Academy; Oxford University Press, 1976), 2; "Pocket Book of Anthony Hammond," British Library MS., Add. 22,584, fos. 4–7, 11; "The Commonplace Book of Henry Calverley," British Library MS., Add. 27,419, fos. 4, 43, 46.

6   The "mystic vitality" quotation is from Thomas Sprat, *History of the Royal Society*, ed. Jackson I. Cope and Harold Whitmore Jones (St. Louis: Washington University Studies, 1958), xxxi; *The Diary of John Evelyn*, ed. and introd. John Bowle (Oxford University Press, 1985), 250.

7   Alexander Chalmers, *General Biographical Dictionary*, 32 vols. (London, 1812–17), xvii, 283; the phrase "laborious Plunder" is from John Hughes, *Complete History*, quoted in Levine, *Humanism and History*, 170. On the religious aspect of Baconianism, see Charles Webster, *The Great Instauration: Science, Medicine and Reform, 1626–1660* (New York: Holmes and Meier, 1975), 1–99; and Shapiro, *Probability and Certainty*, chapter 3; and Richard S. Westfall, *Science and Religion in Seventeenth-Century England* (Ann Arbor: University of Michigan Press, 1973), especially chapter 2.

Yet, as we have seen, the commitment to the principle that history *was* the presentation of matters of fact was subject to revision in all forms of historical discourse, including natural history, in light of ideological or rhetorical desiderata. Thomas Sprat, for example, admitted that he was unwilling to renounce polemic in his *History of the Royal Society* in which he presented the society and its aims to Restoration England. In the "Advertisement to the Reader," Sprat openly declared that his *History* functioned as "a Defence and Recommendation of *Experimental Knowledge*"; he argued that although "the Style . . . in which it is written, is larger and more contentious than becomes that purity and shortness which are the chief beauties of Historical Writings," it deserved to be read as a history "because that was the main end of my Design." P. B. Wood has argued that even Sprat's explanation of the fundamental principles guiding the work of the society served a crucial polemical purpose, since the "stress on empirical evidence and the application of the results for the benefit to mankind" allowed Sprat to characterize "the Society as a vehicle for religious and social unification." Sprat attributed deviations from the purity and austerity of history to the enemies of the society: "the blame of this ought not so much be laid upon me, as upon the Detractors of so noble an Institution: For their Objections and Cavils against it, did make it necessary for me to write of it, not altogether in the way of a plain *History*, but sometimes of an *Apology*."[8] Thus he implied that unadorned, uncolored matters of fact would yield their primacy in history when practical demands, like the need "to make the Royal Society respectable," had to be addressed by the historian.[9]

The faith in particulars, furthermore, led not infrequently to the presentation of dubious "facts" to readers of history. Arthur and Brut were "asserted" in histories, as were stories of avenging crows tracking down killers. One sees this clearly in the natural history of Robert Plot, so much admired by Evelyn.[10] Plot was secretary of the Royal Society, professor of chemistry at Oxford, first curator of the Ashmolean Museum, and historiographer-royal, and thus a considerable figure in the learned world

---

[8] Sprat, *Royal Society*, "Advertisement," n.p.; P. B. Wood, "Methodology and Apologetics: Thomas Sprat's *History of the Royal Society*," *British Journal for the History of Science* 13 (1980), 5–6, 14, 19.

[9] Christopher Hill, "Sir Isaac Newton and His Society," in Hill, *Change and Continuity in Seventeenth-Century England* (London: Weidenfeld and Nicolson, 1974), 258.

[10] A case might be be made that natural history should lie outside the bounds of this study since it was concerned with the laws of nature rather than historical truth. Barbara Shapiro, however, has argued that "the reorientation of English natural philosophy, which gave a new prominence to experience and matters of fact, forced historians and naturalists into closer relationship"; *Probability and Certainty*, 11. See also, Foucault, *Order of Things*, 131; *Les mots et les choses*, 142–43. The "reorientation" to which Shapiro refers was, of course, inaugurated by Bacon, who argued that "History is Natural, Civil, Ecclesiastical, and Literary"; *Selected Writings*, 230.

of Restoration England, and in 1677 he published *The Natural History of Oxford-shire*, a "seminal" work of natural history praised by the *DNB* as "unexcelled by any subsequent writer" ("due regard being had to the time in which he wrote").[11] Nevertheless, Plot's credulity in the face of reports of the marvelous put him at odds not only with such "scientific" natural historians as John Ray, "the father of natural history" in Britain, but also with the historian-apologist Sprat, who decried the inclusion of "the delightful deceit of *Fables*" in natural history.[12] Yet Plot was a typical Baconian historiographer, working within the Baconian agenda by concentrating on the reporting of matters of fact but also drawn to the marvelous and the monstrous, even when he seems to have recognized that some of his "facts" were fabulous.

Plot's *Oxford-shire* was typical of the natural history of this period insofar as it partook of both local history and what would now be called the life and earth sciences; it reported information according to the tripartite structure for observing reality that Bacon himself used: "Natural Things," Nature's "extravagancies and defects," and "Artificial Operations."[13] The *History* consisted of reports of virtually "random collecting" since for Plot, as for many natural historians, this form of learning was more a "store of data from which hypotheses were to be inductively derived" than a vehicle for such abstractions.[14] In discussing the waters of Oxfordshire, for example, Plot catalogued the "considerable Rivers" that traversed the county, celebrated the quality of the county's water, listed the Parliaments and councils that convened there (because of its salubrious location), discussed salt springs and the uses to which salt water might be put, and finally (citing Hugh Plat's *Jewel house of Art and Nature*) told of a poor farmer whose "Seed-corn" fell into the sea and who later harvested a bumper crop from the brine-soaked seed. Plot advised farmers to consider the latter information carefully, "and if they shall think fit, make tryal of them (which I shall gladly accept as the *guerdon* of my labor)" (17–40). The *History of Oxford-shire*, then, was rambling, anecdotal, practical-minded, and teeming with facts.

Plot's text was also replete with reports of the marvelous. In discussing the trees found in the shire, Plot related that "the foundations of two eminent *Religious houses* [were] both occasion'd by *trees*." In the first

---

11   Michael Hunter, *John Aubrey and the Realm of Learning* (New York: Science History Publications, 1975), 100; *DNB*.

12   The comment on Ray is from the *DNB*. Sprat criticized the fables and "monstrous Stories" in Pliny's natural history as "like *Romances*, in respect of *True History*"; *Royal Society*, 62, 90.

13   Robert Plot, *The Natural History of Oxford-shire, Being an Essay toward the Natural History of England* (Oxford, 1677), 1; hereafter cited in the text. On the elements that composed natural history, see Mendyk, *"Speculum Britanniae,"* 177, 193. Bacon divided the history of nature into the "history of Creatures, history of Marvels, and history of Arts"; *Selected Writings*, 231.

14   Hunter, *Science and Society*, 17–18.

instance, the wife of the founder, on repeated walks by a certain tree "was always occupied by a clamorous bunch of Pyes" and when she asked a local cleric what this meant he "cunningly" advised her to build "some *Church* or *Monastery* where the *tree* stood." The second establishment was founded because near a "*triple Elm* . . . Sir Thomas White, Lord Mayor of London (as we have it by Tradition) was warned in a *Dream* he should build a College, for the education of Youth in Religion and Learning" (169). Similarly, in the section "Of Men and Women," Plot reported the recent case of

a child [who] cryed very audibly in its *mothers* womb somtime before the *birth*. For the performance of which action, whether there be a necessity of the *Infants* having respiration whil'st included in the *Amnion*; or whether it may not be done without it? let the *Physitians* dispute: The matter of fact sufficeth me at present that there was such a thing, the people being frighted with it, and expecting some calamity should soon attend such a *Prodigie*.   (192)

Plot's willingness to "let the Physitians dispute" this report demonstrates that he recognized that there were grounds for skepticism in respect to this story. Why report it, then, given his assurance to the reader that "the Curiosities [in the text] . . . are so certain truths, that as many as were portable, or could be procured, are in the hands of the Author" (sig. b$_2$v)?

There are at least two different ways to assess the attention paid to such marvels by members of the Royal Society. The first is to ask whether what Plot was doing deserves to be regarded as in any sense "scientific" or "historical." Many have argued that early modern natural historians were dominated by outmoded ways of thinking, "in thrall to Moses."[15] This was the standard view of seventeenth-century histories of nature from the early nineteenth century down to our own day, and the "formed stones" controversy – the debate over whether fossils were the "real Spoils of once living Animals" or were "generated or wrought by a Plastick virtue" inherent in the earth itself – may induce modern readers to believe that "scientists" of the period were indeed captives of the Mosaic account of creation since the dispute was clearly as much about religion as about natural history. Even John Woodward, who argued the "organic origin thesis," offered "the Universality of the Deluge" as the explanation for the distribution of the fossils upon the earth.[16] Roy Porter, however, has

---

[15] Roy Porter, *The Making of Geology: Earth Science in Britain, 1660–1815* (Cambridge University Press, 1977), 2.

[16] On the formed stones controversy, see Joseph Levine, *Dr. Woodward's Shield: History, Science and Satire in Augustan England* (Berkeley: University of California Press, 1977), chapter 2; Paolo Rossi, *The Dark Abyss of Time: The History of the Earth and the History of Nations from Hooke to Vico*, trans. Lydia G. Cochrane (University of Chicago Press, 1984), pt. 1; and Porter, *Making of Geology*, chapter 2. The first and last quotes are from John Woodward, *An Essay toward a Natural History of the Earth* (London, 1695), sig. A$_5$v, 15; the middle quotes are from Rossi, *Dark Abyss*, 3, 4. In

disputed the claim that seventeenth-century historians of nature were incapable of being "scientific" because they were restrained by the demands of faith or wedded to the emblematic reading of the earth. Porter claims that "attitudes toward the Earth and its investigation underwent great transformation in Britain between the mid-sevententh and the early nineteenth century"; Porter further argues that around the end of the seventeenth century "the Earth became conceptualized as a neutral object, distinct from man, to be studied" and "empirical investigation, putatively independent of theoretical questions, became a norm of scientific study."[17] Some historians, thus, have acknowledged that natural history in this period was linked to theology, but also claimed that the turn away from the emblematic reading of the earth and its contents and toward the collection and ordering of data as a means of comprehending nature was a momentous and irreversible event that took place around 1700.[18]

This view is often to linked to the assertion that many of the most important natural histories written in this period were "scientific" in character. Thus Joseph Levine asserts that even though Woodward cited the Flood in his discussion of fossils and, unlike some of his contemporaries, unequivocally attributed it to providential causes, he was "neither unsophisticated, nor 'unscientific'"; Levine claims that Woodward attempted "to treat the Mosaic account . . . as an hypothesis" like any other.[19] Arguing that the importance of the Mosaic account in Woodward's contribution to the formed stones controversy should not be taken to prove that his approach to the fossil question was flawed, Levine declares that Woodward was "on the right track" because he acted as if "only systematic collection and comparison of the evidence, living and dead, could ever settle the question."[20]

There is much to be said for the argument that seventeenth-century natural history approached such questions in an "authentically scientific" (or, to put the matter in seventeenth-century terms, "genuinely historical") spirit. But this line of thinking runs the risk of familiarizing principles and practices that ought to retain at least a measure of their strangeness. After all, a phalanx of Woodward's contemporaries questioned both his method and assumptions. Edward Lhwyd characterized Woodward's account of

the first instance Rossi is quoting Robert Hooke, who argued against the "thesis of plastic virtues."

[17] Porter, *Making of Geology*, 3, 33.
[18] Westfall, especially, treats this question, viewing Robert Boyle as one who "sought, and found, the hand of God in creation" and wrote to demonstrate that "there is no inconsistency between Christianity and scientific investigation." *Science and Religion*, especially 41, 43, and chapter 2.
[19] Levine, *Woodward's Shield*, 55.
[20] *Ibid.*, 51–52. Similarly, Mendyk argues that Aubrey and Plot practiced a "new scientific antiquarianism" that was embodied in their histories of Oxfordshire and Wiltshire; *Speculum Britanniae*, 179, 193.

the history of the earth as a "romantic theory," and one bold reviewer of Woodward's *Essay* argued that the Mosaic account need not be taken literally but should rather be seen as a "fable" offered to "a rude and ignorant people."[21] Ray, furthermore, wrote to his friend John Aubrey in respect to the latter's *Naturall Historie of Wiltshire*, "I think . . . that you are a little too inclinable to credit strange relations" and observed, "I have found men that are not skilfull in the History of Nature, very credulous, & apt to impose upon themselves & others; & . . . to make a shew of knowing strange things."[22] Thus, in the early modern period itself there were students of natural history who found the practice of Woodward, Aubrey, and Plot unacceptable. K. Theodore Hoppen has captured this conflict nicely by labeling the labors of men like Plot as " 'vulgar' Baconianism."[23] As Hoppen gently puts the matter, in the early Royal Society "there was a significant element who saw the society's work in an extremely eclectic and catholic light," and, as a result, the society could support an expedition in search of dragons in the Alps; a member could report his vision during a dissection of "a beautiful yong man with long flaxen haire to his middle"; and the society's collection could include a tooth removed from a testicle and an herb that grew in a thrush's stomach. Hoppen shows that the society was guided not only by the Baconian faith in knowledge derived from experience but also by the hermeticism, the "preoccupation with the spirit world," and the faith in alchemy of many of its adherents including Aubrey, Joseph Glanvil, Isaac Newton, and Plot.[24] Yet the use of the label "vulgar Baconianism" might suggest (although this was not Hoppen's intent) that Plot's practice was unsound even for his own time, whereas the paradoxical truth is that Plot's practice was within the rules that governed historical discourse and, at the same time, problematic.

Understanding the views of Plot and other like-minded natural historians in respect to suspect marvels takes us to the heart of our discussion of seventeenth-century historiography. Unlike Ray, Plot and Aubrey at least entertained the possibility that such stories might be true or contain a germ of truth. Aubrey's justification for his apparent credulity is instructive; in discussing the material in his miscellanies, which included sections on "Knockings," "Converse with Angels," and "Discovery of two Murthers by Apparitions," Aubrey observed: "The matter of this collection is beyond

---

[21] Levine, *Woodward's Shield*, 36–37, 37–38; on the identity of the author of the text, one L. P., see also 35 and 306–07, n. 68, 70, 71.

[22] Hunter, *Aubrey*, 133–34.

[23] K. Theodore Hoppen, "The Nature of the Early Royal Society," *British Journal for the History of Science* 9 (1976), 6, 258–61, 266; see also Hunter, *Aubrey*, 132.

[24] Hoppen, "Early Royal Society," 2, 8–9. See also Webster, who argues that in the seventeenth century science was frequently "employed to add precision to the millenial outline drawn up by theologians" and "conversely millenial ideas furnished the natural philosophers with new premises and goals"; *Great Instauration*, xvi.

human reach, we being miserably in the dark as to the oeconomy of the invisible world."[25] In other words, Aubrey believed that even the most apparently fabulous material deserved the attention of historians who could never be more than dimly aware of "the oeconomy of the invisible world."

Basil Willey has argued that the capacity of men like Aubrey and Plot to think "scientifically" and yet approach the physical world as an entity teeming with occult meaning is proof that the seventeenth century was a "double-faced age . . . half scientific and half magical."[26] This is a widespread view. Stan Mendyk, too, declares that Plot was "a 'transitional' figure in the history of science and scholarship in general, with a foot in both camps, ancient and modern."[27] To so label these historians and their work is, however, almost inevitably to identify "magic" as that which had to be sloughed off in the next age and "science" as that form of knowledge which every "serious" person attempted to embrace; it is, in short, to valorize the scientist in a figure like Sir Thomas Browne, to whom Willey referred, and to depreciate the magician. Charles Raven has proposed, however, an alternate way to view the attitude toward nature in the works of Browne, Aubrey, and Plot, one that acknowledges the great transformation that was underway but also recognizes the singularity of historical discourse in this period. Raven observes of Browne:

He desired to reject all infallibilities, to test all propositions, to expose all superstitions. But, unlike too many of his successors, he refuses to limit his view of the universe to the realm of the mathematical and mechanistic. Being a man of well-developed and wide interests with a common sense which prevents him from being blinkered by logic or swept off his feet by passion, he insists upon treating the whole of his experience as somehow congruous and explicable. He intends, so far as he can, "to see life steadily and see it whole," and to tell what he has seen. He will not easily call anything "common or unclean" or say that it is no concern of his . . . [and thus] he represents the New Philosophy at its best, before it had been narrowed and desiccated by the pre-eminence of Descartes and Newton; and shows us the quality of those first modern men, the founders of the Royal Society, before Walter Moyle in 1719 [note the date] was compelled to lament that "I find there is no room in Gresham College for Natural History: Mathematics have engrossed all."

For he [i.e., Browne] combines, however incompletely, the two worlds of observed fact and of inferred meaning, of outward sign and inward significance, which had been sundered by the medieval failure to relate its symbolism to actuality and which even then were being driven into conflict.[28]

25 *Biographica Britannica*, 6 vols. (London, 1747–1763), I, 278.
26 Basil Willey, *The Seventeenth Century Background; Studies of the Thought of the Age in Relation to Poetry and Religion* (London: Chatto and Windus, 1934), 41.
27 Mendyk, "*Speculum Britanniae*," 184.
28 Charles E. Raven, *English Naturalists from Neckam to Ray* (Cambridge University Press, 1947), 350.

One hears in this discussion echoes of T. S. Eliot on the "unified sensibility" lost after the seventeenth century (and also of Blake on the Enlightenment: "Mock on, mock on, Voltaire, Rousseau"), but the key point in Raven's comment for our purposes is his focus on the capacity of the historian of this period to "treat the whole of his experience as somehow congruous and explicable," to treat, that is, the fantastic as the factual. Raven also asserts the scientific or historiographical "seriousness" (to use a word that Hoppen also insists upon) of a moment when "scientific" observation and arcane reading of human beings and the world seemed not at odds with one another but of a piece.[29]

A second and related explanation for why fantastic material was treated as matters of fact is found in yet another dimension of the Baconian faith: the conviction that all matters of fact, however "common," or apparently rooted in "barbarism" or "heathenism," were at least potentially useful and worthy of being recorded by historians. Gough collected all sorts of material in the belief that everything might potentially be useful to men and women anxious about property and priority, and in 1692 John Houghton made much the same point about natural history: "gain all the Knowledg that is worth getting," Houghton asserts in his *Collection for Improvement of Husbandry and Trade* (1693), because "the more we know of these *Islands*, the better . . . may they be manag'd."[30] The history of the earth, then, no less than histories of the Civil War, could influence the way men and women acted in the world. Thus, Plot opened his chapter on fossils or "formed stones" by reminding his readers that he "treated only of such [things] as eminently . . . were some way or other useful to *Man*," and Aubrey's attention to "magical recipes" was also "utilitarian": "he valued them because they might work" (69).[31]

Within this general utilitarian frame, one specific end that natural history might serve was to provide a rational basis for belief in God. This goal united the efforts of men like Ray with those of their less exacting fellow natural historians. Ray's "most popular and influential achievement," *The Wisdom of God manifested in the Works of Creation* (1691), was a book that occupied "a primary place in the development of modern science," but also a book in which "the frame of reference built up on the Book of Genesis" remained unchallenged.[32] Furthermore, skepticism in respect to many "strange things" related in natural history was sometimes "tempered" out of a desire to combat atheism and make a case for belief. Michael Hunter argues that Boyle and Henry More endorsed Joseph Glanvil's argument in *Saducismus Triumphatus* (1681) for belief in the existence of witches because

---

[29] Hoppen, "Early Royal Society," 258.   [30] Cited in Hunter, *Aubrey*, 93.
[31] *Ibid.*, 106.
[32] Raven, *John Ray, Naturalist: His Life and Works*, introd. S. M. Walters (Cambridge University Press, 1950), 452, 454–55; see also, Westfall, *Science and Religion*, 62–64.

they "valued evidence of supernatural interference as 'an undeniable Argument, that there be such things as *Spirits* or *Incorporeal Substance* in the World'."[33] And while some natural historians tolerated suspect material on religious grounds, others had political ends in mind. Nathaniel Crouch, for example, used his discussion of "Prodigies on Earth" ("matters of fact, very well attested") in *The General History of Earthquakes* to prove that God favored Protestants (*Earthquakes*, 119–20).[34] Plot, however, seems to have had another end in view: pleasure. His treatment of certain narratives in *Oxford-shire* strongly suggests that he regarded pleasing his readers (and perhaps himself) as a sufficient motive for including fabulous material in historical discourse.

In his discussion of "Brutes," Plot recorded that since antiquity bees had been regarded as "not only the *Prognosticators*, but *Concomitants* of *Eloquence*," and cited Plato, Pindar, Lucan, and St. John Chrysostom as instances of subsequently eloquent individuals "about whose mouths, whil'st Infants, the Bees gathered." Evidence from the history of Oxford for this apiary predictive capacity is given in the shape of:

the *Bees* of Ludovico Vives, who being sent in the year 1520. by *Cardinal Wolsey* to *Oxford*, to be publick *Professor* of *Rhetorick* there, and placed in the *College* of *Bees* (*Corpus Christi* being so called by the *Founder* in his *Statutes*) was welcomed thither by a swarm of *Bees*, which to signifie the incomparable sweetness of his *Eloquence*, setled themselves over his *head* under the leads of his *Study* (at the *west-end* of the *Cloyster*) where they continued about 130 years. (180)

Did Plot believe this story? He specified in detail where the bees took up residence, but the manner in which he presented the material suggests he knew that many of his readers would dismiss it as fancy. He cited both "the general voice of the House [i.e., the College]" and "the special testimony of a worthy Antiquary" in its favor but acknowledged that the first source knew about the bees "by tradition" and that the second also had it second-hand.

There is furthermore a playful aspect to Plot's report that the bees in

33 Hunter, *Aubrey*, 141–42.
34 The texts by Crouch discussed in this chapter (and the abbreviations used in parenthetical citations) are as follows: *The Life of Oliver Cromwell* (London, [1680]) (*Cromwell*); *Historical Remarques, and Observations of the Ancient and Present State of London and Westminster* (London, 1681) (*Remarques*); *England's Monarch's:, or A Compendious Relation of the most Remarkable Transactions, and Observable Passages . . . during the Reigns of the* KINGS *and* QUEENS *of* ENGLAND, *from the Invasion of the Romans under J. Caesar to this present*, 2nd edn. (London, 1685) (*Monarchs*); *The History of the Kingdoms of Scotland and Ireland* (London, 1685) (*Scotland*); *The Kingdom of Darkness: or, The History of Daemons, Specters, Witches, Apparitions, Possessions, Disturbances, and other wonderful and supernatural Delusions, Mischievous Feats, and Malicious Impostures of the Devil* (London, 1688) (*Darkness*); *The History of the Two Late Kings* (London, 1693) (*Kings*); *The General History of Earthquakes* (London, 1694) (*Earthquakes*); *The Wars in England, Scotland, and Ireland*, 6th edn. (London, 1697) (*Wars*); *Admirable Curiosities Rarities and Wonders in England, Scotland and Ireland*, 7th edn. (London, 1710) (*Curiosities*); *Martyrs in Flames: or, The History of Popery*, 3rd edn. (London, 1729) (*Martyrs*).

question swarmed and moved to another location in 1648 when all but two "inhabitants of the *College*" lost their places because they were loyal to the king: "as if the *feminine* [bees] sympathized with the *masculine* Monarchy, they instantly declined, and came shortly to nothing" (181). Plot admitted that some bees took up residence elsewhere in "the same *Cloyster*" at about the same time, but he argued that no one could know if those bees came from "the ancient *Stock*" of bees and he therefore chose, "rather . . . than to give too much credit to uncertainties," to assume that the latter bees departed in 1648 (181). Coming at the end of Plot's account of wonderful bees, which he knew would be viewed skeptically, this comment about not wishing to "credit . . . uncertainties" seems ironic and suggests that Plot included such fabulous material in his natural histories for its entertainment value. One gets the same impression from Plot's treatment of the famous "*Glastenbury thorn.*" Plot indicated that the provenance of this shrub, which "constantly buds, and somtimes blossoms at or near *Christmas,*" was an open question and then averred:

As for the excellent and peculiar quality that it hath [of blossoming on Christmas], some take it as a miraculous remembrance of the Birth of CHRIST, first planted by *Joseph* of *Arimathea*; Others only esteem it as an earlier sort of *Thorn* peculiar to *England*: And others again are of [the] opinion, that it is originally a foreigner of some of the *southern* Countries, and so hardy a Plant, that it still keeps its time of blossoming . . . though removed hither into a much colder *Climat*. Whether of these is most probable, I shall not determin, but leave every *Reader* best to please himself. (156–57)

Effectively announcing that the account of the Glastonbury thorn might be specious but leaving it to the reader to decide, Plot is here reminiscent of Camden commenting on the Galfridian stories; his tolerance for fabulous material amounted to an acceptance of fiction within historical discourse.[35]

To appreciate Plot's playful manner in presenting these marvels, it is useful to recall that when he asserted in his discussion of formed stones that he treated only matters useful to humanity, he also, somewhat paradoxically, acknowledged that he included information about "*Minerals* . . . [that] are for the *ornament*, or *delight* of Mankind" (69). Figure 4 suggests why Plot might have viewed the formed stones in this light. Aesthetic considerations, therefore, might help to explain the inclusion of such stories as those of the Glastonbury thorn or Vives's bees in the *Natural History of Oxford-shire*. Crouch openly presented his many histories, filled with "Strange Accidents, Prodigious Appearances," as works that were both entertaining and informative, and in fact entertaining because they

---

[35] Along the same lines, Michael Hunter argues that "among scientific enthusiasts of the Restoration there were more whose interests were of this heterogeneous and uncritical kind than there were rigorous mechanists like [Henry] Oldenburg or Ray"; *Aubrey*, 100, 136.

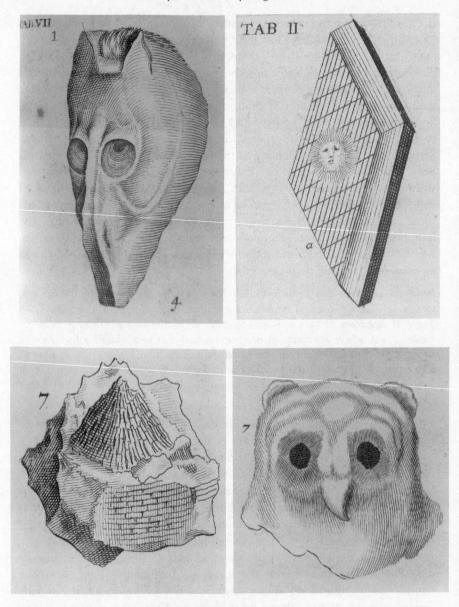

Figure 4   Details from plates of "formed stones" in Robert Plot, *The Natural History of Oxford-shire* (1676).

were informative: "very diverting, since at so small a price, any Person may be accommodated with so many useful particulars" (*Scotland*, t.p.; *Monarchs*, sig. A₂r).

Similarly, Plot's use of entertaining "facts" might well have been conditioned by his argument that fossils were "*lusus naturae*" or tricks of nature, made for mankind's "*admiration*" rather than its "*use*" (80).[36] The earth contained an abundance of formed stones created out of a kind of aesthetic impulse inherent in nature and designed to delight, so why should the historiography of the earth not contain some frivolous material as well? To be sure, the end of delight was conflated in Plot's view, as in Crouch's, with the end of instruction or edification. Discussing the formed stones, Plot observed:

> Whereof the World is beautified with so great variety, that as on the one hand I cannot but wonder at the great Providence of *God*, and his most perfect Workmanship, that has thus created the *Universe* for Mans *delight* as well as *use*: so on the other, I cannot but reprehend the petulant despisers of this innocent sort of Learning, who in derision have called it, *picking of stones*; as if what the Omnipotent and most wise *God* hath thought fit to *create*, were not worth the consideration of weak *Man*. (80)

Plot saw no distinction between viewing God's world as a source of delight and as a collection of potential tools in human hands; thus, in respect to formed stones, Plot asked "who knows but these things may have a use, that hereafter may be discover'd, though not known at present" (80).[37] The *Natural History of Oxford-shire*, then, seems to contain material presented as matters of fact and simultaneously acknowledged to be at least arguably fictive. Ultimately one cannot say with any certainty whether a given narrative or marvel was understood by Plot to be fact, fiction, possibly or potentially true, or tolerably and delightfully false. It seems certain, however, that some of the "facts" reported by Plot and others like him were included in spite of their fabulous character, either because they were potentially useful or because they were pleasing to the author and, it was hoped, to the reader.

II

Such attitudes, I have argued, were not out of place in Baconian historiography, but, on the contrary, were clearly allowed by the rules governing the discourse of history. Yet the view that matters of fact were to

---

[36] On *lusus naturae*, see Rossi, *Dark Abyss*, 19–20, 59–60.

[37] Ray was likewise devoted to the pursuit of useful knowledge, but insofar as he was concerned with pleasure it was because "there is . . . no occupation more worthy and delightful than to contemplate the beauteous works of nature and honour the infinite wisdom and goodness of God"; preface to Ray's *Cambridge Catalogue*, quoted in Raven, *John Ray*, 83.

be valued both because they were useful and because they were diverting was seen as inimical to historical writing by such figures as Ray, who decried the fondness of some historians for "knowing strange things." The taste for the marvelous and the sensational was more evident, then, in popular history than it was in the severer efforts aimed at smaller reader- ships by writers such as Camden, Hearne, or Ray. Not surprisingly, therefore, many of the historians treated in this study might appropriately be described as popular writers, either because the texts they wrote were well received by early modern readers (Milton, Burnet), or because their works were aimed at a general, nonscholarly audience (Churchill, Ha- milton), or because they incorporated popular material in their texts (Gough), or because their practice was a relatively unsophisticated version of the practice of more "eminent" historians and their texts relatively undemanding versions of high-culture historiographical forms (Gough, Hutchinson). *The History of Myddle* was an idiosyncratic version of anti- quarian learning worked out by an intelligent amateur; Clarendon's *History of the Rebellion* was a bestseller; Burnet's secret history was his most widely read work and it continues to be readily available even today; and even Plot's *Oxford-shire* has been characterized as a work "chiefly influential in popularising local natural history."[38] Thus many of the examples of Baconian historiography treated in this study sought to appeal to a popular audience, and even Camden was unwilling to dismiss the Galfridian stories outright because he did not want "to fight against a received opinion."

Popular historiography, then, is an important source for grasping the nature of Baconian historiography. The best source for understanding the shape of historical discourse in popular texts in this period is the work of Crouch, the son of a tailor and a bookseller as well as an historian, a man who "melted down the best of our English Histories into Twelve-penny Books" and in the process became "a celebrated Author."[39] (Many of Crouch's texts were published under the name Richard Burton, sometimes after Crouch's death Robert Burton, and thus were occasionally referred to as "Burton's books.") Crouch has already appeared in this study as a secret historian and in connection with the British History and natural history, and in another setting I have treated his singular popularity as a historian, one who inducted a new class of readers into the ways of history in part by replicating the practice of other Baconian historians.[40] Now I want to use Crouch first to look at the readers of popular historiography of this period and then to discuss what Baconian historiography as practiced

---

[38] Hunter, *Aubrey*, 70.

[39] *The Life and Errors of John Dunton*, 2 vols. (London, 1818), i, 206, ii, 435.

[40] Mayer, "Nathaniel Crouch, Bookseller and Historian: Popular Historiography and Cultural Power in Late Seventeenth-Century England," *Eighteenth-Century Studies* 27 (1993–94), 391–419.

by Crouch taught readers about historiography, reading, and culture in general.

The readers to whom Crouch addressed himself were primarily of the "middling sort," and presumably near the bottom of the middle.[41] The standard one-shilling price for "Burton's books" placed them toward the bottom of the seventeenth-century price scale for books of this length; they cost more than the chapbooks and almanacs (2–6d) that the poorest and least-educated readers were accustomed to buying but much less than most other works of history.[42] Crouch's low prices suggest that he was aiming at the bottom of the market, trying to attract readers habituated to spending as much as sixpence for a slim chapbook or an almanac and also to convince those readers that spending twice that amount for a longer and more serious volume represented a good investment.[43] Presumably, Crouch's readers were primarily Londoners since as an independent London bookseller his primary market would have been the capital, and he clearly assumed that his readers were not only Protestants but of a Puritan cast of mind.[44] In sum, Crouch apparently aimed his texts at a fairly humble version of the kind of readers Richard Altick had in mind when he argued that "'commercial money-getting business, and religious Puritanism' were primary in shaping reading tastes at this time."[45]

Crouch's career suggests, furthermore, that such readers were gravitating at this time away from chapbooks and toward longer texts. His appeals to readers indicate that he was a writer and merchant who was aware of a great transformation taking place, one that entailed a shift from

---

[41] On the amorphous but crucial "middling sort," see Christopher Hill, *A Tinker and a Poor Man: John Bunyan and His Church, 1628–1688* (New York: Knopf, 1989), 16–28; and Keith Wrightson, *English Society, 1580–1680* (New Brunswick NJ: Rutgers University Press, 1982), 37, 223–27.

[42] Generally, small duodecimos and octavos cost 2 to 3s while folios cost 10 to 12s and more. Richard Altick observes that in the 1660s "the smallest books (12mo) usually were 1s6d"; *The English Common Reader: A Social History of the Mass Reading Public, 1800–1900* (University of Chicago Press, 1957), 21–23; and Margaret Spufford, *Small Books and Pleasant Histories: Popular Fiction and Its Readership in Seventeenth-Century England* (Athens: University of Georgia Press, 1981), 48–51 and 91–98. Almanacs, probably the most popular type of book in this period, could cost 6d and more, but they too were much shorter than Crouch's histories; Bernard Capp, *English Almanacs, 1500–1800: Astrology and the Popular Press* (Ithaca: Cornell University Press, 1979), 41. In the late seventeenth century, finally, a 1s "chap-book" *Pilgrim's Progress* was aimed at "rude mechanicals," cottagers, and servants; Frank Mott Harrison, "Editions of *The Pilgrim's Progress*," *The Library*, n.s. 22 (1941–42), 74–75. See also Keeble, *Literary Culture of Nonconformity*, 133–34.

[43] For the debate over changing literacy rates in early modern England, see Lawrence Stone, "Literacy and Education in England, 1640–90," *Past and Present* 42 (1969), 133–46; David Cressy, *Literacy and the Social Order: Reading and Writing in Tudor and Stuart England* (Cambridge University Press, 1980), chapter 7; and Spufford, *Small Books*, chapter 2. Even the most cautious estimates (Cressy, 147, 149–54) suggest that particularly in London, the growth of literacy among women and tradesmen was marked and steady, if gradual.

[44] *Kings*, sig. A$_2$r–v; *Martyrs*, sig. A$_3$r.

[45] Altick, *Common Reader*, 24; the quoted phrase is John Stuart Mill's.

Figures 5 and 6   Scenes of torture from [Nathaniel Crouch], *The History of the Kingdoms of Scotland and Ireland* (1685).

illiteracy to literacy, from chapbook to book, from romance to history. The illustrations in Crouch's texts – crude woodcuts of sensational scenes (see figures 5 and 6) – suggest that these histories were produced with chapbook readers in mind. Identifying a continuum of forms (prints, broadsheets, chapbooks, and "low-price booklets") with varying combinations of words and pictures, the gradual production of which led in the end to the creation of a market for popular literature of all sorts, Roger Chartier argues that pictorial representations like these eased the way for readers making the transition from chapbooks to more substantial texts. Chartier calls the period 1530–1660, when this market was being created in France, a time of progressive "typographic acculturation," when the ability of readers to move in the direction of more text and fewer illustrations was facilitated by the fact that the different classes of texts often looked the same because woodcuts from chapbooks were also used in *livrets bleus*, and by the fact that the material was frequently quite similar: well-known narratives, characters, and situations appeared across the continuum.[46]

Crouch's practice accords strikingly with Chartier's model; Crouch reused the same woodcuts in different texts, and he used illustrations more than once in the same work.[47] These familiar, recyclable visual representations could have helped his English readers make the momentous transition

[46] The print is an illustration with an explanatory title; the broadsheet is a very brief text that "describes" an image; the chapbook is a short text with some illustrations; the booklet is a longer text but still illustrated. Roger Chartier, "Culture as Appropriation: Popular Cultural Uses in Early Modern France," in *Understanding Popular Culture from the Middle Ages to the Nineteenth Century*, ed. Steven Kaplan and David Hall (Berlin: Mouton, 1984), 243–50.

[47] Crouch uses the same portrait of Charles II in *Wars* at 4 and in *Monarchs* at 209; in *Scotland* he uses the same battle scene at 18, 98, and 208.

from chapbooks to book-length histories. Crouch trumpeted his histories as substitutes for less distinguished fare and argued that they had "occasioned many (especially young people) to lay aside those vain and idle Songs and Romances wherewith they were formerly Conversant and to divert their vacant hours with reading the real Transactions, Revolutions and Accidents that are recorded by Authors on the greatest Veracity" (*Earthquakes*, sig. A₂v). He thus claimed to be changing the habits of a whole class of English readers, and later students of the London literary scene credited the assertion. Dr. Johnson said that "Burton's books . . . seem very proper to allure backward readers," and Philip Bliss, the nineteenth-century editor of Wood and Hearne, argued that

although as historical documents these plagiarisms [i.e., Crouch's histories] were comparatively worthless, still the design and execution were undoubtedly commendable; since, besides that the abridgements were executed with no common degree of cleverness, the introduction of this new species of chap-book superseded, in a great measure, the licentious and profane publications which the lower and middling classes had before been accustomed to.[48]

From the seventeenth to the nineteenth centuries, then, Crouch and his most learned readers argued that he was a writer who had made his name by bridging the gap between two cultures. He was particularly important in this respect because, of all the writers of similarly questionable merit who were, at this time, both meeting and shaping the needs of new readers (John Dunton, Ned Ward, William Winstanley, for example, as well as fiction writers like Thomas Deloney, John Bunyan, Aphra Behn, Francis Kirkman, and Daniel Defoe), Crouch almost alone was a popularizer of history at a time when the Baconian program made history the foundation of all learning and when the new fiction that was supplanting romance was presented to readers as a species of history.[49] Crouch, therefore, was introducing his readers not only to a new type of text but also to a new form of discourse, and he was thus engaged in a far-reaching acculturating activity, one that brought his audience into book culture and inducted it into the ways of history.

Introducing his readers to historiography, Crouch conveyed to them the devotion to facts that was the central tenet of Baconian historiography, while at the same time suggesting that sensational material authorized by popular memory had a place in historical discourse. His histories included popular versions of the antiquarian masterpieces of Camden and Stow,

---

48 Philip Bliss, ed., *Reliquiae Hearnianae: The Remains of Thomas Hearne*, 2 vols. (Oxford: Bliss, 1857), I, 298; I, 291; James Boswell, *Life of Samuel Johnson*, 6 vols., 2nd edn., ed. G. B. Hill; rev. L. F. Powell (Oxford University Press, 1964), IV, 258.

49 On Dunton and Ward, see Hunter, *Before Novels*, 99–106, 115–17; on Winstanley and another seventeenth-century popular historian, Alexander Ross, see Mayer, "Nathaniel Crouch," 397–98.

histories of earthquakes and of supernatural phenomena, accounts of Protestant martyrs and of the worthies of England and of the world as well as political histories of England, Scotland, and Ireland and of successive English dynasties. These works were recommended to readers for containing "many particulars," "useful particulars," "matters that then happened," and "matters of fact, without reflection or observation," collected from "Authors of Undoubted Verity" (*Darkness*, t.p.; *Monarchs*, sig. A$_2$r; *Remarques*, sig. A$_2$r; *Wars*, 3; *Cromwell*, t.p.). Crouch's basic historical form was the compendium; titles like *Admirable Curiosities Rarities and Wonders in England* and *Extraordinary Adventures and Discoveries of Several Famous Men* indicate that he was above all a collector and collator of facts. Dunton said of him, "I think I have given you the very soul of his Character when I have told you that his talent lies at *Collection*."[50] His *Kingdom of Darkness* features a defense of compendium as an historical form:

> In this Collection I have no respect to time when these matters were acted, so as to put them into Chronological Order, though I shall set down the years wherein most of them were done; Neither will I divide the Histories that are Domestick from those which happened in Foreign Nations; But only relate bare matters of Fact as I find them recorded by credible Historians, without much enlarging upon Reflections or Advertisements . . . [and] without Distinguishing them into part Heads or Chapters.   (*Darkness*, 1)

For Crouch the collection of unaltered and unsynthesized particulars was the best historical method and the compendium the preferred historical form. Indeed he labeled his histories "abstracts": digests of matters of fact.[51]

Crouch provided his readers, in short, with many "useful particulars" and also with sensational material whose entertaining aspect he celebrated and whose inclusion he clearly regarded as consistent with the writing of history. The title page of the *History of Earthquakes* promises accounts of "the Most Remarkable and Tremendous Earthquakes" and "dreadful Conflagrations and Fiery Irruptions," and that of the *History of the Kingdoms of Scotland and Ireland* informs us that "the most Remarkable Transactions and revolutions" will be "Intermixt with Variety of Excellent Speeches, Strange Accidents, Prodigious Appearances, and other very considerable matters, both delightful and profitable." Disassociating his own work from merely titillating works on devils, Crouch nevertheless promised the readers of *Kingdom of Darkness* "wonderful and supernatural Delusions, Mischievous Feats, [and] . . . Malicious Impostures of the Devil." All this, and illustrations too: "Pictures of several memorable Accidents" (*Darkness*,

---

[50] Dunton, *Life and Errors*, I, 206.
[51] Crouch tells his readers that "the acceptance that Abstracts of this Nature have met with hath encouraged me to proceed"; *Kings*, sig. A$_2$r.

sig. A₃v, t.p.). The frontispiece to the *Kingdom of Darkness* (see figure 7) makes it clear why that text was recommended to readers as "delightful" as well as "profitable," and why Crouch concluded that work with the claim that "it cannot but amuse a man's mind to think what these Officious Spirits should be that so willingly sometimes offer themselves to associate and assist mankind" (167). The scenes depicted in the frontispiece are putatively horrific, but they have an undeniably playful aspect as well. In *Martyrs in Flames*, similarly, Crouch told the story of a man named Burton, a bailiff in Lincolnshire and "a cruel Persecutor of Protestants," who went from being a Protestant during the reign of Edward VI to being a Catholic during the reign of Mary Tudor. One day after joining forces with the Papists, this man was

riding, [when] a Crow flew over his Head, and voided her Excrements just upon his Beard with such a horrible stink, that it caused him to Vomit in a violent manner; he got Home, but could eat nothing, the stink and vomiting still continuing, which made him with dreadful Oaths and Execrations curse the Crow that had poisoned him, and so continued till he died.

This was no idle tale; it served to show that "God's Judgments [fell] upon Popish Persecutors." More evidence for this assertion was taken from the life of Queen Mary: her lack of children, her loss of Calais, the fact that her "Land was grievously afflicted with Tempest, Famine, [and] Plague" during her reign (*Martyrs*, 184, 186).

Crouch used both well-known facts about Bloody Mary and narratives out of folklore as evidence for his assertion about Providence. Furthermore, he defended his use of such stories by asserting that his texts featured information other historians excluded. He offered *Historical Remarques*, for example, as a valuable supplement to Stow, claiming there were no historians "who have written of the[se] particular Accidents" (*Remarques*, sig. A₂v). And although he followed in Camden's footsteps in *Admirable Curiosities*, Crouch also declared that he would provide quite different information:

there cannot be expected an exact description of every Town or considerable place, that having been performed by others; this being only a Collection of the Natural, and Artificial Curiosities, Wonders, and the remarkable *Places*, *Persons*, and *Accidents* in each County. (*Curiosities*, sig. A₁r)

By including these "Wonders," Crouch constructed for his readers what might be called the secret history of Britannia: a history known to many but rarely reported.

Crouch's introduction of readers to historical discourse also conveyed to them a strong sense of history as a utilitarian endeavor; in addition to identifying his histories as "abstracts," he also referred to them as

Figure 7   Frontispiece [Nathaniel Crouch], *The Kingdom of Darkness* (1688).

"Manuals" (*Earthquakes*, sig. A₂v). According to the *OED*, a "manual" is a "small book" or a "concise treatise," but it is also a book "for handy use," as the illustrative quotation from 1663 indicated: "If in your Building, you want instructions for your Clark; pray let him make use of the Manual." By identifying his histories as manuals, then, Crouch implied that they were designed as practical guides, and suggested that the reading of history could be useful not only for statesman but also for ordinary Londoners. His texts conveyed a belief that history would make his readers better subjects of their monarch and better Christians, and would also be of use in more mundane ways. He recommended *England's Monarchs*, for example, on the grounds that in it one was "accommodated with so many particulars both for Instruction and Discourse"; it was presented as a vehicle for self-improvement, promising to increase readers' general knowledge ("Instruction") and improve their conversational facility ("Discourse") (*Monarchs*, sig. A₂r). His "manuals" were in this respect much like the popular almanacs of the period which "filled a wide variety of roles, cheaply and concisely" and "had a largely utilitarian purpose."[52] Literacy in and of itself "allowed men and women to function more effectively in a variety of social contexts," and the same and more could be said of cheap and easy-to-read histories, especially in an age when the reading of history was held to be a worthwhile activity, as Richard Brathwaite commented, "not only in respect of discourse, but in respect of discipline and civill societie."[53]

Crouch told his readers, then, that they could use his histories to make their way in the world, and they presumably took him at his word. J. Paul Hunter argues that the "specific new needs" of the new readers of the late seventeenth and early eighteenth century were addressed by the novel after 1719 and before that date by a wide variety of texts, many of them practically-oriented: "we go far toward comprehending the content, concerns, and directions of the early novel if we imagine ambitious, aspiring, mobile, and increasingly urban young people . . . as among the most ready patrons of the novel, those who were already able to read by the later seventeenth century and poised for reading materials that would address who they were." Crouch's texts did just this; readers of his historical "manuals" were offered texts that explained "how the world works." History and the novel were linked of course from the novel's earliest days; this may help to explain why the novel was a peculiarly utilitarian form of imaginative discourse, why, as Hunter puts it, readers

---

[52] Capp, *English Almanacs*, 23–24.
[53] Thomas Laqueur, "The Cultural Origins of Popular Literacy in England 1500–1850," *Oxford Review of Education* 2 (1976), 255; Brathwaite, *The English Gentleman* (1630), cited in H. S. Bennett, *English Books and Readers 1603–1640. Being a Study of the Book Trade in the Reigns of James I and Charles I* (Cambridge University Press, 1970), 179.

turned to novels in response to " 'real-life' issues."[54] Before this readerly expectation became associated with the novel, a mundanely practical view of historiography was delineated by Crouch in "Burton's books."

III

What we learn from Crouch is how Baconian historiography appeared to the common reader. But as we have seen throughout this study, Baconian historiography encompassed not only popular historians aiming both to entertain and educate unsophisticated readers but also high culture types like Plot and Camden. Thus while Baconian historiography had its popular aspect, it was not merely a popular form produced and read only by marginal figures. "Knowing strange things" was of the very essence of historical discourse in this period.

There is an evident danger in characterizing historical discourse in the period just before the publication of *Robinson Crusoe* as I have here. That danger lies in the possibility that focusing on Baconian historiography can lead to thinking about history as a factual discourse into which the fictive leaked from time to time in ways not authorized by more rigorous historiographical practice. This line of thought leads, almost inevitably, to viewing the factual as that which was authentic, proper, and genuine in history and the fictive as illegitimate, corrupting, and spurious. To overcome this tendency, we must insistently recall that the most stringent "scientific" historians of the period enunciated strict canons of behavior and yet qualified them in practice. Camden explicitly "resolved to remove" all material from historiography that could be traced to "Ignorance" or "doubtfull Uncertainty" or "flat Falsity," but he also informed his readers that "Things doubtfull I have interpreted favourably; [and] Things secret and abstruse I have not pried into."[55] What is more, Camden told stories of Brut and Arthur that he knew were at best dubious and left it to the reader to decide whether to give such stories credence. From such exceptions much followed: openly acknowledging that historiography served political ends and that historians ought to keep those ends in view and alter their practice accordingly provided a theoretical justification for histories of the rebellion written from the perspective of a single, highly-engaged individual, secret histories designed to discredit the last of the Stuart kings, local histories that advanced the interests of local power, and natural histories that promised to improve both the material and the spiritual well-being of their readers. Telling discredited tales so as to avoid fighting "against a received opinion" allowed for the possibility of repre-

---

54 Hunter, *Before Novels*, 68, 81, 79. On the impulse to self-improvement, see Wright, *Middle-Class Culture*, 121–22; Altick, *Common Reader*, 26–27; Wrightson, *English Society*, 196–97.
55 Camden, *Princess Elizabeth*, 5–6.

senting the marvelous in historical discourse even when it was evidently
fictional. It is true that biased or credulous historians might be attacked as
writers of fiction, but it is equally true that devotion to the "scientific"
method of the antiquarians also elicited attacks from historical writers who
believed such methods led not to legitimate history-writing but to compendia of mostly useless facts. In such a historical discourse, fiction was not
the poor relation of history, tolerated but always depreciated; it was simply
one of the means used by writers of history who embraced the Baconian
dictum that all forms of knowledge should be "for the benefit and use of
life" as a literal statement of historiography's end. As we shall see, one of
the most distinctive features of Defoe's historiographical practice was that
he seems to have used fiction, in a more or less untroubled fashion, as one
of the means of historical representation. This aspect of Defoe's practice
linked him to a historical discourse that was giving way to another
discourse of history virtually as he wrote. Certainly, rules of practice were
changing.

As the eighteenth century progressed, the love of the marvelous became
increasingly identified with the "popular" and increasingly unacceptable in
historical discourse, just as "knowing strange things" became the province
of the "vulgar." The taste for the marvelous found in Plot was absent, for
example, from Gilbert White's *Natural History of Selborne* (1788). Like Plot,
White wrote popular natural history and like Plot, White treated both
natural phenomena and antiquities, but unlike his seventeenth-century
forebear, White had almost no tolerance for what he called "superstitious
prejudices," which he saw as fit only for "lower people . . . not invigorated
by a liberal education."[56] In the eighteenth century, White's comment
suggests, the marvelous came to be thought of as the province of the
untutored and the ignorant. This change was registered in *Antiquitates
Vulgares* (1725), in which Henry Bourne asserted in respect to the "Opinions" of the "Common People" that "they are almost all superstitions,
being generally either the Produce of Heathenism; or the Inventions of
Indolent Monks." Bourne claimed to be neither a "reviver" nor an
"abolisher" but a "regulator" of popular antiquities, and yet his characterization of the beliefs of "the Vulgar" suggests that the day when historians
such as Gough and Plot might tolerate fabulous material had come to an

---

[56] Gilbert White, *The Natural History of Selborne*, notes Richard Kearton (London: Arrowsmith,
1924), 171–72. Elizabeth Heckendorn Cook has argued that White's text functions as "a kind
of ideological state apparatus," containing a "model for rural class relations acceptable to the
dominant church and state establishment"; I quote here from the unpublished essay, "Writing
the Space of the 'Natural': *The Natural History of Selborne*" that the author has kindly shared with
me. See also, Clarence Wolfshohl, "Gilbert White's Natural History and History," *CLIO* 20
(1990–91), 271–81.

end.[57] Much the same impression is produced by William Warburton's 1727 tirade against

Prodigies and Portents [which] have infected the best Writings of Antiquity; and have so blotted and deformed our modern Annals, that they may be rather called TRAGEDIES than HISTORY.

Warburton wondered

How it comes to pass that while the other Sciences are daily Purging and Refining themselves from the Pollutions of superstitious Error, that had been collecting throughout a long Winter of Ignorance and Barbarism; *History*, still the longer it runs, contracts the more Filth.[58]

The comments of Bourne and Warburton signal the passing of the heyday of "vulgar Baconianism" – the end of the era in which advanced historical or scientific method was associated with the reporting of marvels and wonders and narratives that were known to be fabulous.

The change that was underway around 1719 is evident in Dennis Todd's study of the uproar surrounding Mary Toft's claim, made in 1726, that she had given birth to seventeen rabbits and the subsequent exposure of the claim as a hoax. Todd points out that one of the effects of the controversy was that the widely held view that the imagination could transform an ordinary fetus into a monster became increasingly difficult to maintain: "most of the assumptions that had explained its [the imagination's] functioning were destroyed by the new philosophical . . . thinking." Discussions of the power of the imaginative faculty gave way to explanations of "more mundane and mechanical causes." Todd argues that the intense reaction to this celebrated case resulted from the story's capacity to suggest how "the imagination could lay us open to alien energies"; Todd further argues that the Toft affair was not an isolated incident: "Some thirty years after the Mary Toft affair, Sterne published *Tristram Shandy*, a novel in which the hero is . . . precipitated into a perpetual whirl of confusion . . . because, at the moment of his conception, the imaginations of his parents were disordered."[59] A discursive transformation is signaled by the fact that Toft's hoax is played out in the medicine and natural history of her day while Tristram's story is told in a novel. The fabulous became increasingly untenable in history at the same time that a new fictional form – capable of accommodating Robinson Crusoe's "surprising

[57] Henry Bourne, *Antiquitates Vulgares; or, The Antiquities of the Common People* (Newcastle, 1725), ix, xi, x.

[58] [William Warburton], *A Critical and Philosophical Enquiry into the Causes of Prodigies and Miracles, as related by Historians. With An Essay Towards Restoring a Method and Purity in History* (London, 1727), 1–2.

[59] Dennis Todd, *Imagining Monsters: Miscreations of the Self in Eighteenth-Century England* (University of Chicago Press, 1995), 63, 112, 104, 105.

adventures" as well as the "life and opinions" of poor, deformed Tristram
– was taking shape on the literary horizon.

What is more, autobiographical historiography largely disappeared
around this time; Clarendon and Burnet were the last great public figures
to produce massive accounts of their own time until Churchill did so in the
twentieth century, and, significantly, Churchill took the epigraph for his
History of the Second World War not from the *History of the Rebellion* but from
Defoe's *Memoirs of a Cavalier*. By the twentieth century, Churchill's
"melange of personal reminiscence . . . accepted chronological fact, and
autobiography" (likened by John Kenyon to Clarendon's *History*), was in
some ways more indebted to fiction than to history.[60] Secret history also
ceased in the eighteenth century to be an important historical form. And
the topics chosen by the historians of the last three quarters of the
eighteenth century were far more removed from immediate events than
were the projects of historians from Bacon to Burnet: Hume and Smollett
treated the whole history of England, not just politically charged recent
events; Robertson wrote a history of Scotland but his most important
works were his histories of Charles V and of America; Gibbon focused on
Rome. These topics suggest that the sense that history could or should be
practically valuable in an immediate sense was on the wane. In both
political and natural history, the inclusion of the fabulous became increasingly indefensible and history ostensibly became a far more disinterested
form of intellectual inquiry. As we have seen, there was no room for stories
of Brut and Arthur in the histories of Hume (1754–62), Robertson (1759),
and Smollett (1757–58). At the same time, the novel made its appearance
in England.

The matrix of that development, as I have been arguing, is in important
part the discourse of history at a particular moment, a moment after facts
were enshrined as the stuff out of which history was made, and the struggle
to identify and record facts became the central task of the historian, but
before the new methodological principles necessitated the *apparent* banish-
ment of fiction, rhetoric, and polemic from historiography. As I shall argue
in discussing Defoe, two developments converged in his work, the transformation of historical thought and writing that I have been treating here,
and the formulation of a key argument in the long debate – discussed in
the next chapter – over whether it was possible for fictional discourse to do
the work of history. Defoe's career is unique in the early history of the
English novel because these developments so clearly impinged on his life as
a writer; after all, he wrote large numbers of both "histories" and
"novels."

What we find in Defoe's corpus is a number of works of history in which

---

[60] Kenyon, *History Men*, 29–30.

the author's conviction that fiction could function as a means of historical representation was plainly evident as well as a number of works that were first offered to readers as species of historical discourse and often initially read as such (sometimes for a long time), but that were gradually read into the tradition of the novel. In Defoe's career, then, one can see the fictive element in Baconian historiography hiving off into another form of discourse, one that acknowledged its fictive character without renouncing its claim to contain matters of fact. Defoe's career suggests, therefore, that the novel emerged from Baconian historiography. In the discursive context in which Defoe's works appeared, fiction had a clear place in historical discourse; eventually the more obvious ways in which writers had used fiction in historical representation became increasingly unacceptable. After Defoe the novel appeared and it featured an urgent claim to be read, as Richardson put it, with "Historical faith." As I shall argue in the ensuing chapters, Defoe's most famous narratives indicate the ways in which the novel in England was constituted upon a dialogue between the fictional and the historical within a new discourse that asserted the power of fiction to do the work of history.

7

"History" before Defoe: Nashe, Deloney, Behn, Manley

Two different sets of developments that animated English culture in the early modern period converged in the career of Daniel Defoe. The first was the transformation of history that eventuated in Baconian historiography; this process has been treated at length, and historiography will again be the focus in the next chapter, where Defoe's historical practice will be discussed. We must now turn to the second set of developments: the history of English fiction in the seventeenth century and particularly the debate, in theoretical statements and in imaginative works, over the relationship between history and fiction that can be said to have begun with Sidney's *Apology for Poetry* and to have reached an important watershed in the works of Defoe. Sidney insisted on the absolute difference between history and poetry, believing that this distinction redounded to the glory of poetry, and Defoe wrote fictional texts that he presented to readers as histories and that only later came to be read as novels. Although scarcely touched upon thus far in this study, the debate over the nature of fiction is crucial to understanding the emergence of the discourse of the novel. Up to now, I have left this debate to one side; as the principal goal of this work is to elucidate the relationship between historical discourse and the discourse of the novel, it was necessary to treat historiography at length before turning to fiction. We now turn, however, from historical discourse to the nature of "history," a form of fiction that asserted its difference from and opposition to romance and stipulated a claim to historicity even as it acknowledged its imaginative status. This brief consideration of various approaches to theorizing the history-fiction link in the age before Defoe will demonstrate that although the writers of "history" or "antiromance" argued for a new form of fiction, nothing about their practice was sufficiently new to require of readers a transformation in their understanding of the possibilities of fiction, whereas Defoe's most famous narratives represented the moment of "sudden redistribution" that made possible the eventual emergence of the discourse of the novel.

"History" – represented in this discussion by the "histories" of Thomas Nashe, Thomas Deloney, Aphra Behn, and Delarivier Manley – has been examined by numerous historians and theoreticians of the novel; these

scholars have generally focused on the tendency of early modern English
fiction writers to deny the fictionality of their works.[1] Many scholars have
insisted upon a continuity between the works that have variously been
identified as species of "antiromance" and "true history" from Nashe to
Defoe.[2] Michael McKeon, for example, has described a "generic instability" in this period that was linked to an epistemological crisis in the
course of which "romance idealism" was subjected to criticism and
displacement by "naive empiricism," both in their turn undermined by
"extreme skepticism."[3] For McKeon this unfolding epistemological shift is
a key to the "dialectical constitution of the novel," and yet in his
discussions of actual works of fiction written in the seventeenth century it
becomes clear that few works can be neatly classified using McKeon's
taxonomy (in the case of fiction, "romance, antiromance, true history").[4]
Repeatedly, individual works, as McKeon construes them, are the site of
an "epistemological double reversal" in the process of which the idealist
position associated with romance is attacked from an empiricist perspective
and then empiricism as well as idealism are subjected to correction by
skepticism. Thus, McKeon argues that an "antiromantic impulse" in the
preface to William Congreve's *Incognita* (1691) "is completed by its
'antihistorical' corollary movement, which effectively punctures both the
claim to historicity and the pretense to verisimilitude."[5] McKeon organizes
his discussion of these texts into a narrative in which romance is dialectically transformed by the respective challenges of empiricism and skepticism, but his own evidence reveals a remarkable sameness in the fiction of
the period: the double reversal is everywhere. According to Homer Obed
Brown, McKeon's "dialectical patterns of two-stage reversals are . . .
curiously ahistorical."[6]

What is more, McKeon, like many other critics and literary historians,
can only see the claim to historicity as uniformly figurative: "the claim to
historicity is no less a rhetorical trope than verisimilitude."[7] Generally, of

---

[1]   Aside from the works by Ballaster, Davis, Foley, Hunter, McKeon, Nelson, and Richetti cited
     in earlier chapters, see Walter Allen, *The English Novel: A Short Critical History* (Harmondsworth:
     Penguin, 1984), chapter 1; Ernest A. Baker, *The History of the English Novel*, 10 vols. (London:
     H. F. and G. Witherby, 1937), vols. II and III; Bridget G. MacCarthy, *Women Writers: Their
     Contribution to the English Novel 1621–1744* (Cork University Press, 1944); Paul Salzman, *English
     Prose Fiction 1558–1700* (Oxford: Clarendon Press, 1985); Jane Spencer, *The Rise of the Woman
     Novelist from Aphra Behn to Jane Austen* (Oxford: Basil Blackwell, 1986); Arthur J. Tieje, "The
     Expressed Aim of the Long Prose Fiction from 1579 to 1740," *Journal of English and German
     Philology* 11 (1912), 402–32; Janet Todd, *The Sign of Angellica: Women, Writing, and Fiction 1660–
     1800* (London: Virago, 1989).
[2]   See, for example, Nelson, *Fact or Fiction*, chapter 5, and Salzman, *English Prose Fiction*, chapters
     15, 18.
[3]   McKeon, *Origins*, 20–22.
[4]   *Ibid.*, 52–64; the first phrase is the title of part 3 of McKeon's book.   [5] *Ibid.*, 63–64.
[6]   Brown, "Of the Title to Things Real: Conflicting Stories," *ELH* 55 (1988), 923.
[7]   McKeon, *Origins*, 53.

course, McKeon is correct, but this study aims to demonstrate that the case of Defoe is different and that, accordingly, his narratives occupy a crucial place in the history of the novel. Therefore, while McKeon's work has had the beneficial effect of forcefully reinserting romance into the history of the novel, his discussion of the dialectical constitution of the novel provides no means to account for the radical difference between the presentation and reception of, on the one hand, the "histories" that appeared in the century before *Robinson Crusoe* and, on the other hand, Defoe's own narratives. I shall argue that although the antiromances are far from being irrelevant to the early history of the novel – since taken together they constituted a prenovelistic fictional critique of romance – they nevertheless remained bound to the discourse they criticized and thus neither constituted nor elicited a fundamental rethinking of the nature of fiction. Defoe's work, however, was a radical departure in the debate over the nature of fiction, a development of such significance that one can legitimately argue that Defoe's narratives signal the emergence of the discourse of the novel.[8]

The fictional form that was "history" has been treated at length by other scholars; therefore, it need not be described in this study in the same detail as was required in delineating Baconian historiography in the century before Defoe published *Robinson Crusoe*. Yet certain aspects of English fiction and of the debate over the nature and value of fiction must be explored here to clarify the nature and significance of the claims to historicity of eighteenth-century novels as well as to make clear why, at this late date in the "institution" of the novel, I have focused my discussion of the emerging discourse of the novel on the lonely figure of Defoe, thereby ignoring so many other writers who might legitimately be called "mothers" or "fathers" of the novel.[9] In what follows, I shall demonstrate that in the debate over the nature of prose fiction that began with Sidney and reached a crucial climax in the work of Defoe, the question of the relationship between fiction and history was the central issue. Then I shall argue that Defoe was the pivotal figure in this debate because he alone wrote narratives that, from the moment of their publication into the twentieth century, pressed the history-fiction question upon readers insistently, so that the production and reception of those texts made the nexus of fiction and history a key feature of the theory of the novel. Finally and most importantly, I shall show that Defoe's impact on the debate over the nature

---

[8] Davis argues that there was "a profound rupture between novel and romance"; *Factual Fictions*, especially 41 and chapter 2.

[9] Dale Spender, *Mothers of the Novel: 100 Good Women Writers Before Jane Austen* (London: Pandora, 1986). For "institution," see Brown, "Title to Things Real," 937–38; and Armstrong, *Desire and Domestic Fiction*, 38, where she quotes from an unpublished manuscript by Brown. The word "institution" refers to the formation or origination of a discourse of the novel by readers representing powerful institutional forces.

of fiction arose from his having approached the issue not as a writer of "histories" or antiromances but as a practitioner of Baconian historiography who employed fiction in such a way as to suggest, ultimately, how fictions that desired to be read as histories had to be written.

The appearance of a revolutionary work, Jauss argues, is marked by a distinct and often alienating challenge to readerly expectations.[10] That moment is *not* to be found in the work of fiction writers from Nashe to Manley, but is inescapably present in Defoe's career. Thus while it is no doubt finally impossible to say that one writer or one book was responsible for the emergence of the discourse of the novel, one can nonetheless argue that Defoe *was* in fact as crucial as he has long been held to be because his work represents the kind of shift that signaled the emergence of a new mode of discourse.

I

Sir Philip Sidney's *Apology for Poetry* (written around 1580 but not published until 1595) was an important statement of Elizabethan poetics, and it bears closely upon our discussion of both fiction and history. Sidney denigrated history as the work of pedants laboring over "mouse eaten records" and did so in order to make a case for poetry. He declared that whereas history was "captived to the truth of a foolish world," poetry "excelleth History, not only in furnishing the mind with knowledge, but in setting it forward to that which deserveth to be called and accounted good."[11] Yet although Sidney's argument was a brilliant rhetorical performance in defense of the value of poetry, it nevertheless left imaginative discourse in a somewhat awkward position.[12] Near the end of the essay, Sidney made what is perhaps his most famous pronouncement about poetry, defending it against the charge that it was "the mother of lies" by asserting: "Now for the poet, he nothing affirms, and therefore never lieth."[13] Although this view accords with modern views of poetry and therefore seems unexceptionable to most modern readers, the *Apology* can be seen as a problematic argument on behalf of fiction in an age when, as Bacon asserted, all forms of learning should be "for the benefit and use of life."[14]

In fact if one considers Sidney's argument in light of Bacon's discussion of poetry in the *Advancement of Learning*, Sidney's case for poetry might be seen as the basis for an attack on poetry rather than a defense of it. Like

[10] Jauss, *Aesthetic of Reception*, 25.

[11] Sir Philip Sidney, *An Apology for Poetry*, ed. Geoffrey Shepherd (London: Nelson, 1965), 111.

[12] Walter Jackson Bate, *Prefaces to Criticism* (Garden City: Doubleday, 1959), 45, 49.

[13] Sidney, *Apologie*, 123–24.

[14] Bacon, *Selected Writings*, 437; Martha Woodmansee, "Speech-Act Theory and the Perpetuation of the Dogma of Literary Autonomy," *Centrum* 6 (1978–79), 75, 76.

Sidney, Bacon named poetry as one of the three principal ways of knowing, but Bacon gave poetry short shrift in his "perambulation of learning" and indicated that it is *not* a form of knowledge founded upon "that commerce between the mind of man and the nature of things, which is more precious than anything on earth." Bacon viewed poetry as an "extremely licensed" form of discourse that "doth truly refer to the Imagination; which, being not tied to the laws of matter, may at pleasure join that which nature hath severed, and sever that which nature hath joined, and so make unlawful matches and divorces of things." Drawing, seemingly, on the language of the Prayer Book in respect to marriage, Bacon implicitly lamented the inevitable "divorce" between reality and representation that was for him a constitutive feature of poetry. One is not surprised, therefore, to find Bacon summing up his view of poetry by declaring that it was best to move on to "the judicial place or palace of the mind, which we are to approach . . . with more reverence" (the realm of philosophy, whose axioms were founded upon history) and warning his readers in respect to fiction that "it is not good to stay too long in the theatre." Thus although Bacon rather formulaically praises poetry, the *Advancement* reveals a "consistent distrust" of poetry and the imagination.[15]

Sidney was an important Elizabethan courtier and poet and his *Arcadia* was a "bestseller" in the century after its appearance, but it was nevertheless Bacon, both "the most important philosophical and scientific authority of the Puritan Revolution" and the guiding intellectual force behind the foundation of the Royal Society after the Restoration, who was the more crucial figure of these two Tudor-Stuart theoreticians of fiction and history.[16] One reason for Bacon's greater influence was undoubtedly the practical orientation of many seventeenth-century readers, readers whose expectations embodied "popular literary taste" and for whom "the demand for information of every conceivable sort" was more important than "the desire for amusement."[17] This disposition on the part of readers also suggests the reason for what Robert Weimann sees as the "vulnerability" of Sidney's position: "this [i.e., the Sidneian] differentiation in the functions of poetical and historiographical modes of discourse presupposed the differing correlations between words and things, writing and experience."[18] In a world shaped by Baconian principles and a passion for useful knowledge, Sidney's argument was something of a cul-de-sac.

[15] Bacon, *Selected Writings*, 243–44, 247; Murray W. Bundy, "Bacon's True Opinion of Poetry," *Studies in Philology* 27 (1930), 254. See also McKeon, *Origins*, 68.

[16] Charles Mish, "Best Sellers in Seventeenth-Century Fiction," *Papers of the Bibliographical Society of America* 47 (1953), 365; on Bacon's importance, see Webster, *Great Instauration*, 25; Westfall, *Science and Religion*, 32–33.

[17] Wright, *Middle-Class Culture*, 103, 83, and chapter 4.

[18] Robert Weimann, "*Fabula* and *Historia*: The Crisis of the 'Universall Consideration' in *The Unfortunate Traveller*," *Representations* 8 (Fall 1984), 16.

It seems not at all surprising, therefore, that from Sidney onward into the eighteenth century, claims for the *marriage* rather than the divorce of history and fiction were a constant feature of the self-presentation of fiction in England.[19] As Weimann and others have shown, virtually from the moment of Sidney's assertion that the poet "affirmeth nothing," there began to appear in England texts that were presented to readers as "histories."[20] Writers in "flight from fiction" were, whether consciously or not, in flight from the Sidneian position, and they used various means to make good their claim to be presenting readers with history not fiction: setting a fictional narrative in a historical setting, making fictional characters take part in "veritable actions," declaring the work to be a true story in the guise of a fiction, or asserting "the story to be . . . of a kind that historians failed to tell."[21] In the introduction I cited the many fiction writers from Behn to Scott who presented their texts to readers as species of "history." Just thirty years before Scott published *Waverley*, James Beattie, in an essay "On Fable and Romance" (1783), distinguished between romance and "fabulous history" like Xenophon's *Cyropaedia* because in the case of the latter "the outlines of the story are true." What is more, before declaring *Robinson Crusoe* a "novel" that could be read "with Pleasure, but also with profit," Beattie argued that Defoe's narrative was founded upon the testimony of Alexander Selkirk.[22] Sidney's argument that the poet "affirmeth nothing," therefore, may be said to have elicited not endorsements from other writers of fiction but, rather, opposing definitions of poetry that asserted the power of imaginative texts to represent ordinary reality. If for Sidney the poet's world was golden, many fiction writers following in his wake seemed determined to lay claim to the "brazen" world to which the author of *Arcadia* consigned the historian.[23]

---

[19] I am not arguing that Sidney's *Apology* "caused" this debate. Sidney is simply the best known of several Renaissance critics who addressed themselves to "the indictment of fiction as lie"; Nelson, *Fact or Fiction*, 1. There are important similarities between Sidney's view and that of George Puttenham; see *The Arte of English Poesie*, introd. Baxter Hathaway (Kent State University Press, 1970), xxvii–xxviii, 19–21.

[20] Weimann, "Crisis of the 'Universall Consideration'," 16; he is thinking about Nashe, Deloney, Dekker, and other "popular pamphleteers." Nelson distinguishes between the "fraudulent" assertions of historicity before 1500 and the superficially similar assertions of the sixteenth century and after, which he construes as a part of a new and extremely consequential debate over the difference between fiction and history; *Fact or Fiction*, 36–37.

[21] Nelson, *Fact or Fiction*, 93.

[22] Geoffrey Day, *From Fiction to the Novel* (London: Routledge and Kegan Paul, 1987), 34, 59; according to Day, Beattie's essay was the most important discussion of the nature of prose fiction written in England at the end of the eighteenth century.

[23] Sidney, *Apologie*, 112.

II

An early example of a writer who argued that his fictional text ought to be regarded as something other than "mere" poetry was Thomas Nashe in *The Unfortunate Traveller* (1594). Nashe related the continental exploits of Jack Wilton, a putative servant of Henry Howard, earl of Surrey, which included participation in several important historical events like the rising and subsequent massacre of Anabaptists in Munster. These incidents are described in the kind of graphic detail one also finds in the description of the execution of the thief and murderer Cutwolfe:

His tongue he [the executioner] puld out, least he should blaspheme in his torment: venimous stinging wormes hee thrust into his eares to keep his head ravingly occupied: with cankers scruzed to pieces hee rubd his mouth and his gums: no lim of his but was lingeringly splintered in shivers. In this horror left they him on the wheele as in hell: where yet living he might beholde his flesh legacied amongst the foules of the aire.[24]

All this is presented to readers as "some reasonable conveyance of historie" as well as a "varietie of mirth." Offering a text to readers that purported to represent historical events of the Henrician period as actually witnessed by a man of low estate, *The Unfortunate Traveller* seemingly contradicted the Sidneian proposition that the poet tells nothing of the real world that is supposedly the realm of the historian, both by telling stories historians did not tell and by treating "people of no fame" and scenes of unspeakable horror.[25] Nevertheless, despite the claim that Jack Wilton's story was a "conveyance of historie," there was no mistaking the fact that Nashe wrote as an imaginative writer in this "history." Stanley Wells argues that Nashe was "conscious of attempting something new," but although the exact nature of the "new vein of writing" was and is difficult to stipulate, it does not seem that anyone ever read this work as a veracious account.[26]

Was Nashe writing a novel, and is *The Unfortunate Traveller* the first English novel or the first historical novel, as some have claimed?[27] Few who read it would be likely to think so, and most are likely to agree with Jonathan Crewe that more than anything else Nashe's text seems like an instance of "sheer performance" based upon "rhetorical amplification and

---

24 Thomas Nashe, *The Unfortunate Traveller*, in *Shorter Novels*, 2 vols., introds. and notes George Saintsbury and Philip Henderson (London: J. M. Dent and Sons, 1930), I, 355–56.

25 *Ibid.*, I, 263; Nelson, *Fact or Fiction*, 93.

26 Stanley Wells, ed., *Thomas Nashe. Selected Writings* (Cambridge MA: Harvard University Press, 1965), 14; Charles Nicholl, *A Cup of News: The Life of Thomas Nashe* (London: Routledge and Kegan Paul, 1984), 154.

27 Nicholl, *A Cup of News*, 154; Merritt Lawlis, ed., *Elizabethan Prose Fiction* (New York: Odyssey, 1967), 435–36.

figures of disorder," a sustained blast of what Crewe calls "unredeemed rhetoric."[28] And yet Nashe was in his way offering an answer to the question propounded to fiction writers by Sidney and answered in a number of ways by writers from Nashe's day to Scott's, the question being: can writers and readers put "words and things," "writing and experience," fiction and history back together again? Weimann has argued that in the wake of the Sidneian divorce of these terms

the tidiness of these differentiations is treated very roughly in some of the narrative texts themselves, and especially in those flowing from the pen of writers like Nashe . . . the respective modes of poetic and historiographical discourse tend to affect and intertwine each other until "the fainted Image of Poetrie" and "the particular truth of things" cease to appear so diametrically opposed.[29]

Thus Nashe was a writer who came at or near the beginning of a dialogue among writers and readers over the capacity of fiction to surmount the barrier between history and poetry; Nashe challenged the history-fiction distinction with his narrative of putatively historical events, and yet he did so within a discourse that was clearly marked as fictional by an outlandish and highly stylized mode of representation. Like other fictionists before Defoe who addressed themselves to this issue, Nashe implicitly argued that he was writing a kind of fiction that could serve as a "conveyance of historie" but not history itself.

Another contributor to the dialogue over the nature of fiction at the beginning of the seventeenth century was Thomas Deloney, whose "pleasant histories" of Jack of Newbery and Thomas of Reading (1597, 1600) likewise claimed that fiction could be historical. Treating clothworkers and yeomen, Deloney presented his readers with stories about the ordinary individuals never treated by historians as well as "notable members in the Commonwealth of this Land." As in Nashe's texts, ordinary men and women rub shoulders with the great and powerful (Henry VIII, Catherine of Aragon, Cardinal Wolsey), and there is even a suggestion that a conversation between Jack of Newbery and Henry VIII led to a change in England's foreign policy. Deloney proclaimed that he treated material neglected by other writers: the "long hidden History" of the "most worthy Clothiers" of England. As we have seen, this claim was also made in secret histories and other popular historical forms, and Deloney's use of the word "compile" in his defense of the work's style suggests that he assembled the work from gossip and similar sources in the manner of a popular historian like Crouch or Gough.[30] But although Jack of Newbery was an actual

---

28 Jonathan V. Crewe, *Unredeemed Rhetoric: Thomas Nashe and the Scandal of Authorship* (Baltimore: Johns Hopkins University Press, 1982), 68. Wells argues that Nashe's model is the jest book; *Thomas Nashe*, 14.

29 Weimann, "Crisis of the 'Universall Consideration'," 16.

30 Deloney claims he wrote "in a plaine and humble manner, that it may be the better understood

clothier of the Henrician period, the roots of Deloney's text in jest books and popular tales was if anything probably clearer to his early modern readers than it is to us.[31] Thus Deloney's texts like Nashe's were "histories" rather than histories because they overtly signaled their fictionality even as they claimed to be historical. The attributive "pleasant," particularly, indicated to Deloney's readers that these texts were fanciful renderings of vaguely historical events.[32] Deloney's texts were neither proffered to readers nor read by them as genuine histories; they remained very much within fictional discourse, requiring little if any reorientation on the part of readers. Indeed, Paul Salzman argues that despite their popularity they exerted almost no influence over subsequent writers: "the most interesting and original fiction of the seventeenth century owed nothing at all to Deloney's attempt to shape a new form."[33]

If Deloney's "pleasant histories" forced no fundamental reorientation upon readers at the beginning of the seventeenth century neither did the works of Behn and Manley at the end of the seventeenth and the beginning of the eighteenth centuries. Behn's most famous work of prose fiction, *Oroonoko* (1688), tells the story of an African prince whose regal qualities shine through even when he is enslaved and transported to Surinam. After leading a slave revolt, Oroonoko is brutally executed; his death is described in a manner reminiscent of Nashe's treatment of the death of Cutwolfe.[34] The narrator of *Oroonoko* declares to her readers that this work is literally true: "I do not pretend, in giving you the history of this royal slave, to entertain my reader with the adventures of a feign'd hero"; rather, she relates her own experience: "I was my self an eye-witness to a great part of what you will find here set down; and what I cou'd not be witness of, I receiv'd from the mouth of the chief actor in this history, the hero himself, who gave us the whole transactions of his youth."[35]

of those for whose sake I took pains to compile it"; Thomas Deloney, *Jack of Newbery*, in *Shorter Novels*, I, 3.

31 Baker, *History of the English Novel*, II, 174–75. See, for example, the incident reported in chapter 7 of *Jack of Newbery* in which an Italian merchant, "greatly inamoured" of one of Jack's young serving girls, is tricked into making love to a sow and thereby taught a lesson; this incident is replete with comic dialogue in broken English ("bee Gossen I tinke you play the knave wid me, and me wil be revenge be Got"); II, 55–62. On the jest books, see F. P. Wilson, "The English Jestbooks of the Sixteenth and Early Seventeenth Centuries," *Huntington Library Quarterly* 2 (1938–39), 121–58.

32 Examples of works published around this time in which the word "pleasant" signals the fictive character of the texts include A. M., *The Honorable, pleasant and rare conceited Historie of Palmendos . . .* (London, 1589), and the pleasant histories in Roger Thomson, ed., *Samuel Pepys' Penny Merriments . . .* (New York: Columbia University Press, 1977). On these pleasant histories, see Spufford, *Small Books and Pleasant Histories*, 219–57; at 238, Spufford classifies Deloney's texts as "realistic novels."

33 Salzman, *English Prose Fiction*, 109 and chapter 9.

34 Aphra Behn, *Oroonoko: or, The Royal Slave. A True History*, in *Shorter Novels*, II, 222–23.

35 *Ibid.*, II, 147.

As a result of these claims, Behn's work has inspired more comment about whether it should be regarded as based on fact than all the other texts presented to readers as "history" in the century before Defoe wrote his most famous narratives. The debate over the factuality or fictionality of *Oroonoko* was in part inspired by Behn's striking description of the principal setting of *Oroonoko*, not unlike Defoe's rendering of Robinson Crusoe's island:

> 'tis there eternal Spring, always the very Months of *April, May,* and *June;* the Shades are perpetual, the Trees bearing at once all degrees of Leaves and Fruit, from blooming Buds to ripe Autumn: Groves of Oranges, Lemons, Citrons Figs, Nutmegs, and noble Aromaticks, continually bearing their Fragrancies. The Trees appearing all like Nosegays adorn'd with Flowers . . . The very Meat we eat, when set on the Table, if it be native, I mean of the Country, perfumes the whole Room; especially a little Beast call'd an *Armadilly*.[36]

As a result of such passages, Behn's biography has figured prominently in the critical commentary on this work: did she go to Surinam? did she know William Byam (a British official in Surinam and an important character in the text)? did she encounter slaves such as the text describes?[37] The case might be made, therefore, that Behn's blend of fact and fiction in *Oroonoko* makes it a precursor of *Robinson Crusoe* and consequently that this work merits Behn the title of "mother" of the novel. Yet criticism of this work has consistently agreed on the romantic character of crucial elements of the text: "Even those who accept the (partial) authenticity of the Surinam scenes are likely to dismiss the African background and the character of the hero as far-fetched romance."[38] This way of viewing *Oroonoko* was, in fact, elicited by Behn who, in introducing her fiction to her readers in the *Epistle Dedicatory* to her collected works, declared: "A Poet is a Painter in his way; he draws to the life, but in another kind; we draw the Nobler Part, the Soul and the Mind." It is true that Behn excuses the "Romantick" elements in *Oroonoko* by pointing to the strangeness of the tropical lands where the story is set, but her identification of herself as a "Poet" who "draw[s] the Nobler part" of her characters clearly invites her readers to read *Oroonoko* as a work of fiction in the Sidneian mold.[39]

Oroonoko is systematically idealized: he "had nothing of Barbarity in his Nature . . . as if his Education had been in some *European* Court";

---

[36] *Ibid.*, II, 194–95; a similar passage from *Robinson Crusoe* is discussed in chapter 9 below.

[37] On this debate, see Katharine M. Rogers, "Fact and Fiction in Aphra Behn's *Oroonoko*," *Studies in the Novel* 20 (1988–89), 1–15; also see Spencer, *Rise of the Woman Novelist*, 47.

[38] Rogers, "Fact or Fiction," 3. See also Allen, *English Novel*, 20; Baker, *History of the English Novel*, III, 89–90; Spencer, *Rise of the Woman Novelist*, 48.

[39] *The Histories and Novels of the Late Ingenious Mrs. Behn* (London, 1696), sig. A₃r, A₅v–A₆r. Sidney had argued that the poet represents not what is but "the divine consideration of what may be or should be"; *Apology for Poetry*, 102.

courting his beloved ("the fair Imoinda"), "he omitted saying nothing to this young Maid, that might persuade her to suffer him to . . . take the Rights of Love"; and in battle "he appear'd like some Divine Power descended to save his Country from Destruction . . . and did such things as will not be believed that Human Strength could perform."[40] This is a protagonist out of heroic drama or a French heroic romance. In fact Vita Sackville-West asserted "Oroonoko resembles those seventeenth-century paintings of negroes in plumes and satins, rather than an actual slave on a practical plantation," and judged, therefore, that Behn "could not wholly escape from [the French romance] 'Le Grand Cyrus'" in writing her most famous composition.[41] Despite its putative roots in Behn's own experience, *Oroonoko* situates itself within the discourse of fiction that putatively opposed itself to romance and asked to be read as history but that did not in fact either constitute a fundamentally new way of writing "history" or represent a real break with romance. Behn's most famous work, therefore, cannot be said to have constituted an originary moment for the history of the novel in English.[42]

For essentially the same reasons, it seems incorrect to argue that Behn's epistolary fiction *Love Letters Between a Nobleman and His Sister* was the "first English novel." Taking issue with this assertion need not arise – as some have suggested – either from a desire to keep "lewd trash" out of the canon or from a conviction that only stories of feminine virtue (not the scandalous narratives of Behn) should be identified with the emerging novel.[43] If the novel was a new form of discourse or a new way of knowing that depended upon the redefinition of fiction in relationship to history, then Behn's *Love Letters* fails to qualify as the first novel since it was so obviously akin to "the romances and scandal novels" of Behn's day. Judith Kegan Gardner's argument that we learn interesting things about the novel by reforming the

---

[40] Behn, *Oroonoko*, II, 153, 156, 169, 176.

[41] Cited, approvingly, in MacCarthy, *Women Writers*, 182.

[42] Frederick Link mounts an argument for Behn's originality and her importance to the rise of the novel, but he cannot deny that Behn's text remained within the discourse of romance in a way that Defoe's did not:

> Defoe . . . did not originate the technique of circumstantial detail for which he is best known, but merely refined and extended it. The difficulty Mrs. Behn has comes from trying to fit an *essentially romantic story* into a realistic mold; *Moll Flanders* is often improbable, but it is not romantic, and therefore it is more successful.   [emphasis added]

Frederick M. Link, *Aphra Behn* (New York: Twayne, 1968), 139; see also McKeon, *Origins*, 112. For our purposes, the point is not whether *Oroonoko* is more or less "successful" than *Moll*, but whether Behn's fiction is qualitatively different from Defoe's fiction as a work of "history."

[43] Judith Kegan Gardner, "The First English Novel: Aphra Behn's *Love Letters*, The Canon, and Women's Tastes," *Tulsa Studies in Women's Literature* 8 (1985), 201; it is Gardner herself who labels Behn's "novel" "a rather wonderful piece of lewd trash." Perhaps her comment is designed to emphasize the degree to which her argument necessitates one's "reimagining the [novel's] form as well as its history" (204).

English canon of novels with *Love Letters* as the initiating work is instructive, but if we are to conceive of a single work as having originary force there has to have been something about its appearance that seemed revolutionary to contemporary readers.[44] No such response is apparent in respect to any of Behn's works; readers seem to have assimilated them easily to the fictional traditions of the day.[45]

Manley's secret histories also laid claim to being read as histories by eighteenth-century readers while at the same time revealing their fictive character. *The New Atalantis* (1709) was presented to readers as a manuscript of uncertain provenance translated first from Italian into French and then from French into English, but the narrative begins "Once upon a time . . ." and relates an earthly visitation of Astrea, the goddess of Justice and daughter of Zeus, who is guided on the earth by Intelligence.[46] Thus, the work functioned as an allegory as well as a secret history akin to the "fictional memoirs" of Mme. d'Aulnoy and Bussy-Rabutin, and indeed like the latter's secret history, *New Atalantis*, it represented the corruption of the despised Whig politicians in and around the English court so blatantly that Manley and her publisher were arrested shortly after the publication of the second part of the work.[47] Defoe, of course, defended *Robinson Crusoe* as "Allegorick History," but the difference between *Atalantis* and *Crusoe* is that the latter text was presented to its early readers as a veracious account, gave its readers reasons aplenty for so reading it, and was initially read as such by a significant number of readers. *Atalantis*, by contrast, reveled in its fictionality; John Richetti argues that the work was "designed for diversion" and "presented . . . an erotically exciting and glittering fantasy world of aristocratic corruption and promiscuity . . . [that] was, in the long run,

44 *Ibid.*, 217–19.
45 The *Biographia Britannica* asserts that both *Oroonoko* and *The Fair Jilt* are "true stories" but nevertheless unequivocally identifies them as "novels"; I, 665. Compare that approach to Behn with the tortured history of the reception of Defoe's "novels," discussed in chapter 10 below.
46 Delarivier Manley, *New Atalantis*, ed. Rosalind Ballaster (London: Penguin, 1991), 1, 4.
47 *Ibid.*, vii. Davis's argument that the "overtly fictional" nature of Manley's texts was due in part to actual and potential legal difficulties is insightful, especially when read in light of his claim that changes in the English libel laws in the early eighteenth century "made it more difficult for narratives to rest in some grey area between fact and fiction"; *Factual Fictions*, 121, 95. Unfortunately for Davis's argument, the chronology does not always support his view of things. The important legal revision took place in 1724; *Robinson Crusoe*, which brought the fact-fiction dispute to at least one important point, was published five years earlier. Perhaps fiction anticipated politico-legal developments; John Bender and Armstrong argue this view of the novel in respect to the discourse of the prison, and "a modern, gendered form of subjectivity [that] developed first as a feminine discourse" respectively. John Bender, *Imagining the Penitentiary*, 1; Armstrong, *Desire and Domestic Fiction*, 14. Or perhaps the legal revision of 1724 was part of a general rethinking of the fact/fiction boundary that altered the nature of both historical and fictional discourse. The emergence of the novel after 1724 is a key part of this larger rethinking.

more important in making the book popular than the specific scandals and libels" alluded to by the author.[48]

An earlier work by Manley, *The Secret History of Queen Zarah, and the Zarazians* (1705) was one of a number of texts (*Incognita* was another) in this period that defended "little histories" and argued their superiority to romance but at the same time flaunted their fictionality and even their debt to the romance form. McKeon argues convincingly that such arguments constituted a version of the claim that a given fiction was in fact "history":

Modern scholars usually treat the romance parody of the discovered manuscript topos as a critique of the claim to historicity. But it is better understood instead as an implicit instance of that claim, the most conventional means by which "modern" romance becomes conscious and skeptical of its own customary conflation of "history" and "romance."

Whether an instance of an actual claim to historicity or a critique of that claim, however, the assertion, according to McKeon, was an evident figure of speech, and the truth of Manley's texts, was "that not of strict historicity but of the historical fruit which stands revealed once we have stripped away the mediating chaff of 'romance'."[49] But the "chaff" of romance sets Manley's secret histories distinctly apart from those of Crouch, Burnet, or Hamilton; Manley's *romans à clef* are assertively fictive even though they relentlessly refer the reader to the corrupt reality they seek to expose.[50]

Thus, all of the authors under discussion here invoked the claim to historicity but presented texts to readers that remained squarely within the fictional discourse of seventeenth-century England; in these texts one finds no confrontation with readerly expectations engendered by the narratives being read. Nor does one discover a subsequent fundamental reshaping of the horizon of expectations in respect to possible kinds of narratives in the history of the reception of those texts. Much the same thing might be said about the political-allegorical romances of the seventeenth century presented to readers as "new," "serious" forms of romance and describing and commenting upon contemporary historical reality. The fact that a work like John Barclay's *Argenis* (1621) clearly functioned as a "fictionalized account of European history . . . in the guise of a Heliodoran romance" and was understood as such by Barclay's readers meant that as a work of fiction it revised the theory of romance rather than theorized a new fictional form.[51] Similarly, among the antiromancers from Nashe to

---

[48] Richetti, *Popular Fiction*, 123–24.   [49] McKeon, *Origins*, 56, 59, 60.
[50] Ballaster, ed., *New Atalantis*, vii; see also, McKeon, *Origins*, 56, 60.
[51] Annabel Patterson, *Censorship and Interpretation: The Conditions of Writing and Reading in Early Modern England* (Madison: University of Wisconsin Press, 1984), 160, 180, 184; see also Salzman, *English Prose Fiction*, chapter 11.

Manley the flight from fiction remained a critique of romance that failed to posit anything fundamentally new.

By contrast, Defoe's claims were, and therefore are, of a very different order from those of the writers of "history" discussed above. To be sure, Defoe's assertions that his most famous narratives were histories have also generally been read figuratively. This is Barbara Foley's point when she argues, first, that early examples of what she calls "pseudofactual" fictions did not elide the difference between history and fiction but "hovered around the borderline" between the two in order to argue for a different kind of fiction, and, second, that in the case of a Defoe "pseudofactual imposture of veracious discourse signaled invocation of a [new] mimetic contract."[52] In other words, Defoe used the claim to historicity in such a way as to effectively create what Foley calls the pseudofactual novel. Yet I will argue that no such mimetic contract was in fact invoked by Defoe and no such contract was understood by his early readers, although in the case of *Robinson Crusoe* such a contract was, as it were, attached to the text shortly after its appearance. What sets Defoe apart from Nashe, Deloney, Behn, and Manley (and also from those who followed him like Haywood, Richardson, Fielding, and Burney) is that while the texts of those writers invoked "fictional contracts" of one sort or another, Defoe's most famous narratives did not.[53] Defoe presented his texts to readers as works of history and only gradually and very problematically were they read into the tradition of the novel; unlike the "histories" that preceded them, therefore, Defoe's narratives did represent a genuine challenge to both narrative taxonomies and readerly expectations. This far from uncontroversial claim will be substantiated in the next three chapters; for the moment I state it only to indicate why I give such short shrift to Defoe's forebears from the late sixteenth through the early eighteenth century. The key figure in this study is Defoe because he and only he wrote works that could be, and at first were, read as histories, that later were read as fictions, and, most paradoxically, that sometimes have been read as both.

III

In a compelling essay on the "elevation" of the English novel in the eighteenth century, William B. Warner argues that scholarship on the

[52] Foley, *Telling the Truth*, 112, 118.

[53] Foley implicitly acknowledges this; she claims that in *The Unfortunate Traveller* Nashe was "breaking new ground" in respect to the subject matter of fiction, and, similarly, that Mme. d'Aulnoy sought in *The Lady ———Travels* (1691) "to expand the province of epistolary fiction." In respect to Defoe's *Journal of the Plague Year*, however, Foley asserts that the text "is essentially a lie" because "it is intended . . . to be read as . . . a historical document." Nevertheless, Foley does not consider the possibility that Defoe's narrative should be regarded as a species of historical discourse; *Telling the Truth*, 115, 116, 119.

novel has been shaped not just by sexist critics more or less incapable of taking women writers seriously, but more fundamentally by an originary "hegemonic articulatory 'moment'" controlled by the "fathers" of the novel, Richardson and Fielding, which resulted in the identification of the "novel of amorous intrigue" written by Behn, Manley, and Haywood not as "a legitimate precursor" but as "the alternative in popular entertainment that . . . [was] put out of play by ethically-enlightened novels." Warner claims that "the contingent decision" to denominate the works of Richardson and Fielding as "novels" is open to "appeal and repeal," that it is "a decision still undergoing review," but he also argues that the hegemonic move by the male novelists of the 1740s stood more or less unchallenged until Hardy and Lawrence argued for a more honest treatment of love and sex in the novel, and he points out too that the principal accounts of the novel's rise written in the last ten years have not significantly altered the literary historical picture.[54]

Despite Warner's assertion that the effects of Richardson and Fielding's maneuver can be reversed, the continued slighting of fiction of "amorous intrigue" is not surprising since the logic of Warner's argument dictates that not only the history of novelistic criticism but also the history of novel-writing itself has unfolded in the wake of the original hegemonic move of the male writers of the 1740s. That is, after the 1740s there are women novelists aplenty, but even those who celebrate the writers of "amatory fiction" – most famously, Virginia Woolf on Aphra Behn – have nevertheless written under the aegis of the eighteenth-century "fathers" of the novel and not that of the "mothers." The inescapable fact of the history of the English novel is that the so-called "novel of amorous intrigue" has been marginalized for two-and-a-half centuries, and no amount of criticism will change that. Paula Backscheider has argued compellingly that Defoe's *Roxana* is fundamentally different from his other narratives because in it he appropriates important elements of the "woman's novel," and Jane Spencer has pointed out that Richardson "was following a long tradition of epistolary fiction, much of it written by women, and his achievement owed much to cultural definitions of feminine writing and to the traditions established by women writers."[55] Thus one could argue that the writers who are seen as inaugurating and establishing a kind of imperial suzerainty over the novel may be said to have *both* appropriated certain features of the "woman's novel" and at the same time marginalized that form, but in any case the works of Behn and Manley *were* marginalized and the subsequent

---

[54] William B. Warner, "The Elevation of the Novel in England: Hegemony and Literary History," *ELH* 59 (1992), 579, 581, 578, 593, 594, n. 1.

[55] Paula Backscheider, "The Genesis of *Roxana*," *The Eighteenth Century: Theory and Interpretation* 27 (1986), 211; Spencer, *Rise of the Woman Novelist*, 89.

history of novel-writing and theorizing the novel unfolded in the wake of that move.

More important for purposes of this study, however, Warner also argues that Fielding and Richardson drew a line of "cultural legitimacy" on one side of which there lay the amorous novel and on the other side of which lay "the new species of . . . writing, consistently tagged by Richardson and Fielding with the term 'history'."[56] As we have seen, however, Behn and Manley also presented their fictions as works of "history." Thus the struggle to define the new form of fiction was like the struggle over the right to invoke the word "history" that we noted in contests between contending historians like Heylyn and Fuller or Nalson and Rushworth. In each case legitimacy consisted of being able to lay claim to the label that suggested the text's participation in this almost hallowed discourse. Behn and Manley had presented their various works as histories and in losing out to Richardson and Fielding they effectively lost the right to have those claims taken seriously. At the very least, then, Warner's "hegemonic moment" serves to underline the fact that the long process of elaborating a discourse of the novel in English consisted, in important part, of the process of describing and theorizing the complicated and difficult-to-specify link between historical discourse and the new literary form that came to be called "novel."

Perhaps understanding that process may help us to grasp the ongoing review of Fielding and Richardson's literary coup de grace; the "histories" of the antiromancers of both genders constituted prenovelistic critiques of romance that never escaped from the fictional discourse they sought to criticize. Defoe provided the basis for a new fictional form by producing works that he presented as legitimate histories for reasons that readers frequently found convincing; Defoe's narratives were not so much situated by the author in a new fictional discourse as they were ultimately read into the discourse of the novel by readers. In thus focusing on Defoe do we thereby pronounce him *the* father of the novel? Decidedly not. Defoe's narratives have never been easily situated within the canon of English novels; they are too strange finally to be identified as *the* originary moment in the history of the novel. Scott, for example, left not only Behn and Manley (and even Burney) but also Defoe out of the first edition of the *Lives of the Novelists*, and the many critics who have branded Defoe a "liar" have implicitly argued, as Davis asserts, that Defoe's "works remain odd to us because they seem not fully novels."[57] What our attention to Defoe does is to establish the debate over the link to historical discourse as a key to understanding the emergence of the novel in early modern England and to demonstrate that that debate was a multivocal dialogue in which no writers

---

[56] Warner, "Elevation of the Novel," 582.   [57] Davis, *Factual Fictions*, 155.

can be said to have played so crucial a role as to exclude any other writers. A proper history of the novel can only be written when we begin to stipulate how the "amatory fiction" of Behn and Manley and the "new species of writing" of Richardson and Fielding – both forms of "history" – fused in the emerging discourse of the novel. That work, however, lies beyond the scope of the present study which aims simply to demonstrate the degree to which and the way in which history was the matrix of that emergent discourse.[58]

From Sidney onward, the debate over fiction focused on the relationship between fiction and history, and increasingly seventeenth-century fiction writers insisted on the historical nature of their texts. Defoe joined that debate obliquely, writing texts that were presented to readers, and read by them, as history. Baconian historiography habituated Defoe to using fiction as a means of historical representation and habituated readers to accepting fiction within historical discourse. Thus Defoe wrote histories that were read into the tradition of the novel; antiromantic writers from Nashe to Manley wrote "histories" that never constituted a clear break with romance and tended until very recently to be read as something other than novels. Unlike the "histories" before *Robinson Crusoe*, Defoe's texts marked a crucial moment before which the novel did not exist but after which it became possible. To that career and to that crucial moment, we now turn.

[58] Armstrong's study, in which she argues that the novel transformed the domestic sphere into a new locus of power and that "domestic fiction could represent an alternative form of political power," is as close as we have yet come to this dimension of the history and theory of the novel; *Desire and Domestic Fiction*, 29.

8

Defoe's historical practice: from "The Ages Humble Servant" to Major Alexander Ramkins

Although in recent years John Robert Moore's landmark *Checklist of the Writings of Daniel Defoe* (1960) has been cast into a very doubtful light, it provided what was for some time regarded as a reasonably reliable account of what Defoe wrote and when. The publication of *The Canonisation of Daniel Defoe* (1988) by P. N. Furbank and W. R. Owens, however, has more or less definitively problematized that list, especially since Furbank and Owens simply enunciated at length and systematized doubts that had already been voiced about Moore's *Checklist.*[1] The question of what is to be done in Defoe scholarship, however, remains to be answered.

Furbank and Owens are preparing their own, presumably much scaled down, list of Defoe's writings, but the appearance of that work will undoubtedly be only the beginning of a long debate in which other scholars will insist on additional attributions, and all of those arguments will have to be assessed by yet other scholars.[2] In the meantime, discussion of Defoe proceeds. If, however, one looks at the problem of the Defoe canon and its relationship to the study of the early English novel from a Foucauldian perspective, the problem seems less serious than it otherwise might. Foucault has challenged our automatic resort to the concept of "author" and recommended instead that we describe and analyze discursive formations instead of focusing on writers, careers, or bodies of work; for Foucault, "the function of an author is to characterize the existence, circulation, and operation of certain discourses within a society."[3] And in a way "Daniel Defoe" has always been something of a covering term for a particular way of writing and, to be more specific, a particular variant of

---

[1] P. N. Furbank and W. R. Owens, *The Canonisation of Daniel Defoe* (New Haven: Yale University Press, 1988). For earlier quarrels with the Moore list, see Rodney M. Baine, *Daniel Defoe and the Supernatural* (Athens: University of Georgia Press, 1968), 137; John Richetti, *Defoe's Narratives: Situations and Structures* (Oxford: Clarendon Press, 1975), 1–2.

[2] A negative version of the new list has appeared; see Furbank and Owens, *Defoe De-Attributions: A Critique of J. R. Moore's Checklist* (London: Hambledon, 1994).

[3] Michel Foucault, "What is an Author?" *Language, Counter-Memory, Practice: Selected Essays and Interviews*, ed. Donald F. Bouchard, trans. Bouchard and Sherry Simon (Ithaca: Cornell University Press, 1977), 124; for the original French, see *Dits et écrits*, I, 798. See also Foucault, *Archaeology of Knowledge*, 92–96; *L'archéologie du savoir*, 121–26.

Baconian historiography. Furbank and Owens acknowledge, for example, that *A True Account of the Proceedings at Perth* was attached to the Defoe canon largely because it belonged to "a genre at which Defoe was an adept": a fictionalized account of historical events told from the perspective of an informed insider and written with a clear political end in view.[4] Similarly, Paula Backscheider discusses the *Minutes of the Negotiations of Monsr. Mesnager*, the histories of Charles XII, *Memoirs of a Cavalier*, and *An Impartial History of Peter*, all attributed to Defoe, as works that came out of a particular political "milieu," and she likewise treats the *True Account*, the *Minutes*, and the *Memoirs of Alexander Ramkins* as a group of Defoe's "fictions designed to discourage Jacobitism."[5]

It is possible, therefore, to set aside the question of what Defoe actually wrote and discuss instead the discursive formations – history and novel – in which "his works" participated, without undermining the Defoe scholarship that for more than a generation has been predicated on the dubious attributions of Moore and his bibliographical forebears. "Defoe," then, may serve as an organizing principle for examining those discourses, and even, quite plausibly, as an example of what Foucault calls an "initiator of discursive practice."[6] Some of the works discussed below were indisputably by Defoe, some were more than likely written by him, some may well have been written by him but will never be attributed to him with certainty, some were undoubtedly attributed to him incorrectly because they resemble other works more confidently associated with Defoe, and some will probably always be contested. In the absence, then, of a satisfactory, stable alternative to Moore, one can still use Defoe as a vehicle for describing a variant of Baconian historiography that is crucial to an understanding of the role Defoe's most important narratives played in the elaboration of the discourse of the novel in English.[7] Whichever list of Defoe's writings one uses, it seems clear that beginning around the year

4   Furbank and Owens, "*A True Account of the Proceedings at Perth*: The Impact of an Historical Novel," *Eighteenth-Century Fiction* 6 (1993–94), 239.
5   Paula Backscheider, *Daniel Defoe: Ambition and Innovation* (Lexington: University Press of Kentucky, 1987), 97; Backscheider, *Daniel Defoe: His Life*, 442.
6   Foucault, *Language, Counter-Memory, Practice*, 131; *Dits et écrits*, i, 804.
7   An earlier version of the present argument about Defoe's historical works was first conceived before the appearance of Furbank and Owens's *Canonisation*; that version was thoroughly reworked before the appearance of *De-Attributions*. The present argument *could* be made using only works they have thus far not challenged. (Even they do not contest the attribution of *The Storm*, the *Minutes of Monsr. Mesnager*, the *History of Discoveries and Improvements*, and [except for the *Secret History of One Year*] the various secret histories. What is more, they acknowledge some evidence for believing that Defoe wrote some of the works they challenge [*Memoirs of John, Duke of Melfort*, *Memoirs of the Church of Scotland*]; see *De-Attributions*, 63–64, 131–32.) My study of Defoe's history is left in its present state both because it seems likely that the Defoe canon will be contested terrain for some time to come even if Furbank and Owens occupy the high ground for the foreseeable future and because the present study focuses more on "the operation of a certain discourse" than on the production of particular works by Defoe or anyone else.

1710, he began to produce a number of works that were presented to readers as works of history.[8] This is not surprising since his extensive written work on behalf of the union of England and Scotland frequently took the form of historical argument and in fact climaxed with the *History of the Union* in 1709.[9] His advocacy of the union must have taught him a good deal about the efficacy of historical argument as a means of persuasion.[10] Although the discussion of Defoe's histories will begin with *The Storm* (1703), this chapter will focus on histories assigned to Defoe from the years 1709–19.

Defoe was a consummate Baconian historian, a recorder of matters of fact but also a writer who plainly believed that fiction could be a legitimate strategy of historical representation, and who saw historiography as a means to an end despite a theoretical commitment to impartiality. Early in his career as a historian, Defoe published a collection of reports somewhat in the manner of the antiquarians, but he gradually came to rely almost exclusively upon long and detailed narratives as the chief tool of the historian, and at the same time he came increasingly to use a fictionalized narrator in his historical texts. Defoe's use of a fictionalized narrator is more or less unique in Baconian historiography, although if Defoe did not write, for example, the *True Account of the Proceedings at Perth* and the histories of Charles XII and Peter the Great, the practice would seem to have been reasonably widespread in his day. Furthermore, since the discourse of history in England at the end of the seventeenth century featured a marked tolerance for elements of fiction within historical texts, and since readers of history were accustomed to encountering putatively historical works the historicity or fictionality of which was open to question, Defoe's practice was within the bounds of the rules governing historical discourse in England at the beginning of the eighteenth century.

Nevertheless, as we shall see, Defoe's historical practice forces the fact-fiction dilemma upon the reader to a degree not seen elsewhere in this study of early modern historical practice. Defoe's practice, therefore, is particularly useful in stipulating how the horizon of expectations against which *Robinson Crusoe* appeared in 1719 illuminates the historical claims of

---

[8]   On Defoe's interest in history throughout his career, see Moore, *Daniel Defoe: Citizen of the World* (University of Chicago Press, 1958), 254–73; Raymond Klopsch, "Daniel Defoe as a Historian" (Dissertation, University of Illinois, 1962), 2–5; Backscheider, *Ambition and Innovation*, 72. I treat nothing as history in this chapter that does not properly belong to the discourse of history as defined in preceding chapters. In considering Defoe as a historian, I have included among his historical works the "histories," "historical accounts," "lives," "secret histories," "true accounts," "essays on history," "memoirs," "journals," "annals," "secret memoirs," "minutes," and "true relations" and "narrations" attributed to Defoe.

[9]   Backscheider, *Life*, 209; Moore, *Citizen of the World*, 176–77, 182–87.

[10] See, for example, *Caledonia: A Poem in Honour of Scotland and the Scots Nation* (1706) and *An Essay at Removing National Prejudices Against a Union with Scotland*, part 1 (1706).

Crusoe and Defoe's other contributions to the discourse of the novel. In this chapter, Defoe's historical practice will be examined; in the next chapter we will see how that practice makes explicable Defoe's claims that those texts we read as novels were, as he saw it, "just histories."

I

Defoe's first major historical work, *The Storm*, was a self-consciously "scientific" effort in which the narrator praises Bacon as an exemplary philosopher.[11] Essentially a collection of "documents" (some of which first appeared in the *Philosophical Transactions*) containing personal testimony on the course and effects of a storm that hit England in the fall of 1703, and therefore part of the "antiquarian enterprise," this early work by Defoe contains a definition of history that is not dissimilar to that delineated by Camden in the *Annals of Elizabeth*.[12] Also, subsequent remarks by Defoe in a variety of historical texts suggest that the "scientific" method of *The Storm* was always an important element in his historical practice.

The author of *The Storm* styles himself "The Ages Humble Servant" and declares that "the proper Duty of an Historian" is "to set everything in its own Light, and to convey matter of fact upon its legitimate Authority." This assertion is echoed in the *Memoirs of the Church of Scotland* (1717), where the author assures his readers, "I have endeavoured carefully to adhere to Truth of Fact."[13] Thus Defoe argues both that the function of history is the provision of matters of fact and that "facts" have to be established and criticized by the historian for his readers. Again in *The Storm*, he declares: "where a Story is vouch'd to him with sufficient Authority, he ought to give the World the special Testimonial of its proper Voucher, or else he is not

---

11 *The Storm: or, A Collection of the Most Remarkable Casualties and Disasters which happen'd in the Late* DREADFUL *Tempest, Both by Sea and Land* (London, 1704), 4 and 9. Defoe also referred to Bacon in other works as well, most notably *A General History of Discoveries and Improvements In Useful Arts* (London, 1726–27), 238. For a discussion of Defoe's intellectual debt to Bacon, see Robert James Merrett, *Daniel Defoe's Moral and Rhetorical Ideas* (Victoria, BC: English Literary Studies, University of Victoria, 1980), 9–13, and, especially, Ilse Vickers, "The Influence of the New Sciences on Defoe," *Literature and History* 13 (1987), 208–10. On Defoe's intellectual training, see Lew Girdler, "Defoe's Education at Newington Green Academy," *Studies in Philology*, 50 (1953), 573–91; Vickers, "New Sciences on Defoe," 200–02; and Backscheider, *Life*, 13–20. Webster discusses the pervasive influence of Bacon on the community of dissenters; *The Great Instauration*, 12.

12 *The Storm*, 26–31; Maximillian E. Novak, *Realism, Myth, and History in Defoe's Fiction* (Lincoln and London: University of Nebraska Press, 1983), 53.

13 *The Storm*, sig. A₃v; *Memoirs of the Church of Scotland* (London, 1717), "Preface," n.p. The latter is a history of the Scottish Kirk that drew upon the best historical accounts of Defoe's day, including Burnet's authoritative *History of the Reformation*. See also the *Review*, in which Defoe promised "a diligent Enquiry after Truth, and laying before the World the Naked Prospect of Fact, as it really is," and tells us that the "Matter of our Account will be real History, and just Observation"; *Defoe's Review*, 22 Facsimile Books, introd. and notes, A. W. Secord (New York: Facsimile Text Society; Columbia University Press, 1938), I, 2–3.

just to the Story: and where it comes without sufficient Authority, he [the historian] ought to say so; otherwise he is not just to himself." Citing the examples of Daedalus and Arthur, Defoe cautions readers that unwarranted credulity on the part of the historian transforms what might otherwise be history into romance: "Matters of Fact are [sometimes] handed down to Posterity with so little Certainty, that nothing is to be depended upon." In the case of *The Storm*, however, "tho' some Things here related shall have equal Wonder due to them, Posterity shall not have equal Occasion to distrust the Verity of the Relation."[14] "The Ages Humble Servant," then, reports wonders and marvels, but they can reliably be read as matters of fact, and the author of the *Memoirs of the Church of Scotland* similarly claims that he has "applied himself . . . by just *Authorities* . . . to make himself sufficiently Master of the Matters of Fact." From *The Storm* to *A General History of the Pyrates* (1724–28) Defoe made extensive use of documents to establish the authority of his historical texts. The various histories of Charles XII, for example, depended heavily upon extracts from treaties, letters, and proclamations and the text signed by Mesnager consists of the kind of "documents" one finds in secret history, the author's own "minutes" of conversations with powerful individuals in England and France.[15]

Yet *The Storm* is hardly *Britannia*; rather, it is a typical example of Baconian historiography in which elements of the "scientific" methodology of the new history are employed in the creation of a work that depends heavily upon narrative and is intended to have popular appeal. The "documents" that "The Ages Humble Servant" presents to his readers are personal accounts of the storm. One "Relation," for example, reports the effects of the storm,

in a well-built brick House in the skirts of the City; and a Stack of Chimneys falling in upon the next Houses, gave the House such a Shock, that they [the inhabitants] thought it was coming down upon their Heads: but opening the Door to attempt to Escape into a Garden, the Danger was so apparent, that they all thought fit to surrender to the Disposal of Almighty Providence, and expect their Graves in the Ruins of the House, rather than to meet most certain Destruction in the open Garden.[16]

Of the earthquake that some said accompanied the storm, a minister of Hull reported:

---

[14] *The Storm*, sig. A₃v, A₄v, A₅r.

[15] *Church of Scotland*, "The Preface," n.p. On Defoe's use of documents in history, see Klopsch, "Defoe as a Historian," chapter 3. Klopsch argues 63 percent of the *History of the Union* was "primary source material" reproduced in the text; 48–49. See also Backscheider, *Ambition and Innovation*, 73–74.

[16] *The Storm*, 32.

It came with a Noise like that of a Coach in the Streets, and mightily shak'd both the Glass Windows, Pewter, *China Pots* and Dishes, and in some places threw them down off the Shelves . . . [so that] Several Persons thought that a great Dog was got under the Chair they sat upon; and others fell from their Seats, for fear of falling.[17]

Like Gough, the author of *The Storm* is a custodian of public memory, and like Plot and Crouch, he is a compiler of "narrativized" data; his practice constitutes a kind of popularized antiquarianism.

Although *The Storm* was a key work by Defoe that reveals his kinship with other important Baconian historiographers of the late seventeenth and the early eighteenth centuries, in many ways it was not typical of his subsequent historical labors. As a record of one event, it was synchronic rather than diachronic, and as a collection of unrelated pieces of testimony, it lacked a narrative; furthermore, although the use of the anonym, "The Ages Humble Servant," anticipated important aspects of Defoe's use of fiction in his later histories, there was no fictionalized narrator in this text. Still, even though Defoe never again produced a text like *The Storm*, it nevertheless contains his clearest statement of his theoretical view of historical practice and demonstrates that he knew about and embraced, if in the same qualified sense of other Baconian historiographers, the principles of the new history.

The History of the Union (1709) marked a departure from the method of *The Storm*. Defoe's account of the achievement of the union of the two parliaments was an early instance of his commitment to what I shall call the genetic method, which became one of the enduring features of his historical practice. The author of the *History of the Union* promises to trace the origins of the idea of the union back to "the very original of it," so as to reveal "all the several steps which have been taken" that led him to conclude that the Union was "the only harbour the ship of state could safely come to an anchor in."[18] Defoe repeatedly insists upon the need to trace the development of a problem, an institution, an idea, or a person from its beginning; the genetic account, then, was a recurring feature of his historiography.[19] This aspect of his practice is anticipated in *The Storm*, where the author opens by discussing (very much in the manner of a report in the *Philosophical Transactions*) the "Original of Winds" and "the Opinion of the Ancients" on storms in Britain, and also in the *Essay upon Projects* (1697), where Defoe treats "the original of the practice" of projecting.[20]

---

17 *Ibid.*, 34, 231–32.
18 *The History of the Union between England and Scotland, with A Collection of Original Papers Relating Thereto* (London, 1786), 33.
19 When he eschews chronological treatment, he explains himself; see *The Secret History of the October Club. From its Original to this Time. By a Member* (London, 1711), 1–2; and *Memoirs of the Life and Eminent Conduct of that Learned and Reverend Divine, Daniel Williams, D.D.* (London, 1718), 1–2.
20 *The Storm*, 1, 13; for examples of reports and "histories" in the *Philosophical Transactions*, see Sprat, *History of the Royal Society*, 260–61, 277.

In the later works, Defoe describes and defends the genetic method. The author of the *Memoirs of the Church of Scotland*, for example, argues that "To give a true and concise Scheme of the State of this Church, it will be needful to go back to its original Constitution," and *A General History of Discoveries and Improvements* (1726–27) traces developments from antiquity to demonstrate "how much Superior every Generation has been, because Wiser than those who went before them."[21] In *An Essay on the History and Reality of Apparitions* (1727), Defoe indicates what he valued in the genetic method; he observes that hitherto there were two incorrect ways of considering apparitions ("our Ancestors laying too much stress upon them, and the present Age endeavouring wholly to explode and despise them") and argues that an appreciation of these two mistaken approaches provides the basis for a correct understanding of the phenomenon under study.[22] Similarly, the *History of Discoveries and Improvements* explores the flourishing commerce of the ancient inhabitants of the Mediterranean basin and its suppression by various conquerors and concludes that a revival of trade in the area will produce a return of ancient prosperity. For Defoe then, history should begin at the beginning and trace subsequent developments, showing how the present state of affairs has been reached and providing the basis for future action.

In addition to revealing Defoe's genetic method, the *History of the Union* also shows that Defoe was beginning to understand history as a narrative form, although the narrative in that work was thin and often merely interrupted the reproduction of documents. Thus although Backscheider describes the *History* as "a work that . . . fails to project a unified painting worthy of contemplation," she also argues that it shows Defoe "turning away from the attempt to produce unadorned compilations of facts and documents."[23] After the composition of this work, Defoe repeatedly proclaims his faith in the efficacy of narrative in historical representation. In the *Annals of King George, Year the Second* (1717), he promises to spare his readers undue "copy[ing] of publick Papers . . . as such Things are very tiresome to the Reader, and a great Interruption to the Thread of the Story."[24] Raymond Klopsch regrets that "Defoe presents historical events

---

21   *The Earlier Life and the Chief Earlier Works of Daniel Defoe*, ed. H. Morley (New York: Burt Franklin, 1970), 38 and 189; *Church of Scotland*, 6; *Discoveries and Improvements*, 2. The *Review*, offered to readers as an example of "history Inch-by Inch," promises "a compleat History of France, [including] the Antient Part"; *Review*, i, 2.

22   *The Secrets of the Invisible World Disclos'd; or, An Universal History of Apparitions Sacred and Prophane . . . By Andrew Moreton, Esq.* (London, 1729), "Preface," n.p.

23   Backscheider, "Cross-Purposes: Defoe's *History of the Union*," *Clio* 11 (1982), 177. Klopsch shows a declining use of raw data after 1709; "Defoe as a Historian," 49.

24   *The* ANNALS *of King George, Year the Second; Being a Faithful* HISTORY *of the Affairs of Great Britain, For the Year* MDCCXVI. *Containing also a full and compleat History of the Rebellion* (London, 1717), iii–iv.

in a basically chronological sequence" because this "practice . . . causes him to neglect . . . to interrupt his continuity in order to analyze an event," but in fact for Defoe a genetic narrative was a form of explanation and even analysis.[25] In *The Review* he offers periodical "Historical Observations" as a "Compleat History of *France*," asserting that he will present "the genuine History of what happens in the Matters of State and war" because "when Matters are thus laid open . . . Men are easily capable to Judge . . . whereas all the Observations or Reflections I ever yet met with, serve but to Amuse Mankind."[26]

Despite the fact that the *History of the Union* was to some extent Defoe's most significant historical work – it was the only such text that he actually signed and it is still useful today – it would seem that in 1709 Defoe had not yet discovered, at least by his own lights, how to write history effectively.[27] One senses him testing different methods: providential explanation was invoked but not really employed, and a reliance upon documents competed with an expanding role for narrative.[28] Before 1711, furthermore, Defoe seldom used the fictionalized narrators that would later become a standard feature of his historical practice. A short work that appeared in that year suggests that Defoe's historical method was evolving away from both antiquarian method and straightforward (and rather dull) historical narration toward a more compelling way of telling a story. *A Short Narrative of the Life and Actions of His Grace, John, Duke of Marlborough*, signed "By an Old Officer in the Army," was the first of the many military memoirs that Defoe wrote and also the first instance of his use of an invented narrator in a history. The putative author of the *Life* provides the reader with details about the common soldier's experience of Marlborough's campaigns, reminding readers that to understand military men (including the Duke), they must "see them in a Rainy Season, when the whole Country about them is trod into a Chaos, and in such intolerable Marches, Men and Horses dying and dead together, and the best of them glad of a bundle of Straw to lay down their wet and weary Limbs." The "Old Officer" recounts a visit to "my Lord's Appartments" and voices his opinions about the Duke, thereby allowing Defoe to make his complicated

---

[25] Klopsch, "Defoe as a Historian," 9. On narrative as an explanatory device, see A. R. Louch, "History as Narrative," *History and Theory* 8 (1969), 56, 58–59; see also J. R. Hale, *The Evolution of British Historiography* (Cleveland: World, 1964), 20.

[26] *The Review*, I, 2–3. [27] Backscheider, "Cross-Purposes," 181.

[28] The *History of the Union* contained a typical assertion by Defoe of a providential view of history, claiming to show "how Providence has led the nations . . . to see this Treaty" (33). For similar assertions, see also *The Storm*, sig. A₂r–A₃r; *The History of the Wars, of his Present Majesty Charles XII* (London, 1715), "The Preface," n.p.; *The Memoirs of Majr. Alexander Ramkins, A Highland Officer, Now in Prison at AVIGNON* (London, 1719), 85–86. In these works the assertion of the providential direction of history seems more an article of faith than a methodological principle; the texts attend almost exclusively to second causes. Backscheider, "Cross-Purposes," 176–77.

argument about Marlborough. The *Life of Marlborough* anticipates the use of invented narrators in later and more substantial works that were presented as works of contemporary history.[29]

Later works were also presented to readers as the memoirs of old soldiers; *The History of the Wars, of His Present Majesty Charles XII* was signed by "a SCOTS Gentleman in the SWEEDISH Service," although little use was made of this invented author except to excuse lacunae in the narrative on the basis of putative gaps in the experiences of the narrator.[30] Similarly, the anonymous author of the *Annals of King George* informs his readers that the text derives from an insider's knowledge of events and promises secret, never before published information.[31] These works drew heavily upon journalistic accounts of military campaigns but no matter how rich they were in matters of fact, they were presented as if written by men who served the monarch in question.[32] Thus, although they have generally been read as examples of historical discourse, they might equally well be regarded as works of fiction. Interestingly, although some critics have treated the works with fictionalized narrators as works of history and others have declared them to be historical novels, both camps seem determined to regard the classification of these texts as a relatively uncomplicated business.[33]

James Sutherland shows that Defoe used fictionalized authorial voices like the "Old Officer" in his political pamphlets, specifically in *The Poor Man's Plea* (1698) which marks the first "use of a persona [that] was genuinely integrated with the argument and affected the presentation of

---

[29] *A Short Narrative of the Life and Actions of His Grace, JOHN, Duke of Marlborough, From the Beginning of the REVOLUTION, to this present Time, with some Remarks on his Conduct By an Old Officer in the Army* (1711), Augustan Reprint Soc. Pub. No. 168, ed. Backscheider (Los Angeles: William Andrews Clark Memorial Library, 1974), 41, 11, ix; Klopsch, "Defoe as a Historian," 45–48, 81–95; Backscheider, *Ambition and Innovation*, 89–106. It might be argued that the *Life* was not a history at all but a political pamphlet since it evidently aimed more at defending Robert Harley than at examining the life of the duke, but the text was a narrative of events in the life of the general; its having a clear political agenda hardly disqualifies it from being classed as a work of Baconian historiography.

[30] Both the 1715 and the 1720 histories of Charles XII and *An Impartial History of the Life and Actions of Peter Alexowitz the Present Czar of Muscovy* (London, 1723) were historical narratives presented to the reader within fictional frames.

[31] *Annals of King George*, iii.

[32] Klopsch shows that Defoe used the *Present State of Europe* in constructing these works; "Defoe as a Historian," 64, 80–81, and 94.

[33] Furbank and Owens admit that *A True Account* was "accepted as true history" by a large number of readers, some of whom acknowledged Defoe to be the author. However, having pointed to a few "puzzling features" in the text that show how it was "cunningly designed to make . . . exactly the points that a Whig would most relish," they declare *A True Account* a historical novel as if that generic classification were entirely unproblematic; "*True Account*," 236, 238. A reader of Scott might well wonder, however, if this text is in the same class with *Waverley*. Similarly, Backscheider divides a number of works that are treated here as fictionalized military memoirs into two categories (histories and historical novels) without really justifying the division; see *Ambition and Innovation*, chapters 4 and 5.

it."[34] Of course, the most famous use of this device by Defoe, as well as the most personally consequential, was in *The Shortest Way with Dissenters*, the satire that landed its author in jail and in the pillory. This use of personae in polemical or sharply satirical compositions like *The Shortest Way* is not surprising, but Defoe's use of a similar pose in history-writing is more remarkable, especially in light of the exacting principles governing historical discourse that he enunciated in *The Storm* and the somewhat austere historical practice of *The History of the Union*. The histories of Charles XII and Peter the Great do not appear to have been controversial works, and therefore did not have to be presented to readers in a surreptitious fashion, so it would seem that Defoe simply viewed this fictional device as a legitimate strategy of historical representation, one that did not undermine the historicity of the text.[35]

As we have seen, ample precedents existed for the use of fiction in historiography. Not only the ancients but also Bacon, in his *History of Henry VII*, regularly employed imaginary scenes or speeches as part of the rhetoric of history. And Baconian historiography, under the proper circumstances, readily tolerated material that was either acknowledged to be fictional, such as the stories of Arthur and Brut, or that was sufficiently sensational or of sufficiently uncertain provenance to be regarded as possibly fictional. At the same time, histories were sometimes classified as species of fictional discourse by readers who thought the works too personal or polemical, and secret history constituted itself on the border between history and fiction. In short, a writer like Defoe who elected to use fictional devices had before him many examples of putative or actual uses of fictional discourse within historical texts. And although in *The Storm* he echoed Camden (who pronounced against this practice in the *History of Princess Elizabeth*), Defoe never explicitly rejected the inclusion of imaginative features in historical texts, and his practice suggests that this feature of ancient practice remained acceptable to him.

Nevertheless, our survey of early modern English history would seem to indicate that the use of fictionalized narrators like the "Old Officer" of *Marlborough* or the "Scots Gentleman" of the *History of Charles XII* was unique to Defoe, although if Furbank and Owens are correct in "de-attributing" these works once assigned to Defoe, there appear to have been other writers whose practice was so similar to Defoe's that their works have been ascribed to the author of *Robinson Crusoe*. Still, Defoe's use of these fictionalized narrators does bear a certain resemblance to Crouch's use of Richard Burton as what I have elsewhere called a "bibliographic persona."

---

[34] James Sutherland, "The Relation of Defoe's Fiction to his Non-Fictional Writings," in *Imagined Worlds: Essays in Honour of John Butt*, ed. Maynard Mack and Ian Gregor (London: Methuen, 1968), 38.

[35] Moore, *Citizen*, 258–59.

Both Crouch and Defoe, of course, were preeminently popular writers, conscious of the necessity and desirability of pleasing a relatively unsophisticated audience. Sutherland reminds us that Defoe wrote "for the small shopkeepers and artisans, the publicans, the footmen and servant wenches, the soldiers and sailors, those who could read but who had neither the time nor the inclination to read very much."[36] Nor, Sutherland might have added, the time or inclination to worry overmuch about the mode of discourse or the generic status of what they were reading. Indeed, it is one of the supreme ironies of literary history that works written by a man and for men and women who cared so little about the rules governing the production and reception of fictional and historical texts should have come to figure so prominently in debates over the nature of the central literary form of the modern period.[37] In any case, Defoe's status as a popular writer provides us with a starting point in searching for an understanding of his use of fiction in historiography.

II

Defoe believed that a good story was the best means to reach and affect his audience. Even in *The Storm*, for example, when he asserts the need for truth in history, he also declares that the historian must be "just to the Story." The value of narrative was a lesson he would have learned at an early age; his teacher, Charles Morton, once wrote that "Romances, & parables, or fables, that have no truth In the Matter, but Morall honesty In the Designe . . . are noe Lyes, but Ingenuous Poesie . . . The better to Inculcate the virtue."[38] Maxmillian Novak has argued, furthermore, albeit in respect to Defoe's "theory of fiction," that Defoe believed "that this effect of representing reality must be achieved through entertaining adventures if it is to find any readers."[39] Thus, we can assume that many of Defoe's histories, and particularly the military memoirs, were offered as compositions written by actual participants in events in the belief that narratives of an individual's adventures would appeal to readers much more than histories weighed down by the historian's overscrupulous

---

[36] Mayer, "Nathaniel Crouch: Bookseller and Historian," 417; James Sutherland, *Defoe* (Philadelphia: Lippincott, 1938), 227–28.

[37] Ian Watt has commented that Defoe "is perhaps a unique example of a great writer who was very little interested in literature, and says nothing of interest about it as literature"; *Rise of the Novel*, 70. However, while Defoe's assertions about literature *and* history were unexceptional, his practice is of great significance. Cf. Maximillian E. Novak, *Realism, Myth, and History in Defoe's Fiction* (Lincoln: University of Nebraska Press, 1983), 1.

[38] Charles Morton, *Of Ethicks and Its End*, Harvard MS. Am. 911*; quoted in Backscheider, *Life*, 17. Alan Dugald McKillop argues that Defoe consciously made "concessions to the popular desire for entertainment" in order to educate and lead his readers; *The Early Masters of English Fiction* (Lawrence: University of Kansas Press, 1956), 14.

[39] Novak, "Defoe's Theory of Fiction," *Studies in Philology* 61 (1964), 655.

practice. Defoe's use of fictional devices in historiography, therefore, can be seen as his response to the criticism leveled at the new history by such historical counterrevolutionaries as Sidney and Butler; like Crouch, Defoe sought to write history that would provide matters of fact *and* delight his readers.

The fact that the military memoirs were supposedly written by soldiers who had fought in the military campaigns treated in the texts points to another reason for Defoe's use of fictionalized narrators: the belief embodied in the texts of writers such as Clarendon and Burnet that the best history was written by those who had participated in great events. According to the title page, the *Annals of King George* offered a "full and compleat History of the Rebellion," in this case, the Jacobite rising of 1715; this apparent allusion to Clarendon, perfectly natural in an account of a rebellion written in 1715, suggests that the two works shared not only a common subject but also a common perspective, that of the knowledge-able insider.[40] Defoe certainly believed that if at all possible history should be written by a person intimately involved in events. In *Mist's Weekly Journal*, he declares: "The Historian . . . is confined to a faithful Relation of Facts whereof he is supposed to be an Eyewitness." Yet although Defoe accepted the view that history should be based upon first-hand knowledge, he also recognized that this was an ideal that could not always be achieved: "if this cannot be strictly comply'd with, he [the historian] is indispensably obliged to deliver nothing of Importance without authentick Memoirs in Writing."[41] Lacking the capacity to write as an eyewitness, the historian should rely upon trustworthy evidence and produce an account equivalent to one written by an actual participant. It was simply one additional step in the elaboration of a rhetoric of historical representation, although admittedly a crucial one, for Defoe to present this second-hand account *as if it were a first-hand account* in order to gain the reader's attention and interest.[42] Thus Defoe's embrace of the Thucydidean precept seems to have led to his frequently posing as an eyewitness, thereby simultaneously observing and violating the principle. Indeed, Defoe acted as if the dictum that history should be written by participants in great events had as much to do with historical narration as with the basis of historical truth; the fact that his Thucydidean stance was often a fiction demonstrates that for him fiction

---

[40] A. W. Secord has documented the importance of Clarendon to Defoe in the making of *Memoirs of a Cavalier*, "The Origin of Defoe's *Memoirs of a Cavalier*" in *Robert Drury's Journal and Other Studies* (Urbana: University of Illinois Press, 1961), 111–24.

[41] Cited in Novak, "Defoe's Theory," 657, 658.

[42] Pat Rogers argues in a similar vein about Defoe's *Tour* (1724–26); Rogers shows that Defoe is writing in imitation of, among others, Camden in the *Tour*, but he also points out that among all the others who undertook the same task as Camden, only Defoe "evolved a literary vehicle (the 'tour' or 'circuit') that could straddle the literal and the imaginative." See Rogers, abr. and ed., *A Tour Through the Whole Island of Great Britain* by Defoe (London: Penguin, 1971), 29.

was simply one among many stategies of historical representation and also that its use in history did not contaminate the text's claim to historicity.

Yet Bacon clearly differentiated between true history and feigned history and labeled the latter poetry. How then could Defoe justify such feigning in historiography, especially since even he had rejected fictions that "cheat the Readers in the Shape or Appearance of Historical Truth"?[43] The answer to this question lies outside these histories, since they contain no explicit admission of the use of fiction and therefore no attempt to justify the use of this strategy in historical writing. In *The Storm*, Defoe prefaces his extended definition of the historian's duty with the assertion that "if a Man tells a Lye in Print, he abuses Mankind, and imposes upon the whole World."[44] Inevitably the student of Defoe asks how, in light of this statement, Defoe could "abuse" his readers by maintaining that historical works were written by participants when these narrators were in fact invented by Defoe. A memorandum that Defoe wrote for Harley in 1704 provides an answer to this question. In defending proposed hypocritical behavior on the part of Harley, Defoe argues that "as a Lye Does Not Consist in the Indirect Position of Words, but in the Design by False Speaking, to Deceiv and Injure my Neighbour, So Dissembling does Not Consist in Putting a Different Face Upon our Actions, but in the further Applying That Concealment to the Prejudice of the Person."[45] As Defoe saw it, then, two things distinguished dissembling from actual prevaricating. First, if the auditor or observer was not injured through the use of false speech or action, there was no lie; more important for our purposes, if the auditor or observer was not materially deceived, then the speaker or actor had not really dissimulated. By Defoe's logic, if a narrative was substantially true, if it was a historical account based on reliable sources, neither a fictional frame, nor a fictionalized narrator, nor even the use of fictional material, altered the narrative's essentially historical character. So the histories of Charles XII and Peter the Great functioned as historical discourse just as they purported to do because their fictional frames did not work to "the Prejudice of" readers. Defoe's practice suggests then that he had a complicated and somewhat idiosyncratic but nonetheless internally consistent view of the relationship between fact and fiction in narratives presented to readers as histories. Feigning within history was not lying so long as the writer actually sought to convey matters of fact.

Defoe also seems to have thought it valid to acknowledge a lack of authority for statements in historical discourse (and surely this would

[43] Defoe's *A New Family Instructor* (1727); cited in Novak, "Defoe's Theory," 653. Novak argues that Defoe accepted fiction as long as it advanced a good moral and did not try to pass itself off as history.

[44] *The Storm*, sig. A₂v.

[45] *Letters of Daniel Defoe*, ed. George Harris Healey (Oxford: Clarendon Press, 1955), 42.

include fictional statements) by covertly signaling readers to be on their guard. Such signals could be either implicit admissions that some of the text was fictional (as in the secret histories, discussed below) or suggestions that the putative authority for the text was only a fictional substitute for the real basis of the historical account. In the *History of Charles XII*, for example, the author argues "these Memoirs" require "no better Appeal for their Authority and Truth, than to the General Knowledge of Mankind" even though the account was supposedly authorized by the author's own participation in events.[46] This assertion, repeated essentially verbatim in *Memoirs of a Cavalier*, amounted to an admission that the basis for the text's authority – the personal knowledge of a participant – was not genuine. A somewhat different claim that had much the same effect was made in texts where Defoe simply appealed to common sense. In *A True Relation of the Apparition of One Mrs. Veal* (1706), for example, the narrator asserted that "this relation is matter of fact, and attended with such circumstances, as may induce any reasonable man to believe it," asking his readers to accept the "relation" as factual because it "appeared" to be true.[47] Appeals to common knowledge and common sense functioned both as covert signals of the partially fictive character of a text and as implied assertions that the historicity of the text was not necessarily compromised by an admission that the historian lacked the requisite authority for the historical narrative he presented.

Defoe's reasons for using fiction in historical accounts were undoubtedly linked to his view of the end of history. The author of the *Annals of King George* called "an unbyas'd Regard to Truth, the greatest Beauty of an Historian," but there probably never was a less disinterested writer than Defoe.[48] In all his histories, he had an agenda: *The History of the Union* was a defense of a policy already achieved and the *Memoirs of the Church of Scotland* a reminder that the Kirk's rights must be protected in the newly united kingdom; the secret histories supported Harley; and the *Annals* and a number of other texts condemned Jacobitism. For Defoe, as for all Baconian historiographers, fidelity to the facts was consistent with the presentation of those facts in what the author regarded as the "true Light."[49] Believing in history as a storehouse of political lessons ("Hystory is fruitful of Examples"), Defoe begins the *Royal Progress* (1724) by discussing the emperor Hadrian as "a Pattern to all wise, just, and beneficent Princes"; argues in *The Storm* that the disaster shows that God is affronted by the spread of atheism in contemporary society; and declares in

46 *Charles XII, "Preface," n.p.*
47 Daniel Defoe and Others, *Accounts of the Apparition of Mrs. Veal*, Augustan Repr. Soc. Pub. No. 115, introd. Manuel Schonhorn (Los Angeles: William Andrews Clark Memorial Library, 1965), n.p.
48 *Annals of King George*, iv.   49 *Marlborough*, 3.

the *History of the Pyrates* that governments must "find employment for the great Numbers of Seamen turn'd adrift at the Conclusion of a War."[50]

Defoe's belief in the instrumental character of history was particularly evident in his *General History of Discoveries and Improvements*, where he surveys developments in trade, agriculture, and navigation in what seems a disinterested fashion until one recognizes that the text was designed to function as a call for rejuvenating North Africa through the intervention of British settlers.[51] Defoe valued historiography for its ability to teach readers how to think and act. Alan Dugald McKillop argues, in fact, that "from first to last didactic emphasis and the claim to literal truth were fixed upon Defoe" and also insists that an "interest in practical moral reform" was evident throughout his career.[52] The most practical-minded of writers, Defoe, like other Baconian historiographers, was willing to countenance the use of fiction in history, so long as it was not deceptive, because he believed that an effective narrative was most likely to engage and therefore shape the thinking and, most important, the action of his readers. His defense of his method in *Robinson Crusoe* is apposite here: "Had the common Way of Writing a . . . History been taken . . . all I could have said would have yielded no Diversion, and perhaps scarce have obtained a Reading, or at best no Attention." Defoe argues that the writer might do whatever was needed to obtain "a Reading" and "Attention," even if that entailed deploying fiction within an historical text.[53]

III

A number of works written in the years just before the appearance of *Robinson Crusoe* demonstrate Defoe's belief that fiction was a legitimate means of historical representation. At least one of his secret histories is a case in point. Most of Defoe's secret histories and memoirs (published between 1711 and 1717 but mostly in 1714 and 1715) are neither of the historical type discussed in chapter 6 nor of the fictional sort treated in chapter 8. *The Secret History of the October Club, Part I*, said on the title page to have been written "By a Member," was in important ways a typical Augustan satire. Harley's ministry was defended in a text that at first seems a straightforward account of events but suddenly becomes a savage, farcical attack (presented in dialogues between club members) on a group "of High Tory members of Parliament who met to drink October ale and abuse the

---

[50] *The Secret History of the White Staff* (London, 1714), 4; *The Royal Progress* (London, 1724), viii; *The Storm*, "Preface," n.p.; *A General History of the Pyrates*, ed. Manuel Schonhorn (Columbia: University of South Carolina Press, 1972), 3.

[51] *Discoveries and Improvements*, 134–39.   [52] McKillop, *Early Masters*, 6–7.

[53] *Robinson Crusoe*, 262; whether in *Robinson Crusoe* he was defending this practice in respect to history or fiction is a question we leave for the next chapter.

Whigs."[54] The October Club was a real political association that, according to G. M. Trevelyan, "was Jacobite when drunk and Hanoverian when sober," but the secret history of the club was presented to readers not as a factual account of the group but as a fantastic rhetorical blast at these antagonists of George I.[55]

Not all of Defoe's secret histories, however, were of this type; at least one was more closely akin to the histories of Crouch, Burnet, and Hamilton than to *October Club* and other such works. *A Secret History of One Year* (1714) was Defoe's final defense of William III as well as an argument in favor of George I, another foreign-born monarch.[56] Lacking the rhetorical eccentricities of many of the other secret histories, this work presented dialogues to explain William's efforts on behalf of the Act of Indemnity (which the Whigs opposed) and his use of men whom the author says were hostile to the king (that is, the Tories). The author implicitly acknowledges the fictional aspect of at least some of the dialogues in promising to relate "to the *Publick, Verbatim*, what I received many Years ago from a Venerable Head, who perhaps was an Ear Witness" and asserting that at the end of William's reign "the following Things, or something like them, happen'd to be discours'd." The hedges in these remarks ("perhaps," "or something like them") indicate that the narrative was partly invented; yet the narrator also claims that he intends "not to act the Politician, but the Historian."[57] The implication is that the fictional element was unimportant: the dialogues were historical because they were based upon a reliable account of events that transpired in 1689.

In this putative reconstruction of actual conversations, a "noble Lord" speaks "with some Warmth of the ill Treatment, which, as he thought, the King [William] met with" upon ascending the throne. The same lord claims that "if his Majesty had not IMMEDIATELY put himself into the Hands of those very Men whom he ought to have put in the Hands of the Executioner, he had not been brought to suffer these ignominious things," and then declares that the king's problems resulted from the fact that he "did not know the *English* Nation: That they were not to be won with Kindness, any more than to be crush'd by Oppression, that the *English* Temper is only to be manag'd by Justice." Finally, the lord tells his auditors that he told the King exactly what he has just told them, but that "His Majesty smiled and told him again that he [the Lord] was too

---

54 *October Club*, 29–31; G. M. Trevelyan, *England under Queen Anne*, 3 vols. (London: Longmans, Green, 1930–34), III, 96.

55 Trevelyan, *England under Queen Anne*, III, 89. Other secret histories similar to *October Club* include the second half of that work, the three parts of *The Secret History of the White Staff*, and *The Secret History of the Secret History of the White Staff*.

56 Sutherland shows that Defoe did have inside information; *Defoe*, 208. On Defoe's relationship with and work for William III, see Backscheider, *Life*, 71–76.

57 *A Secret History of One Year* (London, 1714), 3–4, 8.

censorious . . . That he had such Confidence in the Affection of all his People, that it was below him to fear a few disaffected Party-Men."[58] Defoe here employs the "within Doors" perspective characteristic of secret history, but in this case at least he eschews the outlandish rhetoric that disqualified other secret histories from serious consideration as historical texts. The tone of this work, sober and earnest throughout, suggested that the author was indeed privy to the king's view of English politics and therefore that the text's asserted historicity was a genuine claim.[59] Although it apparently contains invented material, Defoe's practice in *A Secret History of One Year* suggests that at least this secret history was presented to readers as historical discourse, not as a satirical blast nor as a fiction in the manner of Manley. This text, then, suggests how far Defoe might go in inventing portions of historical accounts and yet remain, by his own lights, within the bounds of history.

In 1717 and 1718, there appeared two additional works now attributed to Defoe (one of which goes unchallenged by Furbank and Owens) in which the author seems to invent freely in the process of writing accounts that he apparently hoped would be read as history. These two texts can be classified as Jacobite memoirs, in which the experiences of men in the service of the Pretender, Louis XIV, or both, are related in order to discredit the forces that opposed the Hanoverian succession.[60] In the first of these, the *Minutes of the Negotiations of Monsr. Mesnager* (1717), one of his many defenses of Harley, Defoe treats the contacts between the English and French that led to the Treaty of Utrecht. As in the military memoirs and the secret histories, the putative narrator of the *Minutes* (Nicolas Mesnager, Louis XIV's secret envoy to the English court in 1711) attests to his personal knowledge ("I . . . had the Honour to converse intimately with his Majesty in the greatest and most valuable Confidences"), but unlike the narrators of the earlier works, this putative memoirist was a reasonably well-known public official and an important actor in the represented events.[61] The *Minutes* convey the view that Louis XIV was able to manipulate the English into moves that ran counter to their own interests, but they also exonerate Harley for his participation in the negotiations.

---

58 *One Year*, 8–10.
59 Furbank and Owens note that Sir Walter Scott attributed the *Seceret History of One Year* to Robert Walpole. Their own argument in support of the "de-attribution" of this work is at least partly on grounds of style; *De-Attributions*, 66.
60 Backscheider groups *Minutes of Mesnager* (1717) and the *Memoirs of Alexander Ramkins* (1718), discussed below, with *A True Account of the Proceedings at Perth* and *A Journal of the Earl of Marr's Proceedings* (both 1716) as works "designed to discourage Jacobitism" (*Life*, 442–43). One might add to this list *Memoirs of John, Duke of Melfort* (1714), *Memoirs of the Conduct of her late Majesty* (1715), and *Memoirs of . . . the Duke of Shrewsbury* (1718).
61 Paul Larousse, *Grand Dictionnaire Universel*, 15 vols. (Paris: Administration du Grand Diction-naire Universel, n.d.), XI, 105; *Minutes*, 28–29.

Defoe's Mesnager avers that Harley wanted "*a moderate Administration*" but that this was impossible due to "the Animosity of the Parties," which, according to the narrator of the *Minutes*, did Louis XIV's work for him by dividing the English against themselves, thus rendering them easy to manage. In addition to representing the French as crafty and exploitative, the *Minutes* also suggest, by means at one point of a conversation between Abigail Masham and "an English Person of Honour" supposedly reported to Mesnager by the latter, that most of the Tories were secret Jacobites. Harley, however, is exempted from this charge and represented as one of the few ministers or courtiers who actually served Queen Anne. Mesnager relates that Masham railed against the (Tory) ministers who were incapable of dealing with the Whigs and lamented that "there was not a Man among the whole Ministry, but my Lord Treasurer, that ever spoke a Cheerful word to the Queen."[62]

Mesnager figures prominently in the text, but mainly in recording and reflecting on events. He typifies Defoe's fictionalized Thucydidean historical narrators; the text is almost entirely about the negotiations, not the negotiator. Defoe's Mesnager asserts at the outset that he created the text "not to form it as an History of my Life, which was led in a more private Capacity."[63] Thus one feature of the *Minutes* that differentiates it from works like *Robinson Crusoe* is that Mesnager has no past, no "private Capacity," that would establish him as a character rather than as a fictionalized narrator of a historical text.

Defoe took his use of the fictionalized narrator of a historical text one step further in a work of Jacobite memoirs published in 1718; here he arrived at the point where such fictionalized narrators began to seem (to some readers at least) like characters in a novel instead of rather odd features in his own particular brand of Baconian historiography. *The Memoirs of Major Alexander Ramkins* is an account of Jacobitism in France from 1689 to 1717, ostensibly told by an erstwhile Jacobite who has learned the errors of his ways. Typically for Defoe, the *Memoirs* have a clear political agenda that is more effectively advanced by being presented as the construct of a participant in the events treated in the narrative. The goal of the *Memoirs* is to establish the faithlessness of Louis XIV in respect to the Pretender and his deceived supporters, and to show that a Jacobite could and should transfer his allegiance to the House of Hanover.

Accepted as genuine by many readers until recently but now thought to have been written by Defoe, the *Memoirs* were really two works knitted together by their author.[64] One was an account of political and military

---

62 *Minutes*, 83, 99, 118, 262.   63 *Ibid.*, 142, 3.
64 Ramkins made it into the *Dictionary of National Biography* on the strength of this work; as recently as 1941, a noted scholar of English biography discussed the *Memoirs* as if Ramkins really wrote them. See James Boulton, introd., *Memoirs of an English Officer (The Military Memoirs of Captain*

events on the continent and in Ireland; James Boulton argues in respect to
this part that the *Memoirs* have "a credible historical framework." The
other part of the *Memoirs* was an account of Ramkins's escapades while he
was away from the Pretender's army.[65] Here, for the first time, Defoe gave
one of his invented narrators a reasonably believable life. First, Ramkin's
early life was sketched in: "the martial Spirit of his Family," his consorting
with "several [Highland] Clans," his tutelage by "an old Officer," and his
small inheritance. His father dead, Ramkins took leave of his mother at the
beginning of the narrative; on the continent, his adventures alternated
between the political and the amorous. In a military academy in Stras-
bourg, he received instruction in politics: "the Monarchs of *France* wou'd
look upon themselves as injur'd by the rest of the Princes of *Europe*, till the
imperial Diadem was restor'd to *France*, who were the first Possessors of it
in the Person of *Charles the Great*." In Paris, he learns his first lesson in love,
when "a *Spanish* young Lady" leaves him after a courtship likened to a
series of battles and sieges.[66] Throughout, the narrator alternates between
public events and the diverting life story that make the historical narrative
creditable and the political argument embedded in the text palatable. The
effective combination of these two parts signals a new stage in Defoe's
evolution as a writer of histories with fictionalized narrators. The reader is
assured that the narrative is authentic; in the preface, the editor states that
"these papers were deliver'd into my Hands by a near Kinsman of the
Author, who lately came from France." The hero's transfer of loyalty from
the Pretender to George I suggests that the memoirist is able to treat both
sides with insight and fairness. Defoe lets events (including, of course,
Ramkins's reflections) speak for themselves. The reader arrives, along with
Ramkins, at the perception that "King James was not only . . . the Dupe of
their great Monarch [Louis XIV], but the Sport and Game of his
Ministers."[67]

This is not new; the *Life of Marlborough* was a putative memoir of a man
in the ranks that was fashioned to mount a political argument. What is
unprecedented in the *Memoirs of Ramkins* is the way in which the salient
historical events are related by Ramkins in terms of his own experience.
Much of the political story is left vague; Ramkins excuses himself on this
score by arguing that a participant in a battle has a limited view of a
large action. (This assertion is echoed in *Memoirs of a Cavalier*.) The
Major's private affairs are much better detailed.[68] Yet, as Furbank and

---

*George Carleton) with The History of the Remarkable Life of John Sheppard and The Memoirs of Major
Alexander Ramkins (London: Victor Gollancz, 1970), 3–11; Donald Stauffer, The Art of Biography
in Eighteenth-Century England (Princeton University Press, 1941), 212–18.*
[65] Boulton, *English Officer*, 10–12.   [66] *Ramkins*, 2–16, 21, 70–78.
[67] *Ibid.*, "Publisher to the Reader," n.p.; 85–86; 53–54.
[68] *Ibid.*, 58. Ramkins's account of his first stay in Paris, where he was mistaken for his brother and

Owens observe in respect to *A True Account*, once one begins to consider
the *Memoirs* as a text written by someone other than Ramkins himself, it
becomes clear that the work focuses not on the affairs of its putative
author but on British politics.[69] One need not conclude, however, as
Furbank and Owens do, that the *Memoirs of Ramkins* are therefore an
historical novel since it is also possible, and in terms of the history of the
novel, very productive, to view this text as a species of Baconian
historiography.

Indeed, in the *Memoirs of Ramkins*, Defoe's brand of Baconian historiography achieved something like ideal form. The homely and apparently
guileless account of an obscure participant in great events is in fact a
fabricated account whose putative author is an invention designed to
authorize a text whose historicity might be challenged and whose utility
might be compromised if the real author announced himself and thereby
declared his political agenda. Central to Defoe's historical method at this
point is the elaboration of the participant-narrator's point of view through
an extended treatment of that character's life. The narrator's personal
experience is rendered in great detail although political events finally seem
more important; nevertheless, the attention to private matters entertains
the reader and has the effect of inducing belief in the author's version of
historical events. At the same time, the integration of the life of Ramkins
with known historical events suggests that the life story is true. Thus, the
two aspects of the narrative are mutually authenticating and, taken
together, argue for the historicity of the text, not perhaps for us but
certainly for many readers for a long time. The case is still uncertain; the
most Boulton will assert in a 1970 edition of this text is that "Ramkins's
existence has not yet been established."[70]

That we still cannot say with certainty whether Ramkins was a fictional
character is symptomatic of the way Defoe worked; he constantly elided the
distinction between history and fiction in an apparently careless way
because, as I have argued, he regarded the use of fiction in historical
discourse as a legitimate strategy of historical representation. Of course, to
designate the *Secret History of One Year*, Mesnager's *Minutes*, and Ramkins's
Memoirs as works of history is far from unproblematic; indeed, the issue of
the categorial status of these works is, typically for Defoe, almost endlessly
murky and ambiguous. Backscheider classifies such works as "fictional
journals or memoirs," assuming that the attribution of the works to Defoe
definitively settles the matter. Others are not so sure. Boulton, for example,
accepts Defoe as the author of the *Memoirs* but discusses them as the product
of Defoe's "imaginative ability" and "factual knowledge" and ultimately

consequently forced to fight a duel for his supposed dalliance with "a young French woman," is
typical of the way his personal life is handled; see 33–41.
[69] Furbank and Owens, "*True Account*," 235–36.   [70] Boulton, *English Officer*, 8.

declines to classify them.[71] Paul Dottin preferred to regard the *Minutes* as a species of "mystification," a word that in French implies, to some extent at least, "deception."[72] Yet Dottin highlights the ambiguous nature of these works, celebrating both Defoe's brilliance and his singularity:

De tous les écrivains de l'époque, seul De Foe était capable de telle effronterie. Il était d'ailleurs le seul à pouvoir faire, dans les *Minutes* la part de la fiction et la part de la vérité: en effet, pour donner à son oeuvre un caractère d'authenticité, et mieux dissimuler ses mensonges au milieu d'un flot d'événements réels, il s'était documenté.[73]

Several comments on Dottin's important discussion of the *Minutes* are in order. To some extent, Dottin suggests that in this typical Jacobite memoir Defoe was lying. Yet our study of Baconian historiography suggests that Defoe's historical practice – like that of less problematic historians of the period – allowed for deception of a sort that did not constitute lying because the essential truth was told, matters of fact were adhered to. The essential truth in these works was that "Harley had played a more honourable part in the peace negotiations than was generally supposed," and that the Jacobitism of some men was "an uncurable Distemper."[74] Thus, from Defoe's point of view no deception was involved despite the recourse to fiction. What is also noteworthy about Dottin's comment is his own remarkable ambivalence, although his apparently contradictory views are not likely to surprise anyone familiar with the reception of Defoe's "novels" (examined in chapter 11). Using words and phrases like "fiction," "vérité," "authenticité," "dissimuler," "mensonge," "événements réels," and "était documenté" to describe this work, what Dottin ultimately insists upon is the unclassifiability of the text. So too, I would argue, does Laura Ann Curtis:

Defoe created a work of fiction for which his era provided no aesthetic theory; forced to vacillate between calling his writings non-fiction, history or romance and fable, Defoe was unable to supply a theory . . . for those of his works in which . . . he believed and disbelieved at the same time.[75]

---

[71] Boulton begins his discussion by asserting that "[Dr.] Johnson hated deception," which has the effect of labeling the *Memoirs* as deceptive, but much of the rest of his essay has the effect of vitiating this remark; *English Officer*, 8, 19, 7.

[72] *Le Petit Robert 1* gives the following meanings:

Mystifier: Tromper qqn en abusant de sa crédulité et pour s'amuser à ses dépens (1251).
Tromper: 1st: Induire (qqn) en erreur quant aux faits ou quant à ses intentions, en usant de mensonge, de dissimulation, de ruse
4th: Donner une satisfaction illusoire ou momentanée à (un besoin, un désir) (2027).

[73] Paul Dottin, "Daniel De Foe mystificateur ou Les faux mémoires de Mesnager," *Revue Germanique* 14 (1923), 273, 280.

[74] Sutherland, *Defoe*, 219; *Ramkins*, 157.

[75] Laura Ann Curtis, ed. and introd., *The Versatile Defoe: An Anthology of Uncollected Writings by Daniel Defoe* (Totowa NJ: Rowman and Littlefield, 1979), 347.

Twentieth-century readers of Defoe such as Dottin are both believing and disbelieving critics. This study demonstrates, however, that such disbelief arises at least in part from a failure to appreciate the nature of historical discourse in Defoe's day: Baconian historiography, and Defoe's own particular historical practice, authorized "mystification" in history so long as the historian did not allow "imaginative ability" to obscure what "factual knowledge" suggested to be true. Certainly there were early modern readers who objected; Abel Boyer was a celebrated example, protesting as he did the "Forgery" of the *Minutes*. But Defoe was not alone in being accused of telling lies: Heylyn thought Fuller had failed to tell the truth; Nalson accused Rushworth of having written "History without Truth or with a mixture of Falsehood, [which] degenerates into Romance"; and Oldmixon asserted that Clarendon's great history was "Rotten." Readers were accustomed to such charges and knew that "history" was often a murky affair, one that they, not infrequently, had to sort out. The fact that the *Secret History of One Year*, the *Minutes*, and the *Memoirs* were richly fictional accounts no doubt constituted a stumbling block to their being read as histories, then and now. Yet the reception of these works, then and now, suggests that they could be, were, and sometimes still are, read as histories, even when readers knew (or know) that Defoe used fiction to write history. Similarly, Furbank and Owens report that as recently as 1970 historians acknowledged that Defoe wrote the *True Account* and then quoted the text, "evidently asking the reader to accept it as sober truth."[76]

My argument is not that we ought to put Mesnager's *Minutes* and Ramkins's *Memoirs* on the shelf alongside modern histories of Jacobitism or biographies of Harley any more than the historian of medicine would put the strange treatises of eighteenth-century doctors in a medical library along with modern textbooks of anatomy and physiology. I am arguing, however, that we must reconstruct the meaning of "history" in 1700 lest we end, as many who have studied Defoe have ended, by simply calling him a liar.[77] A study of his practice suggests that his claims that he related matters of facts were serious and, to some extent, demonstrably true. If Defoe used fiction in histories before he wrote those works now frequently designated as novels, should we then simply regard all of the narratives as species of fictional discourse? If we think of fiction and history as two mutually exclusive forms of discourse or ways of knowing, constructed according to different rules and principles, the answer to this question must be yes. Yet it seems more enlightening to recognize that in company with

---

[76] Furbank and Owens, *"True Account,"* 238.
[77] See, most notably, William Minto, *Daniel Defoe* (New York: Harper & Brothers, 1899), 140. More recently, see Foley, *Telling the Truth*, 119; Davis, *Factual Fictions*, 154. Davis's discussion of Defoe is subtitled "Lies as Truth."

his contemporaries Defoe did not regard history and fiction in that light. For Defoe, a writer who was more interested in writing efficacious rather than theoretically correct history, history was a factual discourse, but fiction, although in the end qualitatively different from history, could nevertheless be one of the historian's tools.

To be sure, there was a point at which fact finally became fiction, even for Defoe's contemporaries. It is this point that we examine in the next chapter in looking at how Defoe's most famous narratives were presented to readers in 1719 and the early 1720s. There we will see that Defoe's "novels" were presented to readers as species of historical discourse but also that those texts were qualitatively different from his histories. The differences ended in forcing readers, comfortable with reading Defoe's histories as examples of Baconian historiography, to alter their readerly expectations in respect to the later texts that came to be read as novels. As a result, the presentation and reception of Defoe's narratives, taken together, were a constitutive moment in the history of the early English novel.

9

"Facts that are form'd to touch the Mind": Defoe's novels as forms of historical discourse

In contemporary criticism *Robinson Crusoe* is automatically referred to as a novel. Leo Braudy, for example, while acknowledging that Defoe used a first-person narrator in both his nonfiction and his fiction, distinguishes between the former type that focuses on some "public person" and the latter type that features a "private impersonation" and classifies the latter, including *Crusoe*, as novels.[1] Similarly, in her life of Defoe, Paula Backscheider recognizes that Defoe defended *Crusoe* as "Allegorick History" and that "some readers have always found the book autobiographical," but she nevertheless refers to the text in an untroubled way as a novel.[2] And Michael Seidel has recently asserted:

The literary revolution that Defoe's *Robinson Crusoe* helped instigate is monumental. No matter what talk there is of the forebears of the novel, very little reads like a novel until Defoe develops the form beginning with *Crusoe*.[3]

No matter how much one may agree with Seidel that Defoe's career was the locus of a great transformation that eventuated in the discourse of the novel in English, there is still no question that Defoe's narratives are strikingly different from the works of later novelists like Richardson and Fielding. Those later texts were presented to readers as a "new species of writing" or a new form of fiction, whereas Defoe sought to ensure that his most famous narratives would be read not as fiction but as history.[4]

To be sure, critics have often read the "telling overprotestation[s]" of historicity that one finds in a number of these texts (*Crusoe, Moll Flanders, Memoirs of a Cavalier, Roxana*) as tropological assertions that the works in

---

[1] Leo Braudy, "Daniel Defoe and the Anxieties of Autobiography," *Genre* 6 (1973), 76.
[2] Backscheider, *Life*, 412, 417.
[3] Michael Seidel, *Robinson Crusoe: Island Myths and the Novel* (Boston: Twayne, 1991), 27.
[4] Richardson informed his readers that *Pamela* had its "Foundation in Truth" but also reproduced a letter (from an obscure French writer who lived in London, Jean Baptiste de Freval) that asserted that "this little Book will infallibly be looked upon as the hitherto much-wanted Standard or Pattern for this Kind of Writing"; and Fielding prefaced *Joseph Andrews* with his famous "few Words concerning this kind of Writing." *Pamela*, ed. T. C. Duncan Eaves and Ben D. Kimpel (Boston: Houghton, Mifflin, 1971), 3, 4; *Joseph Andrews and Shamela*, ed. Douglas Brooks-Davies (Oxford University Press, 1970), 30.

181

question were in fact novels.[5] But texts like *Captain Singleton* and *Journal of the Plague Year* contained no such signals of their fictionality, and, more important, not only *Singleton* and the *Journal* but also the narratives with those "overprotestations" were read as factual accounts at some time during the history of their reception, in some cases for a surprisingly long time. Thus, the works we call novels did not at first situate themselves within fictional discourse, and at least some readers (in some cases, most readers) concretized Defoe's novels as forms of historical discourse. Speaking only of *Crusoe* for the moment, we know that Gildon objected to the work in important part because many were reading it as a relation of matters of fact, and in 1753 Robert Shiels commented that "for some time after its publication, it was judged by most people to be a true story."[6]

The great disparity between the way we read Defoe's most celebrated narratives – as works of fiction that lay claim to initiating the discourse of the novel in English – and the way they were read in the first half of the eighteenth century and beyond – as texts situated within the discourse of history – has often been seen as a key to understanding Defoe's contribution to the history of the novel. Lennard Davis, for example, represents "the confusion of attitude toward fact and fiction" as the "quiddity [that] has installed his work in the position of *primum mobile* of the novelistic tradition."[7] That Defoe was the central figure in the emergence of the novel is best explained, to my mind, by examining why Defoe's novels were first read as histories and then how they were were gradually assimilated to the tradition of the novel in English. To that end, I focus in this chapter on the presentation of Defoe's most famous narratives to eighteenth-century readers and then, in the following chapter, treat their reception.[8]

In considering Defoe's novels, however, I do not intend to undertake a standard "reading" of those works, in important part because such an approach would suggest that what I am arguing is simply that Defoe thematized history in his most famous narratives. Instead I shall concentrate on certain familiar elements of the text, crucial to the way it was apprehended by readers in Defoe's day, thereby indicating how *Robinson*

5   Foley, *Telling the Truth*, 122; see also Novak, *Realism, Myth, and History*, 56.
6   Theophilus Cibber, *The Lives of the Poets* (London, 1753), IV, 322; quoted by Rogers, *Critical Heritage*, 49–50. Rogers attributes this work to Shiels, "a friend of Dr Johnson."
7   Davis, *Factual Fictions*, 155. For other arguments that focus on the question of history in Defoe's narratives, see A. W. Secord, *Studies in the Narrative Method of Defoe* (1924; repr. New York: Russell and Russell, 1963), 9–20; Ralph W. Rader, "Defoe, Richardson, Joyce, and the Concept of Form in the Novel," in *Autobiography, Biography, and the Novel* (Los Angeles: William Andrews Clark Memorial Library, 1973), 27–72.
8   I might refer to "production" rather than "presentation," but the latter term emphasizes that a work is both a narrative and a set of signals that helps the reader concretize that narrative. On the relationship between the study of presentation and reception, see Manfred Naumann, "Literary Production and Reception," *New Literary History* 8 (1976–77), 114–15; Robert Weimann, "Reception Aesthetics and the Crisis in Literary History," *CLIO* 5 (1975), 23.

Crusoe and the other novels could have been at least initially concretized as works of history. Defoe's practice provided readers with ample reasons for reading these texts as species of historical discourse. Yet, as Gildon's attack on *Robinson Crusoe* suggests, from the first some readers, and over time more and more of them, sensed that facing the question of whether these texts were fact or fiction was an inescapable part of reading them. By requiring readers to address this issue, Defoe's texts forced them in the end to alter their readerly expectations and allow for the possibility of works that seriously laid claim to being read as history which nevertheless had to be concretized as fiction. This study does not aim to prove that Defoe's novels are in fact histories but rather to demonstrate that they were plausibly presented and received as histories when they first appeared, and only subsequently read into novelistic discourse.

I

To begin, it seems worthwhile to look afresh at the title page of *Robinson Crusoe*, which presents to the reader an account of an unknown individual who was shipwrecked and then lived for twenty-eight years "all alone in an un-inhabited Island"; the narrative is said to have been "Written by Himself."[9] It has often been pointed out that Defoe had many texts to draw upon in composing his own account of an island castaway, including not only the treatments of Alexander Selkirk's story, but also an extensive literature of travel that featured many stories of exile.[10] There is a danger, however, in linking Defoe's text to similar accounts written at the end of the seventeenth or the beginning of the eighteenth century; source studies can create the impression that Defoe's contemporaries had read this extensive literature (a reasonable assumption in the case of some readers of *Crusoe*), and thereby suggest, without ground, that readers would have recognized *Crusoe* as a "compilation" of such works and thus a product of

---

[9] *Robinson Crusoe*, ed. and introd. J. Donald Crowley (Oxford University Press, 1972), iii; hereafter citations will be given in the text.

[10] The accounts of Selkirk are Edward Cooke, *A Voyage to the South Sea and Around the World* (London, 1712); Woodes Rogers, *A Cruising Voyage round the World* (London, 1712); and Richard Steele, "[On Alexander Selkirk]," *The Englishman*, no. 26, December 3, 1713. All are excerpted in Shinagel, ed., *Robinson Crusoe*, 248–57. The travel literature includes, most prominently, William Dampier, *A New Voyage Round the World* (London, 1697), and Robert Knox, *An Historical Relation of . . . Ceylon* (London, 1681). For a recent discussion of this "voyage-literature," see Philip Edwards, *The Story of the Voyage: Sea-Narratives in Eighteenth-Century England* (Cambridge University Press, 1994), 17–43. For discussions of Defoe's use of this literature, see Secord, *Narrative Method*, chapter 2; Burton J. Fishman, "Defoe, Herman Moll and the Geography of South America," *Huntington Library Quarterly* 36 (1973), 227–38; Percy G. Adams, *Travel Literature and the Evolution of the Novel* (Lexington: University Press of Kentucky, 1983), 97–105; 118–26 and chapters 2–4; Seidel, *Island Myths*, chapter 5; Pat Rogers, *Robinson Crusoe* (London: George Allen and Unwin, 1979), 17–20, 27–34; and Backscheider, *Ambition and Innovation*, 219–23. However, Seidel, at 39, observes that "much of Selkirk's story is antithetical to Defoe's."

"the editor's" imagination.[11] However, rather than signaling the fictionality of *Crusoe*, travel narratives and stories of castaways may have simply created a disposition on the part of readers to accept a similar narrative as equally historical so long as nothing obviously prevented its being read as a report of matters of fact.

Certainly, the travel narratives published before *Robinson Crusoe* can help us understand how a reader might have approached that work. Accounts of voyages by William Dampier (1697), Edward Cooke (1712), and Woodes Rogers (1712) were all adventure stories presented by individuals who were unknown to the public before their accounts appeared. Dampier had been a pirate, and Cooke served under Rogers on the expedition that rescued Selkirk; Dampier informs his readers that his *New Voyage Round the World*, like Crusoe's account, is based upon a journal.[12] Thus early modern readers were accustomed to accounts of adventures written by unknown mariners, and while the imaginary voyage was quite common in French literature at this time, the accounts of voyages written in English between 1697 and 1719 tended to be "descriptions of real travels."[13] Readers could then easily have assimilated *Robinson Crusoe* to this type of historical writing.

The famously ambiguous preface to *Crusoe* could have fostered this concretization; the putative editor declares that he believed the work

> to be a just History of Fact; neither is there any Appearance of Fiction in it: And however thinks, because all such things are dispatch'd, that the Improvement of it, as well to the Diversion, as to the Instruction of the Readers, will be the same. (1)

Yet this claim need not have been understood by readers as an admission that what followed was imaginary. John Bulkeley and John Cummins present their *Voyage to the South Seas* (1743) in a way that throws light on *Crusoe*:

> It has been a Thing, usual, in publishing of Voyages, to introduce Abundance of Fiction; and some Authors have been esteemed merely for being marvellous. We have taken to deviate from those, by having a strict Regard for Truth.[14]

Bulkeley and Cummins thus admit that they essay a dubious form but assure their readers that they, uncharacteristically, tell the truth. Readers, therefore, could have read the claim in *Crusoe* as a declaration that although the unnamed editor was unable to swear to the truth of everything that followed, he nevertheless believed the work to be essentially

---

11 McKillop used the word "compilation" to describe Defoe's method; *Early Masters*, 9. See also, Secord, "Origins of Defoe's *Memoirs*," 130.

12 *DNB* entries treating Dampier and Rogers; Dampier, *New Voyage*, sig. A₃r.

13 Dampier, *New Voyage*, sig. A₃r, 26, 285–86, 200–01, 84–88; Peter Earle, *The World of Defoe* (London: Weidenfeld and Nicolson, 1976), 46; Philip Babcock Gove, *The Imaginary Voyage in Prose Fiction* (1941; repr. New York: Arno Press, 1974), 198–223.

14 Cited in Adams, *Travel Literature*, 87.

factual. The twentieth-century reader almost automatically construes the comment of Defoe's editor as an introduction to a novel while reading the defense of *Voyage to the South Seas* as the preface to a "genuine" travel account. Early modern readers, on the other hand, were accustomed to such ambiguous statements in both history and fiction and were used to sorting them out. Most fiction writers before Defoe attached similarly historical claims to texts that announced their fictionality in other ways, but readers of *Crusoe, Memoirs of a Cavalier, Captain Singleton, Moll Flanders,* and *A Journal of the Plague Year* were not similarly apprised by Defoe. A 1719 reader of *Crusoe*, therefore, would have had good cause to read the signals on the title page as an indication that the text ought to be regarded as history.

In addition to the preface, the map that appeared in the fourth edition of *Crusoe*, also published in 1719 (see figure 8), would have tended to induce in Defoe's contemporaries a decision to concretize the text as history. *Gulliver's Travels* also contained maps (see figure 9), but Swift's maps were much less likely to have been taken seriously than Defoe's map, which was authentic even if the voyages plotted upon it was not. The map for *Robinson Crusoe* was virtually identical to the first map in Dampier's *New Voyage* whereas Swift's maps of Lilliput and Brobdingnag were at odds with real maps and, it has been argued, obviously satirical.[15] A fanciful map in *Crusoe* would have had the effect of indicating to the reader that the "telling overprotestation" of the editor of *Crusoe* was just that, but the inclusion of a credible map presumably had the opposite effect; while it would not have settled the matter, it would have functioned as one more inducement to reading the text as a genuine history.

To a reader without a clear sense of whether the work was fiction or history but who was inclined to accept its historical claim, there was much within the text to justify that approach. There were, for example, the many ways in which *Robinson Crusoe* functioned as a record of the experience of an amateur natural historian. Crusoe makes several surveys of his island during which he inventories the flora and fauna. On his first survey, he describes different vegetation zones, first "pleasant *Savana's*, or Meadows; plain, smooth, and cover'd with Grass," next "the higher Grounds, where . . . I found a great deal of Tobacco," and finally the area where "the *Savana's* began to cease, and the Country became more woody than before." Noticing "Plants of Alloes," "several Sugar Canes, but wild," "Mellons upon the Ground," and "Grapes upon the Trees" as well as

---

[15] For the argument for and against the view that Swift's cartography was "fanciful" or "satirical," see J. R. Moore, "The Geography of *Gulliver's Travels*," *Journal of English and Germanic Philology* 40 (1941), 214, 216; A. E. Case, *Four Essays on Gulliver's Travels* (Princeton University Press, 1945), 54; Frederick Bracher, "The Maps in Gulliver's Travels," *Huntington Library Quarterly* 8 (1944), 67, 73. Cf. Adams, *Travel Literature*, 142–44.

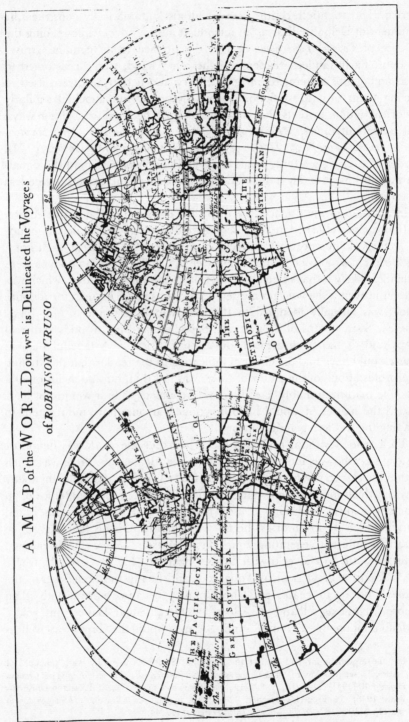

Figure 8 Map, fourth edition of *Robinson Crusoe* (1719).

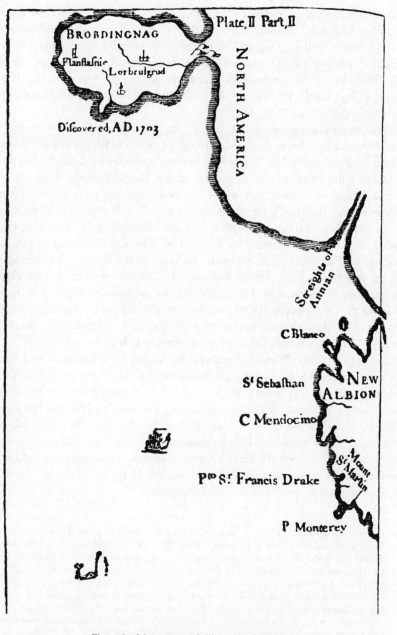

Figure 9   Map, part II, *Gulliver's Travels* (1726).

hares, foxes, goats, "Pidgeons," "innumerable Turtles," and "an infinite Number of Fowls, of many kinds . . . but such as I knew not the Names of, except those called *Penguins*," Crusoe also supplies the reader with a detailed picture of the seasons as he experienced them on the island, "divided, not into *Summer* and *Winter*, as in *Europe*, but into the Rainy Seasons and the Dry Seasons." Finally, all this latter material is presented in a table (98–99, 109–10, 106).

The presentation of this kind of "data" both within the narrative account and in tabular form established a kinship between *Crusoe* and such works as Dampier's *New Voyage* and various histories by Crouch. Dampier dedicates his work to the president of the Royal Society, suggests that perhaps his work does not merit "a place among your more Curious Collections," but finally offers his "plain piece" with its rich facticity out of a "hearty Zeal for the promotion of useful Knowledge." The *New Voyage* contains tables, documents, an account of a bout with illness in the East Indies, and another of a "Moskito Indian" who "lived . . . alone above three years" on Juan Fernandez Island. Crouch's treatments of *English Acquisitions in Guinea* and *The English Empire in America* contain lists of the East India Company's "Forts and Factories," accounts of journeys, royal documents, discussions of such topics as "the Soyl of Jamaica" ("there are many Plains which they call *Savana's* intermixt with Hills and Woods"), and plates representing "strange creatures in America." Dampier's and Crouch's texts were popular works that responded to and fostered the craze for popularized natural history at the end of the seventeenth century. Defoe used the *Philosophical Transactions* in writing *The Storm* and Secord has shown that in *Crusoe* Defoe drew in turn upon Dampier and *The Storm*, but this information has generally led to regarding those historical texts as sources for a novel. However, the links between *Crusoe* and such works would have inclined some early modern readers to regard Defoe's text not as a work of fiction but as the "just History" it claimed to be.[16]

---

[16] Dampier, *New Voyage*, sig. A$_2$r–v; [Crouch], *English Acquisitions in Guinea* (London, 1700), t.p.; *The English Empire in America* (London, 1685), 207, 185. Secord introduced his *Narrative Method*, the model for all source studies, by discussing what he called "the Defoe Problem" (the question asked of "nearly all of Defoe's narratives . . . are they fact or fiction?"), and he sought to solve the problem by providing "a more thorough knowledge of the materials which Defoe utilized in composing his works." In speaking of Defoe's method of composition in *Robinson Crusoe*, Secord concludes that "the courses and geographical matters . . . are based upon more or less authentic relations but the details . . . are largely invented by Defoe from suggestions contained in these relations"; *Narrative Method*, 10, 17. These studies in the end did not solve "the Defoe problem" largely because the sheer volume of "facts" deployed within a text that also has a demonstrable or acknowledged fictional aspect can never provide a satisfactory basis for generic classification; readers make qualitative judgments about the fundamental nature of texts and then accommodate the particular use of "fact" and "fiction" in those texts in accordance with those judgments; Foley, *Telling the Truth*, 27–28. Yet all the same this scholarship does have the (often unintended) effect of

In addition to sketching in the natural history of his island, Crusoe also presented his readers with an outline of the history of human economic activity, one that has been compared with Defoe's treatment of similar material in *The History of Trade* and *The General History of Discoveries and Improvements*.[17] Shortly after he begins to explore his environment, Crusoe's ability to exploit it progressively develops. He starts with hunting and gathering; in respect to these activities, his discovery of grapes on the island is illustrative: "I resolved to lay up a store . . . to furnish myself for the wet season." To accomplish this, he tells us, "I gathered a large quantity of the grapes and hung them up upon the out branches in the sun." Later, having established the pattern of the seasons, Crusoe moves from gathering to cultivating crops, thereby replicating a momentous leap in human economic history: "I dug up a piece of ground as well as I could with my wooden spade, and dividing it into two parts [for barley and rice], I sowed my grain." Crusoe then relates his first attempt at manufacture: "cutting some of the smaller twigs . . . I employed myself in making, as well as I could, a great many baskets . . . and tho' I did not finish them very handsomely, yet I made them sufficiently serviceable for my purposes." The relation is brief and fragmentary at this point, but Crusoe fleshes out the sketch of economic history later as he reports, among other accomplishments, his strides in animal husbandry, in the cultivation of corn, and in pottery (114–15, 118, 120, 128–30, 131–33, and 154). The entire account acts as evidence provided by Crusoe for his declaration of a Baconian belief in the human capacity to master both nature itself and nature "wrought or mechanical":

So I went to work; and here I must needs observe, that as Reason is the Substance and Original of the Mathematicks, so by stating and squaring every thing by Reason, and by making the most rational Judgment of things, every Man may be in time Master of every mechanick Art. (68)

If one reads *Robinson Crusoe* as a novel, the preceding discussion serves to demonstrate how Defoe thematized the Baconian vision in his fictional rendering of a human being *in extremis*. Ilse Vickers argues along these lines, asserting that in *Robinson Crusoe* Defoe "render[ed] the experimental philosophy of things in fictional terms."[18] Once this concretization of the text is initiated, furthermore, the reader readily categorizes all such "historical" features of the narrative as devices employed by Defoe, whether consciously or not, to render his fiction verisimilar. But if one

---

demonstrating how it was possible for eighteenth-century readers to read *Robinson Crusoe* and other Defoe "novels" as veracious accounts.

[17] Sutherland, *Defoe*, 231; Vickers, "New Sciences," 210–14; Novak, *Economics and the Fiction of Daniel Defoe* (Berkeley: University of California Press, 1962), ix.

[18] Vickers, "New Sciences," 210.

approaches the text as a factual account, then the narrative functions not as a fictional thematization but as a lively illustration of the Baconian principle that "commerce between the mind of man and the nature of things" leads to knowledge for "the benefit and use of life."[19] Given the nature of seventeenth- and early eighteenth-century historiography in general, and Defoe's historiography in particular, such a reading was possible not only for readers who believed that Crusoe was an historical individual, but also for those readers who sensed that some of the account was feigned but who had been prepared by the rules of existing historiography to regard fictional material as an acceptable element in historical discourse.

It was not only Defoe's material, however, that encouraged many readers to read *Crusoe* as a work of history; "the agreeable Manner of the Performance" would have had the same effect.[20] Without a clear signal that the work was fictional, those aspects of the narrative that Ian Watt identified in *The Rise of the Novel* as the defining features of novelistic or "formal realism" would have reassured readers that the work in hand was history. It was set in reasonably precise times (1632; twenty-eight years on the island) and locales (York; an island off the coast of South America near the mouth of the Orinoco River); it was an account of a specific person "in particular circumstances" such as, for example, Crusoe himself amidst "the confusion of thought which I felt when I sunk into the water"; and it was written, like Dampier's plain piece, in a language "much more largely referential . . . than in other literary forms" (44).[21] All these features would have supported the editor's claim that the work was historical if a reader were inclined, as the result of readerly experience and of the initial signals offered by the text itself, to concretize the text as history. As in the case of certain histories – *Charles XII* for example where the editor cited common knowledge – the editor of *Robinson Crusoe*, having cited the "modesty" and "seriousness" with which the story was told, recommended the text to his readers because it *appeared* to be true. Defoe's method, therefore, served as an argument not for the author's imaginative powers but for the authenticity of the text's historical claims. Watt himself put the matter succinctly, though to a different end from my own, when he observed that "the novel has less need of historical and literary commentary than other genres . . . [because] its formal convention forces it *to supply its own footnotes*."[22] Thus both the "Manner of the Performance" and the material that was presented in the text recommended it to readers as a factual account.

With a view of how Defoe's most famous narrative could have been read as a "just History" by early modern readers, we can perhaps also set in a

19 Bacon, *Selected Writings*, 423, 437.   20 Shinagel, ed., *Robinson Crusoe*, 258.
21 Watt, *Rise of the Novel*, 15, 30, 32.   22 *Ibid.*, 30; emphasis added.

somewhat different light one of the key features of *Crusoe* and the other "novels" that has been stressed by critics who have argued for Defoe's self-conscious use of the novel form: his appropriation of the "moral and ideological aims" of Puritan guide literature or spiritual autobiography.[23] J. Paul Hunter and George Starr definitively changed our view of Defoe by revealing the extent of his debt to these forms; seeking to demonstrate "the artistry of *Robinson Crusoe*," Hunter shows that the book is "structured on the basis of a familiar Christian pattern of disobedience-punishment-repentance-deliverance" and that "Crusoe's continual appraisal of his situation" in light of that pattern is not "superficial commentary" but "an integral part of the thematic pattern" of the narrative.[24] Defoe's appropriation of the narrative conventions and ideational structures of religious narratives has also been seen as evidence that he imparted "form" to the matters of fact he used in his most famous narratives and that those works consequently deserve to be regarded as well-wrought novels.

Yet one can also argue that the debt of those texts to guide literature and spiritual autobiography was wholly consistent with their presentation as species of historical discourse. An alert early modern reader of Baxter or Hutchinson would have recognized that the former appropriated an incident from Augustine's *Confessions* in presenting his own spiritual progress and that the latter used the life of Moses to tell the story of her husband's life, without concluding that the Life in hand was a work of fiction. These were the models that faith provided both for living a life and for writing a Life. For us *Robinson Crusoe* is more like a novel when we recognize Defoe's importation of form from spiritual autobiographies and the like, but for an eighteenth-century reader *Crusoe*'s kinship with guide literature would not have necessitated its being concretized as fiction. This is especially so since Crusoe derives not only a vital religious (and political and social) lesson ("a *Memento* to those who are touch'd with the general Plague of Mankind . . . I mean, that of not being satisfy'd with the Station wherein God and Nature has placed them") but also what Vickers calls his "philosophy of things" from his struggle for survival and well-being on the island (194).[25] Thus *Robinson Crusoe* could have been read as a history that was "fruitful of Examples."[26]

---

23 The two crucial arguments along these lines are Hunter, *Reluctant Pilgrim*; and Starr, *Defoe and Spiritual Autobiography*; a recent work that is apposite is Leopold Damrosch, *God's Plot and Man's Stories: Studies in the Fictional Imagination from Milton to Fielding* (University of Chicago Press, 1985).

24 Hunter, *Reluctant Pilgrim*, 13, 19–20.

25 Vickers, "New Sciences," 210; on the compatibility of the Baconian faith in knowledge derived from experience with the belief that experience is a record of God's plan for man on earth, see Webster, *Great Instauration*, 1.

26 Much of Defoe criticism has in its way confirmed this point, see, for example, Novak, *Economics*; Novak, *Defoe and the Nature of Man* (Oxford University Press, 1963); Manuel Schonhorn, "Defoe: The Literature of Politics and the Politics of Some Fictions," in *English Literature in the Age of*

There is no reason to argue, however, that *Crusoe* was accepted by all readers as a historical text; Philip Gove observes that "critics throughout Europe recognized it at once as a fiction," citing comments of 1720 from the *Journal des Sçavans* and the *Neue Zeitungen von gelehrten Sachen*. Yet the first such English comment that Gove refers to is from 1725, and he admits that Shiels "had some basis for believing" that initially *Crusoe* was read as a true account.[27] At the very least, then, Defoe did not enable readers unequivocally to place the text within the discourse of fiction or history. Undoubtedly there were some in London who knew, on the day the work appeared, that it had been written by Defoe, and others who guessed that it was imaginary, but there were also apparently many who read it as an account of matters of fact and probably more who were not sure, as both Defoe's preface and Gildon's objections suggest. What makes *Robinson Crusoe* so monumental is the moment of hesitation – brief for some readers, longer for others – during which the horizon of expectations definitively shifted and adjustments were made that ultimately forced such "historical" narratives to be read as works of fiction. Defoe's importance to the history of the novel lies principally in the fact that his narratives were a key part of the process in the course of which readers created a new narrative category, eventually labeled "novel." This category was generated in important part by the need to manage the tricky business of reading and classifying works – like those of Defoe – that at first seemed to function as history and that subsequently were read into fictional discourse.

Yet a fundamental question in respect to this text remains: why was *Crusoe* and not another text, such as the *Memoirs of Ramkins*, the locus of a "literary revolution"? The answer, as has often been implied, may simply have to do with the nature of Defoe's participant-narrator in *Crusoe*. Crusoe was different from all the participant-narrators who preceded him in Defoe's historical texts. Earlier, these putative historians (with the exception of Ramkins) related little of their own experience, and their lives (even in the case of Ramkins) were unimportant except insofar as the representation of their own experiences made the narrative of public events more credible and convincing. *Robinson Crusoe* was like Defoe's earlier histories in deriving its authority largely from its status as an account written by a participant, but it was profoundly different from the earlier histories in having as its narrator an individual who was necessarily the *only* participant in most of the events related, events that did not have a public aspect. For the first time in the evolution of Defoe's historical practice, the focus of the narrative became unavoidably private and personal.

Disguise, ed. Novak (Berkeley: University of California Press, 1973), 15–56, all of which show what "Examples" Defoe was illustrating in his narratives.
[27] Gove, *Imaginary Voyage*, 122.

Defoe had previously written histories in which he treated Jacobite rebellions, court intrigues, and catastrophic phenomena, and in them he did not represent the private experience of fictionalized narrators in such a way as to obscure his political lessons. Thus, even in the Ramkins *Memoirs*, the focus was Jacobite politics, and Ramkins's private adventures were designed to make the anti-Jacobitical argument of that text palatable. In *Robinson Crusoe*, however, Crusoe's experience was reported throughout the text, and Crusoe himself was the focus of the narrative. Defoe still had lessons to draw from his material, and in drawing on texts like Dampier's he gave to *Crusoe* the same rich facticity that characterizes *The Storm* or the *History of Charles XII*. But in this case the lessons derived not from the narrator's involvement in public events but from the private experience of an individual who found himself alone on "an un-inhabited Island."

The centrality of Crusoe in this narrative, and the consequences that flow from it, help to explain why *Robinson Crusoe* has been seen as the first English novel while the *Memoirs of Ramkins* seems at most a peculiar form of historical discourse or an unclassifiable hybrid.[28] McKillop has argued: "A decisive step marking the difference between compilation and fiction is taken when the accumulated detail is related to the intention, interest, and point of view of a character impersonated by the author."[29] Fiction, which earlier had been one of the historian's tools, became in this case the essence of the work, and a change that, from the perspective of the earlier histories, could be perceived as merely quantitative was ultimately qualitative: a new kind of narrative metamorphosed out of Defoe's historiography. In other words, once Defoe's "facts" had the effect of transforming a fictionalized participant-narrator into a "character," the novel may be said to have emerged. This is an important argument, best represented in Defoe criticism by Everett Zimmerman's assertion that "Defoe's novels raise the issue of self and identity prominently," and that in those texts we repeatedly "observe a character's desperate efforts to pull himself together in extremely difficult circumstances."[30] It is essential to recall, however, that even for eighteenth-century readers who read *Crusoe* as fiction, the narrative seemed more a vehicle for the facts and ideas contained in the work than for the representation of "vividly realized characters."[31] James Beattie, for example, focused on what *Robinson Crusoe* taught its readers: "piety and benevolence," "the importance of the mechanick arts," "the horrors of solitude," and "how, by labouring with one's hands, one may secure independence . . . health and amusement."[32] Beattie concentrates on the practical lessons embodied in the narrative, and alludes to

---

[28] Foley, *Telling the Truth*, 40–41.   [29] McKillop, *Early Masters*, 9.

[30] Everett Zimmerman, *Defoe and the Novel* (Berkeley: University of California Press, 1975), 5–6; see also Richetti, *Defoe's Narratives*, 8–12, 240.

[31] *Ibid.*, 17.   [32] Cited in Day, *Fiction to the Novel*, 51–52.

Rousseau's famous celebration of *Crusoe* as a vehicle for learning about the world "not through books, but through things."[33] As late as 1851, furthermore, an anonymous writer in *Chambers's Papers for the People* declared: "the grand peculiarity of the work is its immense display of *wordly wisdom*, its wide and varied representation of the interests, motives, rewards, and considerations whereby men are actuated."[34] Thus, even after readers realized that Defoe had written *Crusoe* and the other "novels," those narratives were still prized because, in Bacon's words, they "rest[ed] on the solid foundation of experience" and proffered a kind of knowledge prized for "its value and utility."[35]

Nevertheless, however much we attempt to understand *Robinson Crusoe* and the other novels as texts that situated themselves in respect to historical discourse for early modern readers, the question of what Defoe himself intended almost inescapably arises. At the very least, the present study can answer that Defoe could have presented this "modest" work – rich in material gleaned from reading in the historical literature of the day, full of "Instruction . . . by . . . example," and having no "Appearance of Fiction in it" – as a "Just History," secure in the belief that it was not a lie by Defoe's lights and that it therefore could be presented and read as matters of fact. Defoe, as has already been observed, seems always to have been more interested in the function than in the form of a text, so perhaps the closest we can come to answering this question is to consider the possibility that he knew that the narratives we call novels were strange and simply put aside questions of definition. McKillop has cogently argued that Defoe's presentation of "novels" to eighteenth-century readers "seems to have appeared as a mere variant of his extensive labors in journalism and pamphleteering"; it is not unreasonable (although it may be unsatisfying) to assume that in some ways it appeared so to the author as well.[36] Pressed to say what Defoe intended, however, I would point to Claudio Guillen's telling conception of form: "form is the presence in a created, man-made object of a 'cause'."[37] If *Crusoe* is examined in light, first, of Baconian historiography and, then, of Defoe's particular historical method, Defoe's desire to write history emerges as the "cause" of *Robinson Crusoe*.

Still, Defoe himself seems to have signaled a fundamental difference between *Crusoe* and earlier works, albeit only after he was compelled by attacks on *Crusoe* to defend and explain that work. In the *Serious Reflections of Robinson Crusoe* (1720), the narrator describes *Robinson Crusoe* as "Allegorick History" and asserts:

---

[33] Ibid., 52; Rousseau comment cited in Rogers, *Critical Heritage*, 52–53.

[34] [Anon.], "Daniel Defoe," *Chambers's Papers for the People*, 7 no. 56 (1851), 28.

[35] Bacon, *Selected Writings*, 427, 429.   [36] McKillop, *Early Masters*, 16.

[37] Claudio Guillen, *Literature as System* (Princeton University Press, 1971), 111.

All these reflections are just history of a State of forc'd confinement, which in my real History is represented by a confined Retreat in an Island; and 'tis as reasonable to represent one kind of Imprisonment by another, as it is to represent any thing that really exists, by that which exists not.

Defoe's fictionalized editor argues that the representation of one action or situation through the use of another action or situation does not relieve the author of the requirement to convey factual truth: "when . . . I mention my Solitudes and Retirements . . . all those Parts of the Story are real Facts in my History."[38] In *The Storm* Defoe asserted that facts were synonymous with truth, but his subsequent practice demonstrates that he saw fiction as a legitimate means of historical representation. What is new about *Crusoe*, is that the editor of *Serious Reflections* argued "that the Story, though Allegorical, is also Historical."[39]

Defoe here implicitly acknowledges that this historical text is somehow different from his earlier histories: a narrative that was *both* historical *and* fictional. He also defends his most famous work as a "private History," written out of "the common Way," using "facts that are *form'd* to touch the Mind . . . done a great Way off."[40] This is an extremely odd and a very important formulation. The new history, which Defoe knew and to whose tenets he at least theoretically subscribed, taught that facts must be uncovered, ascertained, stipulated, but never "form'd."[41] Baconian historiography allowed for fabulous narratives, rhetorical displays, polemical blasts, and sensational stories, all of which might be used by a critic to denounce a particular historical account as in reality a fiction. But neither Baxter, nor Burnet, nor Crouch, nor Gough, nor Hamilton defended their histories as works constructed of "facts . . . form'd to touch the Mind." Even Defoe, who fashioned his narratives out of published sources and presented them as the work of fictionalized narrators, had always insisted that his histories could be verified by referring to known sources, general knowledge, and common sense. In respect to *Robinson Crusoe*, however, he acknowledged that he had "form'd" the facts he presented, thereby seeming to recognize that the text was the site of a fundamental transformation.

And yet – and this point must be insisted upon – Defoe does not thereby yield his prerogative to classify *Robinson Crusoe* as history. It is *both* allegory

---

[38] Shinagel, ed., *Robinson Crusoe*, 261, 260; on Defoe's fiction and allegory, see Angus Fletcher, *Allegory: The Theory of a Symbolic Mode* (Ithaca: Cornell University Press, 1964), 332.

[39] Shinagel, ed., *Robinson Crusoe*, 259.   [40] *Ibid.*, 262; emphasis added.

[41] Twentieth-century theorists of history like Hayden White argue for the "form'd" character of all facts, but in doing so tend to deny the difference between fact and fiction. There is no real evidence for Davis's assertion that "for Defoe, fact was just another form of fiction," although Davis's corollary statement, "fiction was just a particular category of fact" does seem more defensible if one considers Defoe's particular brand of Baconian historiography; *Factual Fictions*, 173.

and history; the facts are "form'd" but they are nevertheless facts: "Matter of real History."Although one might argue that Defoe was backing off here – admitting that *Crusoe* was a work of fiction – in a certain sense nothing that Defoe asserted in his second and third defenses of *Crusoe* was new. In each of the prefatory remarks there was a contradictory assertion, veiled or otherwise, that the work was both fiction and history. Admittedly, by labeling *Robinson Crusoe* "Allegorick History" and informing the reader that it was fashioned from "form'd facts," Defoe brought this contradiction to the fore. Asserting this contradiction, Defoe seems to acknowledge that he is writing the new type of narrative that was anticipated by the seventeenth-century writers of "history" or antiromance. But with Defoe "history" developed in a way the antiromancers did not anticipate: Defoe made fiction historical by working as a historian who used fiction within historical discourse, not as a poet who gave his texts the trappings of history.

It would seem, however, that the transformation acknowledged in Defoe's paradoxical prefaces resulted more from the reception of *Robinson Crusoe* than from its production and presentation; Defoe's practice in *Crusoe* was not that different from his practice in the earlier histories. Attacks and queries like Gildon's forced Defoe to explain himself, but his practice did not change in light of those explanations. After *Crusoe*, he wrote other narratives that continued to lay claim to being read as history despite Defoe's having fashioned them out of "form'd facts." The task of theorizing these narratives was left to his readers. Shortly before *Crusoe* appeared, in J. Read's *Weekly Journal*, Defoe was declared a "Master . . . of forging a Story and imposing it on the World for Truth"; Seidel suggests that when Gildon "surmised that Crusoe was invented out of whole cloth," he was tapping into this already existent criticism of Defoe. Seidel also points out that "Gildon's objection . . . still haunts a good deal of Defoe criticism today."[42] The charge that Defoe was a liar forced readers to ask fundamental questions of this text: those who might have read *Crusoe* as a veracious account were put on notice that this approach to the text was faulty or at least incomplete. The charge reflected, and still reflects, uncertainty, and even anxiety, on the part of readers about Defoe's practice and the texts that he produced. Are they true or false, fact or fiction, lies or matters of fact?

The answer to these questions in the long run has been to associate Defoe's narratives, however uneasily, with the tradition of the novel, but that answer was elicited more by objections to and questions directed at Defoe and his texts than by the author's own signals to readers, which made the paradoxical claim that *Crusoe* could be read both as history and

---

[42] Seidel, *Island Myths*, 20, 22.

as fiction. Defoe presented *Crusoe* as history even though he admitted he used matters of fact of his own fashioning, and as a result his presentation of the text raised more questions than it answered. Defoe's contradiction was only resolved, and then problematically, in the extraordinary course of the reception of those narratives. But before turning to that reception history, we need to examine the presentation of the narratives that came after *Robinson Crusoe* and that have also, over time, been assimilated to the tradition of the novel.

II

Twentieth-century readers resist the idea that *Robinson Crusoe*, often regarded as the ur-novel, was ever read as history. Yet in respect to three other narratives published after *Crusoe* that are also frequently discussed as examples of Defoe' novels, the case is much clearer.[43] The presentation of *Captain Singleton*, *Memoirs of a Cavalier*, and *A Journal of the Plague Year* reveals Defoe doing his best "to ensure that they will be taken as authentic autobiographies" and in fact these texts were for many years read as genuine histories.[44]

Much of what we have observed about *Robinson Crusoe* might equally well be asserted about *Captain Singleton*, another narrative of the adventures of a mariner, who, like Dampier, became a pirate. *Singleton*, however, relates a trek across central Africa by the narrator-protagonist. Secord demonstrated that Defoe drew heavily upon published sources for this text, which featured the same rich facticity of *Crusoe* and like *Crusoe* contained an authentic map, but unlike the earlier work included no ambiguous preface. It is easy for us, at this stage in what Felix Vodička calls the "biography" of this work, to see that *Singleton* is replete with "gross inaccuracies" and that Defoe's skill in this text is revealed "not in his knowledge of Africa but in his creation of the illusion of knowledge by a clever use of background material and dramatic incident," especially in the treatment of regions of Africa about which nothing was known.[45] In 1720, however, quite a different approach to the novel seems to have been common; *Singleton* was serialized in *The Post-Master*, replacing another account of adventures at sea, and it was introduced as "another Treatise of fresher Date," thereby

---

[43] It must be said that after at least a generation during which Defoe's texts have fruitfully been read as novels, there is a current tendency to argue that this classification needs to be reconsidered; see, for example, Davis, *Factual Fictions*; Richetti, *Daniel Defoe*; David Roberts, introd., *A Journal of the Plague Year* (Oxford University Press, 1990); Penelope Wilson, introd., *Captain Singleton* (Oxford University Press, 1990).

[44] Wilson, ed., *Singleton*, ix; the comment refers to all the novels.

[45] Gary J. Scrimgeour, "The Problem of Realism in Defoe's *Captain Singleton*," *Huntington Library Quarterly* 27 (1963–64), 22, 24.

suggesting that *Singleton*, like the earlier work, was initially read as an authentic history.[46]

Memoirs of a Cavalier appeared immediately after *Robinson Crusoe* and but for the fact that it was published after *Crusoe* rather than before, it might never have been read as a novel at all. Generically, *Memoirs of a Cavalier* is much more akin to the earlier military and Jacobite memoirs, especially to *Ramkins*, than to *Crusoe*, and the editor defends the *Memoirs* as authentic and valuable in terms that echo the defense of the *History of Charles XII*: "There can be nothing objected against the general Credit of this Work, seeing its Truth is established upon universal History; and almost all the Facts, especially those of Moment, are confirmed for their general Part by all the Writers of those Times" (4).[47] The preface suggests that anyone familiar with other accounts of the same events will immediately recognize the text's authenticity, and since the text was "almost entirely fabricated from published works," the assertion could well have functioned as a guarantee of the text's historicity rather than as a covert signal of its fictionality.[48]

If we compare the *Memoirs* with Defoe's earlier military and Jacobite memoirs, the cavalier emerges as Defoe's most fully realized participant-narrator; he has a private life and a family history that make it possible to discuss him as a fictional character. Although there is a tendency in this work, similar to that noted in *Ramkins*, to alternate between public events and private experience, Defoe integrates the personal and political more effectively here than in any of the earlier memoirs of this sort. In the winter before he joined the Swedish army, for example, the cavalier "tarried at Milan"; once in Italy he personally experiences the decadence of that society, falling in with a "*courtezan*," who is reminiscent of Ramkins's "young Spanish lady." But whereas the only link between the personal and the public in Ramkins's *Memoirs* is a tendency to write about both in terms of martial metaphors, the Italian experience disposes the cavalier to take the side of the Protestants against "the Popish princes" because he attributes the degeneracy of Italy to the "incoherent devotion, and the grossest of idolatry" practiced there (31–32).

James Boulton argues that "the Cavalier is no mere pasteboard figure . . . [but] an individual, vital character," and certainly the cavalier is a more credible participant-narrator than Defoe's earlier military memoirists.[49] But it is easy to make too much of the cavalier and, by arguing that the *Memoirs* are focused on the narrator, to assert that the work is,

[46] Wilson, introd., *Captain Singleton*, viii.

[47] This language in *Charles XII* and *Memoirs* may support the claim that Defoe wrote both; *Memoirs of a Cavalier*, ed. James Boulton, introd. John Mullan (Oxford University Press, 1991), 4; hereafter citations in the text.

[48] Secord, "Origins," 130.

[49] Boulton, introd., *Memoirs of a Cavalier* (Oxford University Press, 1972), xii.

therefore, an historical novel.[50] Yet, an examination of, for example, the treatment of the battle of Edgehill in the *Memoirs* tends to refute this view and to suggest instead that the focus of the narrative is an investigation of the quality of leadership in the Civil War and of leadership in general. The cavalier informs us, approvingly, that Prince Rupert was eager to fight, and he also points out that at the time of Edgehill the king was contemplating a move on London that might have succeeded, but that Charles "suffered his Judgement to be over-ruled by a Majority of Voices; an Error, I say, the King of *Sweden* was never guilty of." The cavalier and his father debate the wisdom of the battle, and the father sees the situation clearly: "*Parliament will have the Victory; for we have lost more by slipping this Opportunity of getting into* LONDON, *than we shall ever get by ten Battles.*" The cavalier points out a disastrous tactical error on Prince Rupert's part, and concludes his account of Edgehill by arguing that "as to its being a Victory, neither side had much to Boast of." The cavalier reports his own limited role, including the fact that he "spoiled a good horse" (155–63). This account of a crucial battle hardly supports the view that this text is about "one man's response to history."[51] Rather it is a narrative that seeks to expose the flaws in royalist leadership and indicate by contrast (using the Gustavus Adolphus section) what good leadership is, all this in an historical narrative putatively written by an informed insider. Even Boulton, who argues that the cavalier "is given an existence totally independent of facts derived from historians," nevertheless admits that the aims of the text are political and excuses Defoe for the "paucity of imaginative resource" displayed in the work on the grounds that "this is an author who is patently not out to deceive by stylistic contrivance." Looked at as an historical text with a fictionalized narrator, one might argue that the *Memoirs* is a tour de force, but looked at as a novel, it seems fair to characterize it, as Richetti has done, as a "lumpish" and "deadening historical narrative."[52] In any case, we know that many eighteenth-century readers did read this work as history. Thus, considering *Singleton* and the *Memoirs*, it is very difficult to argue that Defoe "developed the form of the novel" in fashioning *Crusoe*, since immediately after *Crusoe* he presented narratives to his readers that, despite their similarities to *Crusoe*, were presented and commonly read as authentic histories.[53]

Similarly, everything about *A Journal of the Plague Year* suggests that it was offered to readers as a genuine account of an outbreak of the plague in Marseilles in the early 1720s. The newspapers of the day allowed readers to monitor closely the course of the outbreak in France, and in

---

[50] See, for example, John J. Burke, Jr., "Observing the Observer in Historical Fictions by Defoe," *Philological Quarterly* 61 (1982), 13–32.

[51] *Ibid.*, 20.   [52] Boulton, introd., *Memoirs*, xii, xiii; Richetti, *Defoe's Narratives*, 191.

[53] Seidel, *Island Myths*, 27.

the same pages in which medical developments on the continent were detailed, books concerning the plague were advertised.[54] Defoe's text was simply one of several books published in 1722 in response to anxieties about a possible recurrence of the disease in London. The presentation in the periodical press of these other works on the plague suggests that the market for such works was shaped by a desire for factual, practical treatises on the subject. Newspapers carried advertisements for *A brief Journal of what passed in the City of Marseilles, while it was Afflicted with the Plague* and Richard Mead's *Short Discourse concerning Pestilential Contagion, and the Methods to be used to prevent it.* Texts written in response to earlier outbreaks of plague were also reprinted and advertised; these included the seventeenth-century work, *A Treatise of the PESTILENCE* (1603), written by Thomas Thayre, and Dr. Nathaniel Hodges's *Loimologia: Or, an Historical Account of the Plague in London in 1665* (1671). And at the same time newspapers carried advertisements for the *Journal of the Plague Year*, "written by a Citizen" but "never made Public before."[55] Such works, then, were associated with Defoe's in the popular press and also, presumably, in the booksellers' shops.

There is no reason to surmise that any of these works were thought of as something other than factual discussions of the plague, functioning as advice on how to behave should the disease appear again in England. In fact, as we shall see, even after the truth about the *Journal*'s provenance became public knowledge, many readers continued to assert its historicity. One need not assume, therefore, that early readers accepted the *Journal* as history simply because Defoe successfully lied about the status of the text. The *Journal*, and *Singleton* and *Memoirs* as well, are what Richetti calls "thickly factual, even grossly truthful" texts, written from the perspective of a fictionalized narrator and containing a considerable admixture of invented material, but also presented in such a way as to ensure that they would be read as species of historical discourse.[56] That we now read these texts as novels or as works that belong more to the discourse of the novel than to the discourse of history says more finally about how we think about the novel than it does about Defoe's practice. What seems certain,

---

54 *The Daily Journal,* January 11, 1722, 2; *The Post Boy,* January 6–9, 1722, [1]; *The Weekly Journal; Or, Saturday's Post,* February 24, 1722, 1012.

55 *Daily Courant,* January 5, 1722, [2]; *Post Boy,* February 13–15, 1722, [2]; March 10–13, [2]; March 15–17, 1722, [2]. That the *Journal* was actually read as a practical guide to facing the problems attendant upon an outbreak of the plague is borne out by the ninth edition of Mead's treatise; see chapter 10 below.

56 Richetti, *Defoe's Narratives,* 240; Richetti is referring to the *Journal.* It might be objected that one cannot make the same assertion about *Singleton* because it is far less clearly a product of Defoe's sources than were the *Journal* and *Memoirs,* especially since, as Scrimgeour shows, the account of the trip across Africa depends more on what was *not* known about the continent than on what was known. Yet as late as 1864, *Singleton* was being treated as a "treatise" even by readers who knew that Defoe was the author; see Wilson, ed., *Singleton,* viii–ix and chapter 10 below.

however, is that many of Defoe's earliest readers concretized these works as histories, and the evidence suggests that they might have done so even if they had known that Defoe was the writer.

III

Finally, there is the case of *Moll Flanders*, often treated as Defoe's finest novelistic achievement.[57] The first thing to be said about *Moll* is that the work is at least putatively an example of criminal biography written at a time when England seemed to be experiencing a terrible crime wave, as a result of which there was "a sustained chorus of anxiety about crime." Defoe responded to this development in the various journals he wrote or edited at the time and then also addressed the issue in longer narratives.[58] This sort of narrative tended to situate itself uncertainly in respect to the fact-fiction boundary: "from its inception . . . criminal biography could seem . . . an especially fragile and suspect discourse." Lincoln Faller argues that these texts worked by "alternatively disordering and distorting the real, endowing it with certain meanings and depriving it of others [and therefore] criminal biography was very much in its own right a kind of fiction." Since what Faller has in mind is the way that criminal biography engaged in the "shaping" or "patterning" of "the real," another way to construe the discourse of crime is to assert that criminal biography – a form that presented matters of fact but allowed the writer much leeway in shaping the material – was simply a brand of Baconian historiography.[59]

Alexander Smith's *Lives of the Highwaymen* (1713–19) was typical of the genre. This work told the life stories of more than 180 recent thieves, at least 60 percent of whom Robert Singleton found in contemporary documents. Many of the biographies, however, bore the marks of the "jest books and picaresque literature" from which they were at least partially derived, while others were "completely serious and copied accurately if without acknowledgement from the original confessions." Also, Secord classified Smith's *Lives* as "the most important work of fiction" published in eighteenth-century England before *Crusoe*, but the eighteenth century was not so sure: Richard Steele treated the work as a collection of genuine biographies and there seems little doubt that "the more ignorant . . .

---

[57] See, most notably, Virginia Woolf, "Defoe," in *The Common Reader*, First Series (New York: Harcourt, Brace and World, 1925), 89–97. See also Watt, *Rise of the Novel*, chapter 4; and McKillop, *Early Masters*, 28–33.

[58] Ian Bell, *Literature and Crime in Augustan England* (London: Routledge, 1991), 17; Novak, *Realism, Myth, and History*, 123, 127–29.

[59] Faller, *Crime and Defoe*, 23, xiii.

readers," who, G. M. Maynadier, says "were imposed upon" by *Moll Flanders*, also read at least part of Smith's *Lives* as history.[60]

Is it legitimate to regard *Moll Flanders* as one of Defoe's criminal biographies, as part of his response to the problem of crime, and as a work apprehended by at least some readers as a work of history? The text, its title page informs the reader, was written from Moll's "own MEMORAN-DUMS," and this assertion was repeated in the advertisements for *Moll Flanders* at the same time that Eliza Haywood's *Love in Excess* was being touted as a novel and the three volumes of *Robinson Crusoe* were being advertised without any mention of Defoe's name.[61] The narrator begins by informing us that Moll Flanders is a pseudonym for a notorious person who is so well known that she must change her name to protect herself against "things of . . . Consequence" pending at Newgate and the Old Bailey (7). Clearly some readers took this claim seriously because several pamphlets appeared in 1723 that asserted the real Moll Flanders was Elizabeth Atkins, who had died in Galway in April, 1722.[62] Defoe's great talent for what James Sutherland has called "imaginative reporting," furthermore, would have convinced many readers that Moll's life was actually "written from her own MEMORANDUMS."[63] The representation in the text of the moment when Moll becomes a thief illustrates the point:

WANDRING thus about I knew not whither, I pass'd by an Apothecary's Shop in *Leadenhall-street*, where I saw lye on a Stool just before the Counter a little Bundle wrapt in a white Cloth; beyond it, stood a Maid Servant with her Back to it, looking up towards the top of the Shop, where the Apothecary's Apprentice, as I suppose, was standing up on the Counter, with his Back also to the Door, and a Candle in his Hand, looking and reaching up to the upper Shelf for Something he wanted, so that both were engag'd mighty earnestly, and nobody else in the Shop.

THIS was the Bait; and the Devil who I said laid the Snare, as readily prompted me, as if he had spoke, for I remember, and shall never forget it, 'twas like a Voice spoken to me over my Shoulder, take the Bundle; be quick; do it this Moment; it was no sooner said but I step'd into the Shop, and with my Back to the Wench, as if I had stood up for a Cart that was going by, I put my Hand behind me and took the Bundle, and went off with it, the Maid or the Fellow not perceiving me, or any one else.

IT is impossible to express the Horror of my Soul all the while I did it: When I went away I had no Heart to run, or scarce to mend my pace; I cross'd the Street indeed, and went down the first turning I came to, and I think it was a Street that

60 Robert Singleton, "English Criminal Biography, 1651–1722," *Harvard Library Bulletin* 18 (1970), 71–72; G. H. Maynadier, introd., *Works of Daniel Defoe*, 16 vols. (New York: George D. Sproul, 1913), VII, vii. The Secord comment is cited in Singleton.
61 *Moll Flanders*, ed. G. A. Starr (Oxford University Press, 1971), 3; hereafter cited in the text. *Mist's Weekly Journal*, February 10, 1722; *Post Boy*, February 24–27, 1722.
62 Gerald Howson, "Who was Moll Flanders?" *TLS*, no. 3438 (January 18, 1968), 63.
63 Sutherland, ed., *Moll Flanders* (Boston: Houghton, Mifflin, 1959), viii.

went thro' into *Fenchurch-street*, from thence I cross'd and thurn'd thro' so many ways and turnings that I could never tell which way it was, nor where I went, for I felt not the Ground I stept on, and the farther I was out of Danger, the faster I went, till tyr'd and out of Breath, I was forc'd to sit down on a little Bench at a Door, and then I began to recover, and found I was got into *Thames-street* near *Billingsgate*.   (191–92)

I quote at length here because this passage is a touchstone for Defoe criticism. The spatial, geographical, physical, and psychological particularity of it make it a hallmark of Defoe's realism. Moll describes with great care not only her plausible path through London and her state of mind but also the disposition and the presumed positions of the two workers in the apothecary's shop, the way she handled the seizure of the bundle, and, most subtle of all, how her movements could have been construed by a glancing passerby or attendant in another shop. Such moments as this led Charles Lamb to exult:

The narrative manner of De Foe has a naturalness about it beyond that of any other novel or romance writer. His fictions have all the air of true stories. It is impossible to believe, while you are reading them, that a real person is not narrating . . . what really happened to himself.[64]

But as I argued in discussing *Crusoe*, anyone at all disposed by a previous familiarity with criminal biography and by the protestations at the beginning of the text to read *Moll Flanders* as a genuine life of an actual person would have found in this passage and others like it a powerful confirming argument for accepting the text as an account of matters of fact. Sutherland's labeling of Defoe's work in *Moll* as "imaginative reporting" nicely captures the potential effect of this passage; even for later readers who know that *Moll* is a work of the imagination, it is hard not to read this account as a species of reporting. Thus Leslie Stephen, in discussing "Defoe's Novels," argues that *Moll Flanders* cannot "fairly claim any higher interest than that which belongs to the ordinary police report, given with infinite fulness and vivacity of detail." Stephen, who considered Defoe a great writer but not an important novelist, argues that the importance of *Moll Flanders* "bears a direct proportion to the intrinsic merit of a plain statement of facts."[65]

Is it any wonder then that many readers, not just Maynadier's "more ignorant" ones, have read *Moll Flanders* as an historical account? That this is so will be documented in the next chapter, but here it is worth noting that recently a number of sophisticated readers of this most novelistic of Defoe's texts have argued that the work was based on documentary evidence or personal experience. Even George Starr, who claims that

[64] Cited in Edward H. Kelly, ed., *Moll Flanders* (New York: W. W. Norton, 1973), 326.
[65] Rogers, *Critical Heritage*, 172.

"within the novel is a romance, which gives the story much of its emotional force," argues that Defoe's text is distinct from other criminal biographies in lacking "the 'Tricks' and 'Pranks' of traditional rogue literature" and that Moll's "career owes less to such semi-fictional narratives than to accounts of actual thefts, which were available to Defoe in newspaper reward-advertisements, in the published proceedings of Old Bailey trials, and in conversations with friends." Starr objects that it is in fact "misleading to imply," as some have done, "that *Moll Flanders* is to any significant degree about [the real thief] Moll King, for the book is even less her history than *Robinson Crusoe* is Alexander Selkirk's." This point cuts both ways, however; perhaps Moll's story is just as much a "compilation" of "formed facts" as is *Robinson Crusoe*. At the very least we can say that this text, putatively Defoe's most successful essay of the novel form, was apparently regarded as a (no doubt problematic) species of historical discourse even by readers who recognized that it had been written by Defoe. No wonder, then, that some readers took Defoe's editor at his word when he carefully positioned the text in the discursive terrain of 1722:

The World is so taken up of late with Novels and Romances, that it will be hard for a private History to be taken for Genuine where the Names and other Circumstances of the Person are concealed.   (1)[66]

Defoe's preface for *Moll* allows readers to situate the text within the discourse of history, but it would be foolish not to acknowledge that the text also suggests the concretization of this text is no simple task. "The original of this story," the editor tells us, "is a little alter'd," and the editor "has had no little difficulty to put" Moll's original memorandums "into a Dress fit to be seen." Concerned that the reader might think Moll's life story "leud" and "immodest," the editor declares "as this Work is chiefly recommended to those who know how to read it . . . it is to be hop'd that such Readers will be much more pleas'd with the Moral, than the Fable . . . and with the End of the Writer, than with the Life of the Person written of" (1–2). Thus Defoe clearly provides a basis for construing *Moll* as a fable as well as a history. As was the case with *Robinson Crusoe*, the assertions of the editor of *Moll Flanders* are contradictory and are allowed to remain so: on the one hand, the work is a "private History" distinct from the "novels and Romances" of the day, and, on the other, it presents itself as a fable designed to advance a moral.

Faller bases his discussion of the "new kind of writing" that emerges from Defoe's treatment of crime upon the ambiguities in the text's presentation. He identifies two principal kinds of criminal biography at this time: "the morally serious and quasi-realistic . . . a kind of spiritual

---

[66] Defoe leaves it to the reader to decide; this laissez-faire attitude is actually more characteristic of Baconian historiography than of seventeenth-century "history" or antiromance.

biography, and the generally frivolous, overtly romantic and often fantastic." Although he argues that Defoe appropriated the "winking claims to be factual" found in *Moll Flanders* from the latter type, Faller sees Defoe's text as more closely akin to the first sort because "his novels mean to be taken quite seriously." Quite tellingly for the argument I am advancing here, Faller describes the "crime novels" (*Moll, Singleton, Colonel Jack,* and *Roxana*) as "versions of criminal biography [that] aim at greater adequacy to the actual" and then asserts: "being novels, they achieve it (or rather, *seeming* to achieve it, they *become* novels, indeed begin to define the very genre 'novel')."[67] In other words, striving to be more "adequate" accounts of the real – asking, that is, to be read as matters of fact – *Moll Flanders* sends such signals to its readers as to require of them that they begin, along with the text itself, to theorize a new form, one that is neither "private history" nor a "romance," but somehow, again paradoxically, both.

IV

The point, once again, is *not* that *Moll Flanders* or any of Defoe's other "novels" *are* histories, but that they *were* plausibly presented as histories when they appeared, both because Defoe, with what Pat Rogers has nicely labeled his "scholarly application of the demotic" – his habit of forming facts for popular histories of thieves, pirates, castaways, and "national convulsions" – presented the texts to readers as works of history, and because many readers early and late were inclined to take him at his word.[68] Many readers, however, have found powerful reasons for reading Defoe's works as novels. Starr, for example, suggests a debt to romance in *Moll,* and his earlier work on spiritual autobiography argued that Defoe used the patterns of that narrative form to impart "the coherence of design" to *Moll* and *Robinson Crusoe.*[69] Some of Defoe's earliest readers must have caught glimpses of this aspect of his practice. The concretization of Defoe's narratives, then, would have presented a real challenge to some in Defoe's initial audience. What we can imagine, therefore, is readers suddenly apprehending that there were inescapable reasons for reading Defoe's narratives not as works of history but as fictional texts constructed wholly of "form'd facts." That realization – sometimes signaled by an angry assertion that Defoe was little better than a liar – and the subsequent realization that such narratives were qualitatively different *both* from other

---

[67] Faller, *Crime and Defoe,* 6, 29, 7.

[68] Rogers, *Literature and Popular Culture in Eighteenth-Century England* (Sussex: Harvester, 1985), 151. The second quote is Scott's characterization of the *Journal* and *Memoirs;* Scott, *On Novelists and Fiction,* 167.

[69] Starr, ed., *Moll,* vii; Starr, *Spiritual Autobiography,* 183.

species of Baconian historiography *and* from other fictional forms with which readers were familiar, made the shift in the horizon of readerly expectations that was necessitated by Defoe's "novels" one of the constitutive moments in the emergence of the English novel.

Thus readers, over time, read Defoe's "just histories" into the tradition of the novel in English. Georges May once argued that the novel emerged from history around this time, specifically from biography as a form of history, and that the crucial transitional form was the invented life story or *mémoires*.[70] May did not discuss Defoe in any detail but he indicated that he thought Defoe was a crucial figure in this transformation and that *Robinson Crusoe* held the key to understanding Defoe's contribution to it; he also singled out Hamilton's *Memoirs of Count Grammont*. This study confirms May's view but it also suggests that the change came about in important part because readers reading Defoe were forced to theorize a new form of discourse: fiction constructed of matters of fact "form'd to touch the mind." The reception of Defoe, to which we now turn, made some of his histories into novels and in the process stipulated an important aspect of novelistic discourse: its capacity to do the work of history.

[70] Georges May, "L'histoire a-t-elle engendré le roman?" *Revue d'histoire littéraire de la France* 55 (1955), 157.

10

From history to the novel: the reception of Defoe

We have seen that the narratives of Defoe that have come to be regarded as novels were presented to readers as histories and were often initially read as such. Yet by the end of the eighteenth century *Robinson Crusoe*, *Moll Flanders*, *A Journal of the Plague Year*, and the other "novels" had been issued under Defoe's name, and works by Anna Laetitia Barbauld, James Beattie, and Sir Walter Scott around the turn of the eighteenth century identified Defoe as a novelist and assigned at least some of his most important texts to the canon of English novels.[1] This process was far from smooth, however; Scott initially left Defoe out of his *Lives of the Novelists*, and there was no entry on Defoe in John Dunlop's groundbreaking *History of Fiction* (1814).[2] Still, as the nineteenth century proceeded, important studies of Defoe as a novelist by the likes of Charles Lamb, Walter Wilson, William Hazlitt, and Leslie Stephen appeared.[3] What is surprising about all this commentary, however, is that it did not really settle what A. W. Secord would later label "the Defoe problem" – the question of how fact and fiction are related in his narratives – nor did it satisfactorily clarify the matter of what generic classification was appropriate for his major texts.[4]

Uncertainty about Defoe has continued to our own day. It seems that if historians and theoreticians of the English novel cannot live without Defoe, they cannot live very comfortably with him either. For Ian Watt, Defoe initiated the English novel with *Robinson Crusoe* and *Moll Flanders*, but for Ralph Rader, Defoe's "stories of the pseudofactual type," especially but not solely *Moll Flanders*, cannot be regarded as novels at all.[5] Defoe presents a case, then, that is crucial and yet singular, peculiar, and vexing, and perhaps no work by Defoe presents as difficult a case as the *Journal of the Plague Year*. In this chapter I shall approach "the Defoe problem" by

---

[1] Anna Laetitia Barbauld, ed., *The British Novelists; with an Essay and Prefaces, Biographical and Critical* (London, 1810), vol. xvi; on Beattie, see chapter 7 above.
[2] Scott, *On Novelists and Fiction*, 15–17; John Dunlop, *The History of Fiction*, 3 vols. (London, 1814).
[3] Rogers, ed., *Critical Heritage*, 18–22.   [4] Secord, *Narrative Method*, 9–20.
[5] Watt, *Rise of the Novel*, 92–94; Rader, "Concept of Form in the Novel," 39–47.

treating the reception of his most famous narratives, concentrating particularly on the *Journal*.[6]

Jauss assumes that even the most innovative works, requiring the greatest amount of adjustment in the reader's horizon of expectations, are, in the normal course of things, successfully assimilated to the literary series to which they pertain, revolutionary works with which readers eventually come to terms often assuming thereby the status of classics. Although he considers the possibility that some texts are so revolutionary "that an audience can only gradually develop for them," Jauss does not contemplate the possibility of a work appearing that more or less permanently resists such assimilation.[7] In the present chapter I shall discuss the various ways that the *Journal* has been concretized by readers and show that although Defoe's narrative of a plague outbreak has in some ways achieved classic status, it has never entirely ceased to be a work with revolutionary potential to unsettle readers by posing questions they find difficult to answer. The fact-or-fiction dilemma has always been of paramount interest to readers of the *Journal*, which is not surprising since, as I argued in chapter 6, if this matter is at issue it is likely to constitute the most important question raised by this text in the minds of readers. Other matters, particularly Defoe's style and his use of a first-person narrator, have been confronted again and again by readers of the *Journal*, but those issues are generally of secondary importance. What is more, most readers' views on such matters tend to be determined by the first step in the concretization of the text, the judgment each reader makes about the *Journal*'s historicity or fictionality. Although regularly identified during much of the history of its reception as a novel, or at the very least as an odd species of fiction, the *Journal* has seemingly left readers permanently divided over the fundamental question of whether it is a work of history or fiction. I shall argue here and in the conclusion that the *Journal of the Plague Year*, by constantly posing this question, has throughout the history of its reception laid bare a key feature of the novel: its link to historical discourse.[8]

---

[6] My work on the reception of Defoe has been greatly facilitated by two bibliographies: John A. Stoler, *Daniel Defoe: An Annotated Bibliography of Modern Criticism, 1900–1980* (New York: Garland, 1984) and Spiro Peterson, *Daniel Defoe: A Reference Guide* (Boston: G. K. Hall, 1987). Earlier studies of the reception of Defoe's work include Charles E. Burch, "British Criticism of Defoe as Novelist 1719–1860," and "Defoe's British Reputation, 1869–1894," *Englische Studien* 67 (1932–33): 178–98 and 68 (1933–34): 410–23, respectively; and Rogers, *Critical Heritage*, 1–30.

[7] Jauss, *Aesthetic of Reception*, 18–20, 26.

[8] Scholars generally have been content, as Robert Weimann has pointed out, to see the horizon of expectations as "itself objectified in the work" and to locate the reception of a text not in "the actual historical activity of the reader, but . . . instead in the echoes of reception built into the artwork itself." Robert Weimann, "Reception Aesthetics and the Crisis in Literary History," *Clio: A Journal of Literature, History and the Philosophy of History* 5 (1975), 23; see also Robert C. Holub, *Reception Theory: A Critical Introduction* (London: Methuen, 1984), 134–46. This is an historical study, however, and will, therefore, focus on what a variety of readers have had

Having shown that Defoe's *Journal* is quite possibly *the* borderline case in English fiction and as such useful in delimiting the contours of novelistic discourse, I shall then show that while that work has produced the most pronounced case of puzzlement on the part of readers over the generic status of a Defoe text, it is far from unique among his texts in the way that it presses the fact-fiction dilemma upon readers.[9] In the epilogue I will argue that the unsettled history of the reception of Defoe's narratives suggested to readers that the novel is founded upon a dialogue between history and fiction enacted within the texts of novels, and that the asserted historicity of fictional texts – repeatedly insisted upon by creators of the novel form from Behn to Scott – is a constitutive feature of that form.

I

A Journal of the Plague Year may be said to have been concretized in three principal ways since 1722: as history, as fiction, and as a hybrid form of history and fiction. For much of the eighteenth century, the prevailing view was that the *Journal* was an authentic piece of historical writing. Although no records of the initial reception of the *Journal* exist, there is every reason to believe that the *Journal* was first read as a genuine memoir of the outbreak of the plague in London in 1665. In light of what has already been said about the presentation of the text, the very silence that surrounds it suggests that its authenticity was taken for granted. That the *Journal* continued for some time to be read as an authentic text is verified by the ninth edition of Mead's *Discourse on the Plague*, published in 1744, in which the *Journal* is cited as a source for a discussion of the shutting up of the houses of the afflicted, as a means of controlling the spread of the disease. Several editions of the *Journal* demonstrate that the work was presented to the public as history for a long time. In 1754, it appeared with a new title, *The History of the Great Plague*, which was said to contain the "Observations and Memorials of . . . a Citizen, who lived the whole Time in London"; this edition also contained the *Journal of the Plague at Marseilles* which appeared in London in 1722. In 1763, furthermore, extracts from

---

to say about Defoe's *Journal*. I shall frequently refer to critics, who, as Vodička points out, are readers who force "a confrontation between . . . the work and the period's literary requirements," but I have also heeded the views of historians, topographers, physicians, moralists, observers of the literary scene, and anonymous correspondents in popular periodicals; "Concretization of the Literary Work," 110–12.

9   On borderline cases, see Barbara Herrnstein Smith, *On the Margins of Discourse: The Relation of Literature to Language* (University of Chicago Press, 1978), 41–50. Smith points out that a marginal case can be a somewhat suspect means for defining the nature of a form or genre. Near the end of this chapter and in the next, I shall indicate why I think the *Journal*'s singularity makes it not only useful but indispensable.

the *Journal* were used in *The Dreadful Visitation*, "A Short account of the Progress and Effects of the PLAGUE . . . in the Year 1665." This use of the *Journal* along with Mead's reliance upon it indicates that the text was being read as an authentic memoir by many readers thirty years after it first appeared; the anonymous editor of *Visitation* declared, for example, that the account "was kept by a Citizen who remained there during the whole Time of the Sickness" and recommended the text as a fit occasion for "a close and serious converse with Death and the Grave."[10]

One might argue, of course, that this concretization of the *Journal* cannot be regarded as an authentic "reflection" in the "consciousness" of the reader of the text since it is predicated upon an apparent deception perpetrated by the author and publisher upon the readers.[11] But, as we have seen, it is not clear that the production of this text involved any deception of readers; Defoe can reasonably be thought of as having presented this narrative to readers as a genuine work of history. Any assumption of bad faith on his part derives from the belief that the fictional elements within the text disqualify it from being reasonably construed as history, but this view is anachronistic with respect to a writer who was a thoroughgoing practitioner of Baconian historiography. And many readers read the *Journal* as history long after it was widely known that Defoe was the author; they were not simply taken in by the "liar" Defoe.

By the 1770s Defoe's authorship of the *Journal* began to be clearly established. In 1768, in his *Anecdotes of British Topography*, the antiquary Richard Gough, who published, among other things, an enlarged edition of Camden's *Britannia*, declared that the *Journal* "is professed to be wrote by a saddler in White-chapel, but the real author was Daniel Defoe." What commentary on the *Journal* there was in the final decades of the eighteenth century indicates increasing awareness of Defoe's authorship of the *Journal* and a growing tendency to concretize the *Journal* as a work of fiction. In 1778, Hester Thrale praised Defoe's account of the plague as "stronger" than Clarendon's rendering of the Great Fire of London, adding however, that "De Foe's Plague . . . is a Romance," and in 1785 an anonymous correspondent with the *Gentleman's Magazine* who signed himself "Langbour-niensis" informed the readers of that periodical that "Defoe wrote 'Memoirs of the Plague-Year,' a Romance of a very peculiar kind."[12]

The first commentator on the *Journal* who acknowledged the fictive

10   Richard Mead, *A Discourse on the Plague*, 9th edn. (London, 1744), 105–06; *History of the Great Plague in London, in the Year 1665 . . . To which is added, a Journal of the Plague in London at Marseilles, in the Year 1720* (London, 1754); *The Dreadful Visitation* (Germantown, 1763).

11   Vodicka, "Concretization of the Literary Work," 110.

12   [Richard Gough], *Anecdotes of British Topography* (London, 1768), 299; *Thraliana: The Diary of Mrs. Hester Lynch Thrale (Later Mrs. Piozzi), 1776–1809*, 2 vols., ed. K. C. Balderston (Oxford: Clarendon Press, 1951), I, 248; Langbourniensis, "Letter to Mr. Urban," *Gentleman's Magazine* 55, part 2 (December 1785), 953.

elements in the narrative while nevertheless asserting its historicity was Edward Wedlake Brayley, a now forgotten English topographer. Brayley argued, in a letter in the *Gentleman's Magazine* of March 1810, that "all the particulars respecting that fatal calamity which I have extracted from the 'Journal of the Plague Year,' . . . are both *essentially and literally true!*" Brayley had been publicly embarrassed by an earlier letter to the editor (published in December 1809) in which one "Londinensis" expressed surprise that Brayley, in his topographical magnum opus *The Beauties of England and Wales*, had referred to the *Journal* "as a genuine piece of History" and claimed that Defoe himself was one of the "Examiners . . . appointed to shut up infected houses." (In 1665 Defoe was five years old.) Brayley's letter was thus an attempt to save face. In it he seems to be both admitting his error, by tracing it to a certain ambiguity in Gough's attribution of the *Journal* to Defoe, and standing his ground, by denying that there is any basis for saying, as Londinensis does, that "De Foe's history is as much a work of imagination as his Robinson Crusoe."

Despite Brayley's claim that the *Journal* was literally true, however, he seems to leave the question of whether the *Journal* should be regarded as fact or fiction up in the air, asserting that the work has "every *appearance* of truth" and is "deserving of credence," while never quite acknowledging that it was written by Defoe more than a half-century after the fact. In the section of the *Beauties of England and Wales* published in 1810, Brayley opined that "Mr. Gough attributes this *Journal* to the celebrated Daniel de Foe, but De Foe could have been only the Editor." Brayley's view – apparently changing at the time of his letter – that while Defoe could not have written the text in 1665, he may well have edited a text in 1722 that was composed at the time of the outbreak, might provide a clue to how some eighteenth-century readers perceived the text. Robert Shiels's mystifying identification of the "*Memoirs of the Plague*, published in 1665" as one of Defoe's "principal performances" may be explicable in this light. The comments of both Shiels and Brayley suggest that early readers of the *Journal* who regarded it as history were aware of a certain ambiguity surrounding the text and nevertheless read it as a species of historical discourse, apparently asuming that Defoe's involvement with this text was more as an editor than as an author. In 1809–10 at least, Brayley seems not to know quite what to say about the *Journal*. At first, he claims that Defoe is "H. F."; then he seems to grant the possibility that the *Journal* is a highly effective piece of fiction, having the "*appearance* of truth" although also well stocked with information that is "literally true." But, in referring to Defoe as its possible editor, Brayley also seems to want to assert the text's authenticity.[13]

---

[13] Londinensis, "Letter to Mr. Urban," *Gentleman's Magazine* 79, part 2 (December 1809),

Whatever he may have thought in 1810, twenty-five years later the matter had become clear to him. Editing the *Journal* in 1835, Brayley both acknowledged Defoe's authorship of the piece and argued that it is "emphatically, not a fiction, not based on fiction" and that "great injustice is done to his [Defoe's] memory so to represent it." Brayley was at some pains to demonstrate that Defoe's account of the plague accorded with a large number of other reliable texts, including Hodges's *Loimologia*, the diaries of Pepys and Evelyn, the collected Bills of Mortality, and Thomas Vincent's *God's Terrible Voice in the City* (1667).[14] Without saying so directly, Brayley took the view that those elements of the narrative that might lead one to view the *Journal* as a work of fiction – the use of H. F., the heightening of effect, the provision of additional details not found in but consonant with the author's sources – were trivial, and that Defoe's demonstrable reliance upon and fidelity to the historical record required readers to construe the *Journal* as a work of history. The case of Brayley is an interesting one because his path to a concretization of the work was so tortured. At first embarrassed and uncertain, Brayley later unequivocally asserted a highly problematic view of the text. His efforts to come to terms with the text strikingly represent the *Journal*'s capacity for pressing funda-mental, vexed questions upon the reader.

Interesting as it is, Brayley's case would be insignificant if later readers had not reasserted the view of the *Journal* that he finally enunciated in the 1835 edition. Well after the controversy between Brayley and Londinensis in the *Gentleman's Magazine*, editions of Defoe's account of the plague continued to present the text to readers as authentic history. In 1824 an abridgment of the *Journal* was published together with an account of the Great Fire derived from John Evelyn's diary. No distinction was made between the two works; Defoe's text, although not attributed to him, was accorded the same status as an authentic memoir, although by this time there were, as we shall see, readers who objected to this presentation of Defoe's text on both historical and moral grounds. Even when the *Journal* was attributed to Defoe, editors were willing to assert its historicity. This was the case in Brayley's 1835 edition; it was also true in an 1879 edition, published in New York, the introduction of which ends by citing Brayley's 1835 assessment and by declaring, as had Brayley, that Defoe probably used "some diary, or manuscript observations" as the source for many elements in the narrative not traceable to known sources.[15]

1126–27; Edward Wedlake Brayley, "Letter to Mr. Urban," *Gentleman's Magazine* 80, part 2 (March 1810), 215–17; Brayley, *The Beauties of England and Wales*, vol. x, part 1 (London: Vernor, Hood, and Sharpe, *et al.*, 1810), 374. For Shiels's comment, see Rogers, *Critical Heritage*, 49–50.

14 Brayley, ed., *A Journal of the Plague Year* (London: Tegg, 1835), iv–xii.

15 *The History of the Plague Year in London, in the Year 1665* (London: Offor, 1819); *An Abridgment of the*

But not only editors acted as if Defoe's text was historical discourse. John Lingard, an important English historian of the mid-nineteenth century, cited Defoe (along with Hodges, Evelyn, and Pepys as well as newspapers and letters) as a source for his account of the plague and dismissed the importance of Defoe's having written "as an eyewitness" by arguing that he did so merely "for dramatic effect." Lingard maintained that Defoe's "narrative, as to the substance of the facts, is confirmed by all other authorities."[16]

More significant than any of these readings of the *Journal*, however, is Watson Nicholson's 1919 study of the text. In a classic source study, Nicholson asserted that "there is not one single statement in the *Journal*, pertinent to the history of the Great Plague in London, that has not been verified" by reference to the historical record; he argued that Defoe's narrative was "a faithful record of historical facts . . . [and] was so intended by the author." It may be true, as Frank Bastian later claimed, that Nicholson weakened his own case by confusing Defoe's genuine sources with works that the author could not possibly have seen, but Nicholson's study is, nevertheless, a crucial example of a concretization of the *Journal* as history, based upon the view that Defoe acted as a historian by scrupulously constructing his narrative from reliable sources. While many critics, including Secord, objected to Nicholson's categorical judgment that the *Journal* was "authentic history," there is no question that he convinced many readers. An anonymous reviewer of Nicholson's book in the *Times Literary Supplement* concluded that in the *Journal* at least, "Defoe is historian, not romancer," and the Dutch scholar W. V. Maanen likewise argued that Nicholson provided "abundant and irrefutable proof . . . of the fact that the *Journal* is history pure and simple."[17] Still, Nicholson's study was in some ways the last major concretization of the *Journal* as a work of history. Although Frank Bastian's 1965 discussion of the *Journal* effectively seconded Nicholson's view of the text, neither Bastian nor anyone else has unequivocally endorsed Nicholson's reading of the text. This is not surprising since Secord, the premier Defoe scholar of his generation, dismissed Nicholson's work out of hand, and Nicholson himself fell silent on the subject of Defoe after 1919.

History of the Great Plague in London, in the Year 1665 . . . with an Account of the Fire in 1666, from the Memoirs of Evelyn (London: Rivington, 1824); Daniel Defoe, *Journal of the Plague in London*, Franklin Square Library, no. 46 (New York: Harper, 1879).

[16] John Lingard, *A History of England from the First Invasion by the Romans*, 13 vols., 4th edn. (London: Baldwin and Craddock, 1839), xi, 284.

[17] Watson Nicholson, *The Historical Sources of Defoe's "Journal of the Plague Year"* (Boston: Stratford, 1919), 97; F. Bastian, "Defoe's *Journal of the Plague Year* Reconsidered," *Review of English Studies*, n.s., 14 (1965): 154; Secord, *Narrative Method*, 231–32; "Defoe as Historian," *TLS* (July 1, 1920), 418; W. V. Maanen, review of Nicholson, *Historical Sources of Defoe's Journal*, *English Studies* 3 (1921), 19.

II

Of early readers who read the *Journal* as fiction, Mrs. Thrale, Langbour-
niensis, and Londinensis have already been cited. Their judgments were
not substantiated by any argumentation and in this respect were typical of
subsequent commentary in the same vein. Readers who have concretized
the *Journal* as fiction generally have not felt compelled to justify their view
of the text. For most readers, identification of Defoe as the author of the
work has apparently constituted sufficient ground for construing the *Journal*
as a work of fiction. The *General Biographical Dictionary* (1813), for example,
cited the deception of "the celebrated Dr. Mead" in the same breath that
it declared Defoe's text "pure fiction." Similarly, an anonymous writer in
Chambers's Papers for the People (1851) echoed Langbourniensis in asserting
that the *Journal* was "often received as a veritable history" even though it
was "in fact as much a fiction as *Robinson Crusoe* or *Captain Singleton*."[18]
Many critics throughout the nineteenth and twentieth centuries almost
automatically treated Defoe as a novelist and the *Journal* as a novel.

A basis for these somewhat unreflective assessments may well have been
provided by Scott, who identified the *Journal* as Defoe's work and acknowledged its "romantic" character.[19] Vodička observes that not only works
but also bodies of work and, indeed, writers themselves are concretized by
readers. Scott, who was, as Pat Rogers has pointed out, "the first critic
sufficiently literal-minded and sufficiently alive to technical matters to be
able to cope with Defoe," seems to have led the way in the concretization
of Defoe as a novelist by participating in the preparation of the first edition
of *The Novels of Daniel Defoe* (1809–10) and also by preparing a study of
Defoe that appeared in 1827.[20] Nevertheless, as we shall see, Scott's view
of the *Journal* was so ambivalent as to prevent one from declaring
unequivocally that he concretized it as fiction.

In any case, by the mid-century, writers of textbooks for students of
imaginative literature regularly identified Defoe as an important writer
because of his prose fictions, including the *Journal*. The authors of these
textbooks included the poet and essayist Leigh Hunt and David Masson,
the biographer of Milton; these authors often discussed the deceptive
quality of Defoe's fictional narratives even as they granted Defoe his (in the
case of Hunt, somewhat dubious) place in the evolution of English
fiction.[21] The fact that the text deceived Dr. Mead and presumably misled

18   Alexander Chalmers, *General Biographical Dictionary*, 32 vols. (London: J. Nichols and Son, *et al.*,
     1812–17), xi, 403; "Daniel De Foe," *Chambers's Papers for the People*, vol. vii, no. 56 (1851), 30.
19   Rogers, *Critical Heritage*, 66.
20   Scott, *On Novels and Novelists*, 164–72; Vodička, "Concretization of the Literary Work," 123,
     129–30; Rogers, *Critical Heritage*, 17, 66.
21   George L. Craik, *Sketches of the History of Literature and Learning in England*, 3rd ser., 2 vols. in 1

other readers was something that weighed heavily against Defoe for many
nineteenth-century readers. Barbauld decried Defoe's use of "H. F." as
"awful": "an exercise of ingenuity not to be commended," and Henry
Southern, a lawyer, diplomat, and man of letters, praised the *Journal* for its
"genuineness" and its agreement with the historical record but lamented
the "repeated asseverations of veracity" by means of which Defoe "does
his best to delude posterity." Similarly, a correspondent with the *Christian
Observer* argued that the reader should be informed "that he is to believe
Evelyn and to disbelieve De Foe"; Hunt called the *Journal* "a lie"; and
Augustine Birrell, statesman and biographer of Charlotte Brontë, labeled
Defoe "a faker" who used "all the now well-known artifices of fakers."[22]
For many critics, then, the identification of Defoe as the author of the
Journal dictated a concretization of the text as fiction, frequently coupled
with a condemnation of Defoe as a liar.

The appearance of Nicholson's study, however, changed this state of
affairs; for a time, at least, critics who read the *Journal* as fiction had to
make their peace with Nicholson first. Secord argued that Nicholson was
wrong, but he explained why, insisting that the *Journal* is fiction because
Defoe's facts are mixed with fictional elements and because "the whole is
related as the actual experiences and recollections of a man who . . .
appears to be entirely imaginary." What was for Nicholson trivial was for
Secord determinative. Similarly, Walter George Bell, writing in 1924 as a
historian of the 1665 plague, was at pains to demonstrate that Defoe could
not be regarded as a historian since he used his sources in an uncritical
fashion; Bell classified the *Journal* as a historical novel. More recently,
Everett Zimmerman has also taken care to assert why the text is *not* history:
"It is the intensity of the focus on the narrator that makes *A Journal of the
Plague Year* something more like a novel than . . . history." Zimmerman's
concretization of the text as fiction is the most widely held view in our own
day. In many editions of the *Journal* presently in use, the text is identified as
a novel, and perhaps the most common assertion about the status of the
text in recent years has been that it is an early example of an historical
novel.[23]

(London: Knight, 1845), 123–27; Leigh Hunt, *Books for a Corner*, 2 vols. (London: Chapman and
Hall, 1849), I, 48; J. Cordy Jeaffreson, *Novels and Novelists from Elizabeth to Victoria*, 2 vols.
(London: Hurst and Blackett, 1858), I, 83–84; David Masson, *British Novelists and Their Styles*
(Cambridge: Macmillan, 1859), 96–97.

22 Barbauld, *British Novelists*, XVI, v; [Henry Southern], "Defoe's History of the Plague," *Retro-
    spective Review* 6 (1822), 2–3; An Old Member [pseud.], "Christian-Knowledge Society's
    Catalogue," *Christian Observer* 30 (1830), 759–60; Hunt, *Books*, I, 48; Augustine Birrell, "Daniel
    Defoe," *The Nation and the Athenaeum* 41 (April to October 1927), 147–48.

23 Secord, *Narrative Method*, 231; Walter George Bell, *The Great Plague in London* (London: The
    Bodley Head, 1924), v; Zimmerman, *Defoe and the Novel*, 124. On the *Journal* as an historical
    novel, see Novak, *Realism, Myth, and History*, 47; Burke, "Observing the Observer," 13–32;
    Backscheider, *Ambition and Innovation*, 135–44.

Nevertheless, Zimmerman's assertion that the *Journal* comes closer to being a novel than anything else reveals an ambivalence in the concretization of this work as fiction, one that is also seen in nineteenth-century commentary. Masson, having asserted that Defoe's narratives (along with Swift's) constituted the beginning of modern British prose fiction, then acknowledged that several of them (including the *Journal* and *Memoirs of a Cavalier*) "are, for the purposes of historical instruction, as good as real." Alfred C. Lyall (anticipating Rader's discussion of *Moll Flanders*) classified the *Journal* as a romance but then argued that it and Defoe's other narratives were "the last examples of the long and inveterate confusion . . . between History and Fable." Quite recently, Michael Boardman has argued that the *Journal* "asks that one 'overlook' for a time the knowledge that the story is a fabrication . . . construing H. F.'s words as if they actually referred."[24] Thus many writers have asserted that the *Journal* is fiction while acknowledging simultaneously that their use of that substantive in this instance is particularly problematic.

The ambivalence of these readers of the *Journal* as fiction seems to be contiguous with the third concretization of this text, as history-fiction. The two views are not, however, identical. Whereas most critics have made a choice between history and fiction in concretizing the *Journal*, a small number of readers have simply refused to decide the issue, content to argue that the *Journal* resides in some ill-defined zone between history and fiction. Scott's assessment of the *Journal* is the most famous instance of the concretization of the text as a hybrid of history and fiction. In classifying Defoe's narratives, Scott grouped the *Journal* with "account[s] of great national convulsions" (war, plague, and storm) and then asserted that it "is one of that particular class of compositions which hovers between romance and history" and declined to say more.[25] Similarly, although Walter Wilson, Defoe's biographer, seemed to class Defoe's account of the plague with the author's "imaginary works," the discussion of the *Journal* in his *Memoirs of the Life and Times of Daniel De Foe* (1830) made it clear that Wilson's view of the *Journal* was decidedly equivocal:

In this affecting narrative he has contrived to mix up so much that is authentic with the fabrications of his own brain, that it is impossible to distinguish the one from the other; and he has given to the whole such a likeness to the dreadful original, as to confound the sceptic, and encircle him in his enchantments.

Wilson acknowledged the fictive element in the *Journal*, but he did not attempt to settle the question of its essential character. Instead he

---

24 Masson, *British Novelists*, 97; [Alfred C. Lyall], "Review of . . . *The Works of Daniel Defoe*," *Quarterly Review* 178, no. 355 (January and April 1894), 40, 41; Michael M. Boardman, *Defoe and the Uses of Narrative* (New Brunswick NJ: Rutgers University Press, 1983), 98.
25 Scott, *On Novels and Novelists*, 167–68.

concluded "that it would baffle the ingenuity of any one but De Foe, to frame a history with so many attributes of truth, upon the basis of fiction." Wilson was trying to have it all ways. First the *Journal* was "history," which, as Wilson used the word here, was to say both "story" and "factual account"; then it was a veracious account with "many [but not all?] attributes of truth"; finally it was obviously constructed "upon the basis of fiction." In this crucial remark in an early major study of Defoe, the *Journal* was seen tumbling out of history into fiction only to tumble back into history one sentence later when Wilson spoke of the "alliance between history and fiction" that characterized this narrative.[26] Wilson saw the *Journal*, then, not as history *or* fiction but as both, by turns, one continually becoming the other.

Wilson was echoed by subsequent critics in a number of ways. An anonymous reader in the *National Review* recommended "resigning yourself to this inevitable confusion of truth and fiction, or rather consoling yourself with the reflection that De Foe's inventions are in such close harmony with the facts that surround them, that we may almost accept the whole as true." A critic in the *Gentleman's Magazine* in 1857 asserted that the *Journal* urgently pressed the reader to decide whether it was fiction or history and then simply refused to make any such judgment himself. And in 1900, the novelist Walter Besant admitted:

I have called this work one of those which belong to Defoe's imagination. This is true; not the less it is a true history, with the full horror of the event brought out as had never been before done, and will never again be done. There have been many plagues in the world. Thucydides wrote the history of one; Defoe of another. The modern historian, for once, has done better than the ancient.[27]

Most readers have found and presumably will find this formulation unsatisfactory; it is difficult if not impossible to read a work as both history and fiction. Still, a small but important class of readers has read the *Journal* as a work that forces us to suspend our need to decide this fundamental issue and requires us to accept, in this case at least, that the line in question cannot be drawn.

This concretization was not, furthermore, simply a nineteenth-century view, one that remained popular while Scott's influence endured. In fact, this view of the *Journal* has been embraced by one of the most important of contemporary Defoe scholars. John Richetti studiously speaks not of Defoe's "novels," but of his "narratives," even though he too, like

[26] Walter Wilson, *Memoirs of the Life and Times of Daniel De Foe*, 3 vols. (London: Hurst, Chance, 1830), III, 511, 513.
[27] "Defoe as Novelist," *National Review* 3 (July and October 1856), 384–87; "Defoe's Novels," *Gentleman's Magazine*, n.s., 3 (September 1857), 239; Walter Besant, introd., *A Journal of the Plague Year* (New York: Century, 1900), xx.

Zimmerman, concentrates on Defoe's various essays of "the self." At the
end of one discussion of the *Journal*, as we have seen, Richetti calls it "a
thickly factual, even grossly truthful, book" but one in which "the
imagination . . . flares up occasionally and dominates those facts." More
recently, Richetti has commented about the *Journal* and some of Defoe's
other works: "Mixed in with Defoe's novels, and in some ways remarkably
similar to them, are narratives we now think of as too firmly based in fact
to be regarded as part of his fiction." In both studies Richetti refers to the
Journal as a species of "pseudo-history."[28] Richetti declines to say either/
or: instead he seems to settle for neither/nor; the *Journal* is too "thickly
factual" to be thought of as fiction and yet it cannot be regarded as
genuine history. It is a pseudomorph, an irregular form that is generally
seen as somehow false. But Richetti does not embrace the negative
connotations of this concretization of the *Journal*; he declines, that is, to
regard the work as deceptive. Instead he countenances the view (unlike
Besant who trumpets the notion) that Defoe's narrative is some third thing,
some hyphenated form of discourse, in between history and fiction.

Another recent scholar echoing Scott is Bastian, whose views are
particularly interesting because he aligns himself with those who read the
Journal as history-fiction even though much of his argument seems designed
to second Nicholson. Looking afresh at the question of whether the *Journal*
is fiction or history, Bastian is critical of both Nicholson and of those who
take issue with him. Nevertheless, Bastian's principal additions to scholarship on the *Journal*, which owe much to informed and reasonable conjecture, are an explanation of how Defoe's uncle and father can justifiably
be identified with H. F. and H. F.'s brother, along with a discussion of
Defoe's sources for "anecdotal material" not traceable to printed sources.
Bastian's scholarship leads him to conclude that "some residue of invented
detail there certainly must be in the *Journal*, but it is small and inessential,"
that the work "stands closer to our idea of history than to that of fiction,"
and that in the *Journal*, "Defoe shows in a high degree some of the qualities
of a true historian." Bastian argues that

any doubts that remain whether to label it "fiction" or "history" arise from the
ambiguities inherent in those words. Fiction implies the invention of incident and
the creation of character. We have seen that the characters and incidents once
confidently asserted to be the products of Defoe's fertile imagination, repeatedly
prove to have been factual.

Bastian seems to agree with Nicholson that Defoe's practice in the writing
of the *Journal* was that of an historian; yet unlike Nicholson, Bastian argues
that "at the core is the basic falsehood that the book was actually the work

of 'a Citizen who continued all the while in London'," and he ends by repeating Scott's assertion that the *Journal* "hovers between history and romance."[29]

Bastian seems to want to assert the historicity of the *Journal* without associating his own work with Nicholson's extreme view. Yet although Bastian indicates what he thinks the word "fiction" implies, he does not consider what "history" signifies. If he had addressed himself to the question of the "ambiguities inherent" in that word, and especially if he had considered the question historically, if, that is, he had asked himself how Defoe thought about history, he might well have asserted that the *Journal* was history by its author's lights if not by those of his twentieth-century readers.[30] In the end, however, although he makes a strong case for reading the *Journal* as a work of history, Bastian seems compelled to assert that its author did not exhibit all "the qualities of a true historian," and he too concretizes the text as a pseudomorph.

III

Variously concretized as history, fiction, or history-fiction, the *Journal*'s generic status has remained undecidable throughout the history of its reception. Vodička contemplates a temporary situation in which the distinct values of succeeding generations overlap and conflict for a period of time, ending with the triumph of a new set of values.[31] Following Vodička, we might expect that changing views of what constitutes historical discourse would explain the different concretizations of the *Journal* and allow us to periodize the history of the text's reception with considerable ease. It is tempting, in fact, to argue that Defoe's account of the plague could only have been concretized as history at a time when vestiges of Baconian historiography led readers to accept the use of fictional elements within historical discourse. And it might be similarly satisfying to argue that the history-fiction concretization has become popular in the twentieth century as modernist or post-structuralist views of history (Dilthey, Collingwood, Barthes, White) took hold in literary studies. These constructions do not, however, square with the data; changing views of the nature of historical discourse do not explain the history of the reception of this text.

In the twentieth century, in full knowledge of who wrote the *Journal* and when and how he wrote it, the text has still been concretized as fiction, as history, and as history-fiction. Recently, it might be argued, the concretization of the text as history has come close to becoming untenable. I would

[29] Bastian, "Defoe's *Journal*," 173.
[30] Joseph M. Levine argues that we must read many medieval authors as writers of fiction even though they may have conceived of their work as history; *Humanism and History*, 53.
[31] Vodička, "Concretization of the Literary Work," 111.

not wish to argue, however, that this view has entirely disappeared since my own position is that even if we cannot read the *Journal* as history, we must nevertheless recognize that the text was presented as history by Defoe and read as such by his contemporaries. And one can also point to the discussion of plagues in which Defoe is used as a historical source; the current interest in the *Journal* as a guide to understanding AIDS as a twentieth-century plague is an example of this use of Defoe's text.[32] Periodization, then, will not solve the problems presented by the history of the text's reception. Despite general agreement in our time that the *Journal* is a highly problematic novel, but a novel nonetheless, the history-fiction concretization is alive and well and the history concretization still survives, if just barely.[33]

Just as Vodička asserts that competing concretizations of a text generally arise from changing literary values, Jauss tells us that it takes some time for a striking and unusual new work to be assimilated to the literary series with which it is associated, but that once it is so assimilated the work constitutes a new norm; the revolutionary work becomes a classic.[34] That the *Journal* is available in the Oxford World Classics Series and in the Penguin English Library and as a Norton Critical Edition demonstrates that it has achieved the status of a classic. But this study of the history of the reception of Defoe's narrative suggests that it has not yet ceased to be revolutionary since it has not yet been unequivocally assimilated to the literary series into which it is now most commonly inserted, the novel. The morsel has been swallowed but not digested.

How can a work that has been associated with a particular literary series for so long retain its revolutionary effect even after it has achieved classic status? The answer to this question lies in an understanding of how revolutionary and classic texts are perceived by readers. Jauss tells us that a revolutionary work forces a "change of horizons, through negation of familiar [literary] experiences or through raising newly articulated [literary] experiences to the level of consciousness," whereas a classic is a work that, having already fundamentally altered readers' horizon of expectations then "conceals its negativity within the retrospective horizon of an exemplary tradition."[35] A work that remains revolutionary after it has become a classic must be a work whose "negativity" has been recognized by, but never completely concealed for, readers. Successful

---

[32] See, for example, Backscheider, ed., *A Journal of the Plague Year* (New York: Norton, 1992), 195–264. For uses of the *Journal* as an historical source, see R. Baehrel, "Epidémie et terreur: histoire et sociologie," *Annales historiques de la révolution française*, (April to June 1951), 113–46; and A. G. E. Jones, "The Great Plague at Croydon," *Notes and Queries* 201 (1956), 332–34.

[33] Virginia Ogden Birdsall concludes there is no putting this issue definitively to rest; *Defoe's Perpetual Seekers: A Study of the Major Fiction* (Lewisburg PA: Bucknell University Press, 1985), 187–88.

[34] Jauss, *Aesthetic of Reception*, 25.   [35] *Ibid.*, 25, 31.

assimilation would lead to the concealment of the text's negativity and its unproblematic insertion into the appropriate literary series. Instead the *Journal* remains a text that is associated with the novel but in a perplexing manner; its negativity remains fully in view. The *Journal* continues to pose questions for readers that cannot satisfactorily be answered.

In the case of the *Journal*, those questions cannot merely refer to the use by Defoe of revolutionary "devices," which is what both Jauss and Vodička generally have in mind when they imagine the move from revolutionary to classic status in the minds of readers. To be sure many who have read the *Journal* as fiction have considered the text's significance to arise from the devices employed by Defoe, but if the difficulties presented by the *Journal* were simply a matter of Defoe's realist techniques, then the history of the reception of this text would long ago have become a much more sedate affair than it is.

Insofar as readers have discussed the revolutionary character of the *Journal* in terms of poetic devices employed by Defoe, they have tended to concentrate on the role of H. F. in the narrative. Indeed as the tendency to read Defoe's most famous narratives as novels grew more dominant, so too did the tendency to focus attention upon H. F. Scott makes no mention of the narrator, but Wilson saw Defoe's use of H. F. as a technique by means of which "Defoe secured to himself many advantages which he could not have hoped for in a *formal* history." In other words, in the *Journal* Defoe used a fictional voice as a means of narrating history. In 1869 another biographer of Defoe, William Lee, was more explicit, arguing that "the fiction of the worthy Saddler" shows that Defoe understood "the importance of bringing forth some person who was trustworthy" and of "allowing him to relate . . . the occurrences in which he had taken part, and the things he had seen with his own eyes." Thus many early commentators treated H. F. as an ingenious historiographical device. But increasingly, H. F. was discussed not as one element of a historical method but as an aspect of Defoe's groundbreaking realism in fiction. What historically-minded readers saw as a means of making historical writing more effective, readers of the *Journal* as fiction construed as an impressive fictional representation of a historical eyewitness. Thus an anonymous critic in the *Gentleman's Magazine* commented that "it is the part of the work which belongs to the eloquent *eye-witness* that gives to it its unspeakable charm," and George Saintsbury celebrated the "rigid attention to vivacity and consistency of characterization" in the *Journal* and other works by Defoe.[36]

H. F. is only one among several elements of Defoe's "realism" that have

---

[36] Wilson, *Life and Times*, III, 512, emphasis added; William Lee, *Daniel Defoe: His Life and Recently Discovered Writings*, 3 vols. (London: Hotten, 1869), I, 359, 97; anon., *Gentleman's Magazine*, n.s., 3 (1857), 238; George Saintsbury, "Daniel Defoe," *Encyclopedia Britannica*, 9th edn., VII, 30.

been singled out both by readers who have concretized the work as fiction and by those who have celebrated Defoe's historical method. Masson cited Defoe's use of "actual reports and registers" and his ability to create a fictional representation that "teems with circumstances in exact keeping with it." Leslie Stephen highlighted Defoe's talent "for manufacturing corroborative evidence" as one of his "peculiar gifts."[37] Defoe's fictional style then has been defined in terms of his fidelity to the known facts; this same faithfulness to the historical record, of course, caused other readers to concretize the *Journal* either as history or as history-fiction.

Yet as this study demonstrates, the *Journal*'s "negativity" derives not from mere fictional devices but from its inherently borderline status, from its insistent confounding of the distinction between history and fiction. The questions posed by the text are: how can this text be read as a novel when it is so demonstrably historiographical, and how, given its undeniably fictive elements, can it be read as anything but fiction? Of course, the *Journal* provides us with no definitive answers to these questions; if it did, the *Journal* would at some point have finally been concretized as either fiction or history. Instead, by relentlessly posing these questions and thus revealing its negativity, the *Journal* constitutes the most forceful assertion in the whole discourse of the novel in English that the nexus of history and fiction is a constitutive feature of the form. The *Journal*, that is, asks one more question: what is the relationship between history and fiction in novelistic discourse? The *Journal*, however, along with Defoe's other narratives, raises the issue of the link between history and the novel in a way that no other novelistic text in English does. It presses us to acknowledge not the rhetorical trope but the actual practice: the paradoxical assertion that the crucial and yet disturbing presence of Defoe's works within the canon of the English novels is a result of his having created historical works that came to be read as novels and thereby negated readers' sense of the fictive by asserting the texts' historicity in a way that could not satisfactorily be denied by referring to those assertions as figures of speech.

Borderline case though it may be, the *Journal* has nevertheless been in some ways an exemplary novel (rather in the way that "*Tristam Shandy* is the most typical novel in world literature" for Victor Shklovsky), by establishing that the claim to historicity was a crucial part of the horizon of expectations of novel readers.[38] The *Journal* has continued to press the historical claim of novels in a way that other works have not in large part because the biography of this text cannot open by identifying it as a revolutionary work within the literary series "novel." Initially the *Journal*

---

[37] Masson, *British Novelists*, 96; Leslie Stephen, "Defoe's Novels," *Cornhill Magazine* 17 (January to June 1868), 294–95.

[38] Shklovsky, "Art as Technique," 57.

challenged no one's notion of what fiction might or should be. Only later, as it was gradually associated with the novel, did it become a work that, through its singularity and marginality, helped readers to theorize this element of the form. A work that came into the world as history has been read into the tradition of the novel. This curious fact should not, however, disqualify the *Journal* from being considered a classic, indeed definitive, unit in the literary series "novel." Rather it should intensify our sense of just what the *Journal* has to tell us about that series. Readers have read Defoe's *Journal* into the tradition of the novel and have thereby isolated a crucial element necessary to its theoretical definition: the proposition that the novel is that fictional form that asserts its capacity to do the work of history.[39]

IV

If the *Journal* were the only work by Defoe to have been so concretized by readers, it might provide an insufficient basis for claiming that Defoe's narratives are so crucial to the history of the novel because they press so forcefully the novel's claim to historicity. In fact, however, Defoe's other narratives have also been assimilated to the tradition of the novel with varying degrees of difficulty. Early readers took *Captain Singleton* to be "a genuine memoir rather than a work of fiction" and the text "seems not to have been advertised as a fictitious work by Defoe until 1780."[40] There was no Charles Gildon, that is, to declare to these readers of *Singleton* that their decision to read the text as a species of historical discourse, consonant though it may have been with the nature of Baconian historiography and Defoe's historical practice, was a mistaken approach to the narrative. *Captain Singleton*, furthermore, was cited in Richard Burton's *Nile Basin* "as a genuine account of travels in Central Africa."[41] Similarly, *Memoirs of a Cavalier* was apparently read as an authentic account until the 1780s; readers of the *Memoirs* repeatedly pointed out that Lord Chatham believed that the text was genuine. Indeed the text pressed its historical claims upon readers so forcibly that as late as 1961 Secord felt compelled to confute the argument that the work was based upon a "manuscript source," finally concluding that although not drawn from manuscripts, the work was taken "almost entirely from published sources."[42] What is more, although he defended Defoe against Nicholson's charge that the *Journal* did not deserve to be regarded as an imaginative work, Secord nevertheless essentially

---

[39] On the distinct claims of epic and novel, see M. M. Bakhtin, *The Dialogic Imagination: Four Essays*, ed. Michael Holquist, trans. Caryl Emerson and Holquist (Austin: University of Texas Press, 1981), 13–21.

[40] Penelope Wilson, introd., *Captain Singleton*, viii.   [41] Stephen, "Defoe's Novels," 294.

[42] On Chatham, see, for example, [C. Barker], "Review of *Memoirs of the Honourable Col. Andrew Newport*," *Retrospective Review* 3, part 2 (1821), 377–78; Secord, *Robert Drury's Journal*, 132, 79.

reduced Defoe's "narrative method" to a matter of borrowing from texts like Dampier's *Voyages* and various accounts of Selkirk and identified all of Defoe's "long narratives" as examples of "fictionized history."[43] The whole vast set of source studies, furthermore, suggests that all Defoe's narratives are rooted in the historical record. Readers of *Robinson Crusoe* not only argued that Defoe based his narrative on published texts by writers like Rogers and Dampier but also repeatedly asserted in the eighteenth and early nineteenth centuries that the text was based upon notes, memoirs, or papers obtained from Selkirk and improperly used by Defoe because he failed to cite his sources.[44] In a similar vein, an anonymous editor of *Robinson Crusoe* in 1829 rejected the charge that *Crusoe* was stolen from Selkirk and concluded that Defoe drew upon actual travel in Spain and personal experience with shipwreck in the making of the narrative. Even more tellingly, a writer for *London Society* in 1870 asked "Who Wrote *Robinson Crusoe*?" and although he or she answered that the author was undoubtedly Defoe, this critic also asserted that the popularity of *Crusoe* was "mainly due to a belief in its thorough truthfulness," citing eighteenth-century commentators who accused Defoe of having stolen his masterwork from Selkirk.[45]

Moll Flanders has been viewed in the same light. The work seems only to have been definitively associated with the name of Defoe at the very end of the eighteenth century, and we have no substantial comments on it for more than sixty years after its publication.[46] In *Lavengro*, George Borrow tells of his encounter with an old woman who is an avid reader of *Moll Flanders*, one whose own life of crime and whose faith that her transported son will someday return to her have been shaped by the credence she has given to Defoe's text. Novak observes that in some respects this old lady was a "bad reader," but she was not alone among nineteenth-century readers of Defoe's texts.[47] The critic William Minto accused Defoe of "lying like the truth" in *Moll* and other texts, implying that Defoe had actually intended the book to be read as history, only to have his deception brought to light by observant readers like Gildon and Minto himself. For Minto, then, Borrow's old woman was not a bad reader because she in fact read *Moll* as the author intended it to be read. What is more, George A. Aitken, the editor of Defoe's *Romances and Narratives* argued in 1895 that the book was based on the life of a real criminal, and in 1914 Ernest Bernbaum

[43] Secord, *Narrative Method*, 107, 11; Secord, *Robert Drury's Journal*, 80.

[44] Peterson, *Daniel Defoe*, 13, 23–24, 43–44, 70.

[45] *Ibid.*, 92–93; anon., "Who Wrote *Robinson Crusoe*?" *London Society* 17 (1870), 68, 69.

[46] There is, for example, no mention of *Moll* in Shiels's book, and a comment in the *Gentleman's Magazine* in 1789 suggests that Defoe's first biographer, George Chalmers, was not aware that Defoe wrote *Moll* when he edited *History of the Union* in 1786; Rogers, *Critical Heritage*, 50, 55.

[47] George Borrow, *Lavengro: The Scholar, The Gypsy, The Priest*, ed. George F. Whicher (New York: Macmillan, 1927), 187–90; Novak, *Realism, Myth, and History*, 71–72.

declared his belief that "journalistic and biographic sources shall be eventually found for all of Defoe's great novels," including *Moll Flanders*. John Freeman asserted in *The Spectator* in 1923 that "it is hard not to receive the story as simple fact." Freeman notes a clear "difference between the style of the story and the style of the preface" and wonders about the vivid scenes and language ("aesthetic beauty") that were "suppressed" by the editor in the name of "moral brightness." He concludes in a manner wholly consonant with the checkered history of the reception of Defoe: "Either *Moll Flanders* is a simple autobiography, with pages infelicitously excised for the benefit of a nicer time than ours, or Defoe was an even greater imaginative artist than the readers of *Robinson Crusoe* have thought him."[48] What is more, quite recently, Gerald Howson asked "Who Was Moll Flanders?" Howson has asserted that she was Mary Godson, alias Mary or Moll King, a real thief who was in Newgate at intervals from 1721 to 1722, and who therefore would have been in a position to relate to Defoe (who frequented Newgate at the time because his employer, Nathaniel Mist, was being held there) the information that he used, according to Howson, in constructing Moll's "life as a London thief."[49] And, finally, in trying to say why we cannot think of *Moll Flanders* as a proper novel, Rader argues that we will understand Defoe's form better "if we think a bit about the form of true stories."

Rader insists on the artistry of *Moll*, but the text does not help him define the "concept of form in the novel" except in a negative sense, by suggesting that before there were novels there were narratives "designed to exploit the interest naturally attaching to true stories."[50] If we recall that many early readers did not conceive of the author of *Moll Flanders* as an artist but as a reporter of matters of fact, then Rader's labelling of *Moll* as a "true story" is perhaps more (or at least differently) suggestive than he intended it to be. As histories that came to be read as novels, *Moll Flanders* and Defoe's other narratives are crucial to understanding the form of discourse that Defoe helped to create not because they represent a kind of prenovelistic fictional form but because they argue forcefully that crucial features of the discourse of the novel result from its links to the discourse of history, a result of Defoe's having situated his "novels" within that discourse. No wonder Lennard Davis has asserted that "Defoe strikes us as necessary to, yet subversive of, the history of the novel."[51]

---

48 Aitken, cited in Starr, ed., *Moll Flanders*, xiii; Ernest Bernbaum, *The Mary Carleton Narratives, 1663–1673: A Missing Chapter in the History of the English Novel* (Cambridge MA: Harvard University Press, 1914), 87; John Freeman, "The Autobiography of Mrs. Flanders," *The Spectator*, August 11, 1923 (131), 192–93; Minto, *Daniel Defoe*, 140.

49 Gerald Howson, "Who Was Moll Flanders?" *TLS*, 3438 (January 18, 1968), 63–64; this brief, speculative "guessing game" is displayed prominently in the Norton Critical Edition of *Moll Flanders* (1973).

50 Rader, "Concept of Form in the Novel," 47.   51 Davis, *Factual Fictions*, 155.

Defoe has been called a liar from his day to our own. This charge is a regular feature of the reception of Defoe because his histories unsettle us so. There was a great disparity between what Defoe did in producing and presenting works like *Crusoe*, the *Journal*, and *Moll* to readers and what readers have done with those texts in the nearly three hundred years they have had to work out the problem of concretizing them and thereby to theorize the novel. That in important respects readers have never satisfactorily accomplished the feat of settling the question of the nature of Defoe's texts demonstrates that Defoe's career was an originary moment in the history of the novel. If Defoe's histories have seemed both necessary to our understanding of the form and at the same time irreconcilable to how we theorize that form, the issue that he thrusts upon readers must be crucial. Although that issue has been most tellingly revealed in the biography of *A Journal of the Plague Year* it is unmistakably present in the reception of Defoe as a whole. That issue is: how is novelistic discourse linked to historical discourse; and what do we make of the novel's claim to do the work of history? Defoe does not answer the question, and in the end the study of his work cannot provide us with a satisfactory account of this function of the novel, in no small part because Defoe himself never even conceived of the question in the way that we do. Yet Defoe's importance in the history of the form, particularly in light of his dual status as both classic and revolutionary writer, suggests that at the very least that crucial question is one that inevitably informs the experience of the readers of novels.

Conclusion

The question of the relationship between history and fiction had been a pressing one in discussions of English prose fiction at least since the end of the sixteenth century when Sidney wrote his *Apology for Poetry*. From Sidney's day down to at least the early eighteenth century, the discourse of history featured certain elements of practice that suggested that fictional material would be tolerated even within putatively "scientific" historical discourse or that fiction could be used as a means of historical representation. These elements of practice included sharp polemic; traditional material tolerated within historical texts despite its fabulous character; gossip and hearsay; rhetorical battles with other historians; the taste for strange things; the habit of telling history from the point of view of a far from disinterested individual; and the capacity of certain historical texts to press against the boundary between history and fiction. Thus the seventeenth century was indeed, as Michael McKeon has argued, a time of "categorial instability," and this unsettled state of affairs was reflected in both fictional and historical discourse. I have shown that in the course of his career as a writer Defoe produced works that participated in both of these discursive formations, arguing, more specifically, that in presenting works initially situated within the discourse of history he came to have a revolutionary impact upon fictional discourse. As a result, Defoe's narratives played a key part in that series of developments that eventuated in a shift in the horizon of expectations of early modern readers that pointed toward the emergence of a discourse of the novel.

It is beyond the scope of this work to do more than hint at the complicated process by means of which the discourse of the novel came into being in the eighteenth century, but it may be concluded here that Defoe's career also suggests that the novel came into being thanks to a discursive realignment that occurred in the first half of the eighteenth century. This shift was signaled in the history of English fiction when Defoe was branded a liar for writing works like *Robinson Crusoe* that situated themselves within the discourse of history even while acknowledging that they were fashioned from "formed facts," and that finally induced readers to concretize them, however problematically, as species of fictional discourse. Many signs indicate that such a realignment took place: historians definitively rejected the British history, the heyday of the secret history came to an end, prominent writers produced no more historical "Lives," and the "marvelous" came under attack in works like *Antiquitates Vulgares* and the *Philosophical Enquiry into the Causes of Prodigies and Miracles*.[1] James Aubrey has shown that in 1727 "commonly received ideas about the generation of monsters" were attacked as "absurd" by the London physician James Augustus Blondel, who criticized, among other extravagances, the idea that "the mother could communicate her thoughts to the mind of a fetus."[2] Blondel's *The Strength of Imagination in Pregnant Women Examin'd* is one of many texts of the period, both historical and scientific, showing that questions about the role of the imagination – what was imaginary and what was real – were particularly pressing at this time. In chapter 6 we looked at one controversy in early eighteenth-century England – the Mary Toft affair – that brought this question into focus. Another was the debate over Psalmanazar's *Historical and Geographical Description of Formosa* (1705) which, Tzvetan Todorov argues, helped define "the frontier separating truth and fiction."[3] Approaching this issue from a radically different angle, Lennard Davis has argued compellingly that "in the first quarter of the eighteenth century there was a concrete and rapid movement toward defining, for legal purposes, factual and fictional narratives," and that a series of legal decisons made it "more difficult for narratives to rest in some gray area between fact and fiction."[4]

Many different developments demonstrate, then, that a hiving off of fictional discourse from the discourse of history took place in the first half of the eighteenth century. Crucial among these events was the set of

[1]   See chapters 2 and 7 above.

[2]   James Aubrey, "Revising the Monstrous: Du Plessis' *Short History of Prodigies* and London Culture in 1730," in *Studies in Eighteenth-Century Culture*, vol. XXIII, ed. Carla H. Hay and Syndy M. Conger (East Lansing: American Society for Eighteenth-Century Studies; Colleagues Press, 1994), 76.

[3]   Tzvetan Todorov, "Fictions and Truths," trans. Jennifer Curtiss Gage, in *Critical Reconstructions: The Relationship of Fiction and Life*, ed. Robert M. Polhemus and Roger B. Henkle (Stanford University Press, 1994), which has an excellent discussion of the Psalmanazar affair. Todorov distinguishes between two kinds of truth: the "truth of correspondence to reality" and the "truth of unveiling," with "the first measured only in terms of all/nothing, the second in terms of more/less." The latter is the truth of fiction, and Todorov denies that Psalmanazar's text possesses either: "it is not *presented* as fiction but as truth, it *is not* fiction, but rather lies and deception." Fair enough in respect to a bogus account of Formosa, but what of a text like Defoe's *Journal* that is a fiction and in some respects a lie, but that nevertheless also possesses for most readers a clear "correspondence to reality"? Todorov does not consider this case but he takes a more-or-less Sidneian view of the question when he argues that the writings of Amerigo Vespucci on the New World (with their undeniable fictions) are "superior to those of his contemporaries," despite their inadequacy as historical documents, because of their "greater truth of unveiling" (50). Defoe's narratives, however, suggest that the novel is a fictional form that asserts both of Todorov's truth claims.

[4]   Davis, *Factual Fictions*, 92, 95.

narratives written by Defoe from 1719 to 1724. Defoe's texts serve as clear markers both of what was becoming untenable within the discourse of history and of what was becoming central to the emergent form of fictional writing that would come to be called the "novel." His narratives embodied the crucial shifts effected within these discursive fields when, first, fiction ceased to be a legitimate means of historical representation and, second, prose fiction successfully established the claim – pressed insistently for at least a hundred years – that "matters of fact" constituted the material out of which that fiction would be formed.

This moment represented a clear instance of discontinuity, a "sudden redistribution" within and among discursive fields which, according to Foucault, signals the appearance of "entirely new forms of positivity."[5] To be sure, there were continuities as well: fiction writers continued to worry and theorize the tie to history and to define how the novel functioned as history; the "amatory fiction" of Behn and Manley did not disappear but was subsumed into the tradition of the novel; and historians drew upon both important examples of Baconian historiography such as Clarendon's *History of the Rebellion* and examples of the new fictional form created in Defoe's wake such as *Tom Jones*.[6] And yet, to use again a word favored by both Jauss and Foucault, *Robinson Crusoe* and Defoe's other novels embodied a profound "shift," both in the expectations of readers who had to decide how to read those narratives and in the practice of writers who had to decode and then answer the "questions" posed by texts like *Robinson Crusoe*. After *Robinson Crusoe*, in short, fiction writers who pondered the relationship of fiction and history did so unequivocally within fictional discourse. Those later writers did not write "history" or antiromance, a type of fictional discourse that after all was incapable of giving a name to itself, but instead unabashedly presented their narratives to readers as a "new species of writing."

Nevertheless history was crucial to the definition of this new kind of fiction, a fact that is evident in key fictional texts produced within two generations of Defoe's publication of *Robinson Crusoe* that are now regarded as founding works in the tradition of the English novel. Richardson, Fielding, Sterne, and Burney, to name only the most prominent, produced *Clarissa* (1747–1748), *Tom Jones* (1749), *Tristram Shandy* (1759–1767) and *Evelina* (1778), and each of these crucial works pressed readers to understand the new form in light of its links to history.[7] Offering *Clarissa* to his

5   Foucault, *Archaeology of Knowledge*, 169; *L'archéologie du savoir*, 221.

6   Ballaster, *Seductive Forms*; Braudy, *Narrative Form*.

7   On the history-fiction link in the eighteenth-century novel after Defoe, see Everett Zimmer-man's forthcoming study, *Sceptical Historiography and the Constitution of the Novel*. For a discussion of Smollett in relation to the argument of this book, see Mayer, "History, *Humphry Clinker*, and the Novel," 240–55.

readers as a history "comprehending the most important concerns of private life," Richardson told his readers that the "double yet separate correspondence" that comprised his masterpiece represented "all the secret purposes of an intriguing head, and resolute heart."[8] And it was as an historian of the human heart that he impressed himself upon his age. Diderot's famous assessment of Richardson in his *Eloge* makes this clear: "Il porte le flambeau au fond de la caverne; c'est lui qui apprend à discerner les motifs subtils et deshonnêtes qui se cachent et se dérobent sous d'autres motifs qui sont honnêtes et qui se hâtent de se montrer les premiers."[9] Voltaire praised Locke for writing the "true history" of the soul where earlier philosophers had written only "the romance of the soul."[10] In effect, Diderot paid the same tribute to Richardson.

Fielding too presented his greatest novel, *Tom Jones*, as a history, although it differed so radically from Richardson's that it has often been regarded as the founding work in a distinct, "anti-Richardsonian" tradition of the novel, both indebted to the epic tradition and richly satirical. Yet Fielding, sounding a note we have heard before, offered his work as a vehicle for material other historians failed to treat:

In reality, there are many little circumstances too often omitted by injudicious historians, from which events of the utmost importance arise. The world may indeed be considered as a vast machine, in which the great wheels are originally set in motion by those which are very minute, and almost imperceptible to any but the strongest eyes.

In discussing the marvelous, the narrator of *Tom Jones* first declared that every writer must keep within the "bounds of possibility," and then added that it was the opinion of Aristotle or "of some wise man whose authority will be as weighty when it is as old, that it is no excuse for a poet who relates what is incredible that the thing related is really matter of fact." Fielding's narrator then went on to assert that although this principle might apply to the poet it could not pertain to the historian who must "record matters as he finds them," and closed by declaring that "if the historian will confine himself to what really happened . . . he will sometimes fall into the marvelous, but never into the incredible."[11] Thus, the author of *Tom Jones*, readers were given to understand, followed the rules laid down for the historian, not the poet, and Leo Braudy has argued that in *Tom Jones*

---

[8] Samuel Richardson, *Clarissa or The History of a Young Lady*, ed. Angus Ross (London: Penguin, 1985), 34, 36.

[9] Diderot, *Eloge à Richardson*, quoted in Rita Goldberg, *Sex and Enlightenment: Women in Richardson and Diderot* (Cambridge University Press, 1984), 122.

[10] Voltaire, *Philosophical Letters*, trans. and introd. Ernest Dilworth (Indianapolis: Bobbs-Merrill, 1961), 53–54.

[11] Henry Fielding, *The History of Tom Jones A Foundling*, aftwd. Frank Kermode (New York: Signet, 1963), 335–38.

Fielding attempted a "renovation of reality" that focused on "private life because he believes public history has served . . . to distort people's appreciation of the world and how it works." According to Braudy, the narrator of *Tom Jones* was a "model historian who constructs from the material of observation, learning, and authority an appropriate causal pattern . . . totally fitted to the varied world in which we must live."[12] In short, Fielding acted as if the "new province of writing" yielded knowledge derived from experience and created for "the benefit and use of life."

Sterne, like Fielding, wrote against the Richardsonian tradition of the novel, but he also rejected Fielding's essay in "the new province of writing." Benjamin Lehman once observed that *Tristram Shandy* was "a deep-laid criticism of the novels of Richardson and Fielding," one that saw their "histories" as "too ordered and too intelligible to be true accounts."[13] Yet Sterne's account, in order to be truer to "disordered" and "unintelligible" reality, drew upon Locke, especially the *Essay Concerning Human Understanding*, which Tristram declared "a history-book . . . of what passes in a man's own mind."[14] Sterne commented that "those who knew the Philosopher well enough to recognize his presence and influence would find them or sense them on every page, in every line."[15] Thus *Tristram Shandy*, in some ways the most atypical of eighteenth-century novels, was nevertheless situated squarely within the unfolding discourse of the novel; it laid claim to being read as a Lockean history of mind.

Burney's *Evelina* was unique among these crucial novels in several respects; among the principal novels of the century, it alone treated in a sustained fashion "the History of a Young Lady's Entrance into the World," as the subtitle put it. Similarly, among the same novels, Burney's gave the amplest account of the London social scene and especially the emerging "leisure industry" in the capital.[16] Arguing that Burney could have attached to *Evelina* the definition of the novel that she used in *The Wanderer* (1814) ("a picture of supposed, but natural and probable human existence" that teaches "the lessons of experience, without its tears"), Edward A. Bloom asserts that for Burney the novel was "a preceptive vehicle."[17] The novel, that is, taught *about* the world so as to equip one *for*

---

12   Braudy, *Narrative Form*, 179, 180.

13   Benjamin H. Lehman, "Of Time, Personality, and the Author," in *Studies in the Comic. University of California Studies in English*, vol. 8, no. 2 (Berkeley: University of California Press, 1941), 241.

14   Laurence Sterne, *The Life and Opinions of Tristram Shandy, Gentleman*, ed. Ian Campbell Ross (Oxford University Press, 1983), 70.

15   Cited in Dorothy Van Ghent, *The English Novel: Form and Function* (New York: Harper and Row, 1961), 107.

16   On this "industry," see J. H. Plumb, *The Commercialisation of Leisure in Eighteenth-Century England* (University of Reading Press, 1974), 9–20.

17   Fanny Burney, *Evelina: or The History of a Young Lady's Entrance into the World*, ed. Edward A. and Lillian D. Bloom (Oxford University Press, 1968), xxiv.

the world. Similarly, Susan Staves has argued that Burney's special subject
was "female difficulties": the "physical limitations" and "psychological
restraints" that taken together constituted "the special helplessness of
women to determine their own fates." Hazlitt saw these as fashioned "out
of nothing," but feminist critics have compellingly argued that they were in
fact "novelistic truths" particular to Burney and "nowhere to be found in
Richardson, Fielding, or Smollett."[18] Like the other eighteenth-century
novelists mentioned here, Burney explicitly claimed to be telling a new
kind of fictional truth ("Let me prepare for disappointment those who, in
the perusal of these sheets, entertain the gentle expectation of being
transported to the fantastic regions of Romance") and offered her heroine
as "the offspring of Nature, and of Nature in her simplest attire."[19] All of
these crucial novelists, then, presented themselves to their readers, in one
fashion or another, as historians.

Yet not for a moment did anyone ever read any of these works as other
than fictional creations. Braudy rightly claims that "the world of *Tom Jones*
is palpably a created world," and Richardson himself, although he claimed
that he wanted *Clarissa* to be read with "Historical Faith," declared he did
not wish "the letters to be *thought* genuine."[20] In the nineteenth century,
furthermore, Hazlitt asserted that Richardson "had the strongest matter-
of-fact imagination" that ever existed, but the substantive in that characterization is "imagination," not "matter of fact."[21] Thus unlike Defoe,
writers like Richardson, Fielding, Sterne, and Burney laid claim to being
read as historians from within novelistic discourse. Each of their works
thematizes in its way the historical claims of novels; in *Clarissa*, *Tristram
Shandy*, and *Evelina* the principal characters struggle to render their own
experience faithfully; indeed Clarissa works hard at being her own
archivist.[22] In *Tom Jones*, Fielding's narrator reflects upon the kind of
history he is writing, and Fielding also intertwines the experiences of the
hero with an important moment in the public history of Britain: the
Jacobite rising of 1745. Nevertheless, these writers were poets – to use the
label of Sidney and Bacon – who essayed an imaginative form that
embodied "a fictional approach to history."[23] Not so Defoe, who wrote
histories that only later were read into the new fictional discourse created
by, among others, Richardson, Fielding, Sterne, and Burney. Yet the
emergence of a new fictional discourse was signaled by Defoe's narratives

18 Susan Staves, "*Evelina*; or, Female Difficulties," *Modern Philology* 73 (1975–76), 379–80; Hazlitt
   is quoted at 369.
19 Burney, *Evelina*, 8.
20 Braudy, *Narrative Form*, 145; *Selected Letters of Samuel Richardson*, ed. John Carroll (Oxford:
   Clarendon, 1964), 85.
21 William Hazlitt, *Lectures on the English Comic Writers* (London: Henry Frowde; Oxford University
   Press, 1907), 154.
22 On this point, see Zimmerman, "Battling of Books," 154.   23 Frye, *Anatomy*, 306.

and particularly by the shift in the horizon of expectations they necessitated. Defoe's "novels" and their reception constituted the revolutionary
act, that, consciously or not, subsequent novelists responded to and built
upon.[24]

The presentation and reception of Defoe's most famous narratives, in
short, figured centrally in the process of elaborating the discourse of the
novel from the eighteenth century to our own day. That process is the stuff
of literary history, but Jauss has argued that literary history should act as a
"provocation" to literary theory because, properly understood, literary
history *is* literary theory. Therefore, to conclude this study of the link
between early modern historiography and the early novel, I need to
indicate what Defoe's revolutionary act contributed to the theory of the
novel.

First, it seems undeniable that novels, in a way that still remains
unaccountable, do indeed convey matters of fact. Half a century and more
of New Critical and post-structuralist theorizing predispose many readers
almost automatically to reject this assertion. Thus, Victor Lange argues
that the use of facts in fictional texts or fiction in historical texts is
insignificant because

> whether or not we are in the presence of a fictional [or historical] field is . . . a
> matter of contextual analysis; it cannot be recognized unless we examine the
> specific aesthetic and logical uses to which the facts that sustain it have been put
> . . . The invented speeches in Tacitus are clearly part of a nonfictional intention;
> the actual letter which Rilke incorporated in *Malte Laurids Brigge* assumes, within
> the purposes of the novel, a distinctly fictional character.[25]

Yet what is one to say about a work like the *Journal of the Plague Year* which
has elicited such different judgments about the discursive field to which it
belongs?

Such a text requires us to confront the fact that the novel, from its

---

24 Pat Rogers claims that there is no reason to believe that Fielding knew Defoe's work, but
   Braudy has argued that Fielding's *Jonathan Wild* is a work written in awareness of Defoe's
   legacy. The narrator of *Wild*, Braudy suggests, functions as a criticism of both "the
   Richardsonian editor and the Defoe-like biographer," and yet *Wild* is also an important step
   toward Fielding's successfully "defining the role of the historian-narrator" in *Tom Jones*.
   Richardson edited Defoe's *Tour*. More important, Pope's famous assessment of Defoe ("The
   first part of *Robinson Crusoe*, good. Defoe wrote many things, and none bad, though none
   excellent") coupled with the oft-quoted rhyme from a March 1, 1729 edition of *The Flying Post*
   ("Down in the kitchen, honest Dick and Doll/Are studying Colonel Jack and Flanders Moll")
   suggest that Defoe's "novels" were known by a broad spectrum of readers, although they were
   not always understood to have been written by him. Braudy, *Narrative Form*, 134; Rogers, *Critical
   Heritage*, 40. Finally, the derisive reference to Defoe in Melopoyn's story in *Roderick Random*
   demonstrates that even those writers who disapproved of Defoe had to come to terms with him
   in shaping their own understanding of the novel; see Tobias Smollett, *The Adventures of Roderick
   Random*, ed. Paul-Gabriel Bouce (Oxford University Press, 1981), 382–85.
25 Victor Lange, "Fact in Fiction," *Comparative Literature Studies* 6 (1969), 260.

inception, has militated against the view that fictionality and historicity are mutually exclusive. Poised at the border between two discourses, the *Journal* requires us to be wary of dismissing the possibility of there being such things as fictional facts – fictive statements that genuinely refer to historical reality. In response, readers have acknowledged the historicity of the *Journal* even as they have read it into the literary series "novel." To be sure, some readers *have* concretized the text as fiction and thereby implicitly denied the possibility of reading it as history. But many others – novelists, critics, historians, topographers – have insisted that one can, indeed must, read the *Journal* as history even while acknowledging its fictive character. That novel readers have done so over a 250-year span of reading makes it clear that they do not regard the idea of fact in fiction as untenable.

But it is not just generic oddities like the *Journal* that demonstrate that novelistic discourse has been understood since Defoe to possess a peculiar referentiality setting it apart from other literary forms. Linda Hutcheon has commented that "of all literary genres, the novel has had the most difficulty in escaping from naive referential theories," which, she argues, are no longer brought to bear on poetry, "rescued from the myth of the instrumentality of language by the Symbolists, [and] the New Critics." Hutcheon treats metafiction as a form of the novel that at first glance seems a hopeful candidate for "short-circuiting" the "referential fallacy" that has nagged the novel since its inception. But her study of metafiction does not yield the anticipated results:

> what metafiction's autoreferentiality appears to do is *not* what one might expect it to, that is, to divert readers from making other references and to limit them to a narcissistic textual formalism. Instead, autoreference and intertextual reference actually combine to direct readers back to an outer reference; in fact, they direct the readers outside the text, by reminding them (paradoxically) that, although what they are reading is only a literary fiction which they themselves are creating through language, this act itself is really a paradigm or an allegory of the ordering, naming processes that are part of their daily experience of coming to terms with reality.[26]

Hutcheon's argument suggests a desire to rescue the novel from the taint of referentiality that metafiction cannot accomplish, despite all the hopes that Hutcheon and others might pin on it. Hence "the major worry" in respect to this aspect of novelistic discourse is that "what metafiction has really done is to make explicit what is a truism of *all* fiction: the overdetermination of novelistic reference."[27]

In other words, try though they might, metafictionists and theoreticians

---

[26] Linda Hutcheon, "Metafictional Implications for Novelistic Reference," in *On Referring in Literature*, ed. Anna Whiteside and Michael Issacharoff (Bloomington: Indiana University Press, 1987), 1, 10.

[27] *Ibid.*, 1.

of the form cannot escape from the novel's incessant claim to historicity. The history of the early English novel and particularly of Defoe's contribution to the elaboration of a discourse of the novel provides a ready explanation for why that is the case. From the sixteenth century onward prenovelistic fiction and then the novel itself stipulated a unique link to history as a fundamental rule governing the writing and reading of novels. Defoe's case is central in this respect because in order for his narratives to be attached to the tradition of the novel it was necessary for readers to read them out of the historical discourse of early eighteenth-century England to which they had plausibly belonged and into the novelistic discourse that made its appearance amid the "sudden redistribution" of discourses that seems to have taken place in the first half of the eighteenth century, a "shift" both partially induced and signaled by Defoe's narratives.

The claim that the novel is uniquely referential is, as Hutcheon says and as I have had occasion to argue more than once, paradoxical.[28] Texts cannot be both history and fiction, and yet novels are. How do we account for this paradoxical but inescapable feature of the novel? I would point to three different accounts of novelistic practice, all of which suggest that the novel is built upon a dialogue between history and fiction, indeed that the novel *is* such a dialogue. First, there is Walter Wilson's acute comment on Defoe's practice in the *Journal*, which, as I argued in the previous chapter, represents Defoe's version of fictional practice in such a way as to suggest at least that the novel is a process in which fiction is constantly becoming history and history is constantly becoming fiction, the two modes of discourse always responding to and renewing each other. Wilson's observation is so important because it not only clarifies the nature of Defoe's narratives but also can be seen as commenting upon (even as it was probably shaped by) the novelistic practice of Sir Walter Scott, whose career as a writer of prose fiction functions as a fulcrum in the history of the novel.

Scott offered his first novel, *Waverley* (1814), as a summation of the eighteenth-century novel, and the Waverley novels as a whole, as Judith Wilt asserts, constituted "the environment of the nineteenth-century novelist." Scott denominates his fictional works both "Novels" and "Romances," and in his monumental apparatus for the Waverley novels in the so-called Magnum edition (perhaps his most interesting work from a theoretical standpoint), Scott offers his readers an account of the "historical facts" upon which the narratives are grounded.[29] He thus continued the argument that the novel was a fictional form that could do the work of

---

[28] Hutcheon, too, finds paradoxical her own assertions about the novel's capacity to "direct the readers outside the text"; 10.

[29] See Sir Walter Scott, *Waverley*, ed. Claire Lamont (Oxford University Press, 1986), 3–4, 348; Judith Wilt, *Secret Leaves: The Novels of Walter Scott* (University of Chicago Press, 1985), 203.

history. As I have argued elsewhere, Scott's novels and their apparatus invite us to see the relationship between fictional and historical discourse in the novel as an unfolding dialogue between the author and the texts and writers that Scott identified as his collaborators and, ultimately, a dialogue of two modes of discourse.[30]

This idea of the novel as a "dialogical" form has become central to current discussion of the form as a result of the work of Mikhail Bakhtin, which has come to seem for many critics the most compelling and productive theory of the novel yet advanced. Yet Bakhtin's concept of dialogue is tied to his use of the word "heteroglossia" – simply put, "social diversity of speech types" – and for Bakhtin it is possible to define the novel as "dialogized heteroglossia" or "a diversity of social speech types . . . and a diversity of individual voices, artistically organized."[31] More to the present point, however, one of the ways Bakhtin argues that the novel enacts "dialogized heteroglossia" is through its appropriation of what he calls "incorporated genres" – the use of both "artistic" genres (lyrics, drama, romance) and of "extra-artistic" genres ("everyday, rhetorical, scholarly, religious genres").[32] Beyond these types of "incorporated genres," Bakhtin identifies "a special group of genres that play an especially significant role in structuring novels," including the diary, the travel account, biography, and the personal letter, and, we might add in light of the present study, various other historical forms such as Thucydidean political history, autobiography, and secret history. This "special group of genres," in short, consists either of "documents" that historians use (diaries, letters) or of historical forms *per se* (lifewriting, political or secret history). Bakhtin comments in respect to this "special group of genres" (which I have expanded to include Baconian historiography):

So great is the role played by these genres that are incorporated into novels that it might seem as if the novel is denied any primary means for verbally appropriating reality, that it has no approach of its own, and therefore requires the help of other genres to re-process reality.[33]

Bakhtin rejects this idea, but his discussion of incorporated genres suggests another way of conceiving of Bakhtinian dialogue that is more germane to the purposes of this study. We can conceive of the novel, that is, as in dialogue with other "genres," and most particularly with genres that in the seventeenth and early eighteenth century were part of the discourse of history. The persistent attempt from the sixteenth to the nineteenth

---

30 Mayer, "The Internal Machinery Displayed: *The Heart of Midlothian* and Scott's Apparatus for the Waverley Novels," *CLIO* 17 (1987–88), 1–20. On the Magnum edition, see also Patricia Gaston, *Prefacing the Waverley Novels: A Reading of Sir Walter Scott's Prefaces to the Waverley Novels* (New York: Peter Lang, 1991); Jane Millgate, *Scott's Last Edition: A Study in Publishing History* (Edinburgh University Press, 1987).

31 Bakhtin, *Dialogic Imagination*, 262–63.   32 *Ibid.*, 320–21.   33 *Ibid.*, 321.

century to define fiction in relation to history – and especially the disruptive and defining fact of Defoe's writing from within the discourse of history and subsequently being read into the discourse of the novel – demonstrates that the novel is founded upon a dialogue that arises not only from its incorporation of other genres but also, and perhaps more fundamentally, upon a dialogue of two modes of discourse that is persistently enacted within the form itself and about which the readers and writers of the form have been self-conscious since at least 1719 when Charles Gildon first called Defoe a liar.

Perhaps this dialogue helps to explain why writers and readers of novels have always treated novels as fictional texts with an unusual capacity to *do* things. Defoe wrote the *Journal of the Plague Year* in part because he "was concerned about the risk of plague and wanted to alert people to it," and Richardson concluded *Pamela* with a long list of the "many Applications, of its most material Incidents," among others that "the Proud and the High-born [would] see the Deformity of unreasonable Passion" and that "the UPPER SERVANTS of great Families may . . . learn what to avoid, and what to chuse, to make themselves valued and esteem'd."[34] Recent studies have shown that twentieth-century novel-readers have continued to value novels for the "applications" they find in them. Janice Radway, for example, studying the presentation of "serious fiction" by the editors of the news-letter of the Book-of-the-Month Club to club members, argues that "serious" novels "function for Club members in a way similar to the many self-help manuals, advice books, and reference volumes that make up the majority of the Club's alternate list." Radway asserts that the value of "serious fiction" for these readers is "a function of its capacity to be used as a map which is . . . a tool for enabling its readers to move about more effectively in the world."[35]

Lest the BOMC readers be dismissed as akin to the "ignorant" readers who took Defoe at his word and read his novels as works of history, it should be recalled that in the United States, at least, academic historians regularly assign novels in their classes to "teach" students about such subjects as nineteenth-century Russian revolutionary movements (Dostoevsky, *The Possessed*), France between the two World Wars (Céline, *Journey to the End of the Night*), and racism in America (the novels of Richard Wright, Ralph Ellison, James Baldwin, and Toni Morrison). Finally, recent

---

[34] David Roberts, ed., *A Journal of the Plague Year*, by Defoe (Oxford University Press, 1990), ix; Samuel Richardson, *Pamela or, Virtue Rewarded*, ed. T. C. Duncan-Eaves and Ben D. Kimpel (Boston: Houghton Mifflin, 1971), 409–10.

[35] Janice Radway, "The Book-of-the-Month Club and the General Reader: On the Uses of 'Serious' Fiction," *Critical Inquiry* 14 (1987–88), 535, 537. See also Pierre Bourdieu, *Distinction: A Social Critique of the Judgement of Taste*, trans. Richard Nice (Cambridge MA: Harvard University Press, 1984), 4, 32; Richard Ohman, "The Shaping of a Canon: U.S. Fiction, 1960–1975," *Critical Inquiry* 10 (1983–84), 201.

scholars of the novel have argued that we should move beyond conceiving of novels as literary artifacts that reflect the historical realities in which they appeared and instead see them as "the vehicles, not the reflections, of social change."[36] These latter studies are hardly rooted in the belief in the "continuity between art and life" that Pierre Bourdieu sees as the hallmark of "the popular 'aesthetic'," but they nevertheless serve to remind us that the novel bears the marks of the discourse from which it came because like the crucial form of learning in the Baconian scheme that history was, the novel seems from its first appearance to the present day, to have been presented and received as a literary form that was intended in a very direct and literal way for "the benefit and use of life."[37]

This view of the novel, then, can be seen as continuous with the resolutely utilitarian cast of historical discourse in early modern Britain, especially as the functional character of history was suggested to readers by Nathaniel Crouch. Crouch offered his "manuals" to readers as vehicles for self-improvement: "accomodated with so many particulars both for Instruction and Discourse."[38] Likewise, Richard Ohman, drawing on Philip H. Ennis's study of *Adult Book Reading in America*, argues that twentieth-century Americans read fiction "for some kind of map to the moral landscape" and to stay abreast of "the book talk of friends and neighbors": in short, twentieth-century readers, like seventeenth-century readers of Crouch's popular history, read novels for "Instruction" and "Discourse."[39]

Defoe would have understood both the promises of the seventeenth-century bookseller and the observations of the twentieth-century academic. In fact, he was the heir of Crouch and played an important role in shaping the form that twentieth-century critics theorize. The case of Defoe demonstrates that readers have given their assent to the claim that the novel is a fictional form that does the work of history. This claim is unsatisfactory if one starts from the view that "formed facts" can, as Lange argues, "function only aesthetically and in a manner entirely different from that of facts existing outside the artistic intention." The historical claim of the novel, however, was never unproblematic; it was always paradoxical. This was especially true of the works of Defoe which have "endured a long crisis of classification" that is not yet and may never be over.[40] Defoe is crucial to the history and theory of the English novel exactly because he forced history upon the novel in a way that readers have found both compelling and strange; the reading of his narratives into the tradition of the novel suggests that the theory of the novel is incomplete without an

[36] Bender, *Imagining the Penitentiary*, 1; see also Nancy Armstrong, *Desire and Domestic Fiction*, 9, 25.
[37] Bourdieu, *Distinction*, 32; Bacon, *Selected Writings*, 437.
[38] [Crouch], *England's Monarchs*, sig. A₂r.
[39] Cited in Ohman, "Shaping of a Canon," 201.
[40] Roberts, ed., *Journal of the Plague Year*, vii.

account of how this form of fiction refers to historical reality. In a way, this issue cannot be laid to rest; that is why the history of the reception of Defoe is so remarkably unsettled. Defoe's narratives and the long history of how they have been read established as a crucial element in the theory of the form the paradoxical and yet inescapable assertion that novels consist of matters of fact.

Index

CAMBRIDGE STUDIES IN EIGHTEENTH-CENTURY
ENGLISH LITERATURE AND THOUGHT

General Editors

Professor HOWARD ERSKINE-HILL LITT.D., FBA, *Pembroke College,*
Cambridge
Professor JOHN RICHETTI, *University of Pennsylvania*